The Mammoth Book of
Soldiers
at War

THE MAMMOTH BOOK OF

Soldiers at War

Firsthand accounts of warfare
from the Age of Napoleon

EDITED BY JON E. LEWIS

ROBINSON
London

Constable Publishers
3 The Lanchesters
162 Fulham Palace Road
London W6 9ER
www.constablerobinson.com

First published in the UK by Robinson,
an imprint of Constable & Robinson Ltd 2001

A copy of the British Library Cataloguing in
Publication Data is available from the British Library.

ISBN 1–84119–181–7

Printed and bound in the EU

"Die hard, 57th, die hard!"
– Lieutenant-Colonel William Inglis
to his battalion, Albuera, Spain, 16 May 1811

For Tristram, Freda and Penny

CONTENTS

INTRODUCTION

Not without reason were the French Revolutionary and Napoleonic Wars once known collectively as the 'Great War'. The campaigns of France from 1793 to 1815 composed the largest military endeavour in European history until the armageddon of 1914.

And, dare one say it, the most interesting. Contemporaries were mesmerised by 'Boney' and exploits, and time has done little to lessen his and their magnetism. Few of us care about the to-ing and fro-ing of the Seven Years War, the Thirty Years War, the Hundred Years War, the War of Jenkin's Ear or the War of the Roses, but the Napoleonic Wars are the stuff of which wargaming, popular war fiction and historical pressing are made.

The allure is not difficult to understand. Aside from their sheer scale – Bonaparte alone had more than a million men under arms in 1812 – the Napoleonic Wars possessed a pearl string of celebrated battles: – Austerlitz, Wagram, Leipzig, Salamanca, Borodino, Jena, Ligney – and had in *le Petit Caporal* himself the most magnetically intriguing warrior of the second millennium.

Something more about the Napoleonic era entices; the recognition of modernity. The Napoleonic Wars, and the French Revolutionary Wars which preceded them, ushered in a new way of warfare. The road to the Somme and Stalingrad began in the eighteenth century, not the twentieth. The new way of war-making was seen most obviously in the French army itself.

After the overthrow of the *ancien regime* of Louis XVI in 1789, the ensuing radical republic was obliged to arm itself with something more than the untrustworthy remnant of the regular royal army it inherited. In its stead was fashioned a new model army of volunteers and conscripts, freed from aristocratic hindrances, where officers were promoted on merit not social ranking. (Some of the talent thus allowed to rise did so all the way to Napoleon's 26-strong marshalate, one of whom, Victor, had been a mere bandsman before the Republic.) Moreover, the ridding of aristocratic influence allowed some changes in military tactics to rise to the fore, notably the use of the 'column' against the 'line'. Mobile and hard-hitting, usually some 50–80 men in width and 9–12 men deep, the French column, supported by artillery, became the scourge of the European battlefield, and later much emulated by France's enemies. Behind the French force on the battlefield toiled an economy geared almost exclusively to military ends.

The French soldier, too, differed from his predecessors. A citizen-in-arms, fired up on transcendent political fervour, he fought for a cause as well as the chance for wages and loot. Moreover, the *soldat* – like his Enlightment fellows in Europe and America – no longer saw himself as a pawn in God's game, but an individual with his own destiny to carve. And accordingly, the Napoleonic Wars, with the partial exception of the American War of Independence, were the first to produce a distinct body of soldiers' personal memoirs.

It is from these memoirs that the current volume is culled. *The Mammoth Book of Soldiers at War* presents fourteen voices of those who fought and lived in the land campaigns of the French Revolutionary Wars (1793–1802), the Napoleonic Wars (1803–1815) and the attendant War of 1812 (1812–1815) in North America. Some of these accounts offer a first-hand account of the most historically important moments of the wars, among them the Russian Retreat of 1812 and the battles of Leipzig and Waterloo. As such, they offer fascinating vignettes (a nervous Napoleon at Marengo flicking stones with his whip in Jean-Roch Coignet's 'notebook' comes to mind, as does the sombre courage of the men about to storm the fortress of Ciudad Rodrigo in Thomas Grattan's memoir) but the primary purpose of this volume is not to chronicle the Napoleonic Wars in eyewitness chapters. It is rather to present the experience of war in the age of Napoleon, what it felt like to be an infantry soldier, a cavalryman, an artilleryman on the battlefield and the marches and bivouacs that led to it. Many of the accounts are by commissioned officers and NCOs for the simple reason that these men were the most likely to be literate and thus pen memoirs, diaries or letters; but this does not negate a 'ground-view' intention. In the Napoleonic Wars, officers led from the front, even when they were as mighty a figure as Marshal Macdonald.

Since the assembled accounts are by those 'who were there', their vantage points are usually limited, sometimes only to the men, smoke, horseflesh and flying lead immediately around them. This makes for an accurate portrait of combat, but few soldiers turned memoirist were able to resist bulking out their passage with turgid historical explanation, sometimes directly cribbed (Napier's *History of the War in the Iberian Peninsula* being a favourite). In the pursuit of the vivid picture I have either avoided or excised such material, making an exception for General Marbot, as lively a writer as he was a cavalryman, the very definition of the *beau sabreur*.

That said, some words of historical context might prove useful here. After the outbreak of the French Revolution, pre-eminent among the army officers who secured the safety of the *nouveau regime* was Corsican officer Napoleon Bonaparte who celebratedly dispersed a royalist mob in 1795 with a 'whiff of grapeshot' – a service the ambitious 26-year-old Corsican parlayed into the command of the Army of the Interior, then the command of the Army of Italy. As military success followed upon military success, so political power fell into Napoleon's hands. By the *coup d'etat de Brumaire* in 1799 he became one of France's three ruling Consuls; by the next year he was First Consul; by 1804 he was Emperor. Napoleon was quick to see the relationship between his rise to power and his military prowess, particularly over the hapless Hapsburgs in the Italian campaigns: 'My power depends on my glory and my glories on the victories I have won. My power will fail if I do not feed it on new glories and new victories. Conquest has made me what I am and only conquest can enable me to hold my position'. Permanent war was also an economic necessity, for Napoleon paid much of the cost of his wars and his regime by plundering subjugated countries.

And so it was that Napoleon led out the *Grande Armée* in 1803 for a long decade of epic campaigning that resulted in 'Boney' becoming the master of Europe from Sicily to the North Sea, from Brest to Odessa.

The wonder is less that the Napoleonic empire fell, than that it managed to last so long. Occupation and sequestration were always likely to provoke nationalist uprisings against French rule and even victories cost France dear in blood (40,000 casualties, including 40 generals at Wagram alone, for example) while Britian's early passage into the Industrial Revolution gave France's chief enemy a degree of prosperity that Napoleon could only dream about. At the end of the day, wars are invariably won by the side with the biggest pockets. The British may have been absent as a military force at the battle of Leipzig in 1813, but their pounds not only subsidised the allied side, but also armed it with 125,000 muskets and 218 artillery pieces. Economics also worked against France in other ways; Napoleon's 'Continental System' of embargoing British goods from Europe proved deeply unpopular amongst French satellites for it ruined trade and stopped the import of such niceties as coffee and sugar. Unfortunately for the older Napoleon, he proved a dismal diplomat, and the elevation of his brother Joseph to the Kingdom of Spain caused a draining 'ulcer' in Iberia that never healed.

So, why did the Eagle fly for so long? The swift-marching *Grande Armée* may not have been the revolutionary force of the 1790s, but it still contained enough volunteers and ideological fervour to achieve the seemingly impossible. As, arguably, the military genius *sans pareil*, Napoleon kept the military reforms which worked and junked those that did not (but not immediately: in 1800, one of Coignet's comrades still felt able to fraternally tell a general, 'If you do not move out of my way I will knock you down with one blow of my crowbar'), and was the veritable master of manoeuvering enemies into the big battle where he could deal the KO. So successful was the French military training system, meanwhile, that even in the dog days of 1814, underage conscripts were being turned into soldiers who could achieve unexpected defensive victories. It also helped the Imperial progress that Britain displayed diplomatic ineptitude of some extraordinary sort, and was frequently friendless in western Europe (with the exception of Portugal, 'the oldest ally') and then provoked America into the War of 1812 by violating her maritime rights. Britain may have ruled the waves, but her military interventions on land tended to be inglorious affairs on the edge of matters (notably the expeditions to Buenos Aires and Walcheren), only excepting Wellington's determined campaign in the Peninsula from 1808.

There was something else in the *Grande Armée* that made it near invincible; a belief in its leader that bordered on idolatry. His mere presence could inspire French soldiers to fight to the bitter end. There is a telling moment in Coignet's recollection of the 1800 Italian campaign – 'the Consul appeared; we felt ourselves strong again.' This veneration of Napoleon scarcely abated amongst the French army – politicians and public were another matter – even after the disastrous 1812 attack on Russia. And it was only after such a disaster, which cost 500,000 French soldiers their lives, that the Eagle began to falter and fall.

In April 1814, with the Allies advancing on Paris, Napoleon was finally forced to abdicate. He then fought back for one more grasp of glory, landing from exile in March 1815 with 1,000 followers. The army was sent against him, but the army still adored him and many rejoined his side. Within a month Napoleon was esconced in Paris as *de facto* Emperor. In a desperate gamble, he then launched the *Armée du Nord* against his gathering Allied foes, and despite a blistering success against the Prussians at Ligny, the French offensive was turned at Waterloo. That battle may have been a closer run thing than is generally recognised, but the war was never seriously in doubt. The French public had little stomach and less money for more years of sustained fighting.

It only remains to say something of the men who fought the 700 or so battles of the French Revolutionary, Napoleonic and 1812 Wars, the men who put the grand designs and ambitions into effect. The staple soldier of the Napoleonic era was the infantryman with his musket, forming between 60 and 90 per cent of the various armies' strength, the remainder of which was largely composed of cavalrymen and artillerymen. Most soldiers were conscripted but plenty volunteered ('adventure' being a great pull), but all tended to have a healthy respect for their opponents rather than a hatred, and such chivalric gestures as Rifleman Harris sharing his water bottle with a dying Frenchman at Rolica were not uncommon. As becomes obvious in the following pages, the soldiers' lot, no matter to which army he belonged, was a hard one, of long marches, harsh discipline and poor food. Battle, when it came was almost a relief, a glamorous break to tedium and sheer slog. Although particular combats could be devastatingly bloody for some units (at Albuera, General Beresford lost 40 per cent of his men), most soldiers would expect to survive the fray. On average, the British mortality rate in battle for the Napoleonic Wars was 3.3 percent.

But other, greater, killers lurked in the shadows. It has been estimated that 85 percent of the 240,000 British soldiers who died between 1793 and 1815 did so from disease. Such a 'casualty' rate was not unique to the British army. A man might escape the enemy's cannon or musket ball, but his chances of avoiding sickness and starvation were much slimmer.

Under such circumstances, men were kept going by drilled discipline, ideology (whether revolutionary fervour as in the young French Republican armies and Corporal Stubbs' Kentucky militia, or straight pro-duty patriotism), and the chances for booty, promotion or even the sheer pleasure of wielding arms. *Esprit de corps* or regimental pride was almost a universal phenomenon. Cut off from his family and country, the soldier relied on his unit and his unit relied upon him. Moreover, a man's regiment was usually composed of his friends and peers. Most soldiers would confess to fear, but few would let their fellows down by open cowardice or desertion.

And few, as becomes transparent in the accounts drawn on here, regretted their time with the colours, despite all that they suffered and saw.

Rifleman Harris might speak for them all: 'For my own part I can only say that I enjoyed life more whilst on active service that I have ever done since; and as I sit at work in my shop in Richmond Street, Soho, I look back upon that portion of my time spent in the fields of the Peninsula as the only part worthy of remembrance. It is at such times that scenes long passed come back upon my mind as if they have taken place but yesterday. I remember even the very appearance of some of the regiments engaged; and comrades, long mouldered to dust, I see again performing the acts of heroes.'

Jon E. Lewis, 2000

WITH NAPOLEON IN ITALY, 1800

Jean-Roch Coignet, 96th Demi-Brigade

A consummate political opportunist, Napoleon inveigled himself to power in the coup d'etat de Brumaire *(9–10 November 1799) as one of France's three Consuls. Within months his co-conspirators had been persuaded to retire from political life, leaving the Corsican general the nation's* de facto *ruler. To consolidate his control, however, Napoleon needed to pacify France's external enemies; accordingly, he placed himself at the head of the Army of the Reserve and headed over the Alps to Italy – the very scene of the string of victories in 1796–7 which had established his military reputation – and attacked the Austrian army in the rear. The Second Italian Campaign was as rapid as it was brilliant, although the crucial battle of Marengo in the Po Valley, on 14 June 1800, was a close run thing when Napoleon rashly underestimated the combativity of the Austrians, whose attack took him by surprise. Only the timely arrival of a mud-splattered General Desaix saved the day for the French. Yet, this victory and that of General Moreau's at Hohenlinden on the German front in the same year was enough to make the Hapsburgs sue for peace. The Treaty of Luneville, 1801, duly followed. Even Britain, despite its successful reconquest of Egypt the same year, was averse to more warring against the French and signed the peace of Amiens in spring 1802.*

Jean-Roch Coignet was conscripted in 1799, beginning a career that would include all Napoleon's major campaigns as First Consul and Emperor, from Italy in 1800 to Waterloo in 1815, via Austerlitz, Wagram, and Russia. He was one of the first soldiers to be decorated with the Legion of Honour and despite his small stature was appointed to the Grenadier Guards. He was commissioned in 1812.

On the sixth Fructidor, year VII,[1] two gendarmes came and left with me a way-bill and an order to start for Fontainebleau on the tenth Fructidor. I immediately made preparations for my departure. My master and mistress wished to procure me a substitute. I thanked them with tears in my eyes. "I promise you that I will bring back a silver musket, or die." It was a sad leave-taking. I was overwhelmed with kindness by the whole household. They accompanied me to the end of the road, and bade me good-bye with many embraces. With my little bundle under my arm, I reached Rozoy, the first military halting-place, where I spent the night. I took my billeting-order, and presented it to my host, who took no notice of me whatever. Then I went out to buy something to make a stew, and the butcher gave it to me. I felt quite desolate when I saw that piece of meat in the palm of my hand. I gave it to my landlady, and asked her to have the kindness to have it cooked for me, and went to find some vegetables for her. At last I got my little stew, and by that time I had won the good graces of my hosts, who were willing to talk to me, but I took no fancy to them.

The next day I reached Fontainebleau, where some very casual officers received us and put us in barracks which were in wretched condition. Our fine battalion was formed within a fortnight; it numbered eighteen hundred men. As there was

1 i.e. 23 August 1799 in the Revolutionary calendar.

no discipline, a mutiny at once occurred, and half of them left and went home. The chief of the battalion reported them at Paris, and each man was allowed fifteen days to rejoin his battalion, or else be regarded as a deserter, and punished accordingly. General Lefebvre[2] was immediately sent to organize us. Companies were formed, and grenadiers selected. I belonged to this latter company, which numbered a hundred and twenty-five men, and we were uniformed at once. We received an entire outfit, and immediately began to drill twice a day. The stragglers were brought back by the gendarmes, and we were brought into order again.

Sunday was the *décadi*[3] for the whole battalion. We had to sing "La Victoire," and the officers flourished their sabres about; the church resounded with them. Then we cried out, "Vive la République!" Every evening, around the liberty-pole in the principal street, we had to sing, "Les aristocrates à la lanterne." It was great sport.

This sort of life had lasted nearly two months, when a report was circulated in the newspapers that General Bonaparte had landed, and was on his way to Paris, and that he was a great general. Our officers were full of excitement, because the chief of our battalion knew him, and the whole battalion was delighted by the news. We were reviewed, and our clothing examined. We were made to carry and present arms and fix bayonets. They undertook to make soldiers of us in two months. We had callouses on our hands from slapping them on the butt-ends of our guns. All day long we were under arms. Our officers took us by the collars and examined our clothing; they took every precaution that we should be lacking in nothing.

At last a courier brought the information that Bonaparte

2 General Francois Lefebvre (1755–1820), commander of the Paris military area. Designated one of the original members of the marshalate in 1804.
3 *décadi*, a day of rest occurring every ten days, was the Revolutionary substitute for Sunday.

would pass by Fontainebleau, and that he would spend the night there. We were kept under arms all day long, but he did not come. We were scarcely allowed time to eat. The bakers and innkeepers on the principal street did a good business. Vedettes were placed in the wood, and every moment there was a cry of "*Aux armes*," and every one rushed out on the balconies, but all for nothing, for Bonaparte did not arrive till midnight.

In the principal street of Fontainebleau, where he dismounted, he was delighted to see such a fine battalion. He called the officers around him, and gave them an order to set out for Courbevoie. He got into his carriage again, and we, shouting "Vive Bonaparte," returned to our barracks to make up our knapsacks, wake up our washer-women, and pay them off.

We slept at Corbeil. The inhabitants received us as if we had been natives of that country, and the next day we started for Courbevoie, where we found the barracks in the most destitute condition, not even straw to sleep on. We were obliged to get trellises from among the vines to warm ourselves and boil our pots.

We remained there only three days, as orders were sent us to go to the École Militaire, where we were put in rooms which had nothing in them but straw mattresses, and at least a hundred men in each room. Then a distribution of cartridges was made: three packages of fifteen cartridges each to each man, and three days after we were made to start for St. Cloud, where we saw cannon everywhere, and troopers wrapped in their cloaks. We were told that they were the *gros talons*,[4] that they came down on the enemy, in a charge, like a thunderbolt, and that they were covered with iron. But this was not really so. They had only ugly three-cornered hats with two iron plates in the form of a cross in front. These men looked like big peasants, with horses so large they made

4 Cuirassiers, so called because of their heavy boots.

the earth shake, and great sabres four feet long. These were our heavy cavalrymen, who afterwards became cuirassiers, and were called the *"gilets de fer."* At last the regiment reached St. Cloud. The grenadiers of the Directory and of the Five Hundred were in line in the front court; a half-brigade of infantry was stationed near the great gate, and four companies of grenadiers behind the guard of the Directory.

Cries of "Vive Bonaparte" were heard on all sides, and he appeared. The drums beat a salute; he passed in front of the fine corps of grenadiers, saluted every one, ordered us into line of battle, and spoke to the officers. He was on foot, and wore a small hat and a short sword. He went up the steps alone. Suddenly we heard cries, and Bonaparte came out, drew his sword, and went up again with a platoon of grenadiers of the guard. Then the noise increased. Grenadiers were on the stairway and in the entrance. We saw stout gentlemen jumping out of the windows: cloaks, fine hats, and plumes were thrown on the ground, and the grenadiers pulled the lace from the elegant cloaks.[5]

At three o'clock orders were sent us to start for Paris, but the grenadiers did not go with us. We were famishing. On our arrival brandy was distributed to us. The Parisians crowded around us to hear the news from St. Cloud. We could scarcely make our way through the streets to the Luxembourg, where we were quartered in a chapel at the entrance of the garden (we had to go upstairs). To the left, after we mounted the stairs, was a great vaulted chamber, which they told us was the sacristy. Here they made us put up big kettles for four hundred soldiers. In front of the main building there were handsome linden trees; but the beautiful square in front of the palace was covered with the ruins of buildings. There was nothing left in this beautiful garden but the old chestnut trees, which are still there, and an outlet in

5 Hats with plumes formed part of the dress of government representatives; the *coup d'etat de Brumaire*, occurred on 9–10 November 1799 and swept Napoleon to power as First Consul.

the rear at the end of our chapel. It was pitiful to see that lovely garden utterly destroyed.

Then a fine-looking grenadier rode up with the battalion commander, who ordered us under arms to receive M. Thomas (or Thomé) as lieutenant in the 96th half-brigade; this man said to us, "My comrade and I saved General Bonaparte's life. The first time he entered the hall, two men rushed upon him with daggers, and it was my comrade and I who parried the blows. Then the general went outside, and they cried, 'Outlaw him.' Whereupon he drew his sword, ordered us to fix bayonets, shouted, 'Clear the hall,' and called for his brother. The whole chicken-hearted lot jumped out of the windows, and we were left masters of the hall." He told us also that Josephine had given him a ring, worth full fifteen thousand francs, forbidding him to sell it, and saying she would attend to all his wants.

Our whole fine battalion was finally incorporated in the 96th half-brigade of the line, composed of old and experienced soldiers, and officers who were very strict. Our colonel was named M. Lepreux, a native of Paris, a good soldier, and kind to his officers. Our captain was named Merle, and he had all the qualities of a soldier. Strict, just, always present when rations were distributed to his grenadiers, on drill twice a day, strict in discipline; he was present at meal-times. He also taught us to shoot. We were at work every moment of our time. In three months our companies were able to go through the drill in presence of the First Consul.

I became very skilful in the use of arms. I was supple, and I had two good training masters who helped me on. They had examined me, and so had felt my belt-pockets; they therefore paid court to me. I paid for their drams. It was necessary to deal in this way with these hard drinkers. However, I had no reason to complain of them, for at the end of two months they put me to a severe test. They made a man pick a quarrel with me, and that without pretext. "Come," said this swaggerer to me, "draw your sabre, and I will spill a little of your blood."

– "We'll see about that, my boy." – "Find your second." – "I have none." Then my instructor, who was in the plot, said to me, "Would you like me to be your second?" – "I would, indeed, Father Palbrois." – "Off we go, then," said he, "and no more ado!" All four of us started out. We went a little way into the garden of the Luxembourg where there were two old tumble-down buildings, and they took me in between two old walls. There with my coat off I stood ready. "Now, strike the first blow," said I to him. – "Not I," he answered. – "All right, look out." Then I rushed upon him, and gave him no time to recover himself. My master ran in between us, sabre in hand. I pushed him aside. "Get away, let me kill him!" – "Come, come, that'll do; shake hands, and we will drink a bottle of wine." – "But that drop of my blood, doesn't he want it any longer?" – "It was all a joke," said my master.

I was now recognized as a good grenadier. I saw what they were after; this was a trick to make me pay my scot, which I did with a good grace, and they set it down to my credit. The grenadier, who wanted to kill me in the morning, was my best friend. He paid me all sorts of attentions and rendered me any number of small services. My two masters pushed me forward; four hours of drilling, two hours in the fencing school, making six hours daily. This life lasted three months, and I paid for many drams for these tipplers. Happily for me, M. and Madame Potier had filled my belt-pouch. I reaped the benefit of their goodness a long time.

We passed the winter in Paris. The First Consul's review took place in the month of February, at the Tuileries; the three half-brigades (24th light, 43rd and 96th of the line) formed a division of fifteen thousand men, the command of which was given to General Chambarlhac.[6] The First Consul

6 General Antoine Chambarlhac de Laubespin (1754–1826), former Bourbon infantry officer who served the Revolution as a lieutenant-colonel of volunteers. Promoted *general de brigade* for his part at Arcola, served under Marshal Victor in Italy. Later a garrison and staff officer.

put us through the evolutions, rode down the ranks and seemed satisfied. He called the colonels, and desired to see the conscripts apart. The company of grenadiers of the battalion of Seine-et-Marne was brought out. He told our captain, Merle, to make us go through the evolutions before him. He was surprised. "But these must be old troops you are drilling?" – "No," answered the captain, "they are a company of the auxiliary battalion formed at Fontainebleau." – "I am greatly pleased with this company; send it back to the battalion. Hold yourselves in readiness to march."

We received orders to set out for the camp of Dijon, which really had no existence, at least we never saw it. The whole division started for Corbeil, where Chambarlhac made us camp among the vines in the good department of Seine-et-Marne, which had made so many sacrifices for our battalion. We camped thus all along the route. From Auxerre he led us to St. Nitasse. The citizens were willing to lodge us, they brought us wagon-loads of wood and straw; but all in vain, we still had to burn their trellises and cut down their poplars. We were called "Chambarlhac's brigands." He, however, never bivouacked with his soldiers. This life continued till we reached Dijon, where we were billeted among the citizens and remained for six weeks.

General Lannes[7] formed his advance guard, and set out for Switzerland. We were the last to leave Dijon for Auxonne, where we lodged. The next day we went to Dôle where we only passed the night, and went on to Poligny. Thence we went to Morez. The next day we slept at Rousses, and thence to Nyon, where we brought all our little force together in a beautiful plain. We were reviewed by the First Consul, assisted by his generals, among whom was Lannes. We were

7 Jean Lannes (1769–1809), *general de brigade* from 1797. Appointed Marshal-in-1804; died of wounds received at Aspern-Essling in 1809. One of Napoleon's most able battlefield commanders, and the only man outside the Consul's family allowed to address him as "tu".

put through the evolutions, and made to form a square. The Consul kept us occupied the whole day; the next morning he marched us out, and started us for Lausanne, a very pretty village. The Consul passed the night there, and we were kindly received. The people were good to the soldiers; we never started out without a good bit of ham wrapped in a paper. We had guides all along our route, for we were in danger of losing our way.

Leaving Lausanne, we went around the end of the Lake of Geneva, and then went up the valley of the Rhone, and arrived at St. Maurice. Thence we started for Martigny. All these villages were as wretched as can possibly be imagined. We went into another valley, which might well have been called the valley of Hell. After that we left the valley of the Rhone, and went into the valley which leads to the St. Bernard, and came to the town of St. Pierre, situated at the foot of the St. Bernard pass. This village was composed entirely of huts covered with planks, and immense barns where we slept pell-mell. Here we dismounted our entire park in the presence of the Consul. Each of the guns was placed in a trough; at the end of the trough there was a large mortise by which to drag the gun, managed by a strong and intelligent gunner with forty grenadiers under his orders. We had to obey in absolute silence every movement made by his piece. If he commanded "Halt," we stood like stones; if he cried "Advance," we had to move on. He was our master.

Next morning at daybreak all was ready, and rations of biscuits were distributed to us. I put them on a string and hung them around my neck (the necklace was very inconvenient), and we had two pairs of shoes given us. That very evening our cannoneer made up his teams, which were composed of forty grenadiers to each gun; twenty to drag the piece (ten on each side, holding on to sticks put through ropes which served for traces), and twenty others who carried the others' muskets and the wheels and caissons of the piece. The Consul had taken the precaution to collect the mountaineers together for the purpose of picking up all the things which should have been left behind, promising them six francs for the journey and two rations a day. In this way everything was brought together at the place of rendezvous, and nothing was lost.

The next morning at daybreak, our master placed us by twenties at our pieces, ten on each side of a gun. I was put in the first place, to the right, in front; it was the most dangerous side, because it was next to the precipices. Then we started off with our three pieces. Two men carried each axle-tree, two carried a wheel, four carried the upper part of the caisson, eight carried the chest, eight others the muskets. Every one had his special duty and position. It was a most terrible journey. From time to time there were commands of "Halt," or "Advance," and not a word was spoken. All this was mere pastime, but when we reached the snow, matters became more serious. The road was covered with ice which cut our shoes, and our gunner could not manage his piece; it slipped constantly. He was obliged to mount it anew. This man needed all his courage to be able to hold out; "Halt!" "Advance!" he cried every moment, and all moved on in silence.

We had gone over a league of this terrible road, and it was necessary to give us a moment to rest and to put on some new shoes, for those we had on were in tatters, and also to take a bite of our biscuits. As I was taking my string from around my neck so as to take one off, the string broke, and all my biscuits went rolling down the precipice. How grieved I was to find myself without bread, and how my forty comrades laughed at my misfortune! "Come," said our gunner, "we must make up a feed for our leading horse, he understands the word of command." This made my comrades laugh again. "All right," they answered, "let each of us give a biscuit to our lead horse!" Then I recovered my spirits. I thanked them with all my heart and found myself richer than my comrades. We started off again well shod. "Come, my horses," said our gunner, "fall in, advance! When we reach the snow fields, we shall move more easily and not have so much trouble."

We did reach those terrible fields of perpetual snow, and found less difficulty; our gun-trough slid along more rapidly. General Chambarlhac came up with us and wanted to hasten us; he stood by the gunner and assumed the tone of command, but was ill received. "You don't command my piece," said the gunner. "I alone am responsible for it. Go your own way! these grenadiers do not belong to you for the present; I alone command them." The general went up to the gunner, but the latter commanded him to halt. "If you do not move out of my way I will knock you down with one blow of my crowbar. Move on, or I will throw you over the precipice!"

He was compelled to go away, and after the greatest exertion we reached the foot of the monastery. For four hundred feet the ascent is very rapid, and we could see that some troops had gone on ahead of us. The road had been opened and paths cut out leading to the monastery. We left our guns there, and four hundred of us grenadiers with a party of our officers entered the house of God, where men devoted to the cause of humanity are stationed to give aid and comfort to travellers. Their dogs are always on hand to guide unfortunate creatures who may have fallen in the avalanches of snow, and conduct them to this house, where every necessary comfort is provided.

While our colonel and other officers were in the halls beside bright fires, we received from these venerable men a bucket of wine for every twelve men, and a quarter of a pound of Gruyère cheese and a loaf of bread for each. We were lodged in the large corridors. The good monks did everything that they possibly could, and I believe they were well treated.

For our part, we pressed the good fathers' hands when we parted from them, and embraced their dogs, which caressed us as if they knew us. I cannot find words to express the veneration I feel for those men.

Our officers decided to take the guns down the descent,

and then our terrible task would be accomplished. Our brave captain, Merle, was appointed to conduct the three companies. As we crossed the lake which is at the foot of the monastery, we saw that in one place the ice had been broken. The good monk who showed us the way told us that it was the first time for forty years that he had seen the water. He pressed our captain's hand and bade us all farewell.

We descended almost perpendicularly, and reached St. Rémy. This village is down in a perfect hell of snow; the houses are very low, and covered with very broad tiles. Here we passed the night. I lay down on the floor of a stable where I found some straw, and passed a comfortable night along with twenty of my comrades; we were not cold. The next morning we had roll-call, and started to go to a place three leagues farther on. We were going to get out of hell and descend to paradise. "Be saving of your biscuits," said our captain, "we are not yet in Piedmont. We must go through many a difficult pass before we reach Italy." We came to the place of general rendezvous for all the regiments; it was a long gorge with a village set against the mountain. To the right, up a steep slope, there was a very high cliff. In two days all our forces were gathered together in this plain. Our brave officers were there without any boots and with no sleeves to their coats; it was pitiful to see them.

But this rendezvous seemed to be the end of the world; there was no way leading out of it. The Consul arrived and immediately ordered some heavy timbers to be brought. He superintended in person, with all the engineers, and they cut a hole in the rock, which was on the edge of a precipice. The cliff was so steep that it seemed as though it had been sawn. A piece of timber was placed in the hole; then he made them put another piece across it (this was more difficult to accomplish), and placed a man at the end to hold it in position. Then, by adding beams to these first two, it was no longer difficult to establish our bridge. Railings were put on the side next the precipice, and this wonderful piece of work was completed in two days. All our pieces were carried over, and nothing was lost.

On the other side the descent was easy to the valley, which led to the fort of Bard, which is surrounded by rocks. This fort is impregnable, it is impossible to batter it down; it is one great rock, with rocks all around it which tower above it, and which cannot be climbed. Here the Consul took many pinches of snuff, and had quite enough to do, with all his genius. His engineers set to work to make a road out of range of the guns. They discovered a foot-path among the rocks which was four hundred yards long, and he had it cleared out and made smooth. This foot-path led to the foot of a mountain; he had a path cut in the side of this mountain with iron sledge-hammers, wide enough for a man to ride through on horseback. But this was not his most difficult task. The artillery was close by, sheltered in a cave, but it could not follow the foot-path, but must pass near the fort. So this is the way he managed it; he first placed two guns on the road in front of the fort and fired into it. He was, however, obliged to withdraw them immediately, for a cannon-ball at once disabled one of our pieces. He sent a flag of truce and summoned the commander to surrender, but received an unfavourable reply. He was then obliged to employ strategy. He chose good sharp-shooters, gave them rations and cartridges, and placed them in the clefts of the rocks or had niches made for them in the rocks which overlooked the fort. Their shot took the garrison in the rear, so that they could not move about in their courtyard. The same day he discovered a very broad flat rock to the left of the fort. He immediately made an examination of it so as to station two guns on it. Men and ropes were called into requisition, and the two guns were placed upon this flat rock which was at least a hundred feet higher than the fort. Grape shot was rained down on it, and their gunners could not move from their casemates during the day; but still, there were our pieces and our caissons which must be taken past the fort.

As soon as Bonaparte learned that the horses belonging to the artillery trains had passed by he made preparations to send his artillery under the walls of the fort; he had the wheels and every part which could make any noise, even the soldiers' shoes, padded with straw, so as not to attract attention. At midnight all was ready. The cannoneers of our half-brigade asked for grenadiers to drag the artillery, and the twenty men who had climbed Mont St. Bernard were detailed for that purpose. I was among those who were under the same gunner under whom I had made the passage of the St. Bernard; he put me at the head of the first piece, and each of the others at his former post. The signal for departure was given; not a breath was heard. We got by without being noticed.

On reaching the opposite side, we turned immediately to the left; along the way for forty feet, we were protected by the rock which overlooked the road and concealed us from the fort. We found the horses all ready; they were hooked in at once and started off. We returned by the same road on tip-toe, holding on to each others' coat-tails; but we were heard, and grenades were thrown upon us over the ramparts. As they fell upon the opposite side of the road, no one was struck; we were only frightened and went back to get our muskets. This was a mistake; we should have been told to put them on the caissons, and go straight on. As it was, we were much exposed; but it is impossible to think of everything.

On our return from this perilous undertaking, the colonel congratulated us upon our success: "I thought you were lost, my brave fellows." Our captain made us form a circle around him, and said, "Grenadiers, you have just accomplished a great work. It is a great credit to the company." He shook us all by the hand, and said to me, "I am much pleased with your first services. I shall remember you." Then he pressed my hand again, saying, "I am very well pleased." We all answered, "Captain, we all love you." – "Ah, you are very kind; I shall not forget it, and I thank you."

We now went up a steep footpath; when we reached the top of the mountain, we saw the beautiful plains of Piedmont. The descent being practicable, we soon found ourselves in that paradise, and went on by forced marches as far as Turin, where the inhabitants were surprised to see an army arrive with its artillery.

This is the best-built city in Europe. All the houses are alike, all built after the same model, with streams of pure water in the gutters; all the streets are straight and very magnificent. Next day we set out for Milan. We made no halt, the march was forced. We made our entrance into the beautiful city of Milan, where all the people lined the streets to see us pass. They are very fine-looking. The street which leads to the Roman gateway is as handsome as can well be imagined. Passing through this gate, and turning to the left, we found a camp already established, and barracks completed. We saw that there was an army there ahead of us. We were made to stack arms, and men were detailed to go for rations, and I was among the number. No one was allowed to enter the city. I stole off, while the rations were being distributed, to go and see the cathedral. There is nothing like it, with all its columns of white marble. I went back to carry my bag of bread, and full rations were distributed to us.

We left there the next morning, and went to the right down to the river Po, which is a very deep stream. Here we found a flying bridge, which would hold five hundred men, and by means of a heavy rope, which was thrown across the river, one could cross by pulling on the rope. This consumed a great deal of time, especially in transferring the artillery. It was very late when we reached the heights, which were completely laid waste, and there we passed the night. Our division was sent on to Piacenza, a superb city. General Lannes was defeating the Austrians, and driving them back upon the Po. As for our division, we were sent from one place to another, and made to march in every direction to assist the divisions of the advance guard, and still we did not fire a shot. We only manoeuvred.

We again marched down to the Po. The Austrians seized upon the heights before reaching Montebello. Their artillery cut down our troops as they came up. We were obliged to send the 24th and 43rd half-brigades forward to take possession of the position. General Lannes finally succeeded in driving them back toward Montebello, and pursued them all night. The next morning he gave them another greeting, and our half-brigade occupied the heights which had cost so much to take, for they were twice as strong as we were. Next morning we started out to follow in the wake of that immense advance-guard, and we were stationed about half a league in rear of Montebello, in a broad walk in a beautiful plantation of mulberry-trees. There we were made to stack arms.

We were regaling ourselves upon the ripe fruit with which the trees were loaded, when suddenly at eleven o'clock we heard cannonading. We thought it was very far off. But we were mistaken, it was coming nearer to us. An aide-de-camp came up with orders for us to advance as rapidly as possible. The general was hard pressed on all sides. "To arms," said our colonel, "fall in, my brave regiment! Our turn has come to distinguish ourselves." And we shouted, "Hurrah for our colonel and all our brave officers!" Our captain, with his one hundred and seventy-four grenadiers, said "I will answer for my company. I will march at their head."

We were made to march by platoons, and load our muskets as we were marching, and here I put the first cartridge in my musket. I made the sign of the cross with my cartridge, and it brought me good luck. We reached the entrance of the village of Montebello, where we saw a great many wounded soldiers, and then we heard the drums beating the charge.

I was in the first platoon in the third rank, according to my height. As we were going out of the village, a cannon gave us a volley of grape-shot, which did no one any harm. I ducked my head at the sound of the gun, but my sergeant-major slapped me on the knapsack with his sabre, and said, "No ducking!" – "No, there shan't be!" I answered.

After the first discharge, Captain Merle cried, "To right and left into the trenches," so as to prevent our receiving another volley. As I did not hear the captain's command, I was left entirely exposed. I rushed past our drummers, towards the gun, and fell upon the gunners. They were loading again, and did not see me. I bayoneted all five of them, then leaped upon the piece, and my captain embraced me as he went by. He told me to guard my cannon, which I did, and our battalions dashed upon the enemy. It was a bloody affair of bayonets, with firing by platoons. The men of our brigade fought like lions.

I did not remain long in that position. General Berthier[8] came galloping up, and said to me, "What are you doing there?" – "General, you see what I've done. This gun is mine, I took it all by myself." – "Do you want something to eat?" – "Yes, general." (He talked through his nose.) Then he turned to his groom, and said, "Give him some bread." And taking out a little green memorandum-book, he asked me my name. "Jean-Roch Coignet." – "Your half-brigade?" – "Ninety-sixth." – "Your battalion?" – "The first." – "Your company?" – "First." – "Your captain?" – "Merle." – "Tell your captain to bring you to see the Consul at ten o'clock. Leave your gun and go and find him."

Then he galloped off, and I, delighted, went as fast as my legs would take me to rejoin my company, which had turned into a road to the right. This road was a sunk road, bordered on each side with hedges and occupied by some Austrian grenadiers. Our grenadiers were fighting them with bayonets. They were in complete disorder. I went up to my captain, and told him that my name had been taken down.

8 General Louis-Alexandre Berthier (1753–1815), Bonaparte's Chief-of-Staff from 1796; Commander-in-Chief of the Army of Reserve during the Second Italian campaign; appointed Marshal 1804; Chief-of-Staff to the *Grand Armée* from 1805 to 1814.

"That is good," said he. "Now, come through this opening, so that we can get ahead of the company; they are marching too fast, they will be cut off. Follow me." We went together through the opening. About a hundred steps off, on the other side of the road, there was a large wild pear-tree, and behind it a Hungarian grenadier, who was waiting till my captain came in front of him to fire upon him. But as he saw him, he cried to me, "Fire, grenadier." As I was behind the Hungarian, I took aim at a distance of only ten paces, and he fell, stone dead. Then my captain embraced me. "Don't leave me to-day," said he; "you have saved my life." And we hastened on to get ahead of the company which had advanced too rapidly.

A sergeant came out from the road as we had. Three grenadiers surrounded him. I ran to help him. They had hold of him, and called on me to surrender. I pointed my musket at them with my left hand, and using my right as a lever, plunged my bayonet into the belly of first one and then a second of the grenadiers. The third was thrown down by the sergeant, who took him by the head, and laid him flat. The captain finished the work. The sergeant recovered his belt and his watch, and in his turn plundered the three Austrians. We left him to look after himself, and put on his clothes, and hastened forward to get in front of the company, which was filing into an open field, where the captain once more took command, and rejoined the battalion, which was advancing at a quick step.

We were encumbered with three hundred prisoners, who had surrendered on the sunk road. We turned them over to some of the *hussars de la mort* who had escaped, for they had been cut to pieces that morning, and only two hundred out of a thousand were left. We took more prisoners; we did not know what to do with them; no one wanted to take charge of them, and they went along unguarded. They were routed completely.[9] They ceased firing upon us, and ran like rabbits,

9 The French inflicted 4,000 casualties on the Austrians for the loss of 500.

especially the cavalry, which caused a panic throughout the infantry. The Consul came up in time to see the battle won, and General Lannes covered with blood[10] (he looked dreadful), for he had been constantly in the thick of the fight, and it was he who made the last charge. If we had had two regiments of cavalry, all their infantry might have been taken.

That evening, the captain took me by the arm, presented me to the colonel, and told him what I had done during the day. He answered, "Why, captain, I knew nothing about this!" Then he shook me by the hand, and said, "I must make a note of it." – "General Berthier wishes to present him to the Consul at ten o'clock this evening," said my captain; "I am going to take him." – "Ah! I am glad of it, grenadier."

We went to see General Berthier, and my captain said to him, "Here is my grenadier who captured the gun, and since then he has saved my life and that of my first sergeant. He killed three Hungarian grenadiers." – "I will present him to the Consul." Then General Berthier and my captain went to see the Consul, and after talking a while with him they called me in. The Consul came up to me, and took me by the ear. I thought he was going to scold me, but, on the contrary, he was very kind; and still holding me by the ear, he said, "How long have you been in the service?" – "This is my first battle." – "Ah, indeed! it is a good beginning. Berthier, put him down for a musket of honour. You are too young to be in my Guard; for that, one must have made four campaigns. Berthier, make a note of him at once, and put it on the file. You may go now," said he to me, "but you shall one day be one of my guards."

Then my captain took me away, and we went off arm in arm as if I had been his equal. "Can you write?" said he. – "No, captain." – "Oh, that is a pity; if you did, your fortune would be made. But, never mind, you will be specially remembered." – "Thank you, captain."

10 Lannes was later created duc de Montebello for his part in the battle.

All the officers shook hands with me, and the brave sergeant, whose life I had saved, embraced me before the whole company, who cheered me. How proud I was!

Thus ended the battle of Montebello.

The next night we slept on the field of battle. On the morning of the 10th, the drums beat to arms. Lannes and Murat[11] set out with the vanguard to bid the Austrians good morning, but could not find them. They had not slept, and had marched all night. Our half-brigade finished picking up the wounded Austrians and French whom we had not found the night before. We carried them off to the ambulances, and it was very late before we left the battlefield.

We were all night on the march along cross roads. At midnight, M. Lepreux, our colonel, called a halt, and passed down the ranks saying, "Maintain absolute silence." Then he ordered the first battalion to move. We passed through narrow roads where we could not even see each other. The officers, who were on horseback, had dismounted, and the most profound silence reigned through the ranks. We filed out, and found ourselves in ploughed fields. We were still forbidden to make any noise, or to light any fire. We were obliged to lie down among the great clods of dirt, with our heads on our knapsacks, and wait for the day.

The next morning we were ordered on, with empty stomachs. We advanced only to find villages completely pillaged. We crossed ditches and marshes, a large stream, and came to villages filled with shrubbery. No provisions anywhere. All the houses were deserted. Our officers were overcome with fatigue and hunger. We left these marshy places, and turned to the left, into a village surrounded by

11 Joachim Murat (1767–1815), flamboyant cavalry leader and the archetypal *beau sabre* of the age; *general de brigade* May 1796; married Napoleon's sister Caroline, 1800; commanded the cavalry at Marengo; appointed Marshal in 1804; King of Naples from 1808. Executed in Italy, 1815.

orchards and gardens. Here we found some flour, a little bread, and a few animals. It was time, for we were dying of hunger.

On the 12th our two half-brigades came up on our right wing, and our division was reunited. We were told that the name of the village was Marengo. In the morning the breakfast-drum beat. What joy! Twenty-seven wagons filled with bread had arrived. What happiness for the starving men! Every one was willing to do extra duty. But what was our disappointment! The bread was all damp and mouldy. We had to put up with it though.

On the 13th, at break of day, we were made to march forward into an open plain, and at two o'clock we were placed in line of battle and piled arms. Aides-de-camp arrived from our right, who flew around in every direction. A general engagement was beginning; the 24th half-brigade was detached and sent forward unsupported. It marched a long distance, came up with the Austrians, and had a serious encounter, in which it lost heavily. It was obliged to form square in order to resist the attack of the enemy. Bonaparte abandoned it in this terrible position. It was said that he desired to leave it to be destroyed. The reason was this. At the time of the battle of Montebello, this half-brigade, having been ordered to advance by General Lannes, began by firing upon its officers. The soldiers spared only one lieutenant. I do not know what could have been the motive for this terrible vengeance. The Consul, informed of what had taken place, concealed his indignation. He could not give way to it when in face of the enemy. The lieutenant who had survived the destruction of his comrades was appointed captain; the staff immediately re-formed. But, nevertheless, it was understood that Bonaparte had not forgotten.

About five or six o'clock in the evening we were sent to extricate the 24th. When we arrived, soldiers and officers heaped insults upon us, declaring that we had wantonly left them to destruction, as if it depended upon us to march to their assistance. They had been overwhelmed. I suppose they had lost half their men; but this did not prevent their fighting still better the next day.

The Austrians had occupied the city of Alessandria. All night long we were under arms; the outposts were placed as far forward as possible, and small covering-parties advanced. On the 14th, at three o'clock in the morning, they surprised two of our small posts of four men and killed them. This was the signal for the morning reveille. At four o'clock there was firing on our right. Our drums beat to arms all along the line, and the aides-de-camp came and ordered us to form our lines of battle.[12] We were made to fall back a little behind a fine field of wheat, which was on a slightly rising ground and concealed us, and there we waited a little while. Suddenly their sharpshooters came out from behind the willows and from the marshes, and then the artillery opened fire. A shell burst in the first company and killed seven men; a bullet killed the orderly near General Chambarlhac, who galloped off at full speed. We saw him no more all day.

A little general came up, who had fine moustaches: he found our colonel, and asked where was our general. We answered, "He is gone." – "Very well, I will take command of the division." And he immediately took charge of the company of grenadiers of whom I was one, and led us to the attack in one rank. We opened fire. "Do not halt while loading," said he. "I will recall you by beat of drum." And he hastened to rejoin his division. He had scarcely returned to his post when the column of Austrians started from behind the willows, deployed in front of us, fired by

12 The surrender of the French garrison, under Massena, at Genoa on 4 June had allowed General Melas to bring his main army to bear against Napoleon. Blithely unaware that some 31,000 Austrians were nearby, Napoleon had detached two divisions, reducing the Reserve's strength to 23,700; he had also failed to anticipate that Melas might attack, which he did at 3 a.m. on the 14th. Not until 11 a.m. did Napoleon concede that the attack was not a bluff.

battalions, and riddled us with small shot. Our little general answered, and there we were between two fires, sacrificed . . . I ran behind a big willow-tree, and fired into that column, but I could not stand it. The balls came from every direction, and I was obliged to lie down with my head on the ground in order to shield myself from the small shot, which were making the twigs fall all over me; I was covered with them. I believed myself lost.

Fortunately our whole division now advanced by battalions. I got up and found myself in a musket-company; I continued in it all the rest of the day, for not more than fourteen of our hundred and seventy grenadiers remained; the rest were killed or wounded. We were obliged to resume our first position, riddled by small shot. Everything fell upon us who held the left wing of the army, opposite the high road to Alessandria, and we had the most difficult position to maintain. They constantly endeavoured to outflank us, and we were obliged to close up continually, in order to prevent them from surprising us in the rear.

Our colonel ran up and down the line, inspiring us with his presence; our captain, who had lost his company and who was wounded in the arm, performed the duties of orderly officer to our intrepid general. We could not see one another in the smoke. The guns set the wheatfield on fire, and this caused a general commotion in the ranks. Some cartridge-boxes exploded; we were obliged to fall back and form again as quickly as possible. This weakened our position, but the situation was restored by the intrepidity of our chiefs, who looked out for everything.

In the centre of the division was a barn surrounded by high walls, where a regiment of Austrian dragoons had concealed themselves; they burst upon a battalion of the 43rd brigade and surrounded it; every man of it was captured and taken to Alessandria. Fortunately General Kellermann[13] came up

13 Francois Kellermann (1770–1835); promoted *general de brigade* for his cavalry charge at Marengo.

with his dragoons and restored order. His charges silenced the Austrian cavalry.

Nevertheless, their numerous artillery overwhelmed us and we could hold out no longer. Our ranks were thinned visibly; all about us there were only wounded men to be seen, and the soldiers who bore them away did not return to their ranks; this weakened us very much. We had to yield ground. Their columns were constantly reinforced; no one came to our support. Our musket-barrels were so hot that it became impossible to load for fear of igniting the cartridges. There was nothing for it but to piss into the barrels to cool them, and then to dry them by pouring in loose powder and setting it alight unrammed. Then, as soon as we could fire again, we retired in good order. Our cartridges were giving out and we had already lost an ambulance when the consular guard arrived with eight hundred men having their linen overalls filled with cartridges; they passed along our rear and gave us the cartridges. This saved our lives.

Then our fire redoubled and the Consul appeared; we felt ourselves strong again. He placed his guard in line in the centre of the army and sent it forward. They immediately held the enemy, forming square and marching in battle order. The splendid horse-grenadiers came up at a gallop, charged the enemy at once and cut their cavalry to pieces. Ah! that gave us a moment to breathe, it gave us confidence for an hour. But not being able to hold out against the consular horse-grenadiers, they turned upon our half-brigade and drove in the first platoons, sabring them. I received such a blow from a sabre on my neck that my queue was almost cut off; fortunately I had the thickest one in the regiment. My epaulet was cut off with a piece of my coat and shirt, and the flesh a little scratched. I fell head over heels into a ditch.

The cavalry charges were terrible. Kellermann made three in succession with his dragoons; he led them forward and led them back. The whole of that body of cavalry leaped over me as I lay stunned in the ditch. I got rid of my knapsack, my cartridge-pouch, and my sabre. I took hold of the tail of a retreating dragoon's horse, leaving all my belongings in the ditch. I made a few strides behind that horse which carried me away, and then fell senseless, not being able to breathe any longer. But, thank God, I was saved! But for my head of hair, which I still have at seventy-two years of age, I should have been killed.

I had time to find a musket, a cartridge-pouch, and a knapsack (the ground was covered with them). I resumed my place in the second company of grenadiers, who received me with cordiality. The captain came and shook hands with me. "I thought you were lost, my brave fellow," said he; "you got a famous sabre stroke, for you have no queue and your shoulder is badly hurt. You must go to the rear." – "I thank you, I have plenty of cartridges, and I am going to revenge myself upon such troopers as I meet; they have done me too much harm; they shall pay for it."

We retreated in good order, but the battalions were visibly reduced, and quite ready to give up but for the encouragement of their officers. We held out till noon without being disordered. Looking behind, we saw the Consul seated on the bank of the ditch by the highway to Alessandria, holding his horse by the bridle, and flirting up little stones with his riding-whip. The cannon-balls which rolled along the road he did not seem to see. When we came near him he mounted his horse and set off at a gallop behind our ranks. "Courage, soldiers," said he, "the reserves are coming. Stand firm!" Then he was off to the right of the army. The soldiers were shouting, "Vive Bonaparte!" But the plain was filled with the dead and wounded, for we had no time to gather them up; we had to face in all directions. Battalion fire from échelons formed in the rear, arrested the enemy, but those cursed cartridges would no longer go into our fouled and heated musket barrels. We had to piss into them again. This caused us to lose time.

My brave captain, Merle, passed behind the second battalion, and the captain said to him, "I have one of your grenadiers; he has received a famous sabre-cut." – "Where is he? Bring him out, so that I may see him. Ah! it is you, is it, Coignet?" – "Yes, captain." – "I thought you were among the dead, I saw you fall into the ditch." – "They gave me a famous sabre-cut; see, they have cut off my queue." – "Look here, feel in my knapsack, take my 'life-preserver,' and drink a cup of rum to restore you. This evening, if we live, I shall come and seek you out." – "Now I am saved for the day, captain; I shall fight finely." The other captain said, "I wanted him to go to the rear, but he would not." – "I can readily believe it; he saved my life at Montebello." They took me by the hand. There's nothing like appreciation! I shall feel the value of it all my life.

Meanwhile, do all we could, we were beginning to fail. It was two o'clock. "The battle is lost," said our officers, when suddenly an aide-de-camp arrived at a sweeping gallop. He cried, "Where is the First Consul? The reserves are up. Courage! you will be reinforced at once, within half an hour." Then up came the Consul. "Steady," said he, as he passed along, "reserves are at hand." Our poor little platoons gazed down the road to Montebello every time we turned around.

Finally came the joyful cry, "Here they are, here they are!" That splendid division came up, carrying arms.[14] It was like a forest swayed by the wind. The troops marched at a steady pace, with batteries of guns in the spaces between the half-brigades, and a regiment of heavy cavalry bringing up the rear. Having reached their position, they took possession of it as though they had chosen it expressly for their line of battle. On our left, to the left of the highway, a very tall hedge concealed them; not even the cavalry could be seen.

14 General Desaix – having intelligently disobeyed orders to march to Novi – arrived at the battlefield with his division at around 3 p.m. General Boudet's division arrived two hours later.

Meanwhile we continued our withdrawal. The Consul gave his orders, and the Austrians came along as though they were on their way home, with sloped arms; they paid no attention to us; they believed us to be utterly routed. We had gone three hundred paces past the division of General Desaix, and the Austrians were also about to pass the line, when the thunderbolt descended upon the head of their column. Grape-shot, shells, and musket-fire rained upon them. Our drums beat a general charge; the whole line wheeled about and ran forward. We did not shout, we yelled.

The men of the brave 9th demi-brigade dashed like rabbits through the hedge; they rushed with their bayonets upon the Hungarian grenadiers, and gave them no time to recover. The 30th and 59th fell in their turn upon the enemy and took four thousand prisoners.[15] The regiment of heavy cavalry charged in turn. Their whole army was routed. Every man did his duty, but the 9th excelled them all. Our other cavalry came up, and rushed in solid column upon the Austrian cavalry, whom they so completely routed that they rode off at full gallop to Alessandria. An Austrian division coming from the right wing charged us with bayonets. We ran up also and crossed bayonets with them. We overcame them, and I received a small cut in the right eyelid, as I was parrying a thrust from a grenadier. I did not miss him, but the blood blinded my eyes (they had a grudge against my head that day). It was a small matter. I continued to march and did not suffer from it. We followed them until nine o'clock in the evening: we threw them into the ditches full of water. Their bodies served as a bridge upon which others could cross over. It was frightful to see these unfortunate wretches drowning, and the bridge all blocked with them. We could hear nothing but their cries; they were cut off from the city, and we took their wagon-trains and guns. At ten o'clock, my captain sent

15 The Austrians lost approximately 7,000 troops as prisoner in total; killed and wounded numbered another 7,000. French losses were upwards of 7,000 – about a quarter of the troops deployed.

his servant to ask me to take supper with him, and my eye was dressed and my hair put in good condition.

We slept on the battlefield, and the next day at four o'clock in the morning, a party with flags of truce came out of the city. They demanded an armistice, and went to the headquarters of the Consul. They were well escorted. The camp became gay once more. I said to my captain, "If you please, I would like to go to headquarters." – "What for?" – "I have some acquaintances among the guard. Let me have a man to go with me." – "But it's a long way." – "No matter, we will return early, I promise you." – "Very well, go."

We set out, our sabres at our sides. Upon reaching the grille of the château of Marengo, I asked for a cavalry sergeant who had been long in the corps, and a very handsome man appeared. "What do you want with me?" said he. – "I wish to know how long you have been in the guard of the Directory." – "Nine years." – "It was I who trained your horses, and who rode them at the Luxembourg. If you remember, it was M. Potier who sold them to you." – "That is so," said he to me; "come in, I will present you to my captain." He told my comrade to wait, and introduced me as follows: "Here is the young man who trained our horses at Paris." – "And who rode so well," added the captain. – "Yes, captain." – "But you are wounded." – "Ah! it is a bayonet thrust from a Hungarian. I punished him. But they cut my queue half off. If I had been on horseback that would not have happened to me." – "I dare say," said he, "I know your skill in that respect. Sergeant, give him a drink." – "Have you any bread, captain?" – "Get four loaves for him. I am going to show you your horses and see if you will recognize them." I pointed out twelve of them to him. "That's right," said he, "you recognized them very easily." – "Yes, captain. If I had been mounted on one of those horses, they would not have cut off my hair; but they shall answer for it. I shall enter the Consul's guard. I am marked out for a silver musket, and when I have made four campaigns, the Consul has promised to put me in his guard." – "Very likely, my brave grenadier. If you ever come to Paris there is my address. What is your captain's name?" – "Merle, first company of grenadiers of the 96th half-brigade of the line." – "There are five francs to drink my health. I promise to write to your captain. Give him this bottle of brandy with my compliments." – "I thank you for your kindness, now I must go; my comrade is waiting for me at the grille, I must take him some bread at once." – "I did not know it, off you go, then. Take another loaf and be off to join your corps." – "Farewell, captain, you saved the army by your splendid charges. I saw you at it." – "That is so," said he.

He, with his sergeant, accompanied me as far as the grille. The wounded of the guard were stretched on some straw in the courtyard, and amputations were being made. It was heart-rending to hear their cries on all sides. I came out with my heart rent with grief, but a more horrible spectacle was to be seen on the plain. We saw the battlefield covered with Austrian and French soldiers who were picking up the dead and placing them in piles and dragging them along with their musket straps. Men and horses were laid pell-mell in the same heap, and set on fire in order to preserve us from pestilence. The scattered bodies had a little earth thrown over them to cover them.

I was stopped by a lieutenant, who said to me, "Where are you going?" – "I am taking some bread to my captain." – "You got it at the Consul's headquarters. Could you give me a bit?" – "Yes." I said to my comrade, "You have a small piece, give it to the lieutenant." – "Thank you, my brave grenadier, you have saved my life. Go down the road to the left." And he had the kindness to accompany us a good bit of the way, fearing we might be arrested. I thanked him for his goodness, and soon reached my captain, who smiled when he saw my package. "Have you been on a looting party?" – "Yes, captain, I have brought you some bread and some brandy." – "And where did you find it?" I related my adventure. "Ah," said he, "you were born under a lucky star." – "See, here is a loaf and a bottle of good brandy. Put some in your 'life-preserver.' If you want a loaf for the colonel and the general, you can divide with them; they are likely to need it." – "That's a good idea; I will do so with pleasure, and I thank you on their behalf." – "But do you first eat and drink some of this good brandy, sir. I am delighted to be able to return the service you rendered me and the good meal you enabled me to enjoy." – "You shall tell me all that some other time. I am going to take this bread to the colonel and the general."

All this the captain set down to my account. On the 16th the army received orders to carry laurels, and the oak-trees had a hard time. At noon we marched past before the First Consul, with our excellent general on foot in front of the remnant of his division. General Chambarlhac had appeared on horseback at the head of his division, but he was saluted with a volley from our half-brigade, and he disappeared. We never saw him again, and the sequel of that story is unknown to us.[16] But we gave three cheers for our little general who had led us so bravely on the day of the battle.

On the morning of the 16th, General Melas sent back our prisoners (there were about twelve hundred of them) and this was a great delight to us. Provisions had been given them, and they were triumphantly received on their arrival. On the 26th, the first Austrian column filed before us, and we watched them go by. What a superb column it was! there were men enough in it to have overwhelmed us at that moment, seeing how few of us there were. It was fearsome to see such a body of cavalry and artillery; they were three days in passing. They had no artillery left, only baggage-wagons. They left us half of their stores; we got considerable

16 Chambarlac was appointed to garrison posts; Baron, 1911.

provisions and ammunition. They yielded to us forty leagues of country, and retired behind the Mincio. We brought up the rear of the last column. We travelled along together; our lame men mounted on their carriages; they marched on the left and we on the right side of the road. No one quarrelled, and we were the best friends in the world.

Marching thus, we came to the flying bridge over the river Po. As only five hundred men could cross at one time over this flying bridge, we lost no time, and continued our march to Cremona, the place which we were to garrison during the three months of truce agreed upon. Cremona is a beautiful city which is proof against surprise. Splendid ramparts and solid gates. The town is considerable; there is a handsome cathedral with an immense dial; an arrow-hand makes the circuit of it once in a hundred years. In the markets they weigh everything; even onions and grass; it is filled with delicious melons called watermelons; there are milk taverns there. But it is the worst garrison in Italy; we slept on the ground, on straw filled with vermin. Breeches, jackets and undervests were in a deplorable condition. I conceived the idea of killing the vermin which bit me. I made some lye in a copper boiler and put my jacket in it. Alas for me! The jacket melted away like paper, nothing was left me but the lining. There I was entirely naked, and nothing in my knapsack to put on.

My good comrades came to my assistance. I at once had letters written to my father and my uncle; I informed them of my distress, and begged them to send me a little money. Their answers were long delayed but came at last. I received both letters at the same time (not prepaid); they each cost me a franc and a half, in all three francs for postage. My old sergeant happened to be present. "Do me the kindness to read them." He took my two letters. My father said, "If you were a little nearer I would send you a little money." And my uncle said, "I have just paid my taxes, I can send you nothing." Such were my two charming letters! I never wrote to them again in my life. After the truce, I had to mount guard at the outposts four times, as a forward sentinel on the bank of the Mincio, at fifteen sous a watch, in order to pay this debt.

A FOOT SOLDIER
IN EGYPT, 1801

Sergeant David Robertson, 92nd Foot

Born in 1777, Robertson, a Scottish shoemaker, began his military career with the Duke of Atholl's Company of Volunteers but, by his own admission finding home duty lacking "bustle and variety," he then enlisted in the Caithness Highlanders and thence in a line regiment, the 92nd Highlanders. It was with the 92nd that Robertson arrived in Egypt in 1801.

The guerre *in Egypt was always a sideshow of the Napoleonic conflagration, even if a bloody and disease-ridden one for those obliged to fight it. Begun in 1798 chiefly to sate Napoleon's desire to enhance his career through continued military glory, (although he persuaded the Directory in Paris that a campaign there would break Britain's commerce with the Levant, even threaten India), the indecent haste with which he quit the country after defeating the Marmelukes at the Pyramids, 21 July 1798, and the Turks at the first battle of Aboukir, 25 July 1799, to pursue his political schemes in France only proved its strategic unimportance. Nevertheless, unloved and undersupplied, the* Armée d'Orient *was not to be easily beaten by the British when they ordered Sir Ralph Abercromby and his 18,000-strong force to remove it from Egyptian soil in 1801. The four hour "Night Battle of Aboukir" on 22 March, the centrepiece of Robertson's memoir and the decisive encounter in the British re-occupation of Egypt, cost the British 1,376 casualties – among them the commander-in-chief, mortally shot in the thigh – and reduced Robertson's own regiment to a bare 100 men fit for duty. French losses were upwards of 3,000 killed and wounded.*

Robertson served throughout the remainder of the campaign in Egypt, with its parched desert and dysentery, which culminated in the capitulation of Alexandria on 20 August 1801. Thereafter Robertson saw service in the Walcheren, Danish, Peninsular, and Waterloo campaigns. He was discharged on a pension of 1s 10d on 22 June 1818.

Being brought up in troublous times, and the war arising out of the French Revolution fast approaching, when I arrived at manhood, I became fond of a military life; and in the year 1797, at which period the disturbances in the north country arose about the balloting of the militia, I entered a company of volunteers which the Duke of Atholl had obtained permission to raise; but after being some time in it, I found the life not such as I was led to expect – there was not enough of bustle and variety in it for me; and the same changeless routine of duty, and scene of the Grampians, induced me to leave the corps, which I did, and entered into the Caithness Highlanders, then commanded by Sir John Sinclair, and in which I had not been many days enlisted, when I was ordered to Ireland along with the regiment. It was immediately at the close of the rebellion in that unhappy country when we arrived there, and we had little or no duty to perform. When the expedition under Sir Ralph Abercromby was formed, the several regiments of which it was composed, were found so weak, from the affair in Holland in 1799, that in the beginning of the year 1800, an offer was given to most of the Fencible regiments then in Ireland to enter into regiments of the line. I immediately took advantage of the offer, and volunteered into the 92nd Highlanders, then on board of ship, and ready to sail for Egypt.

After a passage of three weeks we arrived at Malta. There, those regiments that had not been engaged to serve out of Europe, had an offer of returning or accompanying the expedition. Several embraced the former offer, and were sent to Minorca and Gibraltar. The entrance to the harbour of Malta is very narrow, and is strongly guarded with heavy batteries on each side, from the water's edge to the top of the rock. When the entrance is passed, however, you reach a capacious basin, – the finest anchorage, for ships of any class, that could possibly be imagined. Even close to the quay, the largest ships can ride in safety and security. The basin or harbour is surrounded with storehouses, merchants' shops, &c.; and rising behind these are beautiful vineyards and gardens, raised in terraces with earth brought from the island of Sicily in boats. This arises from the nature of the soil of Malta being so thin and sandy of itself, that nothing could grow upon it to any perfection, or in abundance. There are several very excellent edifices in Malta, particularly St. John's church, which is a very fine building, and which, like all the Roman Catholic churches, has relics of one or other of the different saints to show. It is in possession, as its priests say, of the head of its patron saint, John, which is held in high veneration by them, and shown to the curious in these things. The Mason Lodge is also a fine structure.

After remaining on the island a week, we were ordered to embark on board the fleet for our destination, which we did, and immediately set sail for it. We passed a number of islands in our way, such as Candia, Rhodes, &c. On passing the latter, we were pointed out the strait, where the first wonder of the world, the huge Colossus, stretched from side to side his mighty legs. On passing Rhodes, we shaped our course for the coast of Asia Minor. On reaching it, it was so rocky and precipitous, that a considerable time elapsed before any place of safe anchorage could be found; but at length an opening in the ridge of rocks was discovered, on which, – as no one would venture to pilot the fleet through it, – Sir Sidney Smith, observing a small Turkish fishing boat at a short distance, with some fishermen in it, ordered it to be brought to him. This was no sooner done, than making the necessary inquiries at the fishermen as to the possibility of getting through the rocks, and being satisfied with the answers, he gave the necessary orders, and followed the boat with the *Tiger* of 80 guns. The channel was so narrow, that only one ship could go through it at a time, but all passed safely. The bay that we then entered was one of the finest we could wish to behold. It is large and capacious enough to contain the most extensive navy that Britain could ever boast of. It was at this bay that Bonaparte escaped from Lord Nelson in 1798. The country around it abounds in wood and water, with which necessaries the fleet was ordered to be provided. The sick, of which there were a great many, were ordered to be encamped on shore for the recovery of their health, so that, for a while, we had a bustling time of it, between erecting camps and carrying wood and water to the ships. The camps were erected close by the sea-side, in order that the invalids would take advantage of bathing daily, which the most of them did, and many improved greatly, and recovered their health; those that died were buried at the bay-side.

While at this place, we were visited by one of the most awful storms of hail I ever remember to have witnessed. The storm was accompanied with thunder and lightning: the former so loud, and the latter so vivid and frequent, that it seemed as if all the elements of nature would rend. A considerable part of the small shipping, and also some of the large, broke from their anchorages, and were drifted on shore; but these sustained less damage than might have been expected from the fury of the storm. One of the gunboats was struck by the lightning and went on fire, but before it had extended to any length, it was, through considerable exertion, got under; and, with the exception of the burning of the greater portion of the rigging, no other damage was sustained. The tents erected on shore were either torn up, knocked down, or blown away, which left the sick in sad circumstances, more especially as it was night; how many of them recovered its effects, it is not easy to say. It was in the month of January, and the wind was piercing cold, which, contrasted with the generally hot sun through the day, made it, without shelter of any sort, doubly ill to bear; but the long looked for dawn, by many a poor fellow, at length arrived, and the tents were set about being re-erected, or other ones put in their place, and in a short time every thing was, as far as possible, in the same situation as it had been the day before. A little money was issued to the troops while here, which, by degrees, became the means of inducing the inhabitants to form a market at the bay. There was a tolerable supply of almost every thing we wanted, especially of goats and sheep, which we purchased at a dollar each; also plenty of fruits and vegetables. Little afterwards occurred which would interest the reader during the remainder of our stay here, which was up to about the middle of February, when we were again ordered to embark.

On our way to our destination we captured a French vessel, loaded with cocked hats and hussar boots, proceeding to Egypt, for Napoleon's army. After being eight days at sea, we at length descried the Egyptian coast; and, on the same evening, March 1, 1801, anchored in Aboukir Bay. The land, about the bay, lies rather low; and the first object we descried, on making it, was the ruins of the village of Aboukir, which is situated on an eminence somewhat higher than any ground lying immediately around it, nearer the Nile. We remained in the bay from the evening of the 1st, until the evening of the 7th March, busily employed in making every preparation for effecting a landing. During these undertakings, the weather was so stormy that, although every thing had been in readiness, a landing could not have been attempted earlier; however, on that evening, the troops were transferred in boats to a line of small vessels, that approached nearly to the shore, and about six o'clock on the morning of the 8th, all were ready to land. The small vessels were formed in a line to the right, extending towards the village and fort of Aboukir, and a signal was flying from a boat in the centre of it, as an object for the seamen to push past, but to keep the line as nearly as possible circumstances would allow. We were transferred from the vessels to the beats, and, all being ready, a musket was fired from the signal boat, and the seamen pushed forward, while three cheers were given by the whole of the troops. The moment the enemy saw our immediate intention to land, they commenced a heavy fire from the fort of Aboukir, and also from a number of field pieces in front on the shore, while squadrons of cavalry were drawn up prepared to receive us, the moment the boats would take the ground. We were not permitted to load our muskets until we landed or got out of the boats, and this proved to be a far less easy affair than we imagined. For a long way in, the water was extremely shallow, and the boats took the ground sooner than was expected; but the troops leaped out of them when they struck, and not a few, owing to the weight of ammunition and accoutrements they had to carry, the hurry, and one thing or another, lost their lives. The water, in several places, reached their middle. The instant the troops leaped out of the boats, all that could do so, loaded, and smartly prepared to charge. Meanwhile the French cavalry had advanced into the water, and were making considerable havoc among the British troops, during the bustle of disembarkation. But the confusion being partially got over, a loud "hurra" was given, and we pushed for the land, driving the cavalry before us; but they had no sooner given way, than a tremendous fire from the French infantry opened upon us. Fortunately, however, at this juncture, the troops on the right having gained the shore, the enemy's front fell back, and those opposed to them, among whom was myself, gained the beach, and pursued them for about two hundred yards, leaving the beach strewed with dead, dying, and wounded. We were then ordered to halt and pile arms. When we did so, I went to view the havoc that had been made, and, never having seen the effects of a battle before, I was struck with horror at the sight. During the time we were actively engaged with the enemy, I had no time to observe particularly what was going on, or to think of my own situation. I felt all eager to reach the shore along with the rest of my comrades; but after reaching it, and when the affray was over, feelings arose in my breast such as never penetrated it before. The first man I saw killed was a French officer, who no sooner fell than several soldiers stripped him, so as to leave him almost naked. At that time I wished, however anxious I formerly was to be one, that I had never become a soldier; but it was too late to repent, and I felt I must just submit to the life with the best possible nerve I could. The groans of the dying and the wounded, with the ghastly visages of the dead, that lay upon the field, were fearful to hear and witness. My very heart shuddered at the sound and at the sight, and I felt thankful and greatly relieved when we were called from the sad scene, to a duty which had the effect of partially erasing it from my mind.

A little to our right, and on our front, were a number of huts made of planks from the date tree, which had been occupied by the enemy; who, not anticipating that we would be able to effect a landing, had made a provision against such a result for carrying off their baggage &c. The consequence was that in our endeavours to procure fresh water, (the duty our company was required to perform) for what with the effects of the powder in our mouths, in biting off the ends of the cartridges, and the heat of the day, our throats were parched and burning, on reaching the huts, found, to our inexpressible joy, not only plenty of water, but every thing to fill a hungry stomach also, that could be desired. Poultry, goats, and sheep, in numbers, were *lounging*, (if I may use the expression) about the doors of the wooden tenements. To finish this gladdening sight, we found, in the inside of the huts, the camp kettles of the enemy on fires, containing mutton and other edibles, in process of preparation for a meal, entirely *a la Francois*. We remained until we supposed the contents of the kettles had been long enough on the fires, and then falling to in the best way that we could, managed to make a very hearty diet after the fatigue we had undergone, and cracking many a merry joke over the mortification the French would feel at losing so good a meal, especially when it was so nearly ready to be devoured by their epicurish maws. In the huts we found a considerable number of trunks and portmanteaus, but, on examining them, they contained nothing of consequence or value.

Towards evening we moved forward after the enemy; but darkness rapidly coming on, before we proceeded far, we were ordered to form into line, and take up our camp for the night. When I lay down upon my weary pallet, I could not help thinking on my present situation, and interweaving with it what might be my future career. I imagined myself as having fallen into the hands of the enemy, – a prisoner, and wounded; being rudely treated, and subjected to many hardships. But such thoughts had no sooner taken possession of my breast, or had lingered in it for a little while, than others of hope again returned. A handful of raw troops had beat the best troops in Europe – the conquerors of Italy – the Invincibles of the "Great General;" and why should I despair, or indulge in forlorn anticipations. Altogether, while lying on or near the spot where a French army had been routed or slain, by the rawest soldiers, taking them as a whole, that could be collected together, sufficed to cheer my spirits very considerably. In fact, I began to look forward to success attending us, with a good deal of confidence; and the more especially when I reflected that we were under the guidance of the gallant Sir Ralph Abercromby.

As we had no tents ashore, owing to the boats being

employed during the whole night in landing the cavalry, we lay exposed to the air, with nothing more for protection against its effects than our usual clothes. As might be expected, we were otherwise than comfortable; at least, for myself and several of my comrades, we were exceedingly cold, and slept but little. The wind was blowing from the sea, and, from our situation, we had not the slightest protection or shelter from it. But morning at length came, and we were ordered to get under arms. Although I have said "morning," it was an hour before daylight when this order was given; and we were subjected to the same unpleasant duty every morning while we were in the country: it is called an "alarm post parade." Seeing our cold and out-of-sort like appearance, when we had mustered together, the Commander-in-Chief ordered one-half allowance of rum to each man, – in quantity a gill.

In a short time after we had swallowed our allowance, the 92nd Regiment, with a small party of dragoons, were ordered to advance in pursuit of the enemy, under the directions of Lieutenant-Colonel Erskine, and Major, now Sir R. Wilson. When we had proceeded on our march for about an hour, we came in sight of a flag-staff, on a little eminence, or piece of rising ground, where a battery had been erected; but, anticipating our approach, the enemy had deserted it, taking with them their guns, and any thing serviceable to them. They had retreated to Alexandria, which city we came in sight of just as the sun was shining in full splendour over it. The roofs of the mosques and houses glittered in refulgence – giving to us the appearance of its being a rather magnificent city. Here we halted and refreshed ourselves.

The country, from the beach to where we had arrived, was little else than a sandy desert. Here and there, however, a few date trees might have been seen growing, or rather standing, as if it were to contrast the blessings of vegetation with a sterile soil.

By this time preparations had been made by the enemy, in

the Fort of Aboukir[1], to stand a siege, as we ascertained that
the 2nd Regiment had been sent to blockade it. At the same
time munitions of war of every description had been landed
from the ships for the army; but great difficulty and labour
was experienced in getting forward the artillery, although
only a few pieces, from the nature of the ground over which
they had to be conveyed. By this time the supply of water,
which we had fallen in with, was consumed, and there was no
well except in the neighbourhood of the fort, and to which we
could not get. The consequence was, that so thirsty were
several of the men, that they adopted the expedient of trying
to allay their parched throats with salt water; but the result
may be imagined – instead of benefiting them, it made them
infinitely worse. Two days were the troops thus in want of
water, roasting under a burning sun; but some of them, while
digging at the sea side, fortunately discovered a fresh-water
spring. The news soon spread, and were communicated
through the army; and in almost less time than I have taken
to relate it, bayonets, spades, and instruments of every
description, were put in requisition to obtain a proper
supply, and with so much success, that in a short time there
was not a man but had abundance to quench his thirst. We
considered it somewhat remarkable that we should discover
freshwater springs, (for we fell in with a number of them) so
close to the sea, that when the tide was at its height we could
have placed one foot into one of the springs, and another into
the salt water, at the same time.

We remained from the 8th to the 12th March in this place,
when the 90th and 92nd Regiments, being the junior regiments, were ordered to advance and act as riflemen, there
being none of these troops with the army. Accordingly, the
two regiments commenced their march in extended line, the
90th Regiment on the right, and the 92nd on the left. We

1 Commanded by General Louis Friant (1758–1829), later Inspector
General of Infantry and head of the Grenadiers of the Old Guard at
Waterloo.

were partially engaged with several bodies of the enemy
during the whole day, but only in the matter of exchanging
a few shots at intervals, or when an opportunity occurred. As
the company to which I belonged, and some others, were
moving forward, we passed over a great number of bleached
human bodies, scattered over more than an acre of ground.
How they had come there we knew not, for it was evident that
they had lain exposed for a considerable period. We kept
moving forward, covered by the remainder of the army, in
two columns, one on the right led, as said, by the 90th
Regiment, and the other on the left, by the 92nd. We
continued our march, until at length we came in sight of
the French army, formed in line on a rising ground; and they
appeared to be strongly posted. They were well articled –
although an unmilitary expression – in cavalry and artillery,
while we were much deficient in both these dependencies
upon success. We immediately halted, when we were within
gun-shot of the enemy, and formed in line, in case of an
attack being made upon us; but at the same time, as the right
wing was pretty well advanced, we partook of some refreshment. I cannot forget, while writing this journal, to remember one appalling and horrifying accident, or rather incident,
that I was witness of, while we were at our supper. The
enemy were now and then pitching a shot amongst us, which
made us somewhat uneasy, when one of them carried away
the head of a comrade, who was sitting by my side, and while
I was speaking to him, with the masticated bit of bread in his
mouth. I was stunned at the occurrence, and felt relieved
when we were ordered a little way back, to be without the
range of their shot, which although they did no great execution, were very annoying.

After moving a little way back we passed the night there.
Strong picquets were posted, and whole companies were put
upon patrol. We were not even allowed to lie down, nor
permitted to divest ourselves of our knapsacks, although we
had not been off our feet for ten hours during the day. We

continued in our standing posture until daylight, when the enemy's line was reconnoitered by the General and staff officers; but at the same time an order was given for an allowance of rum to each man, and also an order for our knapsacks to be thrown off, and placed in heaps, under the charge of the most weakly soldiers, one taken from each company. We were then formed in order of battle, and commanded to advance, the 90th and 92nd Regiments still acting as rifle brigades on the right and left of the army. On approaching the French lines, a large body of cavalry came sweeping down on the right against the 90th, who received them warmly; after which they passed on to the 92nd, but that regiment, on perceiving their approach, with steadiness, coolness, and precision, threw a volley of musketry amongst them with terrible effect. In fact, few of them escaped to tell the reception they had met with. But I forgot to observe, in their charge upon the 90th, that that regiment was dreadfully cut up by them; nor did the 92nd pass with little loss by them either. The former had about 400 killed and wounded, and the latter about 200. It was altogether a painful sight to witness; the wounded horses of the French cavalry were galloping about snorting in agony, some with riders, and some without them; others with wounded riders who had fallen off their backs, their feet entangled in the stirrups, dragged along the ground, their heads being beaten to pieces with the velocity with which the maddened horses galloped along; while the British bayonet was doing death-work among the uninjured dismounted, who were attempting to defend themselves. It is necessary here to mention, that when the 90th and 92nd entered the field, the former was a thousand strong, and the latter about five hundred and fifty.

While this work was going on, the line was advancing to our support. On the approach of the 17th and 79th Regiments, we were ordered to lie down to allow them to pass over us; which being done, we proceeded to the left, where the Dillon Regiment was engaged with the enemy, near an old tower, which the Arabs called Mandora, where the French had two field pieces, covered by some cavalry, and which, in spite of the efforts made to protect them, were captured by us. For this exploit, the 90th, 92nd, and Dillon Regiments were honourably noticed in general orders on the subsequent day.

In the meantime both armies were fully engaged; fearful havoc was going on – men and horses falling on all hands; but notwithstanding the most determined resistance on the part of the enemy, we kept advancing, and latterly drove them from their position. They commenced a retreat slowly, and in tolerable order, across a long plain in front of Alexandria. The British still kept pressing forward, the 90th, 92nd, and Dillons keeping the left. On reaching a stagnant lake of salt water, near which was a piece of rising ground, a party of the enemy seemed inclined to make a stand; but with the assistance of the 44th Regiment to those on the left, we, after a warm contest, compelled them to abandon their position, after which the whole of the enemy gave way and retreated within the works before Alexandria. We there received orders to rest ourselves, but were not permitted to remain quiet, for the French commenced a heavy cannonade upon us, (we being pretty close to the works,) by which many were killed, and which compelled us to retire as far as the heights the French quitted in the morning. During this retrograde movement, I observed a ball carry off both the feet of one poor fellow; and another, who imagining a ball was spent, in attempting to stop it, had his leg carried away above the knee. The latter was tailor to the 92nd.

We at length arrived at the heights. On or about this place, there had apparently existed some town, as there were ruins indicative of numerous buildings having been at one time there, among which were many large marble slabs with inscriptions upon them, but we, of course, could make nothing of them. On plaistered portions of the ruins also, were various hieroglyphic carvings, and, lying about, broken pieces of earthenware. As we had no tents ashore, we were still subjected to the night air, lying on the bare ground, with a slight blanket for our covering; but several of us imagining that our condition might be made somewhat more comfortable, adopted a curious expedient to make ourselves so; it was that of covering ourselves with sand above the blanket; this, however, did not realise our anticipations of the project. During the evening, large parties were sent out to collect the wounded, and bury the dead. It was remarked, that on the persons of the French soldiers, there were almost invariably found packs of cards, which led us to believe they were very much addicted to gambling.

We were once more very badly off for water, which we had far more difficulty in getting than on the former occasion, as we were on high ground. None could be had that night, but in the morning every regiment was ordered to dig for it; and, being at length successful, we obtained an excellent supply.

We remained, from the 13th to the 20th, in forming entrenchments for defending ourselves from the attacks of the enemy's cavalry, and in bringing up some cannon and provisions from the ships. Through the exertions of the seamen, we also got a number of tents conveyed to us, which protected us from the heat of the day, as well as from the dews of the night. On the 18th, several reinforcements belonging to the enemy were discovered proceeding to Alexandria, on which occasion a few of our dragoons went to annoy them; but nothing farther than a few slight skirmishes took place, in which no party sustained any particular damage, although the British were generally worsted.

About this time the Arabs came down from the high country, with sheep to dispose of. As we had not seen any of them before, we were much struck with their curious appearance. Their clothing consisted of nothing more than a large mantle or plaid, thrown carelessly over their shoulders, with a flat cap upon their heads, while their complexion was quite tawny. We bought their sheep at half a dollar each, being about 2s. 3d. English money. Ostriches were also brought to the market, and fetched a dollar each, these being principally bought by the Highland soldiers, for the use of the feathers in decorating their bonnets. We were likewise supplied with vegetables indigenous to the country.

During the construction of several works upon the left, the men that were employed, had to keep their arms and accoutrements by them in case of an attack, which was apprehended, would take place on the 20th. The 92nd, in the meantime, having been so dreadfully cut up, and affected by dimness of sight, the greater part of them were ordered to fall back to the place of landing, to be recruited in their health by getting better provisions. At this time this regiment did not number more than 250 effective men.

On the morning of the 21st, about two o'clock, we got up and had just begun to march, when several shots were heard on the left, where the works above alluded to, were being constructed. The shots were those of musketry; but in a little while the long boom of cannon swelled on the breeze, which induced the Commander-in-Chief to order the regiment to halt. The firing still continuing, the men expressed an open wish to get placed in the line. The Commander-in-Chief called the other officers around him, and informed them that we must proceed on our route, as the firing heard was only an affair of picquets; but as there was still no abatement in it, and as it was beginning to extend to the right, coming upon our ears like the roll of distant drums, Sir Ralph mounted his horse, which was always ready saddled, and proceeded to the scene of alarm; but ere doing so, he, at the loud calls from the ranks, to permit them to take their stations in the line, consented to their request. Accordingly we proceeded to our posts, by which time daylight was breaking, and a battle raging with dreadful fury.[2]

2 "The Night Battle of Aboukir", begun when 12,000 French troops secretly filed out of Aboukir and unleashed an attack on the British positions, with Major-General Sir John Moore's reserves on the British right receiving the brunt of French attention.

As we were marching to our stations, we lost several men from the shot of the enemy, which came over the line; and as we reached it, the Royal and the 54th Regiments were preparing to charge, and were closing into the centre, from which cause the 92nd could hardly get placed in it. However, we at last got our desires accomplished, and were no sooner in our places than we heard the French beating a charge with great spirit. The General thought it better to receive the enemy in our present position, than to advance and meet them, as we occupied a rising ground, and had the most decided advantage over them. He desired us to be cool and steady, and to give them our fire with as much precision as possible. When they had at length approached sufficiently near for our muskets to *tell*, we poured in a volley with staggering effect; but they still continued, notwithstanding, to advance, and we were necessitated to prepare to receive them with the bayonet. But no sooner did they see preparations to charge, than they fell back a little, but approached again; and they repeated this several times, always keeping up a continual fire of musketry upon us. Seeing, however, that they were unable to force us from our position, they brought up two field pieces to aid them. These they loaded with grape, which made dreadful havoc among our ranks; in fact, the musketry was hardly anything to be compared to the murderous effects of the grape-shot. My comrades were falling around me on every hand, while heads, and arms, and all describable portions of the human body, were flying about, to use a correct although it may be a coarse expression, in every direction.

For the purpose of keeping the enemy in check, and to clear the front, we threw out a few skirmishers from each regiment, which made the French retire to the plain; but being poorly provided with cannon, we were obliged to let them go without much annoyance. Meantime, their two field pieces kept playing upon us, and we were desired to lie down to avoid the grape-shot, which was flying like hail. This hot work was at length brought to a close by the explosion of one of the enemy's guns, which spread death and destruction among the gunners, as we could perceive their bodies blown into the air. The other cannon was then drawn off, the infantry ordered to retire, and few cavalry was left to protect the rear. We were so sorely cut up, that we thought it prudent to remain in our position. The battle meanwhile was going on very warmly on the right, where the Commander-in-Chief had taken his station; for to the left, and on the plain, the affair was comparatively trifling. The French got within the walls of Alexandria, and we remained where we were without gaining any ground. A short time after the battle was over, Sir Ralph Abercromby was carried down the rear, by a party of the 92nd who had been guarding his baggage. When it was known that our respected Commander was dangerously wounded, the interest excited was so great that every one ran to get a sight of him whom we all loved. I assisted in taking him to the boat to go aboard ship, where he died on the 28th of the same month. After the action was over, we were ordered to go and take all the wounded of both armies, and carry them to the boats. While engaged in this necessary and humane work, I observed that the two cannon alluded to above had made dreadful havoc among us. It was truly a horrible sight to see French and British writhing in the agonies of death, and making friendship, who had only a few minutes before been filled with rage and hatred at one another – all their fierce passions stilled, and, like a hushed child, taking one another into their dying arms.

When we were mustered the 92nd had only 100 men fit to do duty; and as we expected the French would attack us again the next day, all hands were employed in bringing ashore more guns – an article so much in request that even the small carronades fixed in the boats were taken out, brought up, and placed in the line. The enemy did not feel inclined to trouble us again; and on the 25th the 92nd commenced its march to Aboukir, according to former orders. We started about three o'clock in the morning, and arrived at the fort and village of Aboukir, where we encamped at night. A guard was ordered to take charge of the stores and guns that were in the fort; and it being my turn for that duty, curiosity induced me to look at the implements of death that had been employed against us. There were two very fine brass 18-inch mortars, and six brass guns, with every thing required for working them. Ammunition was not very abundant; but they had not been unprovided with that necessary of life, bread, for there was a great quantity of excellent biscuit, and some pipes of wine. There was also one of the best wells of fresh water that I saw in the country, and as useful to them no doubt as it was to us.

In battering the place, our guns had done a great deal of mischief. There was a breach made in the tower sufficiently large to admit of the entrance of a section, for the closing up of which, the French were so badly off for materials, that they had filled a number of bags with biscuit, and built it up with them; and as the bags were of the same colour as the stones of which the fort was built, the deception was very ingenious. There was not a living human resident in the village when we entered it; but after a few days, some of its former aged male inhabitants, in a very miserable condition, came to see where they probably were once happy – their homes a heap of ruins, and overrun by scorpions, which were very numerous. At a little distance from the village, towards the spot where our camp was pitched, the spot lies where the French, after their landing, according to the report of the inhabitants, put some thousands of Turks to death. It was a horrible looking place where they were buried. The bodies had been thrown promiscuously into a large pit, and a quantity of sand scattered over them; but as the sand was very dry, the least breath of wind blew it off, and the decaying remains of what had been breathing, living, thinking, and feeling men like ourselves, were exposed to view in all the ghastliness of corruption and death. The place might with great propriety be called the place of skulls, from the number of skeletons lying about it.

While the French lay in this place, a contagious and deadly malady broke out amongst them, which generally proved fatal after an hour's illness. We also lost a great many by it, among whom were one of our surgeons, a sergeant, and almost the whole of the hospital attendants. Indeed, so alarming were its ravages, that scarcely any one could be got to wait upon the sick, except some of the wounded, who were so far recovered as to be able to perform that duty, and who it appeared were not so liable to the infection as those that went in from the fresh air.

Among the many annoyances to which we were subject, there was one of Egypt's ancient plagues – that of flies – with which we were very much annoyed. These insects are exceedingly numerous, and withal, somewhat dangerous. Some of our men having indulged in sleep exposed to the open air, had their mouths and throats made a thoroughfare of by these troublesome creatures. One of them died almost instantly, and another was confined six months in the hospital, in consequence of lying out of their tents. We caught a number of chameleons among the bushes, which rid us in a great measure of these noxious insects within the tents. The men were dying every day in great numbers on board the fleet; and when thrown overboard without sufficient weight being attached to cause them to sink, the bodies were frequently washed ashore, on account of which we were obliged to send parties along the beach for the purpose of burying them.

We remained here till the 2nd of May, when an order reached us from headquarters, to remove and join a portion of the army assembling at or near Rosetta, in pursuance of which order we marched over a sandy desert along the sea side. On our way we suffered very much from want of water, but after great privation, we arrived at a village called Hamet, in the neighbourhood of which we encamped. There were about 7,000 soldiers assembled in this place, for the purpose of proceeding up to Cairo; but we had to wait a few days until our artillery, which came to us by water, were put into order for marching. When all things were got in readiness, we recommenced our route on the 8th of May, and had not proceeded far before we got out of the sandy desert where we had been ever since our landing. On coming to a place where the earth was clothed with grass, no one who has not been similarly situated can imagine how cool and refreshing it was to us, so long scorched among the arid sands, and who had not seen the verdant face of nature for a long time; – we all felt joy and delight.

In this part of Egypt the fields are all surrounded with ditches, filled with water from the Nile, along the banks of which our march extended. The water is raised from the river by means of wheels driven by buffaloes; and in some places there are three tiers, the one above the other. We formed our camp upon the bank of the river, and close to a field where there was abundance of water melons, which were a great delicacy to us as well as a novelty, very few of the men ever having eaten any of them before. There were also fields in which onions and tobacco were growing in great plenty. An incident occurred here to some of us of rather a ludicrous nature, occasioned by our ignorance of the vegetable productions of that part of the world. The men who were cooks for the day, never having seen tobacco growing before, imagined that it was a species of kale, and accordingly put into the kettle as such; but I need hardly mention that the broth was spoiled for that day.

On the 9th we moved off after the enemy, until we came within sight of Rahmanee, a fortified village, where the French had some gun-boats on the river, and a few small pieces of artillery on the mud wall of the place. The Turkish riflemen were sent out in front to cover the formation of the Turkish and British armies; but when the French saw it was with the Turks they had to deal, they sallied out of the fort in great force, and in high spirits, giving them three cheers and a volley, which speedily put them to the right-about, and made them fall back upon the line. The French still kept moving onward, until one of the Turkish officers took a standard, and advancing, got a few to follow him. The British were now ordered to put off their knapsacks, and prepare for action. The Turks had, by this time, got up a number of field pieces, and were so liberal with their shot, that they would discharge a 6-pounder at a single dragoon. The French seemed no ways disposed to come into collision with the British, but bent all their force against the Turks, whom they pressed so hard, that the light companies of the British were ordered to advance to their support, when, upon seeing the onward movement of the British, after the exchange of a few shots on both sides, the French laid down their arms, and surrendered themselves prisoners of war.

I had here an opportunity of seeing a little of the Turkish mode of warfare, which was rather out of our way of doing the business. When a Turk happened to be wounded, there were six or eight of his comrades who carried him off to the surgeon; and if there were many that needed assistance in that way, it would speedily weaken a pretty strong army, and which conduct, no doubt, contributed in no small degree in enabling the French to gain so many victories over them.

At the time that this part of the enemy was engaged, another portion had commenced its retreat to Cairo; and on the morrow we advanced towards that city. On this day's march I witnessed one of the most horrifying sights that had as yet come under my observation. Two French soldiers, who had fallen in the rear, either from fatigue or sickness, were overtaken by some Turks, who had been hovering about the retreating army like so many vultures. That they might get their penchant for cruelty fully indulged, and to protract the agonies of their victims, they had been cutting off their heads by the back of the neck with their sabres and long knives, which they always carry along with them in their belts. When we came up and perceived the barbarous work in which they had been engaged, we soon put an end to it; but it was too late to save the lives of the poor Frenchmen, for they were so severely mangled that they did not survive. The Turks seemed to take a delight in the horrid act; for although we expressed our detestation at them by giving them a sound drubbing, they did not show any regret for what they had done.

We continued our march until the 14th, when we halted for several days. During that time we could not but remark the great want of regularity that prevailed among our Turkish neighbours; for whenever the *revellie* sounded the first that was ready went off, while others would remain in the camp till seven in the morning. At a place where we halted for some time, the Turks were daily bringing in those Arabs who had joined the French army, on whom a courtmartial, composed of Turks, immediately sat for trial. Every criminal was dragged into the court by a rope round his neck. From the preliminaries to the trial, I need hardly say, that the sentence invariably was death, which was carried into effect by hanging the criminals upon the nearest tree. Indeed, the whole proceedings put me in mind of Cupar justice.

Throughout the whole of this march, the Turkish peasantry, as well as the soldiers, were bringing occasionally the heads of such of the Arabs that were so unfortunate as to fall into their hands, for every one of which there was a price given. On the 16th, while the whole army was bathing, – a practice in which we indulged as often as we could, – an Arab came into the camp carrying a white flag, and with whom the Commander-in-Chief had a conference by means of an interpreter. The Arab informed the Commander that a party of the French had been at the river in the morning for the purpose of watering, which, when they had effected, they moved off to the desert. The alarm was sounded immediately, and all preparations made for marching; but so sudden was the order given, that the most of us had not time to take a supply of water in our canteens; likewise, it being the day on which the rations should have been served out, and which had not yet been issued, we had to march without them, the want of which, especially of the water, we afterwards felt severely. We entered the desert about a league from the camp, and continued our march straight onward. We had not gone far, when the sand got so loose and hot, that it seemed as if we were travelling among quicklime; – every step that we advanced was up to the calf of the leg, so that we made very little progress, but we still kept moving on. The want of water was now a desideratum that we had no means of supplying; and I have no doubt that many a poor fellow, suffering from burning thirst – his throat parched, and his tongue cleaving to the roof of his mouth – was, like myself, thinking of the hills and rills of our dear loved Scotia, "the land of the mountain and the flood." To give still greater poignancy to our sufferings, and tantalize us with the hope of relief, the desert, a short distance before us, looked like a vast sheet of water, which deceptive appearance is caused by the reflection of the sun's rays from the sand. Like a great many of our fondly cherished hopes, as we thought we neared the place where our thirst was to be allayed, it was still as far from us as ever. By this time our suffering had become so intolerable, that a number of the men had died of thirst, and others had gone mad from the effects. As we were progressing slowly, to our surprise a gun was unexpectedly heard a little to our right, from behind a sand hill. A few dragoons that had accompanied us, rode out to reconnoitre, and found the party of the enemy that we were in quest of, drawn up in a hollow square, with all the camels and baggage in the centre, with the apparent intention of giving us battle. From the difficulty we had in marching, we were so straggled, that the front was obliged to halt until the rear closed; but the result showed that Monsieur had no intention of engaging us at this time, for when we were all in order, and ready to advance, the French Commanding Officer surrendered himself, and all under his command, prisoners of war.

We found that this was a convoy going from Alexaudria to Cairo, which had been keeping the desert all day, and marching by the river all night, and they had been all mounted on camels or other beasts of burden. We returned with our capture to the camp, which, besides the prisoners, consisted of 400 camels, and a great number of horses and asses. The camels and horses were sold to the commissariat; but the asses, not being saleable, were turned loose, and some of the men took them to carry their knapsacks, – a service for which they were very useful. Each of the regiments got a camel to carry its tents.

We moved forward on the 18th, and in the course of the day came in sight of those stupendous fabrics, the pyramids, far exceeding in magnitude any building that we had ever beheld, and which were distinctly seen at a very great distance. When commencing our march on the 19th, we encountered that dreadful and deadly scourge of the desert traveller – the hot wind. It began to blow about sunrise, and increased in violence towards meridian. So insupportable became the heat, that we were obliged to pitch our tents, which, although formed of thick canvass, afforded us a very insufficient protection from the sand, that fell upon us thick as snow-drift, even although we used our blankets also as a defence. The simoon continued to blow with unabated fury during the 19th, 20th, and 21st, so that it was at the risk of suffocation if any person or animal was exposed to it; in fact, it formed altogether the opposite extreme of a Highland snow storm, – sand and heat instead of snow and cold.

On the 22nd we moved off for Cairo, with the pyramids full in view. On our journey we were joined by a party of Mamelukes, who kept with us till we came opposite to Cairo, where we encamped, when they and the Turks crossed the river by a bridge, with the intention of investing the city. We began to open some works, but before we had proceeded far or many shots fired, the enemy held out a flag of truce, and made proposals of capitulation, which were agreed to with gladness on the part of all concerned. We were joined at this time by the army from India, under the command of Major-

General Baird, which came over land. After things were thus amicably settled, we were allowed to go in small parties to see the pyramids; and the Commander-in-Chief was so anxious that all should have an opportunity of seeing those wonderful edifices, that three parties at different times of the day went, until all who wished to do so had examined them. On the 5th of June, I, along with a few of my comrades, went to survey those gigantic piles, whose size have astonished every beholder – whose date is lost in the obscurity of past ages – the name of whose founder is now matter of doubt – even the purpose for which they were erected is mere conjecture. The greatest of the pyramids of Giza was about two hours' travel distant from the camp, and we reached it a little before sunrise. There were a great many visitors from all the regiments in the army, and among them the late Sir Allan Cameron, then Colonel of the 79th, and a number of other officers. They had provided themselves with a sledge-hammer and some torches, with the design of exploring the interior. After effecting an entrance, we went in by a passage which descended at the mouth, and the floor of which was paved with a bluish sort of marble. The Arab who was our guide led the way, carrying a lighted torch. We had not gone far when we ascended another passage, so narrow that Colonel Cameron, who was rather a stout built man, was brought to a dead stand; however, with a little difficulty we all proceeded forward, until we reached a large room. As there was a great number of us in the place, and having only one light, I could get but a very imperfect survey taken of the place. The only object that attached our attention was a marble chest or coffin, from which Colonel Cameron desired one of his men to break off a piece with the hammer which he carried. The Arab who acted as guide cried out most hideously on the first blow being given, and wished the man to desist, but to no purpose, as we all seemed determined to have something as a memorial of our visit to the pyramids. Colonel Cameron and the most of us possessed ourselves of part of the above-mentioned coffin; and I still retain my share of the spoil, which I am willing to show to those interested in antiquities.

After indulging our curiosity for a time, we were glad to get into the light and breath of heaven, as the place was warm and close to suffocation. From the many lengthened and accurate descriptions which have been given of the size and dimensions of these enormous erections, it is not necessary for to give a long detail of particulars; suffice it to say, that after pacing one angle of the base of the largest, I found that it measured 282 paces of 30 inches. The ascent which I next attempted I found to be no easy matter, as the steps are about breast high; so, after going half way to the summit, on looking up, the height was rather too much for my head, which became somewhat giddy, and I was obliged to give up the attempt. I called to one of my comrades, who had gained the top, to measure the extent, and he found that it contained 12 paces, and it was with difficulty that he could throw a stone beyond the basis. There is a building at the side of one of the pyramids that contains the catacombs, but which we did not enter. We then visited the sphynx, – another of the stupendous wonders of Egyptian art – being a huge mass of rock cut into the form of a woman's bust, but as a great part of it was covered up by the sand, we could not make out what it had been intended to represent. We returned to the camp highly gratified with our excursion, and astonished at what we had seen. For my own part, not having read much, and never having even heard that there were such colossal structures in the world, I felt a degree of surprise, not unmingled with awe, on beholding the vastness and grandeur of what will ever continue to strike every spectator as the greatest effort of architectural labour that has yet been reared.

While we lay before Cairo, a good many of the men went into the city, but I did not avail myself of the opportunity. Apparently, on the outside, it seemed to be in rather a dilapidated condition. There was a castle that protected the place, on the top of which the French flag was placed, besides which there was a gun that was fired at noon for the purpose of giving notice of meridian to the army. While here we were much amused at witnessing the dexterity of a number of jugglers that came into the camp and displayed their slight-of-hand tricks, at which they were very expert. As there was a market established in the place, we were well supplied with every thing that we needed; and among the commodities offered for sale, there was one altogether new to us, I mean women, who although long a subject of traffic in the eastern countries, are happily not so used in ours. From the fashion of always wearing a veil, I was not gratified with a sight of the faces of those daughters of the sunny east, and they seemed particularly anxious that no one should see them unveiled.

We remained here till July, when the French army evacuated the city, and we escorted them as prisoners to the mouth of the Nile, whence they embarked for France, and we returned by the desert to our camp at Alexandria. During our absence, several reinforcements had been sent to the army from England, of which there was a number belonging to the 92nd Regiment, now greatly reduced in strength. Soon after our arrival, it was proposed by the Commander-in-Chief to remove nearer to the city; and accordingly arrangements were made about the beginning of August for that purpose, by sending a strong detachment, under the command of General Coote, to the other side of the town by water. While we were up the country, the French had cut the embankment that separated the Bay of Aboukir from the plain that lies around Alexandria, and in which the aqueduct runs all the way from the Nile, a distance of nearly forty miles; so that what had been a plain was now converted into a vast lake, upon which gun-boats and small craft of all descriptions could sail. Taking advantage of this change made upon the face of the country, General Coote's detachment embarked on board the gun-boats and armed launches, and sailed to its destination on the other side of the city, while the remainder of the army was ready to co-operate as circumstances might require. To elude the observation of the enemy, we intended to make our attack during the night; and having sent out skirmishers in extended order, from the lake already mentioned to the sea shore, the whole line advanced to make a feint, with the design of drawing the attention of the enemy away from the place where General Coote was to disembark. When we had pushed on to the French outposts, their sentry challenged; but no answer being returned, he gave the alarm by discharging his piece, and immediately all was in a blaze of light from right to left, by means of fire-ball, so that we were completely exposed to the view of the enemy, who instantly opened their batteries upon us. As it was not intended to storm the garrison at that time, but merely to divert the attention of the enemy from the other side of the city, whither General Coote had gone, we did not move within range of their shot, but the purpose for which we made the movement was effected. By this time General Coote was securely established on the other side of Alexandria, which was now firmly invested round about. It was then thought necessary to take possession of a small green hill on our left, and a little in front, which, since the 21st of March, had been occupied by a strong piquet of the French, and, while possessed by them, formed an obstruction to our operations.

On the 17th of August, at two in the morning, we were under arms, and a party sent to carry the hill alluded to – the light company of the 30th leading the advance, and the 92nd covering the attack. Upon coming up to the advanced sentinel, he challenged different times, but receiving no reply, he fired and killed the officer who led on the party, but was himself immediately brought down by one of our men. The French were now all under arms, and as day had begun to break, regular work went on. The light company of the 30th were nearly all cut down; still the line advanced steadily, and after some hard fighting, the French gave way, and we drove them before us to the wall of Alexandria. By following the pursuit of the enemy too far, we suffered considerable loss; but by retiring in loose files, we escaped more safely than we otherwise would have done. After the affair was over, we formed on the place formerly occupied by the French piquet, which was a large redoubt composed of stones and earth, and which we now turned to our own use.

General Coote had now placed himself within range of shot, on the west side of the city, so that the enemy was closely hemmed in in that direction. On our side we worked vigorously night and day, forming redoubts and breast-works, on which we placed a few 24-pounders, that we brought from on board ship. It was no easy matter to bring these pieces along, as the wheels of the carriages were far too low; and it was with the greatest difficulty that 300 men on the drag-ropes could get them forward. About dusk, on the evening of the 19th, when all was ready, the signal was given to the forces on both sea and land to open their fire, which was so promptly obeyed, and so completely acted upon, that the shot was meeting in all directions in the city, which capitulated on the morning of the 20th, and taken possession of by a number of our troops. The 92nd was one of the regiments that first entered the place, accompanied by a few dragoons; but on reaching the outworks we were stopped by a French officer – whether at his own instigation or ordered to do so, I did not know; but if we had done as he requested us to do, we would probably all have perished, as trains of powder were laid under all the batteries, and a great number of shells, with lighted matches ready to cause them explode. It was thought that the scoundrel wished to detain us until the plot would take effect; but fortunately, information of the murderous design was given in time by some of our men, who had been prisoners in the place. We fell back, and in a short time the two largest batteries blew up with a tremendous noise, scattering the materials of which they were built in all directions.

After making arrangements we went in, and fatigue parties were sent to gather the shells which had been laid down by the enemy for the purpose of destruction, and which we discovered by the trains of powder, that were laid so as to communicate with them; and before night we had them all put out of the way of doing any harm. We now pitched our tents between the outer or modern and the inner or ancient wall of Alexandria, posting strong piquets, to whom orders were given to fire upon any Frenchmen who should be found doing mischief. A few of them were unfortunately killed in attempting to climb the walls, which, although nearly 30 feet in height, they tried to scale, impelled, as we afterwards learned, by the irresistible cravings of hunger. So badly off were they for provisions by this time, that they were reduced to the necessity of eating horse flesh, and would gladly have purchased any sort of food that we had to spare.

As the line of communication was by far too extensive, we got some additional regiments sent in, to assist us in doing the duty of the place; – there were also a number of Turks attached to the different corps when on guard. After the eastern fashion, the Turks, when on sentry, sat down and smoked their pipes, giving themselves little trouble about what was going on. The French and British soldiers used to laugh heartily at their slovenly habits, but all to no purpose, as they would not upon any account give up their favourite practice of smoking when on duty. The French as well as ourselves had a guard posted at the Rosetta gate, which gave us an opportunity of mixing and conversing with them, as a few could speak English, although but imperfectly. We now got upon very friendly terms, sharing our provisions and exchanging articles with one another.

A great many of us now began to suffer from dysentery, occasioned by the brackish water, and I also was very much reduced by it. One night when on guard, I felt a stinging sensation in my left temple, and before morning I had lost the sight of my left eye. I was now obliged to go to hospital, and had not been many days there, when the right eye also became affected. I was rendered totally blind for some time, during which I suffered very great agony. To heighten the pain I was enduring, I was stung by a scorpion on the right hand, which caused my arm to swell to such a size, that in a few minutes my coat had to be cut off. I got better in a few days from the effects of the sting, but my eyes were still as bad as ever. This trouble being quite a new malady to us, a considerable deal of ignorance prevailed as to the proper mode of treatment, and which, I have no doubt, in regard to it, rendered matters rather worse than better. All the sick and blind were ordered on board ship, preparatory to the embarking of the British army, as the French had been all embarked.

THE ROAD TO CORUNNA, 1808–9

Rifleman Benjamin Harris, 95th Rifles

In the summer of 1807, courtesy of his stunning victories over Russia, Prussia and Austria, Napoleon dominated mainland Europe. There was, alas, one weakspot: the Iberian Peninsula, where Portugal – "Britain's oldest ally", by virtue of a relationship that stretched back to the Middle Ages – refused to implement Napoleon's Continental System, a blockade of British exports designed to bring that nation to its knees. And then there was Portugal's neighbour Spain, whose ardour for France had cooled of late and whose administration was so corrupt that it was adhering to the Continental System more in name than effect. (Napoleon also had a jealous eye on the Spanish treasury, which he imagined filled with gold; in fact, the Bourbon regime was near bankrupt). After the French government had served a number of impossible ultimatums on Portugal, General Jean Junot, Napoleon's former aide-de-camp, led 24,000 French troops over the Pyrenees in October to march through Spain for Portugal. On 30 November, after meeting only scattered resistance, Junot reached Lisbon, and soon all of Portugal was under French occupation. The invasion, as one observer noted, "was an armed parade, not a war."

The ease with which Junot took Portugal led Napoleon to believe that Spain would fall as easily. And so, on 16 February

1808, Napoleon ordered French troops to seize key positions in northern Spain, in particular the frontier fortresses, after which massed Imperial ranks marched into Spain with impunity. The Spanish government plunged into a bickering crisis, the crowds cheered the invader and on 24 March Marshal Joachim Murat, commander-in-chief of French forces in Spain, arrived in Madrid. All augured well for Napoleon's big gamble.

However, Le Tondu then threw away an easy victory for a long, hard war. Having lost his best diplomatic advisor in the shape of Count Talleyrand and his own diplomatic touch to the beginnings of megalomania, Napoleon installed his unwilling brother Joseph onto the Spanish throne. The Spanish disliked their autocratic Bourbon rulers; but they disliked a French imposition even more. At the beginning of May a minor rising in Madrid, the "Dos de May", was brutally suppressed by Marshal Murat, at which a nationalist revolt swept Spain. On 25 May the Asturias declared war on France, with other provinces quickly following suit.

The Peninsular War had begun. Within weeks, some 100,000 regular Spanish troops were under arms. With characteristic zealousness, Napoleon ordered all opposition crushed, particularly the Spanish armies under General Joachim Blake in Galicia and General Castanos in Andalusia. Blake was duly beaten at Rio Seco, but Castanos earned a singular victory at arid Baylen on 19 July 1808, with more than 20,000 Imperial troops passing into captivity. "There has never been anything so stupid, so foolish or so cowardly since the world began", fumed Napoleon on hearing the news.

If Baylen galvanized the Spanish by ending the myth of French invincibility, they were similarly heartened by the arrival in Iberia of a British expeditionary force under Sir Arthur Wellesley. On 1 August 1808, 8,500 troops and three artillery batteries struggled throught the pounding surf at Portugal's Mondego Bay to begin Britain's participation in the Peninsular War.

Benjamin Harris, of the green-jacketed 95th Rifles was

among those who landed at Mondego Bay and who, on 9 August – by which time the expeditionary force had swollen to 13,500 men, 30 guns and been joined by a Portuguese brigade – set off down the coastal highway towards Lisbon in search of Junot's Imperial troops.

These, as Harris relates, were soon encountered. On 17 August 1808 the French offered battle at Roliça where, outnumbered, they were unable to halt Wellesley's march. Junot himself then advanced from Lisbon at the head of 13,000 men, intercepting Wellesley at Vimeiro where the lieutenant-general had, in what would become the classic British tactic in the Peninsula, carefully selected a defensive, elevated position from which he awaited the French onslaught. This duly came on 21 August, with the main French columns attacking Vimeiro itself, while 3,000 men and 600 troopers under General Brennier tried to outflank Wellesley from the north. Although the French managed to penetrate as far as Vimeiro village, after two and half hours of furious battle they had sustained over 2,000 casualties (to Wellesley's 720), and only managed an orderly retreat thanks to powerful cavalry cover. Defeated by the British and surrounded by a hostile populace, Junot sought terms from the new Allied commander, Sir Harry Burrard. By the subsequent "Convention of Cintra," Junot agreed to vacate Portugal; in return, the British Royal Navy evacuated Junot's entire "Army of Portugal" (some 25, 747 troops) back to France.

The generous terms of the Convention caused a furore in Britain, and Burrard and Wellesley (who had opposed the Convention) were called back to London, while the expeditionary force itself lounged around Lisbon. The loss of Portugal and continued French reverses in Spain, notably the withdrawal from Madrid, provoked Napoleon into reaction. In November 1808, the Emperor placed himself at the head of the Army in Spain (shortly to grow to 200,000 men) and began a grand offensive which restored Joseph to the throne, and defeated the Spanish armies at a string of shining victories – Espinosa,

Reynosa, Tudela, Somosierra. Meanwhile, in a desperate at-
tempt to aid the Spanish, the British expeditionary force, now
under Sir John Moore, had left Lisbon and, after some weeks of
hesitant inaction at Salamanca, moved to engage Marshal
Soult's divisions and block the Madrid–Bayenne highway.
There was a small but glorious British cavalry action at Saha-
gun on 21 December; but then Moore was forced to beat a
desperate retreat northward over the mountains towards Cor-
unna when it transpired that Napoleon was marching over the
Guadarrama Pass to meet him, with 80,000 men at his back.

The retreat to Corunna was effected amidst bitter weather
and privation, an eerie portent of the travail awaiting the
Grande Armée itself in Russia only four years later. After
some 5,000 deaths along the road to Corunna, part of Moore's
army was evacuated from nearby Vigo, and the remainder from
Corunna itself, the embarkation taking place while Moore's
tattered, redcoated rearguard fought a spirited battle outside the
town on 16 January 1809. The French were forced to withdraw,
but Moore paid with his life. "I hope the [British] people will be
satisfied," he said before he died. They were. The embarkation
completed, 27,000 British troops reached the safety of home.
They would return to the Peninsula to fight again.

My father was a shepherd, and I was a sheep-boy from my
earliest youth. Indeed, as soon almost as I could run, I began
helping my father to look after the sheep on the downs of
Blandford, in Dorsetshire, where I was born. Whilst I
continued to tend the flocks and herds under my charge,
and occasionally (in the long winter nights) to learn the art of
making shoes, I grew a hardy little chap, and was one fine day
in the year 1802 drawn as a soldier for the Army of Reserve.[1]
Thus, without troubling myself much about the change

1 The Militia Act of 1802 raised 51,500 men by ballot.

which was to take place in the hitherto quiet routine of my days, I was drafted into the 66th Regiment of Foot, bid good-bye to my shepherd companions, and was obliged to leave my father without an assistant to collect his flocks, just as he was beginning more than ever to require one; nay, indeed, I may say to want tending and looking after himself, for old age and infirmity were coming on him; his hair was growing as white as the sleet of our downs, and his countenance becoming as furrowed as the ploughed fields around. However, as I had no choice in the matter, it was quite as well that I did not grieve over my fate.

My father tried hard to buy me off, and would have persuaded the sergeant of the 66th that I was of no use as a soldier, from having maimed my right hand (by breaking a forefinger when a child). The sergeant, however, said I was just the sort of little chap he wanted, and off he went, carrying me (amongst a batch of recruits he had collected) away with him.

Almost the first soldiers I ever saw were those belonging to the corps in which I was now enrolled a member, and, on arriving at Winchester, we found the whole regiment there in quarters. Whilst lying at Winchester (where we remained three months), young as I was in the profession, I was picked out, amongst others, to perform a piece of duty that, for many years afterwards, remained deeply impressed upon my mind, and gave me the first impression of the stern duties of a soldier's life. A private of the 70th Regiment had deserted from that corps, and afterwards enlisted into several other regiments; indeed, I was told at the time (though I cannot answer for so great a number) that sixteen different times he had received the bounty and then stolen off. Being, however, caught at last, he was brought to trial at Portsmouth, and sentenced by general court-martial to be shot.

The 66th received a route to Portsmouth to be present on the occasion, and, as the execution would be a good hint to us young 'uns, there were four lads picked out of our corps to assist in this piece of duty, myself being one of the number chosen.

Besides these men, four soldiers from three other regiments were ordered on the firing-party, making sixteen in all. The place of execution was Portsdown Hill, near Hilsea Barracks, and the different regiments assembled must have composed a force of about fifteen thousand men, having been assembled from the Isle of Wight, from Chichester, Gosport, and other places. The sight was very imposing, and appeared to make a deep impression on all there. As for myself, I felt that I would have given a good round sum (had I possessed it) to have been in any situation rather than the one in which I now found myself; and when I looked into the faces of my companions I saw, by the pallor and anxiety depicted in each countenance, the reflection of my own feelings. When all was ready, we were moved to the front, and the culprit was brought out. He made a short speech to the parade, acknowledging the justice of his sentence, and that drinking and evil company had brought the punishment upon him.

He behaved himself firmly and well, and did not seem at all to flinch. After being blindfolded, he was desired to kneel down behind a coffin, which was placed on the ground, and the drum-major of the Hilsea depot, giving us an expressive glance, we immediately commenced loading.

This was done in the deepest silence, and, the next moment, we were primed and ready. There was then a dreadful pause for a few moments, and the drum-major, again looking towards us, gave the signal before agreed upon (a flourish of his cane), and we levelled and fired. We had been previously strictly enjoined to be steady, and take good aim, and the poor fellow, pierced by several balls, fell heavily upon his back; and as he lay, with his arms pinioned to his sides, I observed that his hands wavered for a few moments, like the fins of a fish when in the agonies of death. The drum-major also observed the movement, and, making another signal, four of our party immediately stepped up to the prostrate body, and placing the muzzles of their pieces to the head, fired, and put him out of his misery. The different regiments then fell back by companies, and the word being given to march past in slow time, when each company came in line with the body, the word was given to "mark time," and then "eyes left," in order that we might all observe the terrible example. We then moved onwards, and marched from the ground to our different quarters. The 66th stopped that night about three miles from Portsdown Hill, and in the morning we returned to Winchester. The officer in command that day, I remember, was General Whitelocke, who was afterwards brought to court-martial himself.[2] This was the first time of our seeing that officer. The next meeting was at Buenos Ayres [*sic*], and during the confusion of that day one of us received an order from the fiery Craufurd[3] to shoot the traitor dead if he could see him in the battle, many others of the Rifles receiving the same order from that fine and chivalrous officer.

The unfortunate issue of the Buenos Ayres affair is a matter of history, and I have nothing to say about it; but I well remember the impression it made upon us all at the time, and that Sir John Moore[4] was present at Whitelocke's court-martial; General Craufurd, and I think General Auchmuty, Captain Eleder of the Rifles, Captain Dickson, and one of our privates, being witnesses. We were at Hythe at the time, and I recollect our officers going off to appear against Whitelocke.

2 Lieutenant-General John Whitelocke (1757–1853). His pompous and incompetent handling of the attack on Buenos Aires in 1807 led to a court martial, at which he was found "totally unfit to serve his Majesty in any military capacity whatever."

3 Major-General Robert Crauford (1764–1812), martinet and commander of the Light Brigade in the Peninsula, nicknamed "Black Bob" for his looks and moods. Killed during the siege of Ciudad Rodrigo.

4 Lieutenant-General Sir John Moore (1761–1809); served as brigadier-general in West Indies; major-general in Ireland 1798; divisional commander in Egypt 1801; commander of British forces in the Peninsula from October 1808 until his death at Corunna. See page 67.

So enraged was Craufurd against him, that I heard say he strove hard to have him shot. Whitelocke's father I also heard was at his son's trial, and cried like an infant during the proceedings. Whitelocke's sword was broken over his head I was told; and for months afterwards, when our men took their glass, they used to give as a toast "Success to *grey hairs*, but bad luck to *White-locks*." Indeed that toast was drunk in all the public-houses around for many a day.

Everything was new to me, I remember, and I was filled with astonishment at the bustling contrast I was so suddenly called into from the tranquil and quiet of my former life.

Whilst in Winchester, we got a route for Ireland, and embarking at Portsmouth, crossed over and landed at Cork. There we remained nine weeks; and being a smart figure and very active, I was put into the light company of the 66th, and, together with the light corps of other regiments, we were formed into light battalions, and sent off to Dublin. Whilst in Dublin, I one day saw a corps of the 95th Rifles,[5] and fell so in love with their smart, dashing, and devil-may-care appearance, that nothing would serve me till I was a Rifleman myself; so, on arriving at Cashel one day, and falling in with a recruiting-party of that regiment, I volunteered into the second battalion. This recruiting-party were all Irishmen, and had been sent over from England to collect (amongst others) men from the Irish Militia, and were just about to return to England. I think they were as reckless and devil-may-care a set of men as ever I beheld, either before or since.

Being joined by a sergeant of the 92nd Highlanders, and a Highland piper of the same regiment (also a pair of real rollicking blades), I thought we should all have gone mad together. We started on our journey, one beautiful morning, in tip-top spirits from the Royal Oak at Cashel; the whole lot of us (early as it was) being three sheets in the wind. When we

5 The 95th Rifles had been formed in 1801; the regiment was equipped with the Baker rifle, as opposed to the standard British Army smooth-bore musket.

paraded before the door of the Royal Oak, the landlord and landlady of the inn, who were quite as lively, came reeling forth, with two decanters of whisky, which they thrust into the fists of the sergeants, making them a present of decanters and all to carry along with them, and refresh themselves on the march. The piper then struck up, the sergeants flourished their decanters, and the whole route commenced a terrific yell. We then all began to dance, and danced through the town, every now and then stopping for another pull at the whisky decanters. Thus we kept it up till we had danced, drank, shouted, and piped thirteen Irish miles, from Cashel to Clonmel. Such a day, I think, I never spent, as I enjoyed with these fellows; and on arriving at Clonmel we were as glorious as any soldiers in all Christendom need wish to be. In about ten days after this, our sergeants had collected together a good batch of recruits, and we started for England. Some few days before we embarked (as if we had not been bothered enough already with the unruly Paddies), we were nearly pestered to death with a detachment of old Irish women, who came from different parts (on hearing of their sons having enlisted), in order to endeavour to get them away from us. Following us down to the water's edge, they hung to their offspring, and, dragging them away, sent forth such dismal howls and moans that it was quite distracting to hear them. The lieutenant commanding the party ordered me (being the only Englishman present) to endeavour to keep them back. It was, however, as much as I could do to preserve myself from being torn to pieces by them, and I was glad to escape out of their hands.

At length we got our lads safe on board, and set sail for England.

No sooner were we out at sea, however, than our troubles began afresh with these hot-headed Paddies; for, having now nothing else to do, they got up a dreadful quarrel amongst themselves, and a religious row immediately took place, the Catholics reviling the Protestants to such a degree that a general fight ensued. The poor Protestants (being few in number) soon got the worst of it, and as fast as we made matters up among them, they broke out afresh and began the riot again.

From Pill, where we landed, we marched to Bristol, and thence to Bath. Whilst in Bath, our Irish recruits roamed about the town, staring at and admiring everything they saw, as if they had just been taken wild in the woods. They all carried immense shillelaghs in their fists, which they would not quit for a moment. Indeed they seemed to think their very lives depended on possession of these bludgeons, being ready enough to make use of them on the slightest occasion.

From Bath we marched to Andover, and when we came upon Salisbury Plain, our Irish friends got up a fresh row. At first they appeared uncommonly pleased with the scene, and, dispersing over the soft carpet of the Downs, commenced a series of Irish jigs, till at length as one of the Catholics was setting to his partner (a Protestant), he gave a whoop, and a leap into the air, and at the same time (as if he couldn't bear the partnership of a heretic any longer) dealt him a tremendous blow with his shillelagh, and stretched him upon the sod. This was quite enough, and the bludgeons immediately began playing away at a tremendous rate.

The poor Protestants were again quickly disposed of, and then arose a cry of Huzza for the Wicklow boys, Huzza for the Connaught boys, Huzza for Munster, and Huzza for Ulster! They then recommenced the fight as if they were determined to make an end of their soldiering altogether upon Salisbury Plains. We had, I remember, four officers with us, and they did their best to pacify their pugnacious recruits. One thrust himself amongst them, but was instantly knocked down for his pains, so that he was glad enough to escape. After they had completely tired themselves, they began to slacken in their endeavours, and apparently to feel the effect of the blows they dealt each other, and at length suffering themselves to be pacified, the officers got them into Andover.

Scarcely had we been a couple of hours there, and obtained some refreshment, ere these incorrigible blackguards again commenced quarrelling, and, collecting together in the streets, created so serious a disturbance that the officers, getting together a body of constables, seized some of the most violent and succeeded in thrusting them into the town jail; upon this their companions again collected, and endeavoured to break open the prison gates.

Baffled in this attempt, they rushed through the streets knocking down everybody they met. The drums now commenced beating up for a volunteer corps of the town, which, quickly mustering, drew up in the street before the jail, and immediately were ordered to load with ball.

This somewhat pacified the rioters, and our officers persuading them to listen to a promise of pardon for the past, peace was at length restored amongst them.

The next day we marched for Ashford, in Kent, where I joined the 95th Rifles, and about six months after my joining, four companies of the second battalion were ordered on the expedition to Denmark.[6] We embarked at Deal, and sailing for the hostile shores, landed on a little place called, I think, Scarlet Island, somewhere between Elsineur and Copenhagen.

The expedition consisted of about 30,000 men, and at the moment of our getting on shore, the whole force set up one simultaneous and tremendous cheer, a sound I cannot describe, it seemed so inspiring. This, indeed, was the first time of my hearing the style in which our men give tongue when they get near the enemy, though afterwards my ears became pretty well accustomed to such sounds.

6 Denmark had refused to surrender her fleet to Britain for the duration of the war with France; Britain accordingly launched an invasion of Denmark in 1807.

As soon as we got on shore, the Rifles were pushed forward as the advance, in chain order, through some thick woods of fir, and when we had cleared these woods and approached Copenhagen, sentries were posted on the roads and openings leading towards the town, in order to intercept all comers, and prevent all supplies. Such posts we occupied for about three days and nights, whilst the town was being fired on by our shipping. I rather think this was the first time of Congreve rockets being brought into play, and as they rushed through the air in the dark, they appeared like so many fiery serpents, creating, I should think, terrible dismay among the besieged.[7]

As the main army came up, we advanced and got as near under the walls of the place as we could without being endangered by the fire from our own shipping. We now received orders ourselves to commence firing, and the rattling of the guns I shall not easily forget.

I felt so much exhilarated that I could hardly keep back, and was checked by the commander of the company (Capt. Leech), who called to me by name to keep my place. About this time, my front-rank man, a tall fellow named Jack Johnson, showed a disposition as though the firing had on him an effect the reverse of what it had on many others of the company, for he seemed inclined to hang back, and once or twice turned round in my face. I was a rear-rank man, and porting my piece, in the excitement of the moment I swore that if he did not keep his ground, I would shoot him dead on the spot; so that he found it would be quite as dangerous for him to return as to go on.

I feel sorry to record the want of courage of this man, but I do so with the less pain as it gives me the opportunity of saying that during many years' arduous service, it is the only instance I remember of a British soldier endeavouring to hold back when his comrades were going forward.

7 Congreve rockets were actually first used against Boulogne in 1806.

Indeed, Johnson was never again held in estimation amongst the Rifle corps; for the story got wind that I had threatened to shoot him for cowardice in the field, and Lieut. Cox mentioned to the colonel that he had overheard my doing so; and such was the contempt the man was held in by the Rifles, that he was soon afterwards removed from amongst us to a veteran battalion.

Whilst in Denmark we led a tolerably active life, the Rifles being continually on the alert – ordered hither to-day, and countermanded the next. Occasionally, too, when wanted in a hurry, we were placed in carts and rattled over the face of the country, in company with the dragoons of the German Legion;[8] so that, if we had not so much fighting as afterwards in the Peninsula, we had plenty of work to keep us from idleness.

Occasionally, also, we had some pleasant adventures among the blue-eyed Danish lasses, for the Rifles were always terrible fellows in that way.

One night, I remember, a party of us had possession of a gentleman's house, in which his family were residing. The family consisted of the owner of the mansion, his wife, and five very handsome daughters, besides their servants.

The first night of our occupation of the premises the party was treated with the utmost civility, and everything was set before us as if we had been their equals; for although it was not very pleasant to have a company of foreign soldiers in the house, it was doubtless thought best to do everything possible to conciliate such guests. Accordingly, on this night, a large party of the green-jackets unceremoniously sat down to tea with the family.

Five beautiful girls in a drawing-room were rather awkward companions for a set of rough and ready Riflemen, unscrupulous and bold, and I cannot say I felt easy. All went on very comfortably for some time; our fellows drank their

8 The King's German Legion, largely officered by Germans from states defeated by Napoleon in 1805–6.

tea very genteelly, whilst one young lady presided at the urn to serve it out, and the others sat on each side of their father and mother, chatting to us, and endeavouring to make themselves as agreeable as they could.

By and bye, however, some of our men expressed themselves dissatisfied with tea and toast, and demanded something stronger; and liquors were accordingly served to them. This was followed by more familiarity, and, the ice once broken, all respect for the host and hostess was quickly lost. I had feared this would prove the case, and on seeing several of the men commence pulling the young ladies about, kissing them, and proceeding to other acts of rudeness, I saw that matters would quickly get worse, unless I interfered. Jumping up, therefore, I endeavoured to restore order, and upbraided them with the blackguardism of their behaviour after the kindness with which we had been used.

This remonstrance had some effect; and when I added that I would immediately go in quest of an officer, and report the first man I saw ill-use the ladies, I at length succeeded in extricating them from their persecutors.

The father and mother were extremely grateful to me for my interference, and I kept careful guard over the family whilst we remained in that house, which luckily was not long.

Soon after this the expedition returned to England, and I came, with others of the Rifles, in a Danish man-of-war (the *Princess Caroline*), and landed at Deal, from whence we had started.

From Deal we marched to Hythe, and there we lay until the year 1808, and in that year four companies of the second battalion, to which I belonged, were ordered to Portugal.

In that year I first saw the French.

I wish I could picture the splendid sight of the shipping in the Downs at the time we embarked with about 20,000 men. Those were times which the soldiers of our own more peaceable days have little conception of.

At Cork, where our ships cast anchor, we lay for something like six weeks, during which time the expedition was not disembarked, with the exception of our four companies of Rifles, who were every day landed for the purpose of drill. On such occasions our merry bugles sounded over the country, and we were skirmished about in very lively fashion, always being embarked again at night.

At the expiration of the time I have mentioned our sails were given to the wind, and amidst the cheers of our comrades, we sailed majestically out of the Cove of Cork for the hostile shore, where we arrived safely [in August 1808], and disembarked at Mondego Bay.

The Rifles were the first out of the vessels, for we were, indeed, always in the front in advance, and in the rear in the retreat. Like the Kentish men of old, we claimed the post of honour in the field.

Being immediately pushed forwards up the country in advance of the main body, many of us, in this hot climate, very soon began to find out the misery of the frightful load we were condemned to march and fight under, with a burning sun above our heads, and our feet sinking every step into the hot sand.

The weight I myself toiled under was tremendous, and I often wonder at the strength I possessed at this period, which enabled me to endure it; for, indeed, I am convinced that many of our infantry sank and died under the weight of their knapsacks alone. For my own part, being a handicraft, I marched under a weight sufficient to impede the free motions of a donkey; for besides my well-filled kit, there was the greatcoat rolled on its top, my blanket and camp kettle, my haversack, stuffed full of leather for repairing the men's shoes, together with a hammer and other tools (the lapstone I took the liberty of flinging to the devil), ship-biscuit and beef for three days. I also carried my canteen filled with water, my hatchet and rifle, and eighty rounds of ball cartridge in my pouch; this last, except the beef and biscuit, being the best thing I owned, and which I always gave the enemy the benefit of, when opportunity offered.

Altogether the quantity of things I had on my shoulders was enough and more than enough for my wants, sufficient, indeed, to sink a little fellow of five feet seven inches into the earth. Nay, so awkwardly was the load our men bore in those days placed upon their backs, that the free motion of the body was impeded, the head held down from the pile at the back of the neck, and the soldier half beaten before he came to the scratch.

We marched till it was nearly dark, and then halted for the night. I myself was immediately posted sentinel between two hedges, and in a short time General Fane came up, and himself cautioned me to be alert.

"Remember, sentinel," he said, "that we are now near an active enemy; therefore be careful here, and mind what you are about."

Next day the peasantry sent into our camp a great quantity of the good things of their country, so that our men regaled themselves upon oranges, grapes, melons, and figs, and we had an abundance of delicacies which many of us had never before tasted. Amongst other presents, a live calf was presented to the Rifles, so that altogether we feasted in our first entrance into Portugal like a company of aldermen.

The next day we again advanced, and being in a state of the utmost anxiety to come up with the French, neither the heat of the burning sun, long miles, or heavy knapsacks were able to diminish our ardour. Indeed, I often look back with wonder at the light-hearted style, the jollity, and reckless indifference with which men who were destined in so short a time to fall, hurried onwards to the field of strife; seemingly without a thought of anything but the sheer love of meeting the foe and the excitement of the battle.

It was five or six days before the battle of Roliça, the army was on the march, and we were pushing on pretty fast. The whole force had slept the night before in the open fields;

indeed, as far as I know (for the Rifles were always in the front at this time), they had been for many days without any covering but the sky. We were pelting along through the streets of a village, the name of which I do not think I ever knew, so I cannot name it; I was in the front, and had just cleared the village, when I recollect observing General Hill (afterwards Lord Hill) and another officer ride up to a house, and give their horses to some of the soldiery to hold. Our bugles at that moment sounded the halt, and I stood leaning upon my rifle near the door of the mansion which General Hill had entered: there was a little garden before the house, and I stood by the gate. Whilst I remained there, the officer who had entered with General Hill came to the door, and called to me. "Rifleman," said he, "come here." I entered the gate, and approached him. "Go," he continued, handing me a dollar, "and try if you can get some wine; for we are devilish thirsty here." Taking the dollar, I made my way back to the village. At a wine-house, where the men were crowding around the door, and clamouring for drink (for the day was intensely hot), I succeeded, after some little difficulty, in getting a small pipkin full of wine; but the crowd was so great, that I found as much trouble in paying for it as in getting it; so I returned back as fast as I was able, fearing that the general would be impatient, and move off before I reached him. I remember Lord Hill was loosening his sword-belt as I handed him the wine. "Drink first, Rifleman," said he; and I took a good pull at the pipkin, and held it to him again. He looked at it as I did so, and told me I might drink it all up, for it appeared greasy; so I swallowed the remainder, and handed him back the dollar which I had received from the officer. "Keep the money," he said, "my man. Go back to the village once more, and try if you cannot get me another draught." Saying this, he handed me a second dollar, and told me to be quick. I made my way back to the village, got another pipkin full, and returned as fast as I could. The general was pleased with my promptness, and drank with great satisfaction, handing the remainder to the officer who attended him; and I dare say, if he ever recollected the circumstance afterwards, that was as sweet a draught, after the toil of the morning march, as he has drank at many a nobleman's board in Old England since.

It was on the 15th of August when we first came up with the French, and their skirmishers immediately commenced operations by raining a shower of balls upon us as we advanced, which we returned without delay.

The first man that was hit was Lieutenant Bunbury; he fell pierced through the head with a musket-ball, and died almost immediately. I thought I never heard such a tremendous noise as the firing made on this occasion, and the men on both sides of me, I could occasionally observe, were falling fast. Being overmatched, we retired to a rising ground, or hillock, in our rear, and formed there all round its summit, standing three deep, the front rank kneeling. In this position we remained all night, expecting the whole host upon us every moment. At daybreak, however, we received instructions to fall back as quickly as possible upon the main body. Having done so, we now lay down for a few hours' rest, and then again advanced to feel for the enemy.

On the 17th, being still in front, we again came up with the French, and I remember observing the pleasing effect afforded by the sun's rays glancing upon their arms, as they formed in order of battle to receive us. Moving on in extended order, under whatever cover the nature of the ground afforded, together with some companies of the 60th, we began a sharp fire upon them; and thus commenced the battle of Roliça.[9]

I do not pretend to give a description of this or any other battle I have been present at. All I can do is to tell the things

9 At Roliça, Allied forces totalled 14,850; the French under Delaborde numbered 4,400, plus 5 cannon. Losses were, respectively, 485 and 700.

which happened immediately around me, and that, I think, is as much as a private soldier can be expected to do.

Soon afterwards the firing commenced, and we had advanced pretty close upon the enemy. Taking advantage of whatever cover I could find, I threw myself down behind a small bank, where I lay so secure, that, although the Frenchmen's bullets fell pretty thickly around, I was enabled to knock several over without being dislodged; in fact, I fired away every round I had in my pouch whilst lying on this spot.

At length, after a sharp contest, we forced them to give ground, and, following them up, drove them from their position in the heights, and hung upon their skirts till they made another stand, and then the game began again.

The Rifles, indeed, fought well this day, and we lost many men. They seemed in high spirits, and delighted at having driven the enemy before them. Joseph Cochan was by my side loading and firing very industriously about this period of the day. Thirsting with heat and action, he lifted his canteen to his mouth; "Here's to you, old boy," he said, as he took a pull at its contents. As he did so a bullet went through the canteen, and perforating his brain, killed him in a moment. Another man fell close to him almost immediately, struck by a ball in the thigh.

Indeed we caught it severely just here, and the old iron was also playing its part amongst our poor fellows very merrily. I saw a man named Symmonds struck full in the face by a round shot, and he came to the ground a headless trunk. Meanwhile, many large balls bounded along the ground amongst us so deliberately that we could occasionally evade them without difficulty. I could relate many more of the casualties I witnessed on this day, but the above will suffice. When the roll was called after the battle, the females who missed their husbands came along the front of the line to inquire of the survivors whether they knew anything about them.[10] Amongst other

10 It was common in the Napoleonic Wars for wives to accompany their husbands on campaign.

names I heard that of Cochan called in a female voice, without being replied to.

The name struck me, and I observed the poor woman who had called it, as she stood sobbing before us, and apparently afraid to make further inquiries about her husband. No man had answered to his name, or had any account to give of his fate. I myself had observed him fall, as related before, whilst drinking from his canteen; but as I looked at the poor sobbing creature before me, I felt unable to tell her of his death. At length Captain Leech observed her, and called out to the company:

"Does any man here know what has happened to Cochan? If so, let him speak out at once."

Upon this order I immediately related what I had seen, and told the manner of his death. After a while Mrs Cochan appeared anxious to seek the spot where her husband fell, and in the hope of still finding him alive, asked me to accompany her over the field. She trusted, notwithstanding what I had told her, to find him yet alive.

"Do you think you could find it?" said Captain Leech, upon being referred to.

I told him I was sure I could, as I had remarked many objects whilst looking for cover during the skirmishing.

"Go then," said the captain, "and show the poor woman the spot, as she seems so desirous of finding the body."

I accordingly took my way over the ground we had fought upon, she following and sobbing after me, and, quickly reaching the spot where her husband's body lay, pointed it out to her.

She now soon discovered all her hopes were in vain; she embraced a stiffened corpse, and after rising and contemplating his disfigured face for some minutes, with hands clasped and tears streaming down her cheeks she took a prayer-book from her pocket, and kneeling down, repeated the service for the dead over the body. When she had finished she appeared a good deal comforted, and I took the oppor-

tunity of beckoning to a pioneer I saw near with some other
men, and together we dug a hole, and quickly buried the
body. Mrs Cochan then returned with me to the company to
which her husband had been attached, and laid herself down
upon the heath near us. She lay amongst some other females,
who were in the same distressing circumstances with herself,
with the sky for her canopy, and a turf for her pillow, for we
had no tents with us. Poor woman! I pitied her much; but
there was no remedy. If she had been a duchess she must
have fared the same. She was a handsome woman, I remember, and the circumstance of my having seen her husband
fall, and accompanied her to find his body, begot a sort of
intimacy between us. The company to which Cochan had
belonged, bereaved as she was, was now her home, and she
marched and took equal fortune with us to Vimeiro. She
hovered about us during that battle, and then went with us to
Lisbon, where she succeeded in procuring a passage to
England. Such was my first acquaintance with Mrs Cochan.
The circumstances of our intimacy were singular, and an
attachment grew between us during the short time we remained together. What little attention I could pay her during
the hardships of the march I did, and I also offered on the
first opportunity to marry her. "She had, however, received
too great a shock on the occasion of her husband's death ever
to think of another soldier," she said; she therefore thanked
me for my good feeling towards her, but declined my offer,
and left us soon afterwards for England.

It was on the 21st of August that we commenced fighting the
battle of Vimeiro.

The French came down upon us in a column, and the
Riflemen immediately commenced a sharp fire upon them
from whatever cover they could get a shelter behind, whilst
our cannon played upon them from our rear. I saw regular
lanes torn through their ranks as they advanced, which were
immediately closed up again as they marched steadily on.

Whenever we saw a round shot thus go through the mass, we raised a shout of delight.

One of our corporals, named Murphy, was the first man in the Rifles who was hit that morning, and I remember more particularly remarking the circumstances from his apparently having a presentiment of his fate before the battle began. He was usually an active fellow, and up to this time had shown himself a good and brave soldier, but on this morning he seemed unequal to his duty. General Fane and Major Travers were standing together on an early part of this day. The general had a spy-glass in his hand, and for some time looked anxiously at the enemy. Suddenly he gave the word to fall in, and immediately all was bustle amongst us. The Honourable Captain Pakenham[11] spoke very sharply to Murphy, who appeared quite dejected and out of spirits, I observed. He had a presentiment of death, which is by no means an uncommon circumstance, and I have observed it once or twice since this battle.

Others besides myself noticed Murphy on this morning, and, as we had reason to know he was not ordinarily deficient in courage, the circumstance was talked of after the battle was over. He was the first man shot that day.

Early on the morning of the battle I remember being relieved from picket, and throwing myself down to gain a few hours' repose before the expected engagement. So wearied was I with watching that I was hardly prostrate before I was in a sound sleep – a sleep which those only who have toiled in the field can know. I was not, however, destined to enjoy a very long repose before one of our sergeants, poking me with the muzzle of his rifle, desired me to get up, as many of the men wanted their shoes repaired immediately. This was by no means an uncommon occurrence, and I would fain have declined the job, but as several of the Riflemen who had followed the sergeant soon afterwards came round me and

11 Captain the Hon. Hercules Pakenham (1781–1850), brother-in-law of Wellington.

threw their shoes and boots at my head, I was fain to scramble on my legs, and make up my mind to go to work.

On looking around, in order to observe if there was any hut or shed in which I could more conveniently exercise my craft, I espied a house near at hand, on the rise of a small hill. So I gathered up several pairs of the dilapidated boots and shoes, and immediately made for it. Seating myself down in a small room as soon as I entered, I took the tools from my haversack and prepared to work; and as the boots of the captain of my company were amongst the bad lot, and he was barefooted for want of them, I commenced with *them*.

Hardly had I worked a quarter of an hour, when a cannon-ball (the first announcement of the coming battle) came crashing through the walls of the house, just above my head, and completely covered the captain's boot (as it lay between my knees) with dust and fragments of the building. There were only two persons in the room at the time, an old and a young woman, and they were so dreadfully scared at this sudden visitation that they ran about the room, making the house echo with their shrieks, till at length they rushed out into the open air, leaving me alone with the boots around me on the floor.

For my own part, although I was more used to such sounds, I thought it was no time and place to mend boots and shoes in, so, being thus left alone in my glory, I shook the dust from my apron, gathered up the whole stock-in-trade from the floor, and hastily replacing my tools in my haversack, followed the example of the mistress of the mansion and her daughter, and bolted out of the house. When I got into the open air, I found all in a state of bustle and activity, the men falling in, and the officers busily engaged, whilst twenty or thirty mouths opened at me the moment I appeared calling out for their boots and shoes. "Where's my boots, Harris, you humbug?" cried one. "Give me my shoes, you old sinner," said another. "The captain's boots here, Harris, instantly," cried the sergeant. "Make haste, and fall into the ranks as fast as you can."

There was, indeed, no time for ceremony, so, letting go the corners of my apron, I threw down the whole lot of boots and shoes for the men to choose for themselves; the captain's being amongst the lot, with the wax-ends hanging to them (as I had left them when the cannon-ball so unceremoniously put a stop to my work), and quickly shouldering my piece, I fell into the ranks as I was ordered.

Just before the battle commenced in earnest, and whilst the officers were busily engaged with their companies, shouting the word of command, and arranging matters of moment, Captain Leech ordered a section of our men to move off, at double quick, and take possession of a windmill, which was on our left. I was amongst this section, and set off full cry towards the mill, when Captain Leech espied and roared out to me by name to return. – "Hallo! there, you Harris!" he called, "fall out of that section directly. We want you here, my man." I, therefore, wheeled out of the rank, and returned to him. "You fall in amongst the men here, Harris," he said. "I shall not send you to that post. The cannon will play upon the mill in a few moments like hail; and what shall we do," he continued, laughing, "without our head shoemaker to repair our shoes?"

It is long since these transactions took place. But I remember the words of the captain as if they had been uttered but yesterday; for that which was spoken in former years in the field has made a singular impression on my mind. As I looked about me, whilst standing enranked, and just before the commencement of the battle, I thought it the most imposing sight the world could produce. Our lines glittering with bright arms; the stern features of the men, as they stood with their eyes fixed unalterably upon the enemy, the proud colours of England floating over the heads of the different battalions, and the dark cannon on the rising ground, and all in readiness to commence the awful work of death, with a noise that would deafen the whole multitude. Altogether, the sight had a singular and terrible effect upon the feelings of a youth who, a few short months before, had been a solitary shepherd upon the Downs of Dorsetshire, and had never contemplated any other sort of life than the peaceful occupation of watching the innocent sheep as they fed upon the grassy turf.

The first cannon-shot I saw fired I remember was a miss. The artilleryman made a sad bungle, and the ball went wide of the mark. We were all looking anxiously to see the effect of this shot; and another of the gunners (a red-haired man) rushed at the fellow who had fired, and in the excitement of the moment, knocked him head over heels with his fist. "D—you, for a fool," he said; "what sort of a shot do you call that? Let me take the gun." He accordingly fired the next shot himself, as soon as the gun was loaded, and so truly did he point it at the French column on the hill-side, that we saw the fatal effect of the destructive missile, by the lane it made and the confusion it caused.

Our Riflemen (who at the moment were amongst the guns), upon seeing this, set up a tremendous shout of delight, and the battle commencing immediately, we were all soon hard at work.

I myself was very soon so hotly engaged, loading and firing away, enveloped in the smoke I created, and the cloud which hung about me from the continued fire of my comrades, that I could see nothing for a few minutes but the red flash of my own piece amongst the white vapour clinging to my very clothes. This has often seemed to me the greatest drawback upon our present system of fighting; for whilst in such state, on a calm day, until some friendly breeze of wind clears the space around, a soldier knows no more of his position and what is about to happen in his front, or what *has* happened (even amongst his own companions) than the very dead lying around. The Rifles, as usual, were pretty busy in this battle. The French, in great numbers, came steadily down upon us, and we pelted away upon them like a shower of leaden hail. Under any cover we could find we lay; firing one moment, jumping up and running for it the next; and, when we could see before us, we observed the cannon-balls making a lane through the enemy's columns as they advanced, huzzaing and shouting like madmen.

Such is my remembrance of the commencement of the battle of Vimeiro. The battle began on a fine bright day, and the sun played on the arms of the enemy's battalions, as they came on, as if they had been tipped with gold. The battle soon became general; the smoke thickened around, and often I was obliged to stop firing, and dash it aside from my face, and try in vain to get a sight of what was going on, whilst groans and shouts and a noise of cannon and musketry appeared almost to shake the very ground. It seemed hell upon earth, I thought.

A man named John Low stood before me at this moment, and he turned round during a pause in our exertions, and addressed me: "Harris, you humbug," he said, "you have got plenty of money about you, I know; for you are always staying about and picking up what you can find on the field. But I think this will be your last field-day, old boy. A good many of us will catch it, I suspect, to-day." "You are right, Low," I said. "I have got nine guineas in my pack, and if I am shot to-day, and you yourself escape, it's quite at your service. In the meantime, however, if you see any symptoms of my wishing to flinch in this business I hope you will shoot me with your own hand." Low, as well as myself, survived this battle, and after it was over, whilst we sat down with our comrades and rested, amongst other matters talked over, Low told them of our conversation during the heat of the day, and the money I had collected, and the Rifles from that time had a great respect for me. It is, indeed, singular, how a man loses or gains caste with his comrades from his behaviour, and how closely he is observed in the field. The officers, too, are commented upon and closely observed.

The men are very proud of those who are brave in the field, and kind and considerate to the soldiers under them. An act of kindness done by an officer has often during the battle been the cause of his life being saved. Nay, whatever folks may say upon the matter, I know from experience, that in *our* army the men like best to be officered by gentlemen, men whose education has rendered them more kind in manners than your coarse officer, sprung from obscure origin, and whose style is brutal and overbearing.

. . . During this day I myself narrowly escaped being killed by our own dragoons, for somehow or other, in the confusion, I fell whilst they were charging, and the whole squadron thundering past just missed me, as I lay amongst the dead and wounded. Tired and overweighted with my knapsack and all my shoe-making implements, I lay where I had fallen for a short time, and watched the cavalry as they gained the enemy. I observed a fine, gallant-looking officer leading them on in that charge. He was a brave fellow, and bore himself like a hero; with his sword waving in the air, he cheered the men on, as he went dashing upon the enemy, and hewing and slashing at them in tremendous style. I watched for him as the dragoons came off after that charge, *but saw him no more*; he had fallen. Fine fellow! his conduct indeed made an impression upon me that I shall never forget, and I was told afterwards that he was a brother of Sir John Eustace.

A French soldier was lying beside me at this time; he was badly wounded, and hearing him moan as he lay, after I had done looking at the cavalry, I turned my attention to him, and getting up, lifted his head, and poured some water into his mouth. He was dying fast; but he thanked me in a foreign language, which, although I did not exactly understand, I could easily make out by the look he gave me. Mullins, of the Rifles, who stepped up whilst I supported his head, d–d me for a fool for my pains. "Better knock out his brains, Harris," said he; "he has done *us* mischief enough, I'll be bound for it, to-day."

After the battle I strolled about the field in order to see if there was anything to be found worth picking up amongst the dead. The first thing I saw was a three-pronged silver fork, which, as it lay by itself, had most likely been dropped by some person who had been on the look-out before me. A little further on I saw a French soldier sitting against a small rise in the ground or bank. He was wounded in the throat, and appeared very faint, the bosom of his coat being saturated with the blood which had flowed down. By his side lay his cap, and close to that was a bundle containing a quantity of gold and silver crosses, which I concluded he had plundered from some convent or church. He looked the picture of a sacrilegious thief, dying hopelessly, and overtaken by Divine wrath. I kicked over his cap, which was also full of plunder, but I declined taking anything from him. I felt fearful of incurring the wrath of Heaven for the like offence, so I left him, and passed on. A little further off lay an officer of the 50th regiment. I knew him by sight, and recognised him as he lay. He was quite dead, and lying on his back. He had been plundered, and his clothes were torn open. Three bullet-holes were close together in the pit of his stomach: beside him lay an empty pocket-book, and his epaulette had been pulled from his shoulder.

I had moved on but a few paces when I recollected that perhaps the officer's shoes might serve me, my own being considerably the worse for wear, so I returned again, went back, pulled one of his shoes off, and knelt down on one knee to try it on. It was not much better than my own; however, I determined on the exchange, and proceeded to take off its fellow. As I did so I was startled by the sharp report of a firelock, and, at the same moment, a bullet whistled close by my head. Instantly starting up, I turned, and looked in the direction whence the shot had come. There was no person near me in this part of the field. The dead and the dying lay thickly all around; but nothing else could I see. I looked to the priming of my rifle, and again turned to the dead officer of the 50th. It was evident that some plundering scoundrel had taken a shot at me, and the fact of his doing so proclaimed him one of the enemy. To distinguish him amongst the bodies strewn about was impossible; perhaps he might himself be one of the wounded. Hardly had I effected the exchange, put on the dead officer's shoes, and resumed my rifle, when another shot took place, and a second ball whistled past me. This time I was ready, and turning quickly, I saw my man: he was just about to squat down behind a small mound, about twenty paces from me. I took a haphazard shot at him, and instantly knocked him over. I immediately ran up to him; he had fallen on his face, and I heaved him over on his back, bestrode his body, and drew my sword-bayonet. There was, however, no occasion for the precaution as he was even then in the agonies of death.

It was a relief to me to find I had not been mistaken. He was a French light-infantry man, and I therefore took it quite in the way of business – he had attempted my life, and lost his own. It was the fortune of war; so, stooping down, with my sword I cut the green string that sustained his calibash, and took a hearty pull to quench my thirst.

After I had shot the French light-infantry man, and quenched my thirst from his calibash, finding he was quite dead, I proceeded to search him. Whilst I turned him about in the endeavour at finding the booty I felt pretty certain he had gathered from the slain, an officer of the 60th approached, and accosted me.

"What! looking for money, my lad," said he, "eh?"

"I am, sir," I answered; "but I cannot discover where this fellow has hid his hoard."

"You knocked him over, my man," he said, "in good style, and deserve something for the shot. Here," he continued, stooping down and feeling in the lining of the Frenchman's coat, "this is the place where these rascals generally carry their coin. Rip up the lining of his coat, and then search in his stock. I know them better than you seem to do."

Thanking the officer for his courtesy, I proceeded to cut open the lining of his jacket with my sword-bayonet, and was quickly rewarded for my labour by finding a yellow silk purse, wrapped up in an old black silk handkerchief. The purse contained several doubloons, three or four napoleons, and a few dollars. Whilst I was counting the money, the value of which, except the dollars, I did not then know, I heard the bugle of the Rifles sound out the assembly, so I touched my cap to the officer, and returned towards them.

The men were standing at ease, with the officers in front. As I approached them, Major Travers, who was in command of the four companies, called me to him.

"What have you got there, sir?" he said. "Show me."

I handed him the purse, expecting a reprimand for my pains. He, however, only laughed as he examined it, and, turning, showed it to his brother officers.

"You did that well, Harris," he said, "and I am sorry the purse is not better filled. Fall in." In saying this, he handed me back the purse, and I joined my company. Soon afterwards, the roll being called, we were all ordered to lie down and gain a little rest after our day's work.

We lay as we had stood enranked upon the field, and in a few minutes, I dare say, one half of that green line, over-wearied with their exertions, were asleep upon the ground they had so short a time before been fighting on. After we had lain for some little time, I saw several men strolling about the fields so I again quietly rose, with one or two others of the Rifles, and once more looked about me to see what I could pick up amongst the slain.

I had rambled some distance, when I saw a French officer running towards me with all his might, pursued by at least half a dozen horsemen. The Frenchman was a tall, hand-some-looking man, dressed in a blue uniform; he ran as swiftly as a wild Indian, turning and doubling like a hare. I held up my hand, and called to his pursuers not to hurt him. One of the horsemen, however, cut him down with a desperate blow, when close beside me, and the next wheeling round, as he leaned from his saddle, passed his sword through the body.

I am sorry to say there was an English dragoon amongst these scoundrels; the rest, by their dress, I judged to be Portuguese cavalry. Whether the Frenchman thus slaughtered was a prisoner trying to escape, or what was the cause of this cold-blooded piece of cruelty, I know not, as the horsemen immediately galloped off without a word of explanation; and feeling quite disgusted with the scene I had witnessed, I returned to my comrades, and again throwing myself down, was soon as fast asleep as any there.

I might have slept perhaps half an hour, when, the bugles again sounding, we all started to our feet, and were soon afterwards marched off to form the picquets. Towards evening I was posted upon a rising ground, amongst a clump of tall trees. There seemed to have been a sharp skirmish here, as three Frenchmen were lying dead amongst the long grass upon the spot where I was standing. As I threw my rifle to my shoulder, and walked past them on my beat, I observed they had been plundered, and the haversacks having been torn off, some of the contents were scattered about. Among other things, a small quantity of biscuit lay at my feet.

War is a sad blunter of the feelings I have often thought since those days. The contemplation of three ghastly bodies in this lonely spot failed then in making the slightest impression upon me. The sight had become, even in the short time I had been engaged in the trade, but too familiar. The biscuits, however, which lay in my path, I thought a blessed windfall, and, stooping, I gathered them up, scraped off the blood with which they were sprinkled with my bayonet, and ate them ravenously.

As I stood at the edge of the little plantation, and looked over to the enemy's side, I observed a large body of their cavalry drawn up. I love to call to mind the most trivial circumstances which I observed whilst in the Peninsula, and

I remember many things, of small importance in themselves, and, indeed, hardly remarked at the time, as forcibly as if they had been branded into my memory. I recollect keeping a very sharp look-out at the French cavalry on that evening, for I thought them rather too near my post; and whilst I stood beneath one of the tall trees and watched them, it commenced raining, and they were ordered to cloak up.

General Kellermann and his trumpets at this moment returned to the French side; and soon afterwards, the picquets being withdrawn, I was relieved from my post, and marched off to join my company. A truce, I now found, had been concluded, and we lay down to rest for the night. Next day was devoted to the duty of burying the dead and assisting the wounded, carrying the latter off the field into a church-yard near Vimeiro.

The scene in this churchyard was somewhat singular. Two long tables had been procured from some houses near, and were placed end to end amongst the graves, and upon them were laid the men whose limbs it was found necessary to amputate. Both French and English were constantly lifted on and off these tables. As soon as the operation was performed upon one lot, they were carried off, and those in waiting hoisted up: the surgeons with their sleeves turned up, and their hands and arms covered with blood, looking like butchers in the shambles. I saw as I passed at least twenty legs lying on the ground, many of them being clothed in the long black gaiters then worn by the infantry of the line. The surgeons had plenty of work on hand that day, and not having time to take off the clothes of the wounded, they merely ripped the seams and turned the cloth back, proceeding with the operation as fast as they could.

Many of the wounded came straggling into this church-yard in search of assistance, by themselves. I saw one man, faint with loss of blood, staggering along, and turned to assist him. He was severely wounded in the head, his face being completely incrusted with the blood which had flowed during the night, and had now dried. One eyeball was knocked out of the socket, and hung down upon his cheek.

Another man I observed who had been brought in, and propped against a grave-mound. He seemed very badly hurt. The men who had carried him into the churchyard had placed his cap filled with fragments of biscuit close beside his head, and as he lay he occasionally turned his mouth towards it, got hold of a piece of biscuit, and munched it.

As I was about to leave the churchyard, Dr Ridgeway, one of the surgeons, called me back, to assist in holding a man he was endeavouring to operate upon.

"Come and help me with this man," he said, "or I shall be all day cutting a ball out of his shoulder."

The patient's name was Doubter, an Irishman. He disliked the doctor's efforts, and writhed and twisted so much during the operation that it was with difficulty Dr Ridgeway could perform it. He found it necessary to cut very deep, and Doubter made a terrible outcry at every fresh incision.

"Oh, doctor dear!" he said, "it's murdering me you are! Blood an' 'ounds! I shall die! – I shall die! For the love of the Lord don't cut me all to pieces!"

Doubter was not altogether wrong; for, although he survived the operation, he died shortly afterwards from the effects of his wounds. After I was dismissed by the doctor, I gladly left the churchyard, and returning to the hill where the Rifles were bivouacked, was soon afterwards ordered by Captain Leech to get my shoe-making implements from my pack, and commence work upon the men's waist-belts, many of which had been much torn during the action, and I continued to be so employed as long as there was light enough to see by, after which I lay down amongst them to rest.

We lay that night upon the hill-side, many of the men breaking boughs from the trees at hand, in order to make a slight cover for their heads; the tents not being then with us.

I remember it was intensely cold during that night. So much so that I could not sleep, but lay with my feet drawn up, as if I had a fit of the cramp. I was indeed compelled more than once during the night to get up and run about, in order to put warmth into my benumbed limbs.

Three days' march brought us without the walls of Lisbon, where we halted, and, the tents soon after coming up, were encamped. The second day after our arrival, as I was lying in my tent, Captain Leech and Lieutenant Cox entering it, desired me to rise and follow them. We took the way towards the town, and wandered about the streets for some time. Both these officers were good-looking men, and, in their Rifle uniform, with the pelisse hanging from one shoulder, and hessian-boots then worn, cut a dash, I thought, in the streets of Lisbon. There were no other English that I could observe in the town this day; and, what with the glances of the black-eyed lasses from the windows, and the sulky scowl of the French sentinels as we passed, I thought we caused quite a sensation in the place. Indeed I believe we were the first men that entered Lisbon after the arrival of the army without its walls.

After some little time had been spent in looking about us, the officers spied an hotel, and entering it, walked upstairs. I myself entered a sort of taproom below, and found myself in the midst of a large assemblage of French soldiers, many of whom were wounded, some with their arms hanging in scarfs, and others bandaged about the head and face. In short, one half of them appeared to carry tokens of our bullets of a few days before.

At first they appeared inclined to be civil to me, although my appearance amongst them caused rather a sensation, I observed, and three or four rose from their seats, and with all the swagger of Frenchmen strutted up, and offered to drink with me. I was young then, and full of the natural animosity against the enemy so prevalent with John Bull. I hated the

French with a deadly hatred, and refused to drink with them, showing by my discourteous manner the feelings I entertained; so they turned off, with a "*Sacré!*" and a "*Bah!*" and, reseating themselves, commenced talking at an amazing rate all at once, and no man listening to his fellow.

Although I could not comprehend a word of the language they uttered, I could pretty well make out that I myself was the subject of the noise around me. My discourteous manners had offended them, and they seemed to be working themselves up into a violent rage. One fellow, in particular, wearing an immense pair of mustachios, and his coat loosely thrown over his shoulders, his arm being wounded and in a sling, rose up, and attempted to harangue the company. He pointed to the pouch at my waist, which contained my bullets, then to my rifle, and then to his own wounded arm, and I began to suspect that I should probably get more than I had bargained for on entering the house, unless I speedily managed to remove myself out of it, when, luckily, Lieutenant Cox and Captain Leech entered the room in search of me. They saw at a glance the state of affairs, and instantly ordered me to quit the room, themselves covering my retreat.

"Better take care, Harris," said the captain, "how you get amongst such a party as that again. You do not understand their language; I do: they meant mischief."

After progressing through various streets, buying leather and implements for mending our shoes, the two officers desired me again to await them in the street, and entered a shop close at hand. The day was hot, and a wine-house being directly opposite me, after waiting some time, I crossed over, and, going in, called for a cup of wine. Here I again found myself in the midst of a large assemblage of French soldiers, and once more an object of curiosity and dislike. Nevertheless, I paid for my wine, and drank it, regardless of the clamour my intrusion had again called forth. The host, however, seemed to understand his guests better than I did, and evidently anticipated mischief. After in vain trying to make me understand him, he suddenly jumped from behind his bar, and seizing me by the shoulder without ceremony, thrust me into the street. I found the two officers looking anxiously for me when I got out, and not quite easy at my disappearance. I, however, excused myself by pleading the heat of the day, and my anxiety to taste the good wines of Lisbon, and together we left the town, with our purchases, and reached the camp.

Next morning Captain Leech again entered my tent, and desired me to pick out three good workmen from the company, take them into the town, and seek out a shoemaker's shop as near the camp as possible.

"You must get leave to work in the first shop you can find," he said, "as we have a long march before us, and many of the men without shoes to their feet."

Accordingly, we carried with us three small sacks filled with old boots and shoes, and entering Lisbon went into the first shoemaker's shop we saw. Here I endeavoured in vain to make myself understood for some time. There was a master shoemaker at work and three men. They did not seem to like our intrusion, and looked very sulky, asking us various questions, which I could not understand; the only words I could at all comprehend being "*Bonos Irelandos, Brutu Englisa.*" I thought, considering we had come so far to fight their battles for them, that this was the north side of civil; so I signed to the men, and, by way of explanation of our wishes, and in order to cut the matter short, they emptied the three sacksful of boots and shoes upon the floor. We now explained what we would be at; the boots and shoes of the Rifles spoke for themselves, and, seating ourselves, we commenced work forthwith.

In this way we continued employed whilst the army lay near Lisbon, every morning coming in to work, and returning to the camp every night to sleep.

After we had been there several days, our landlord's family

had the curiosity to come occasionally and take a peep at us. My companions were noisy, good-tempered, jolly fellows, and usually sang all the time they hammered and strapped. The mistress of the house, seeing I was the head man, occasionally came and sat down beside me as I worked, bringing her daughter, a very handsome dark-eyed Spanish girl, and as a matter of course I fell in love.

We soon became better acquainted, and the mother, one evening, after having sat and chattered to me, serving me with wine, and other good things, on my rising to leave the shop, made a signal for me to follow her. She had managed to pick up a little English, and I knew a few words of the Spanish language, so that we could pretty well comprehend each other's meaning; and after leading me into their sitting-room, she brought her handsome daughter, and, without more circumstance, offered her to me for a wife. The offer was a tempting one; but the conditions of the marriage made it impossible for me to comply, since I was to change my religion, and desert my colours. The old dame proposed to conceal me effectually when the army marched; after which I was to live like a gentleman, with the handsome Maria for a wife.

It was hard to refuse so tempting an offer, with the pretty Maria endeavouring to back her mother's proposal. I, however, made them understand that nothing would tempt me to desert; and, promising to try and get my discharge when I returned to England, protested I would then return and marry Maria.

Soon after this the army marched for Spain,[11] the Rifles paraded in the very street where the shop I had so long worked at was situated, and I saw Maria at the window. As our bugles struck up, she waved her handkerchief; I returned the salute, and in half an hour had forgotten all about her. So

11 Moore's forces departed Lisbon in mid-October; a second British column, under General Sir David Baird struck out from Corunna for the rendezvous near Valladolid in early November.

much for a soldier's love. Our marches were now long and fatiguing. I do not know how many miles we traversed ere we reached Almeida, which I was told was the last town in Portugal: some of my companions said we had come five hundred miles since we left Lisbon.

We now passed to the left, and bade adieu to Portugal for ever. We had fought and conquered, and felt elated accordingly. Spain was before us, and every man in the Rifles seemed only anxious to get a rap at the French again. On and on we toiled, till we reached Salamanca. I love to remember the appearance of that army, as we moved along at this time. It was a glorious sight to see our colours spread in these fields. The men seemed invincible; nothing, I thought, could have beaten them. We had some of as desperate fellows in the Rifles along as had ever toiled under the burning sun of an enemy's country in any age; but I lived to see hardship and toil lay hundreds of them low, before a few weeks were over our heads. At Salamanca we stayed seven or eight days, and during this time the shoemakers were again wanted, and I worked with my men incessantly during their short halt.

Our marches were now still more arduous; fourteen leagues a day, I have heard the men say, we accomplished before we halted and many of us were found out, and floored in the road. It became every one for himself. The load we carried was too great, and we staggered on, looking neither to the right nor the left. If a man dropped, he found it no easy matter to get up again, unless his companion assisted him, and many died of fatigue. As for myself, I was nearly floored by this march; and on reaching a town one night, which I think was called Zamora, I fell at the entrance of the first street we came to; the sight left my eyes, my brain reeled, and I came down like a dead man. When I recovered my senses, I remember that I crawled into a door I found open, and, being too ill to rise, lay for some time in the passage unregarded by the inhabitants.

★   ★   ★

At Sahagun we fell in with the army under command of Sir John Moore.[12] I forget how many thousand men there were; but they were lying in and around the town when we arrived. The Rifles marched to an old convent, some two miles from Sahagun, where we were quartered, together with a part of the 15th Hussars, some of the Welsh fusileers and straggling bodies of men belonging to various other regiments; all seeming on the *qui vive*, and expecting the French to fall in with them every hour. As our small and way-worn party came to a halt before the walls of the convent, the men from these different regiments came swarming out to greet us, loudly cheering us as they rushed up and seized our hands. The difference in appearance between ourselves and these new-comers was indeed (just then) very great. *They* looked fresh, from good quarters, and good rations. Their clothes and accoutrements were comparatively new and clean, and their cheeks ruddy with the glow of health and strength; whilst our men, on the contrary, were gaunt-looking, way-worn, and ragged; our faces burnt almost to the hue of an Asiatic's by the sun; our accoutrements rent and torn; and many without even shoes to their feet. However, we had some work in us yet; and perhaps were in better condition for it than our more fresh-looking comrades. And now our butchers tucked up their sleeves, and quickly set to work, slaughtering oxen and sheep, which we found within the convent walls; whilst others of our men, lighting fires in the open air upon the snow, commenced cooking the fragments, which were cut up, and distributing to them; so that very soon after our arrival, we were more sumptuously regaled than we had been for many days.

12 After massing around Salamanca, Moore decided to attack Marshal Soult's isolated and scattered II Corps, and had marched north on 11 December with 21,000 infantry, 2,500 cavalry and 66 guns, reaching Sahagun ten days later. The action against Soult's II Corps was opened by the British cavalry advance under Lord Paget, who overran a French piquet on 21 December, near annihilating two squadrons of Imperial cavalry.

After this meal we were ordered into the convent and, with knapsacks on our backs, and arms in our hands, threw ourselves down to rest upon the floor of a long passage. Overcome with hard toil and long miles, our wearied men were soon buried in a deep and heavy sleep. In the middle of the night I remember, as well as if the sounds were at this moment in my ear, that my name was called out many times without my being completely awakened by the summons. The repeated call seemed mixed up with some circumstance in my dreams; and it was not until the noise awoke some of the men lying nearer to the entrance of the passage, and they took up the cry, that I was effectually aroused. From weariness, and the weight of my knapsack, and the quantity of implements I carried, I was at first quite unable to gain my legs; but when I did so I found that Quartermaster Surtees[13] was the person who was thus disturbing my rest.

"Come, be quick there, Harris!" said he, as I picked my way by the light of the candle he held in his hand; "look amongst the men, and rouse up all the shoemakers you have in the four companies. I have a job for them, which must be done instantly."

With some little trouble, and not a few curses from them as I stirred them up with the butt of my rifle, I succeeded in waking several of our snoring handicrafts; and the quartermaster bidding us instantly follow him, led the way to the very top of the convent stairs. Passing then into a ruinous-looking apartment, along which we walked upon the rafters, there being no flooring, he stopped when he arrived at its further extremity. Here he proceeded to call our attention to a quantity of barrels of gunpowder lying beside a large heap of raw bullocks' hides.

"Now, Harris," said he, "keep your eyes open, and mind what you are about here. General Craufurd orders you instantly to set to work, and sew up every one of these barrels

13 William Surtees, the author of *Twenty-Five Years in The Rifle Brigade* (1833).

in the hides lying before you. You are to sew the skins with the hair outwards, and be quick about it, for the general swears that if the job is not finished in half an hour he will hang you."

The latter part of this order was anything but pleasant; and whether the general ever really gave it I never had an opportunity of ascertaining. I only know that I give the words as they were given me; and, well knowing the stuff Craufurd was made of, I received the candle from the hands of Surtees, and bidding the men get needles and waxed thread from their knapsacks, as the quartermaster withdrew, I instantly prepared to set about the job.

I often think of that night's work as I sit strapping away in my little shop in Richmond Street, Soho. It was a curious scene to look at, and the task neither very easy nor safe. The Riflemen were wearied, unwilling, and out of temper; and it was as much as I could do to get them to assist me. Moreover, they were so reckless that they seemed rather to wish to blow the convent into the air than to get on with their work. One moment the candle was dropped, and nearly extinguished; the next they lost their implements between the rafters of the floor, flaring the light about amongst the barrels; and wishing, as I remonstrated with them, that the powder might ignite, and blow me, themselves, and the general to—. Such were the Riflemen of the Peninsular War – daring, gallant, reckless fellows. I had a hard task to get the work safely finished; but at length, between coaxing and bullying these dare-devils, I managed to do so, and together we returned down the convent stairs; and, finding Surtees awaiting us in the passage below, he reported to General Craufurd that his order had been obeyed. After which we were permitted again to lie down, and sleep till the bugle awoke us next morning.

We remained in the convent part of the next day, and towards evening received orders to leave all our women and baggage behind, and advance towards the enemy. Our four companies accordingly were quickly upon the move, and before long we came up with the remainder of the Rifle corps, which had recently arrived from England with Sir John Moore. As these men saw us coming up they halted for the moment, and gave us one hearty cheer, allowing our four companies to pass to the front, as the post of honour, calling us "The heroes of Portugal." As we passed to the front we returned their cheer with pride. Our worn appearance and sunburnt look gave us the advantage over our comrades, we thought, and we marched in the van of the vanguard.

War is a sad blunter of the feelings of men. We felt eager to be at it again. Nay, I am afraid we longed for blood as the cheer of our comrades sounded in our ears; and yet, amidst all this, softer feelings occasionally filled the breasts of those gallant fellows, even whilst they were thirsting for a sight of the enemy. Some of the men near me suddenly recollected, as they saw the snow lying thickly in our path, that this was Christmas Eve. The recollection soon spread amongst the men; and many talked of home, and scenes upon that night in other days in Old England, shedding tears as they spoke of the relatives and friends never to be seen by them again.

As the night approached we became less talkative. The increasing weariness of our limbs kept our tongues quieter, and we were many of us half asleep as we walked, when suddenly a shout arose in front that the French were upon us. In an instant every man was on the alert, and we were rushing forward, in extended order, to oppose them. It proved a false alarm, but it nearly cost me a broken bone or two. The honourable Captain Pakenham (now Sir Hercules Pakenham), on the first sound of the enemy being in sight, made a dash to get to the front, at the same moment I myself was scrambling up a bank on the road side. In the darkness and hurry the mule the captain was mounted on bore me to the ground, and, getting his fore-feet fast fixed somehow between my neck and my pack, we were fairly hampered for some moments. The captain swore, the mule floundered, and I bellowed with alarm lest the animal should dig his feet into my back, and quite disable me. At length, however, the captain succeeded in getting clear, and spurred over the bank, as I rolled back into the road. It might be somewhere about two o'clock in the morning that our advance into Spain was, for that time, checked, and the retreat to Coruña might be said to commence.[14] General Craufurd was in command of the brigade, and riding in front, when I observed a dragoon come spurring furiously along the road to meet us. He delivered a letter to the general, who turned round in his saddle the moment he had read a few lines, and thundered out the word "to halt!" A few minutes more and we were all turned to the right-about and retracing our steps of the night before – the contents of that epistle serving to furnish our men with many a surmise during the retrograde movement. When we again neared Sahagun, I remember seeing the wives and children of the men come rushing into the ranks, and embracing the husbands and fathers they expected never to see again.

The entire Rifle corps entered the same convent we had before been quartered in; but this time we remained en-ranked in its apartments and passages, no man being allowed to quit his arms or lie down. We stood leaning upon the muzzles of our rifles, and dozed as we stood. After remaining thus for about an hour, we were then ordered out of the convent, and the word was again given to march. There was a sort of thaw on this day, and the rain fell fast. As we passed the walls of the convent, I observed our General (Craufurd) as he sat upon his horse, looking at us on the march, and remarked the peculiar sternness of his features: he did not like to see us going rearwards at all; and many of us judged

14 Only hours before an intended dawn attack on the 24th, Moore had discovered that Napoleon was advancing against him with some 80,000 troops, spearheaded by Marshal Ney's VI Corps. Surprised by the speed of Napoleon's reaction and cogniscent of his inferior numbers, Moore ordered a full-scale retreat to Corunna on the coast. Harris's battalion left Sahagun on Christmas Day 1808.

there must be something wrong by his severe look and scowling eye.

"Keep your ranks there, men!" he said, spurring his horse towards some Riflemen who were avoiding a small rivulet. "Keep your ranks and move on – *no straggling* from the main body."

We pushed on all that day without halting; and I recollect the first thing that struck us as somewhat odd was our passing one of the commissariat wagons, overturned and stuck fast in the mud, and which was abandoned without an effort to save any of its contents. A sergeant of the 92nd Highlanders, just about this time, fell dead with fatigue, and no one stopped, as we passed, to offer him any assistance. Night came down upon us, without our having tasted food, or halted – I speak for myself, and those around me – and all night long we continued this dreadful march. Men began to look into each other's faces, and ask the question, "Are we ever to be halted again?" and many of the weaker sort were now seen to stagger, make a few desperate efforts, and then fall, perhaps to rise no more. Most of us had devoured all we carried in our haversacks, and endeavoured to catch up anything we could snatch from hut or cottage in our route. Many, even at this period, would have straggled from the ranks, and perished, had not Craufurd held them together with a firm rein. One such bold and stern commander in the East during a memorable disaster, and that devoted army had reached its refuge unbroken! Thus we staggered on, night and day, for about four days, before we discovered the reason of this continued forced march. The discovery was made to our company by a good-tempered, jolly fellow, named Patrick M'Lauchlan. He inquired of an officer, marching directly in his front, the destination intended.

"By J—s! Musther Hills," I heard him say, "where the d—l is this you're taking us to?"

"To England, M'Lauchlan," returned the officer with a

melancholy smile upon his face as he gave the answer – "*if we can get there.*"

"More luck and grace to you," said M'Lauchlan; "and it's that you're maning, is it?"

This M'Lauchlan was a good specimen of a thorough Irish soldier. Nothing could disturb his good humour and high spirits; and even during a part of this dreadful march, he had ever some piece of Irish humour upon his tongue's end, whilst he staggered under the weight of his pack. He would in all probability have been amongst the few who did reach England; but, during the march, he was attacked with the racking pains of acute rheumatism, and frequently fell to the ground screaming with agony. On such occasions his companions would do that for him which they omitted to perform towards others. They many times halted, heaved him up, and assisted him forwards. Sir Dudley Hill, too, was greatly interested for M'Lauchlan, trying to cheer him on, whilst the men could scarcely refrain from laughter at the extraordinary things he gave utterance to whilst racked with pain, and staggering with fatigue. At length, however, M'Lauchlan fell one dark night, as we hurried through the streets of a village, and we could not again raise him.

"It's no use, Harris," I heard him say in a faint voice, "I can do no more."

Next morning, when day broke, he was no longer seen in the ranks, and as I never saw him again I conclude he quickly perished.

The information M'Lauchlan obtained from Lieutenant Hill quickly spread amongst us, and we now began to see more clearly the horrors of our situation, and the men to murmur at not being permitted to turn and stand at bay – cursing the French, and swearing they would rather die ten thousand deaths, with their rifles in their hands in opposition, than endure the present toil. We were in the rear at this time, and following that part of the army which made for Vigo,[15] whilst the other portion of the British, being on the main road to Coruña, were at this moment closely pursued and harassed by the enemy, as I should judge from the continued thunder of their cannon and rattle of their musketry. Craufurd seemed to sniff the sound of battle from afar with peculiar feelings. He halted us for a few minutes occasionally when the distant clamour became more distinct, and his face turned towards the sound and seemed to light up and become less stern. It was then indeed that every poor fellow clutched his weapon more firmly, and wished for a sight of the enemy.

Before long they had their wish: the enemy's cavalry were on our skirts that night; and as we rushed out of a small village, the name of which I cannot now recollect, we turned to bay.[16] Behind broken-down carts and tumbrils, huge trunks of trees, and everything we could scrape together, the Rifles lay and blazed away at the advancing cavalry, whilst the inhabitants, suddenly aroused from their beds to behold their village almost on fire with our continued discharges, and nearly distracted with the sound, ran from their houses, crying "*Viva l'Englisa!*" and "*Viva la Franca!*" in a breath; men, women, and children flying to the open country in their alarm.

We passed the night thus engaged, holding our own as well as we could, together with the 43rd Light Infantry, the 52nd, a portion of the German Legion, part of the 10th Hussars, and the 15th Dragoons. Towards morning we moved down towards a small bridge, still followed by the enemy, whom, however, we had sharply galled, and obliged to be more wary in their efforts. The rain was pouring down in torrents on this morning I recollect, and we remained many hours with

15 General Craufurd's light brigades and General Alten's King's German Legion were detached from the main column at Astorga on 31 December, partly to guard the southern flank, partly to reduce the demands on the commissariat, and sent west to Vigo.
16 Castro Gonzalo

our arms ported, standing in this manner, and staring the French cavalry in the face, the water actually running out of the muzzles of our rifles. I do not recollect seeing a single regiment of infantry amongst the French force on this day; it seemed to me a tremendous body of cavalry – some said nine or ten thousand strong – commanded, as I heard, by General Lefebvre.

Whilst we stood thus, face to face, I remember the horsemen of the enemy sat watching us very intently, as if waiting for a favourable moment to dash upon us like beasts of prey; and every now and then their trumpets would ring out a lively strain of music, as if to encourage them. As the night drew on, our cavalry moved a little to the front, together with several field-pieces, and succeeded in crossing the bridge; after which we also advanced, and threw ourselves into some hilly ground on either side the road; whilst the 43rd and 52nd lay behind some carts, trunks of trees, and other materials with which they had formed a barrier.

General Craufurd was standing behind this barricade, when he ordered the Rifles to push still further in front, and conceal themselves amongst the hills on either side. A man named Higgins was my front-rank man at this moment. "Harris," said he, "let you and I gain the very top of the mountain, and look out what those French thieves are at on the other side."

My feet were sore and bleeding, and the sinews of my legs ached as if they would burst, but I resolved to accompany him. In our wearied state the task was not easy, but, by the aid of Higgins, a tall and powerful fellow, I managed to reach the top of the mountain, where we placed ourselves in a sort of gully, or ditch, and looked over to the enemy's side, concealing ourselves by lying flat in the ditch, as we did so. Thus, in favourable situations, like cats watching for their prey, were the rest of the Rifles lying *perdu* upon the hills that night. The mountain, we found, was neither so steep nor so precipitous on the enemy's side. The ascent, on the contrary, was so easy, that one or two of the videttes of the French cavalry were prowling about very near where we lay. As we had received orders not to make more noise than we could help, not even to speak to each other except in whispers, although one of these horsemen approached close to where I lay, I forbore to fire upon him. At length he stopped so near me that I saw it was almost impossible he could avoid discovering that the Rifles were in such close proximity to his person. He gazed cautiously along the ridge, took off his helmet, and wiped his face, as he appeared to meditate upon the propriety of crossing the ditch in which we lay; when suddenly our eyes met, and in an instant he plucked a pistol from his holster, fired it in my face, and, wheeling his horse, plunged down the hillside. For the moment I thought I was hit, as the ball grazed my neck, and stuck fast in my knapsack, where I found it, when, many days afterwards, I unpacked my kit on ship-board. About a quarter of an hour after this, as we still lay in the gully, I heard some person clambering up behind us, and, upon turning quickly round, I found it was General Craufurd. The general was wrapped in his greatcoat, and, like ourselves, had been for many hours drenched to the skin, for the rain was coming down furiously. He carried in his hand a canteen full of rum, and a small cup, with which he was occasionally endeavouring to refresh some of the men. He offered me a drink as he passed, and then proceeded onwards along the ridge. After he had emptied his canteen he came past us again, and himself gave us instructions as to our future proceedings.

"When all is ready, Riflemen," said he, "you will immediately get the word, and pass over the bridge. Be careful, and mind what you are about."

Accordingly, a short time after he had left us, we were ordered to descend the mountain-side in single file, and having gained the road, were quickly upon the bridge. Meanwhile the Staff Corps had been hard at work mining the very centre of the structure, which was filled with gunpowder, a narrow plank being all the aid we had by which to pass over. For my own part, I was now so utterly helpless that I felt as if all was nearly up with me, and that, if I could steady myself so as to reach the further end of the plank, it would be all I should be able to accomplish. However, we managed all of us to reach the other side in safety, when, almost immediately afterwards, the bridge blew up with a tremendous report, and a house at its extremity burst into flames. What with the concussion of the explosion, and the tremulous state of my limbs, I was thrown to the ground, and lay flat upon my face for some time, almost in a state of insensibility. After awhile I somewhat recovered; but it was not without extreme difficulty, and many times falling again, that I succeeded in regaining the column. Soon after I had done so, we reached Benevento [Benavente], and immediately took refuge in a convent. Already three parts of it were filled with other troops, among which were mingled the 10th Hussars, the German Legion, and the 15th Dragoons; the horses of these regiments standing as close as they could stand, with the men dismounted between each horse, the animals' heads to the walls of the building, and all in readiness to turn out on the instant. Liquor was handed to us by the Dragoons, but having had nothing for some time to eat, many of our men became sick, instead of receiving any benefit from it.

Before we had been in the convent as long a time as I have been describing our arrival, every man of us was down on the floor, and wellnigh asleep; and before we had slept half an hour, we were again aroused from our slumbers by the clatter of the horses, the clash of the men's sabres, and their shouts for us to clear the way.

"The enemy! The enemy!" I heard shouted out.

"Clear the way, Rifles! Up boys, and clear the way!"

In short, the Dragoons hardly gave us time to rise, before they were leading their horses amongst us, and getting out of the convent as fast as they could scamper, whilst we ourselves were not long in following their example. As we did so, we discovered that the French cavalry, having found the bridge blown up, had dashed into the stream, and succeeded in crossing. Our cavalry, however, quickly formed, and charged them in gallant style.

The shock of that encounter[17] was tremendous to look upon, and we stood for some time enranked, watching the combatants. The horsemen had it all to themselves; our Dragoons fought like tigers, and, although greatly over-matched, drove the enemy back like a torrent, and forced them again into the river. A private of the 10th Hussars – his name, I think, was Franklin – dashed into the stream after their general (Lefebvre),[18] assailed him, sword in hand, in the water, captured, and brought him a prisoner on shore again. If I remember rightly, Franklin, or whatever else was his name, was made a sergeant on the spot. The French general was delivered into our custody on that occasion, and we cheered the 10th men heartily as we received him.

After the enemy had received this check from our cavalry, and which considerably damped their ardour, making them a trifle more shy of us for a while, we pushed onwards on our painful march. I remember marching close beside the French general during some part of this day, and observing his chapfallen and dejected look as he rode along in the midst of the green-jackets.

Being constantly in rear of the main body, the scenes of distress and misery I witnessed were dreadful to contemplate, particularly amongst the women and children, who were lagging and falling behind, their husbands and fathers being in the main body in our front. We now came to the edge of a deep ravine, the descent so steep and precipitous, that it was impossible to keep our feet in getting down, and we were

17 This was the battle of Benavente, 29 December 1808.
18 i.e. General Charles Lefebvre-Desnouttes (1773–1822). He was wounded by a pistol shot before being taken prisoner. He later escaped from England and resumed command of his *chasseurs à cheval*. From 1813 he commanded the cavalry of the Young Guard.

sometimes obliged to sit and slide along on our backs; whilst before us rose a ridge of mountains quite as steep and difficult of ascent. There was, however, no pause in our exertion, but, slinging our rifles round our necks, down the hill we went; whilst mules with the baggage on their backs, wearied and urged beyond their strength, were seen rolling from top to bottom, many of them breaking their necks with the fall, and the baggage crushed, smashed, and abandoned.

I remember, as I descended this hill, remarking the extraordinary sight afforded by the thousands of our red-coats, who were creeping like snails, and toiling up the ascent before us, their muskets slung round their necks, and clambering with both hands as they hauled themselves up. As soon as we ourselves had gained the ascent we were halted for a few minutes, in order to give us breath for another effort, and then onwards we moved again.

It is impossible for me to keep any account of time in this description, as I never exactly knew how many days and nights we marched; but I well know we kept on for many successive days and nights, without rest, or much in the way of food. The long day found us still pushing on, and the night caused us no halt.

After leaving the hills I have mentioned, and which I heard at the time were called the Mountains of Galicia, as we passed through a village our major resolved to try and get us something in the shape of a better meal than we had been able hitherto to procure. He accordingly despatched a small party, who were somewhat more fresh than their comrades, to try and procure something from the houses around; and they accordingly purchased, shot, and bayoneted somewhere about a score of pigs, which we lugged along with us to a convent just without the town; and, halting for a short time, proceeded to cook them. The men, however, were too hungry to wait whilst they were being properly dressed and served out.

After this hasty meal we again pushed on, still cursing the

enemy for not again showing themselves, that we might revenge some of our present miseries upon their heads.

"Why don't they come on like men," they cried, "whilst we've strength left in us to fight them?"

We were now upon the mountains; the night was bitter cold, and the snow falling fast. As day broke, I remember hearing Lieutenant Hill say to another officer (who, by the way, afterwards sank down and died):

"This is New Year's Day; and I think if we live to see another we shall not easily forget it."

The mountains were now becoming more wild-looking and steep as we proceeded; whilst those few huts we occasionally passed seemed so utterly forlorn and wretched-looking, it appeared quite a wonder how human beings could live in so desolate a home. After the snow commenced, the hills became so slippery (being in many parts covered with ice), that several of our men frequently slipped and fell, and being unable to rise, gave themselves up to despair, and died. There was now no endeavour to assist one another after a fall; it was everyone for himself, and God for us all!

The enemy, I should think, were at this time frequently close upon our trail; and I thought at times I heard their trumpets come down the wind as we marched. Towards the dusk of the evening of this day I remember passing a man and woman lying clasped in each other's arms, and dying in the snow. I knew them both; but it was impossible to help them. They belonged to the Rifles, and were man and wife. The man's name was Joseph Sitdown. During this retreat, as he had not been in good health previously, himself and wife had been allowed to get on in the best way they could in the front. They had, however, now given in, and the last we ever saw of poor Sitdown and his wife was on that night lying perishing in each other's arms in the snow.

Many trivial things which happened during the retreat to Coruña, and which on any other occasion might have entirely passed from my memory, have been, as it were, branded into my remembrance, and I recollect the most trifling incidents which occurred from day to day during that march. I remember, amongst other matters, that we were joined, if I may so term it, by a young recruit, when such an addition was anything but wished for during the disasters of the hour. One of the men's wives (who was struggling forward in the ranks with us, presenting a ghastly picture of illness, misery, and fatigue), being very large in the family-way, towards evening stepped from amongst the crowd, and lay herself down amidst the snow, a little out of the main road. Her husband remained with her; and I heard one or two hasty observations amongst our men that they had taken possession of their last resting-place. The enemy were, indeed, not far behind at this time, the night was coming down, and their chance seemed in truth but a bad one. To remain behind the column of march in such weather was to perish, and we accordingly soon forgot all about them. To my surprise, however, I, some little time afterwards (being myself then in the rear of our party), again saw the woman. She was hurrying, with her husband, after us, and in her arms she carried the babe she had just given birth to. Her husband and herself, between them, managed to carry that infant to the end of the retreat, where we embarked. God tempers the wind, it is said, to the shorn lamb; and many years afterwards I saw that boy, a strong and healthy lad. The woman's name was M'Guire, a sturdy and hardy Irishwoman; and lucky was it for herself and babe that she was so, as that night of cold and sleet was in itself sufficient to try the constitution of most females. I lost sight of her, I recollect, on this night, when the darkness came upon us; but with the dawn, to my surprise, she was still amongst us.

The shoes and boots of our party were now mostly either destroyed or useless to us, from foul roads and long miles, and many of the men were entirely barefooted, with knapsacks and accoutrements altogether in a dilapidated state.

The officers were also, for the most part, in as miserable a plight. They were pallid, way-worn, their feet bleeding, and their faces overgrown with beards of many days' growth. What a contrast did our corps display, even at this period of the retreat, to my remembrance of them on the morning their dashing appearance captivated my fancy in Ireland! Many of the poor fellows, now near sinking with fatigue, reeled as if in a state of drunkenness, and altogether I thought we looked the ghosts of our former selves; still we held on resolutely: our officers behaved nobly; and Craufurd was not to be daunted by long miles, fatigue, or fine weather. Many a man in that retreat caught courage from his stern eye and gallant bearing. Indeed, I do not think the world ever saw a more perfect soldier than General Craufurd. It might be on the night following the disaster I have just narrated that we came to a halt for about a couple of hours in a small village, and together with several others, I sought shelter in the stable of a sort of farm-house, the first roof I saw near. Here, however, we found nothing to refresh ourselves with, by way of food, but some raw potatoes lying in a heap in one of the empty stalls, and which, for want of better rations, we made a meal of, before we threw ourselves down upon the stones with which the place was paved. Meanwhile, others of the men, together with two or three of our officers, more fortunate than ourselves, had possession of the rooms of the adjoining building, where they found at least a fire to warm themselves. Lieutenant Hill had a black servant with him in this retreat, a youth he had brought with him from Monte Video, where, I heard, the Rifles had found him tied to a gun they had captured there. This lad came and aroused me as I lay in the mule-stable, and desired me to speak with his master in the adjoining room. I found the lieutenant seated in a chair by the fire when I entered. He was one of the few amongst us who rejoiced in the possession of a tolerably decent pair of boots, and he had sent for me to put a few stitches in them, in order to keep them from flying to pieces.

I was so utterly wearied that I at first refused to have anything to do with them; but the officer, taking off his boots, insisted upon my getting out my wax threads and mending them; and himself and servant, thrusting me into the chair he arose from, put the boots into my hands, got out my shoemaking implements, and held me up as I attempted to cobble up the boots. It was, however, in vain that I tried to do my best towards the lieutenant's boots. After a few stitches, I fell asleep as I worked, the awl and wax-ends falling to the ground. I remember there were two other officers present at the time, Lieutenants Molloy and Keppel, the latter of whom soon afterwards fell dead from fatigue during this retreat. At the present time, however, they all saw it was in vain to urge me to mend Lieutenant Hill's boots. He therefore put them on again with a woeful face and a curse, and dismissed me to my repose. Our rest was not, however, of long duration. The French were upon our trail, and before long we were up and hurrying onwards again.

As the day began to dawn, we passed through another village – a long, straggling place. The houses were all closed at this early hour, and the inhabitants mostly buried in sleep, and, I dare say, unconscious of the armed thousands who were pouring through their silent streets. When about a couple of miles from this village, Craufurd again halted us for about a quarter of an hour. It appeared to me that, with returning daylight, he wished to have a good look at us this morning, for he mingled amongst the men as we stood leaning upon our rifles, gazing earnestly in our faces as he passed, in order to judge of our plight by our countenances. He himself appeared anxious, but full of fire and spirit, occasionally giving directions to the different officers, and then speaking words of encouragement to the men. It is my pride now to remember that General Craufurd seldom omitted a word in passing to myself. On this occasion he stopped in the midst and addressed a few words to me, and glancing down at my feet, observed:

"What! no shoes, Harris, I see, eh?"

"None, sir," I replied; "they have been gone many days back." He smiled, and passing on, spoke to another man, and so on through the whole body.

Craufurd was, I remember, terribly severe, during this retreat, if he caught anything like pilfering amongst the men. As we stood, however, during this short halt, a very tempting turnip-field was close on the side of us, and several of the men were so ravenous, that although he was in our very ranks, they stepped into the field and helped themselves to the turnips, devouring them like famishing wolves. He either did not or would not observe the delinquency this time, and soon afterwards gave the word, and we moved on once more.

About this period I remember another sight, which I shall not to my dying day forget; and it causes me a sore heart, even now, as I remember it. Soon after our halt beside the turnip-field the screams of a child near me caught my ear, and drew my attention to one of our women, who was endeavouring to drag along a little boy of about seven or eight years of age. The poor child was apparently completely exhausted, and his legs failing under him. The mother had occasionally, up to this time, been assisted by some of the men, taking it in turn to help the little fellow on; but now all further appeal was vain. No man had more strength than was necessary for the support of his own carcass, and the mother could no longer raise the child in her arms, as her reeling pace too plainly showed. Still, however, she continued to drag the child along with her. It was a pitiable sight, and wonderful to behold the efforts the poor woman made to keep the boy amongst us. At last the little fellow had not even strength to cry, but, with mouth wide open, stumbled onwards, until both sank down to rise no more. The poor woman herself had, for some time, looked a moving corpse; and when the shades of evening came down, they were far behind amongst the dead or dying in the road. This was not the only scene of the sort I witnessed amongst the women and children during that retreat. Poor creatures! they must have bitterly regretted not having accepted the offer which was made to them to embark at Lisbon for England, instead of accompanying their husbands into Spain. The women, however, I have often observed, are most persevering in such cases, and are not to be persuaded that their presence is often a source of anxiety to the corps they belong to.

I do not think I ever admired any man who wore the British uniform more than I did General Craufurd.

I could fill a book with descriptions of him; for I frequently had my eye upon him in the hurry of action. It was gratifying to me, too, to think he did not altogether think ill of me, since he has often addressed me kindly when, from adverse circumstances, you might have thought that he had scarcely spirits to cheer up the men under him. The Rifles liked him, but they also feared him; for he could be terrible when insubordination showed itself in the ranks. "You think, because you are Riflemen, you may do whatever you think proper," said he one day to the miserable and savage-looking crew around him in the retreat to Coruña; "but I'll teach you the difference before I have done with you." I remember one evening, during the retreat, he detected two men straying away from the main body: it was in the early stage of that disastrous flight, and Craufurd knew well that he must do his utmost to keep the division together. He halted the brigade with a voice of thunder, ordered a drum-head court-martial on the instant, and they were sentenced to a hundred a-piece. Whilst this hasty trial was taking place, Craufurd, dismounting from his horse, stood in the midst, looking stern and angry as a worried bulldog. He did not like retreating at all, that man.

The three men nearest him, as he stood, were Jagger, Dan Howans, and myself. All were worn, dejected, and savage, though nothing to what we were after a few days more of the retreat. The whole brigade were in a grumbling and discontented mood; and Craufurd, doubtless, felt ill-pleased with the aspect of affairs altogether.

"D – n his eyes!" muttered Howans, "he had much better try to get us something to eat and drink than harass us in this way."

No sooner had Howans disburdened his conscience of this growl, than Craufurd, who had overheard it, turning sharply round, seized the rifle out of Jagger's hand, and felled him to the earth with the butt-end.

"It was not I who spoke," said Jagger, getting up, and shaking his head. "You shouldn't knock me about."

"I heard you, sir," said Craufurd; "and I will bring you also to a court-martial."

"I am the man who spoke," said Howans. "Ben Jagger never said a word."

"Very well," returned Craufurd, "then I'll try you, sir."

And, accordingly, when the other affair was disposed of, Howans' case came on. By the time the three men were tried, it was too dark to inflict the punishment. Howans, however, had got the complement of three hundred promised to him; so Craufurd gave the word to the brigade to move on. He marched all that night on foot; and when the morning dawned, I remember that, like the rest of us, his hair, beard, and eyebrows were covered with the frost as if he had grown white with age. We were, indeed, all of us in the same condition. Scarcely had I time to notice the appearance of morning before the general once more called a halt – we were then on the hills. Ordering a square to be formed, he spoke to the brigade, as well as I can remember, in these words, after having ordered the three before-named men of the 95th to be brought into the square:

"Although," said he, "I should obtain the goodwill neither of the officers nor the men of the brigade here by so doing, I am resolved to punish these three men, according to the sentence awarded, even though the French are at our heels. Begin with Daniel Howans."

This was indeed no time to be lax in discipline, and the general knew it. The men, as I said, were, some of them, becoming careless and ruffianly in their demeanour; whilst others again I saw with the tears falling down their cheeks from the agony of their bleeding feet, and many were ill with dysentery from the effects of the bad food they had got hold of and devoured on the road. Our knapsacks, too, were a bitter enemy on this prolonged march. Many a man died, I am convinced, who would have borne up well to the end of the retreat but for the infernal load we carried on our backs. My own knapsack was my bitterest enemy; I felt it press me to the earth almost at times, and more than once felt as if I should die under its deadly embrace. The knapsacks, in my opinion, should have been abandoned at the very commencement of the retrograde movement, as it would have been better to have lost them altogether, if, by such loss, we could have saved the poor fellows who, as it was, died strapped to them on the road.

There was some difficulty in finding a place to tie Howans up, as the light brigade carried no halberts. However, they led him to a slender ash tree which grew near at hand.

"Don't trouble yourselves about tying *me* up," said Howans, folding his arms; "I'll take my punishment like a man!"

He did so without a murmur, receiving the whole three hundred. His wife, who was present with us, I remember, was a strong, hardy Irishwoman. When it was over, she stepped up and covered Howans with his grey great-coat. The general then gave the word to move on. I rather think he knew the enemy was too near to punish the other two delinquents just then; so we proceeded out of the cornfield in which we had been halted, and toiled away upon the hills once more, Howans' wife carrying the jacket, knapsack, and pouch, which the lacerated state of the man's back would not permit him to bear.

It could not have been, I should think, more than an hour after the punishment had been inflicted upon Howans, when the general again gave the word for the brigade to halt, and once more formed them into a square. We had begun to suppose that he intended to allow the other two delinquents to escape under the present difficulties and hardships of the retreat. He was not, however, one of the forgetful sort, when the discipline of the army under him made severity necessary.

"Bring out the two other men of the 95th," said he, "who were tried last night."

The men were brought forth accordingly, and their lieutenant-colonel, Hamilton Wade, at the same time stepped forth. He walked up to the general, and lowering his sword, requested that he would forgive these men, as they were both of them good soldiers, and had fought in all the battles of Portugal.

"I order *you*, sir," said the general, "to do your duty. These men shall be punished."

The lieutenant-colonel, therefore, recovering his sword, turned about, and fell back to the front of the Rifles. One of the men, upon this (I think it was Armstrong), immediately began to unstrap his knapsack and prepare for the lash. Craufurd had turned about meanwhile, and walked up to one side of the square. Apparently he suddenly relented a little, and, again turning sharp round, returned towards the two prisoners. "Stop," said he. "In consequence of the intercession of your lieutenant-colonel, I will allow you thus much: you shall draw lots, and the winner shall escape; but one of the two I am determined to make an example of."

The square was formed in a stubble-field, and the sergeant-major of the Rifles, immediately stooping down, plucked up two straws, and the men, coming forward, drew. I cannot be quite certain, but I think it was Armstrong who drew the longest straw, and won the safety of his hide; and his fellow gamester was in quick time tied to a tree, and the punishment commenced. A hundred was the sentence; but when the bugler had counted seventy-five, the general granted him a further indulgence, and ordered him to be taken down, and to join his company. The general calling for his horse now mounted for the first time for many hours, for he had not ridden all night, not, indeed, since the drum-head court-martial had taken place. Before he put the brigade in motion again, he gave us another short specimen of his eloquence, pretty much, I remember, after this style:

"I give you all notice," said he, "that I will halt the brigade again the very first moment I perceive any man disobeying my orders, and try him by court-martial on the spot." He then gave us the word, and we resumed our march.

Many who read this, especially in these peaceful times, may suppose this was a cruel and unnecessary severity under the dreadful and harassing circumstances of that retreat; but I, who was there, and was, besides, a common soldier of the very regiment to which these men belonged, say *it was quite necessary*. No man but one formed of stuff like General Craufurd could have saved the brigade from perishing altogether; and, if he flogged two, he saved hundreds from death by his management. I detest the sight of the lash; but I am convinced the British army can never go on without it. Late events have taught us the necessity of such measures.

It was perhaps a couple of days after this had taken place that we came to a river. It was tolerably wide, but not very deep, which was just as well for us; for, had it been deep as the dark regions, we must have somehow or other got through. The avenger was behind us, and Craufurd was along with us, and the two together kept us moving, whatever was in the road. Accordingly into the stream went the light brigade, and Craufurd, as busy as a shepherd with his flock, riding in and out of the water to keep his wearied band from being drowned as they crossed over. Presently he spied an officer who, to save himself from being wet through, I suppose, and wearing a damp pair of breeches for the remainder of the day, had mounted on the back of one of his men. The sight of such a piece of effeminacy was enough to raise the choler of the general, and in a very short time he was plunging and splashing through the water after them both.

"Put him down, sir! put him down! I desire you to put that officer down instantly!" And the soldier in an instant, I dare say nothing loth, dropping his burden like a hot potato into the stream, continued his progress through. "Return back, sir," said Craufurd to the officer, "and go through the water like the others. I will not allow my officers to ride upon the men's backs through the rivers: all must take their share alike here."

Wearied as we were, this affair caused all who saw it to shout almost with laughter, and was never forgotten by those who survived the retreat.

General Craufurd was, indeed, one of the few men who was apparently created for command during such dreadful scenes as we were familiar with in this retreat. He seemed an iron man; nothing daunted him – nothing turned him from his purpose. War was his very element, and toil and danger seemed to call forth only an increasing determination to surmount them. I was sometimes amused with his appearance, and that of the men around us; for, the Rifles being always at his heels, he seemed to think them his familiars. If he stopped his horse, and halted to deliver one of his stern reprimands, you would see half a dozen lean, unshaven, shoeless, and savage Riflemen standing for the moment leaning upon their weapons, and scowling up in his face as he scolded; and when he dashed the spurs into his reeking horse, they would throw up their rifles upon their shoulders, and hobble after him again. He was sometimes to be seen in the front, then in the rear, and then you would fall in with him again in the midst, dismounted, and marching on foot, that the men might see he took an equal share in the toils which they were enduring. He had a mortal dislike, I remember, to a commissary. Many a time have I heard him storming at the neglect of those gentry when the men were starving for rations, and nothing but excuses forthcoming.

"Send the commissary to me!" he would roar. "D – n him! I will hang him if the provisions are not up this night!"

Twice I remember he was in command of the light brigade. The second time he joined them he made, I heard, something like these remarks, after they had been some little time in Spain:

"When I commanded you before," he said, "I know full well that you disliked me, for you thought me severe. *This time I am glad to find there is a change in yourselves.*"

Towards evening of the same day Howans was punished, we came to a part of the country of a yet wilder and more desolate appearance even than that we had already traversed; a dreary wilderness it appeared at this inclement season: and our men, in spite of the vigilance of the general, seemed many of them resolved to stray into the open country rather than traverse the road before them. The coming night favoured their designs, and many were, before morning, lost to us through their own wilfulness. Amongst others, I found myself completely bewildered and lost upon the heath, and should doubtless have perished had I not fallen in with another of our corps in the same situation. As soon as we recognised each other, I found my companion in adversity was a strapping resolute fellow named James Brooks, a north of Ireland man. He was afterwards killed at Toulouse by a musket-ball which struck him in the thigh. He was delighted at having met with me, and we resolved not to desert each other during the night. Brooks, as I have said, was a strong, active, and resolute fellow as indeed I had, on more occasions than one, witnessed in Portugal. At the present time his strength was useful to both of us.

"Catch hold of my jacket, Harris," said he: "the ground here is soft, and we must help each other to-night, or we shall be lost in the bogs."

Before long, that which Brooks feared, happened, and he found himself stuck so fast in the morass, that although I used my best efforts to draw him out I only shared in the same disaster; so that, leaving him, I turned and endeavoured to save my own life if possible, calling to him to follow before he sank over head and ears. This was an unlucky chance in our wearied state, as the more we floundered in the dark, not knowing which way to gain a firmer foundation, the faster we fixed ourselves. Poor Brooks was so disheartened, that he actually blubbered like a child. At length, during a pause in our exertions, I thought I heard something like the bark of a dog come down the wind. I bade Brooks listen, and we both distinctly heard it – the sound gave us new hope, just as we were about to abandon ourselves to our fate. I advised Brooks to lay himself as flat as he could, and drag himself out of the slough, as I had found some hard tufts of grass in the direction I tried; and so, by degrees, we gained a firmer footing, and eventually succeeded in extricating ourselves, though in such an exhausted state, that for some time we lay helplessly upon the ground, unable to proceed.

At length with great caution, we ventured to move forwards in the direction of the sounds we had just heard. We found, however, that our situation was still very perilous; for in the darkness we hardly dared to move a step in any direction without probing the ground with our rifles, lest we should again sink, and be eventually smothered in the morasses we had strayed amongst. On a sudden, however (as we carefully felt our way), we heard voices shouting in the distance, and calling out "*Men* lost! *men* lost!" which we immediately concluded were the cries of some of our own people, who were situated like ourselves.

After awhile I thought I saw, far away, something like a dancing light, which seemed to flicker about, vanish, and reappear, similar to a Jack-o'-lantern. I pointed it out to Brooks, and we agreed to alter our course, and move towards it. As we did so, the light seemed to approach us, and grow larger, and presently another and another appeared, like small twinkling stars, till they looked something like the lamps upon one of our London bridges, as seen from afar. The sight revived our spirits, more especially as we could now distinctly hear the shouts of people, who appeared in search of the stragglers, and as they approached us, we perceived that such was indeed the case. The lights, we now discovered, were furnished by bundles of straw and dried twigs, tied on the ends of long poles, and dipped in tar. They were borne in the hands of several Spanish peasants, from a village near at hand, whom Craufurd had thus sent to our rescue.

He had discovered, on reaching and halting in this village, the number of men that had strayed from the main body, and immediately ordering the torches I have mentioned to be prepared, he collected together a party of Spanish peasants, and obliged them to go out into the open country, and seek for his men, as I have said; by which means he saved (on that night) many from death.

To return to my own adventures on this night. When Brooks and myself reached the village I have mentioned we found it filled with soldiers, standing and lying, huddled together like cattle in a fair. A most extraordinary sight it appeared as the torches of the peasants flashed upon the wayworn and gaunt figures of our army. The rain was coming down, too, on this night, I remember; and soon after I reached our corps, I fell helplessly to the ground in a miserable plight. Brooks was himself greatly exhausted, but he behaved nobly, and remained beside me, trying to persuade some of our men to assist him in lifting me up, and gaining shelter in one of the houses at hand. "May I be –!" I heard him say, "if I leave Harris to be butchered in the streets by the cowardly Spaniards the moment our division leaves the town." At length Brooks succeeded in getting a man to help him, and together they supported me into the passage of a house, where I lay upon the floor for some time. After awhile, by the help of some wine they procured, I rallied and sat up, till eventually I got once more upon my legs, and, arm in arm, we proceeded again into the streets, and joined our corps. Poor Brooks certainly saved my life that night. He was one of the many good fellows whom I have seen out, and I often think of him with feelings of gratitude as I sit at my work in Richmond Street, Soho.

When the division got the order to proceed again, we were still linked arm in arm, and thus we proceeded; sometimes, when the day appeared, stopping for a short time and resting ourselves, and then hurrying on again.

I remember Sir Dudley Hill passing me on a mule this day. He wore a Spanish straw-hat, and had his cloak on. He looked back when he had passed, and addressed me. "Harris," said he, "I see you cannot keep up." He appeared sorry for me, for he knew me well. "You must do your best," he said, "my man, and keep with us, or you will fall into the hands of the enemy." As the day wore on, I grew weaker and weaker; and at last, spite of all my efforts, I saw the main body leave me hopelessly in the lurch. Brooks himself was getting weaker too; he saw it was of little use to urge me on, and at length, assenting to my repeated request to be left behind, he hurried on as well as he was able without a word of farewell. I now soon sank down in the road and lay beside another man who had also fallen, and was apparently dead, and whom I recognised as one of our sergeants, named Taylor, belonging to the Honourable Captain Pakenham's (now General Sir Hercules Pakenham) company.

Whilst we lay exhausted in the road, the rear guard, which was now endeavouring to drive on the stragglers, approached, and a sergeant of the Rifles came up and stopped to look at us. He addressed himself to me, and ordered me to rise; but I told him it was useless for him to trouble himself about me, as I was unable to move a step further. Whilst he was urging me to endeavour to rise up, the officer in command of the rear guard also stepped up. The name of this officer was Lieutenant Cox; he was a brave and good man, and observing that the sergeant was rough in his language and manner towards me he silenced him, and bade the guard proceed, and leave me. "Let him die quietly, Hicks" he said to the sergeant. "I know him well; he's not the man to lie here if he could get on. I am sorry, Harris," he said, "to see you reduced to this, for I fear there is no help to be had now." He then moved on after his men, and left me to my fate.

After lying still for awhile, I felt somewhat restored, and sat up to look about me. The sight was by no means cheering. On the road behind me I saw men, women, mules, and horses, lying at intervals, both dead and dying; whilst far away in front I could just discern the enfeebled army crawling out of sight, the women huddled together in its rear, trying their best to get forward amongst those of the sick soldiery, who were now unable to keep up with the main body. Some of these poor wretches cut a ludicrous figure, having the men's great-coats buttoned over their heads, whilst their clothing being extremely ragged and scanty, their naked legs were very conspicuous. They looked a tribe of travelling beggars. After a while, I found that my companion, the sergeant, who lay beside me, had also recovered a little, and I tried to cheer him up. I told him that opposite to where we were lying there was a lane down which we might possibly find some place of shelter, if we could muster strength to explore it. The sergeant consented to make the effort, but after two or three attempts to rise, gave it up. I myself was more fortunate: with the aid of my rifle I got upon my legs, and seeing death in my companion's face, I resolved to try and save myself, since it was quite evident to me that I could render him no assistance.

After hobbling some distance down the lane, to my great joy I espied a small hut or cabin, with a little garden in its front; I therefore opened the small door of the hovel, and was about to enter, when I considered that most likely I should be immediately knocked on the head by the inmates if I did so. The rain, I remember, was coming down in torrents at this time, and, reflecting that to remain outside was but to die, I resolved at all events to try my luck within. I had not much strength left; but I resolved to sell myself as dearly as I could. I therefore brought up my rifle, and stepped across the threshold. As soon as I had done so, I observed an old woman seated beside a small fire upon the hearth. She turned her head as I entered, and immediately upon seeing a strange soldier, she arose, and filled the hovel with her screams. As I drew back within the doorway, an elderly man, followed by two, who were apparently his sons, rushed from a room in the interior. They immediately approached me; but I brought up my rifle again, and cocked it, bidding them keep their distance.

After I had thus brought them to a parley, I got together what little Spanish I was master of, and begged for shelter for the night and a morsel of food, at the same time lifting my feet and displaying them a mass of bleeding sores. It was not, however, till they had held a tolerably long conversation among themselves that they consented to afford me shelter; and then only upon the condition that I left by daylight on the following morning. I accepted the conditions with joy. Had they refused me, I should indeed not have been here to tell the tale. Knowing the treachery of the Spanish character, I however refused to relinquish possession of my rifle, and my right hand was ready in an instant to unsheath my bayonet as they sat and stared at me whilst I devoured the food they offered.

All they gave me was some coarse black bread, and a pitcher of sour wine. It was, however, acceptable to a half-famished man; and I felt greatly revived by it. Whilst I supped, the old hag, who sat close beside the hearth, stirred up the embers that they might have a better view of their guest, and the party meanwhile overwhelmed me with questions, which I could neither comprehend nor had strength to answer. I soon made signs to them that I was unable to maintain the conversation, and begged of them, as well as I could, to show me some place where I might lay my wearied limbs till dawn.

Notwithstanding the weariness which pervaded my whole body, I was unable for some time to sleep except by fitful snatches, such was the fear I entertained of having my throat cut by the savage-looking wretches still seated before the fire. Besides which, the place they had permitted me to crawl into was more like an oven than anything else, and being merely a sort of berth scooped out of the wall was so filled with fleas and other vermin that I was stung and tormented most miserably all night long.

Bad as they had been, however, I felt somewhat restored by my lodging and supper, and with the dawn I crawled out of my lair, left the hut, retraced my steps along the lane, and once more emerged upon the high-road, where I found my companion, the sergeant, dead, and lying where I had left him the night before.

I now made the best of my way along the road in the direction in which I had last seen our army retreating the night before. A solitary individual, I seemed left behind amongst those who had perished. It was still raining, I remember, on this morning, and the very dead looked comfortless in their last sleep, as I passed them occasionally lying on the line of march.

It had pleased Heaven to give me an iron constitution, or I must have failed, I think, on this day, for the solitary journey and the miserable spectacles I beheld rather damped my spirits.

After progressing some miles, I came up with a cluster of poor devils who were still alive, but apparently, both men and women, unable to proceed. They were sitting huddled together in the road, their heads drooping forward, and apparently patiently awaiting their end.

Soon after passing these unfortunates, I overtook a party who were being urged forward under charge of an officer of the 42nd Highlanders. He was pushing them along pretty much as a drover would keep together a tired flock of sheep. They presented a curious example of a retreating force. Many of them had thrown away their weapons, and were linked together arm in arm, in order to support each other, like a party of drunkards. They were, I saw, composed of various regiments; many were bare-headed, and without shoes; and some with their heads tied up in old rags and fragments of handkerchiefs.

I marched in company with this party for some time, but as I felt after my night's lodging and refreshment in better condition I ventured to push forwards, in the hope of rejoining the main body, and which I once more came up with in the streets of a village.

On falling in with the Rifles I again found Brooks, who was surprised at seeing me still alive; and we both entered a house, and begged for something to drink. I remember that I had a shirt upon my back at this time, which I had purchased of a drummer of the 9th regiment before the commencement of the retreat. It was the only good one I had; I stripped, with the assistance of Brooks, and took it off, and exchanged it with a Spanish woman for a loaf of bread, which Brooks, myself, and two other men shared amongst us.

I remember to have again remarked Craufurd at this period of the retreat. He was no whit altered in his desire to keep the force together I thought; but still active and vigilant as ever he seemed to keep his eye upon those who were now most likely to hold out. I myself marched during many hours close beside him this day. He looked stern and pale; but the very picture of a warrior. I shall never forget Craufurd if I live to a hundred years I think. He was in everything a soldier.

Slowly and dejectedly crawled our army along. Their spirit of endurance was now considerably worn out, and judging from my own sensations, I felt confident that if the sea was much further from us, we must be content to come to a halt at last without gaining it. I felt something like the approach of death as I proceeded – a sort of horror, mixed up with my sense of illness – a reeling I have never experienced before or since. Still I held on; but with all my efforts, the main body again left me behind. Had the enemy's cavalry come up at this time I think they would have had little else to do but ride us down without striking a blow.

It is, however, indeed astonishing how man clings to life. I am certain that had I lain down at this period, I should have found my last billet on the spot I sank upon. Suddenly I heard a shout in front, which was prolonged in a sort of hubbub. Even the stragglers whom I saw dotting the road in front of me seemed to have caught at something like hope; and as the poor fellows now reached the top of a hill we were ascending, I heard an occasional exclamation of joy – the first note of the sort I had heard for many days. When I reached the top of the hill the thing spoke for itself. There, far away in our front, the English shipping lay in sight.

Its view had indeed acted like a restorative to our force, and the men, at the prospect of a termination to the march, had plucked up spirit for a last effort. Fellows who, like myself, seemed to have hardly strength in their legs to creep up the ascent seemed now to have picked up a fresh pair to get down with. Such is hope to us poor mortals!

There was, I recollect, a man of the name of Bell, of the Rifles, who had been during this day holding a sort of creeping race with me – we had passed and repassed each other, as our strength served. Bell was rather a discontented fellow at the best of times; but during this retreat he had given full scope to his ill-temper, cursing the hour he was born, and wishing his mother had strangled him when he came into the world, in order to have saved him from his present toil. He had not now spoken for some time, and the sight of the English shipping had apparently a very beneficial effect upon him. He burst into tears as he stood and looked at it.

"Harris," he said, "if it pleases God to let me reach those

ships, I swear never to utter a bad or discontented word again."

As we proceeded down the hill we now met with the first symptoms of good feeling from the inhabitants it was our fortune to experience during our retreat. A number of old women stood on either side of the road, and occasionally handed us fragments of bread as we passed them. It was on this day, and whilst I looked anxiously upon the English shipping in the distance, that I first began to find my eyesight failing, and it appeared to me that I was fast growing blind. The thought was alarming; and I made desperate efforts to get on. Bell, however, won the race this time. He was a very athletic and strong-built fellow, and left me far behind, so that I believe at that time I was the very last of the retreating force that reached the beach, though doubtless many stragglers came dropping up after the ships had sailed, and were left behind.

As it was, when I did manage to gain the sea-shore, it was only by the aid of my rifle that I could stand, and my eyes were now so dim and heavy that with difficulty I made out a boat which seemed the last that had put off.

Fearful of being left half blind in the lurch, I took off my cap, and placed it on the muzzle of my rifle as a signal, for I was totally unable to call out. Luckily, Lieutenant Cox, who was aboard the boat, saw me, and ordered the men to return, and, making one more effort, I walked into the water, and a sailor stretching his body over the gunwale, seized me as if I had been an infant, and hauled me on board. His words were characteristic of the English sailor, I thought.

"Hollo there, you lazy lubber!" he said, as he grasped hold of me, "who the h—ll do you think is to stay humbugging all day for such a fellow as you?"

The boat, I found, was crowded with our exhausted men, who lay helplessly at the bottom, the heavy sea every moment drenching them to the skin. As soon as we reached the vessel's side, the sailors immediately aided us to get on board, which in our exhausted state was not a very easy matter, as they were obliged to place ropes in our hands, and heave us up by setting their shoulders under us, and hoisting away as if they had been pushing bales of goods on board.

"Heave away!" cried one of the boat's crew, as I clung to a rope, quite unable to pull myself up, "heave away, you lubber!"

The tar placed his shoulder beneath me as he spoke, and hoisted me up against the ship's side; I lost my grasp of the rope and should have fallen into the sea had it not been for two of the crew. These men grasped me as I was falling, and drew me into the port-hole like a bundle of foul clothes, tearing away my belt and bayonet in the effort, which fell into the sea.

It was not very many minutes after I was on board, for I lay where the sailors had first placed me after dragging me through the port-hole, ere I was sound asleep. I slept long and heavily, and it was only the terrible noise and bustle on board consequent upon a gale having sprung up, that at length awoke me. The wind increased as the night came on, and soon we had to experience all the horrors of a storm at sea. The pumps were set to work; the sails were torn to shreds; the coppers were overset; and we appeared in a fair way, I thought, of going to the bottom. Meanwhile, the pumps were kept at work night and day incessantly till they were choked; and the gale growing worse and worse, all the soldiery were ordered below, and the hatches closed; soon after which the vessel turned over on one side, and lay a helpless log upon the water. In this situation an officer was placed over us, with his sword drawn in one hand, and a lantern in the other, in order to keep us on the side which was uppermost, so as to give the vessel a chance of righting herself in the roaring tide. The officer's task was not an easy one as the heaving waves frequently sent us sprawling from the part we clung to, over to the lowermost part of the hold where he stood, and he was obliged every minute to drive us back.

We remained in this painful situation for, I should think, five or six hours, expecting every instant to be our last, when, to our great joy, the sea suddenly grew calm, the wind abated, the vessel righted herself, and we were once more released from our prison, having tasted nothing in the shape of food for at least forty-eight hours. Soon after this we arrived in sight of Spithead, where we saw nine of our convoy, laden with troops, which had been driven on shore in the gale. After remaining off Spithead for about five or six days, one fine morning we received orders to disembark, and our poor bare feet once more touched English ground. The inhabitants flocked down to the beach to see us as we did so, and they must have been a good deal surprised at the spectacle we presented. Our beards were long and ragged; almost all were without shoes and stockings; many had their clothes and accoutrements in fragments, with their heads swathed in old rags, and our weapons were covered with rust; whilst not a few had now, from toil and fatigue, become quite blind.

Let not the reader, however, think that even now we were to be despised as soldiers. Long marches, inclement weather, and want of food, had done their work upon us; but we were perhaps better than we appeared, as the sequel showed. Under the gallant Craufurd we had made some tremendous marches, and even galled our enemies severely making good our retreat by the way of Vigo. But our comrades in adversity, and who had retired by the other road to Coruña, under General Moore, turned to bay there, and showed the enemy that the English soldier is not to be beaten even under the most adverse circumstances.

The field of death and slaughter, the march, the bivouac, and the retreat, are no bad places in which to judge of men. I have had some opportunities of judging them in all these situations, and I should say that the British are amongst the most splendid soldiers in the world. Give them fair play, and they are unconquerable. For my own part I can only say that I enjoyed life more whilst on active service than I have ever done since; and as I sit at work in my shop in Richmond Street, Soho, I look back upon that portion of my time spent in the fields of the Peninsula as the only part worthy of remembrance. It is at such times that scenes long passed come back upon my mind as if they had taken place but yesterday. I remember even the very appearance of some of the regiments engaged; and comrades, long mouldered to dust, I see again performing the acts of heroes.

"I TRUST WE SHALL RETURN SUCCESSFUL": A DRAGOON IN THE PENINSULA, 1809

Captain Thomas C. Fenton, 4th Dragoons

Although Sir John Moore's army was evacuated from Vigo and Corunna, the British had not entirely departed the Peninsula and small forces remained in Portugal, under Sir John Craddock, while the Portuguese Army itself was being reconstructed by General William Beresford. These Allied forces were joined on 22 April 1809 by Wellesley, freshly exonerated by the Cintra enquiry, and bringing with him the first of a substantial number of reinforcements. Realizing that the French offensive had become diluted by the increasing numbers of troops detailed to garrison conquered territories and guard supply lines, Wellesley decided to launch a blow against Marshal Soult, stalled north of Lisbon on the River Douro. Wellesley had some 30,000 British troops, plus 16,000 Portuguese organized by Beresford. Strategically, Wellesley's concern was defensive, to clear Portugal of the French and establish the safety of Lisbon as a supply base.

And so, in the early hours of 10 May, Wellesley led his main column up the Oporto highway, before making an undetected crossing of the Duoro to assault Soult, ensconced in Oporto, on the morning of 12 May. By 2 p.m. Soult conceded that his position was hopeless and began a retreat towards Vallonga, leaving behind 600 casualties, plus 1,500 sick and 58 guns. Save for some isolated garrisons, the French were now driven from Portugal, and Wellington (as Wellesley became with the Barony awarded after Oporto) sought a fresh target. This was Marshal Victor's I Corps, positioned across the border on the Tagus. Advancing into Spain, Wellington linked up with the Spanish General, Gregario Cuesta, and won the battle of Talavera on 27–8 July – but at tremendous cost, with nearly 5,500 British casualties. Moreover, Wellington's supply lines were overstretched and his troops down to one-third rations. When a captured French dispatch informed him that Marshal Soult was about to envelop him with 30,000 troops, Wellington decided upon discretion and ordered an immediate withdrawal. His army, reduced by hunger and exhaustion, limped back to Badajoz, its confidence severely shaken. To protect Lisbon against the tide of French troops likely to be released by the Imperial victory over the Austrians at Wagram, Wellington ordered a series of concentric fortifications to be built around the city. A year later, the Lines of Torres Vedras would stop Wellington from being swept into the sea.

Thomas Charles Fenton was nineteen when, in 1809, he embarked for the Peninsula as a subaltern in the 4th Dragoons. Like other British cavalry units in the Peninsula, the 4th Dragoons averaged 400 officers and men; as heavy cavalry, the 4th Dragoons were largely kept for battlefield charges, though they were not spared other duties. Fenton, promoted captain by purchase, later exchanged to the Royal Scots Greys and by dint of his Peninsula days became the only officer with the Greys at Waterloo who had previously been under fire.

On Board the *Britannia*. 6th April 1809.

My dear Father,

I know it will give you pleasure to hear that I am on board an uncommon good transport, of four hundred tons. Many of them are not so; I am therefore very lucky. We hourly expect to sail, and as Sir Arthur Wellesley who commands the Army is a very brave and excellent officer, I trust we shall return successful. George Dalbiac, who goes out as Brigade Major, says we shall march into Madrid in less than three months; he was as sanguine the last expedition. John Dalton takes his troop.

I never will lose any opportunity of writing to you, and let me entreat of you to rest perfectly easy on my account, for I can assure you, there is very little danger in the service we shall be employed upon, and I hope I shall never do anything that would not be pleasing to you or my family. I shall never run my head into danger without necessity requires it. They will expect a great deal from the Fourth; we go out very strong of officers, but a great number of them young. Our sea stock has cost us twenty guineas, after paying everything. I have 15 guineas left. They say we shall not want money in Portugal. I wish I may find it so.

Give my kindest love to every part of my family, and I am
My dear Father,
Truly and affectionately your son
Thomas C. Fenton.

Abrantes. May 31st 1809.

My dearest Mother,

You I hope received my letter from Belém. It was written the night before we commenced our first day's march. Nothing can equal the beauty of the country we have marched through. Our first day's march was through a vineyard garden the whole way, but the roads were so bad it took away in a great measure the gratification we should otherwise have experienced. They are paved and stoney and the hills are very high but they are liberally supplied with trees, which gives them a pleasing appearance. The villages (which they here call towns) are very bad and dirty; the streets are narrow and not uniform, the houses are chiefly white-washed, and were it not for the filth of the streets, would have a very neat effect. The inhabitants are very civil, but so very poor they cannot pay us that attention they are inclined to do were it not for this circumstance.

The only tolerable quarter I have as yet been in is Golegã, where we remained a fortnight. We are at present stationed at Abrantes, upon the Tagus; its situation is grand and majestic; the hill which it stands upon rises from the bank of the river nearly two miles from which you can see to the distance of 20 miles. The castle which General . . . destroyed overlooks the whole town, and I can for hours sit and admire the grandeur of the scene. I then think of all at home and guess their employment. I fancy my father and William busy in rubbish; Harry of course making sermons. I suppose he has written, or rather composed, volumes.

I now begin to think the old Fourth are soldiers. I am confident no one can have any idea what service is till they have experienced it. What we have as yet seen is trifling, but I can form a good idea from it what we have to expect. There is a great advantage in service; you are so much employed that it keeps both body and mind in health. At least I can answer for myself, for I never was in better health or better spirits. The officers are allowed the same rations as the men, which we all live upon, for there are no inns where we can get anything to eat. They have many coffee houses, but they are miserable places. The lower class meet there; as such the society is not select. I, however, have got accustomed to them and can make as good a breakfast as in England.

Richard is an excellent cook; he makes famous broth. I dine under old George's head, who generally shares with me in my allowance of bread. You will be glad to hear how good a servant Richard is abroad; much better than at home, and, as usual, a great favourite of the ladies. I told him this morning I was sure you would let his family know he is perfectly well. You are happy in hearing from me; his mother will have equal pleasure in hearing from him.

The weather is so intensely hot I shall be quite a genteel figure before I return. I have taken my sword belt in three inches and I hope soon to lose three or four more. I have also lost my heart to a little Portuguese beauty that lives opposite my billet, but unfortunately we cannot understand each other. All we can say is "star bon" which is Spanish is "very good" till I am actually sick of the words.

Who do you think I have been writing to? My old friend Mr Stopford. I am certain he would have pleasure in hearing from me. Perhaps my letters may not reach him. Do pray therefore write to him. I shall now send my Father what little news we know here respecting the movements of Sir A. Wellesley. You will have the particulars much sooner and more correct in England than we shall have here. Sir A. Wellesley has taken Oporto and given the French a good drubbing. It is reported Soult[1] is taken prisoner, and that the greatest part of his army have laid down their arms. If this is true he will join our division and march against Victor[2], who is retreating into Spain as fast as possible. Victor has passed the Tagus at the bridge of Alcántara, about sixty miles from this place, and is retreating through the mountains on the north side of the Tagus.

May 16th. I had not time to finish this the other day, being called away upon duty. You would smile to see the place I am now writing in. We have an outlying picquet under the command of a subaltern, which is relieved every twenty-four hours. It is my turn and I take this opportunity to finish this. Yesterday was the first day of my service, as till last

1 Marshal Nicolas Soult (1769–1851), Duke of Dalmatia; the rumour was wrong, Soult escaped the battle of Oporto, 12 May 1809.
2 Marshal Claude Victor (1764–1841), commander of I Corps.

night I had never slept in the open air. If I always sleep as well as I did last night I shall never take any harm.

It is now quite certain Sir A. Wellesley is marching this way; the advanced guard will be at Abrantes in a few days. The 14th Light Dragoons are completely done up,[3] and are to be left at Oporto. Major Stanhope of the 16th Dragoons is wounded, but not seriously. I hope to write to you in less than a fortnight. It is generally expected we shall be in Spain about that time. I hear it is not improbable that the 4th will lead the way into Madrid, provided we can preserve our horses, but this country does not agree with them. We have more than eighty unfit for service, and should we march immediately that number will be doubled. Not having an opportunity, this as I expected, I did not close it. We have this moment got the order to march. We cross the Tagus. Six thousand men came in yesterday. Sir A. Wellesley with four thousand more came in today.

Give my best and kindest love to my father and all at home, and believe me, my dearest Mother, ever your Most affectionate son,

Thomas C. Fenton.

God bless you all.

Castelo-Branco, 3rd July, 1809.

My dearest Mother.

I hope ere this you have received my letter from Abrantes, tho' I am rather inclined to doubt it, as William in his letter to Col. [J. C.] Dalbiac complains of my not writing. I sent three letters to England before I received yours. You may imagine what pleasure it affords all to hear from England. When an orderly arrives in the camp with a packet of letters what anxious faces you see, the greater the distance the greater the anxiety.

I was truly concerned to hear such bad accounts respecting my kind friends at Leeds. I trust most sincerely their affairs

3 The 14th Light Dragoons had attacked Soult's rearguard at Oporto, taking 300 prisoners but sustaining heavy casualties themselves.

will turn out much better than William's letter leads us to expect. As to the 12 thousand pounds which you name, I cannot perfectly understand, I should have thought money placed in the hands of Trustees would have been secured so as to prevent his turning it to his own advantage. William, however, conceives it probable we shall soon get it.

You will be anxious to hear what we are doing. I have not seen the inside of a house for the last month. Our horses are picquetted, and the men and officers make themselves huts of the branches of trees, and very comfortable they are. What I hinted in my last respecting our marching into Madrid will probably prove true, for we are now on our road to Spain. In three days we shall be at Zarza la Mayor, which you will see by the map is a frontier town. We shall halt there one day and then proceed in a line with Madrid. We subalterns are totally ignorant of Sir A. Wellesley's movements, therefore I cannot pretend to give you any account of them. My intention was to have written part of this after every day's march, but this has been the only one I could find a moment to spare in, for after a long and hot march I have had to go out to procure forage for the horses, which in this part of the country is difficult to get. The poor horses frequently go without for a day. It is not possible for any country to be more barren or uncultivated. Our line of march has been over nothing but mountains, and I do not suppose we have met half a dozen people the whole of the march. We cannot get anything, not even wine which is the chief produce of the country. I do not mean to insinuate by this we are starving; far otherwise, for we have lb of good beef and lb and a half of bread each day. But I mean luxuries, as eggs, milk, etc, etc. I find tea and milk the greatest luxury imaginable, for the climate is so hot it occasions great thirst. We were told it never rains after April. If this is actually the case we have hitherto been unlucky, for we have generally a thunderstorm every other day, and the heat that succeeds is intolerable. It was ever my idea that I should not be able to bear heat but, thank God, I never was better in my life, and should at this moment be as happy as possible could I see you all reading this, but I hope you and I may read them over together before the end of the year. Dalbiac has this moment called to say he can get me this sent to England.

We are now in Spain, everyone looks forward to a glorious campaign. We halt here tomorrow and march the next day to join Cuesta's[4] army. We are in General Sherbrooke's[5] division, consisting of ten thousand men. The Guards are also in the same division. I saw Walker and Hervey today as we passed on the march. Both were well. It was a grand sight to see a column of ten thousand men marching in the greatest regularity. I like the appearance of Spain much better than Portugal. The inhabitants have a much better appearance, and the town of Zarza la Mayor is more regularly built than any in Portugal.

I shall fill the rest of my paper to my Father. God bless you, my dearest Mother, and may you ever have reason to believe me, your most affectionate son,

Thomas C. Fenton.

Mérida, Sept. 14th.

My dear Father,

I am in great hope that my letter from Talavera[6] which was written immediately after the action, would arrive at P. [ark] Hill as soon as Sir A. Wellesley's despatches. I sent it by Lord R. Somerset's servant with a promise of a guinea if it came safe. You would have heard from me sooner could I have given a good account of myself. I was taken ill at Trujillo with a complaint which numbers in the army have

---

4 General Gregorio Cuesta (1740–1812), Captain General of Old Castile.
5 General Sir John Sherbrooke (1764–1830), Wellington's second-in-command.
6 The battle of Talavera, 27–28 July 1809, considered by Wellington as one of the hardest he fought, pitting 55,000 Allied troops against 46,150 under King Joseph Bonaparte and Marshal Victor. See page 151.

had, and I did not join until four days ago. You may rest perfectly easy as I am now as well as ever. It was a bowel complaint, which I believe is more painful than dangerous unless attended with fever. I am sorry to say we have lost a very worthy young man, Lieut. Baker. He died a few days ago, and is universally lamented.

I am afraid this expedition will be the cause of sorrow to many a family, and little or no advantage to England. I wished my letter to arrive in time for you to reveal the death of poor [Samuel] Walker and [Robert] Beckett to Mrs Bruin, that she might escape the shock of reading it in the papers. After our return on the evening of the 27th from covering the retreat of General Sherbrooke's division over the River Alberche I passed Walker and Hervey and shook hands with them both. The latter was in very low spirits, but Walker appeared uncommonly low and in his manner seemed as if he apprehended what was to befall him. With our long acquaintance with the family, and also being so near, I thought it my duty to enquire if I could be of any service by taking charge of anything that was to be sent to his friends. In the army it is a rule for things belonging to an officer killed in action to be sold by auction at the head of his regiment. Therefore all his things were sold, but I believe Sir W. W. Dalling, an officer in the same regiment [3rd Guards], who appears to have been a friend of his, has taken charge of a pocket-book, and also what papers were thought necessary to be saved, which he will on his return to England give to his family.

You will ere this have heard of our retreat which we commenced a few days after the action. We crossed the Tagus at Arzobispo, and did not halt until we arrived at Trujillo. Our situation at Talavera was rather perilous. The army which we had just defeated was in our front and though we had eased it of more than sixteen thousand men, there still remained between thirty and forty, Soult with thirty-three thousand men advancing from Plasencia on our rear it was therefore quite out of the question our remaining at Talavera. Indeed, had this not been the case we could not have remained long, for in the first place provisions were very dear, and in the second, I do not believe Sir A. Wellesley and Cuesta agreed in any one point. They may talk in England of the patriotism of the Spanish nation, but it is the opinion of every individual in the army that they are most rascally cowards in existence. I will give you one instance. We left them in possession of the bridge of Arzobispo, which is an uncommon strong position, strengthened by nature as well as art. They had thirteen pieces of cannon placed in such a situation to protect the bridge that it would have been impossible for the French army to have passed had they done their duty. The French commander had sent a small patrol of cavalry over a ford he had found out, which the Spaniards no sooner perceived than they fled from the strong position, leaving the guns all loaded and the matches burning. It was some time before the French could believe that they were such cowards. The guns remained some time in this state, they supposing it a manoeuvre of the Spaniards.

Our march from Arzobispo was very harassing. The first three days we passed over mountains apparently impassable. It took three days with the assistance of the whole of the infantry to get the guns and ammunition wagons over one, and after all, we were under the necessity of destroying a great quantity of ammunition, not being able to carry it forward. We were two-and-twenty hours on horseback, halted two hours, and then proceeded on our march. We expected the French to have crossed the Tagus at the bridge of Almaraz, and by that means have annoyed us on our retreat. However, to our no small satisfaction they remained on the other side, and we retreated unmolested. I am confident they have received such a drubbing from our little army that they will not be in such a hurry to try their strength again. Indeed, it can be of no advantage to Bonaparte to sacrifice a number of men in endeavouring to drive us out of the country at present when in a very short time he may do it without the loss of a man.

We were in hopes we should be recalled for it is the general opinion we can be of no further use in this country, and as to our forming a second junction with the Spaniards is ridiculous, but John Bull is so delighted with the action of Talavera that he will not be satisfied without such another.

I should like to know how you send your letters to me for I have not received one since I entered Spain. All that ever reached me are one from my mother, the other from William at Abrantes. Col. Dalbiac gets his very regularly. The plan, I believe, is to send them to the agents and they will forward them immediately. I am indeed anxious to hear from home as John Dalton's last letter from the Grange names Mary Anne's having been very ill. I hope to hear every day expecting and hoping for a good account.

George Luard has been ill with the complaint I had but I am happy to add is now considerably better. Perhaps his family may not have heard of it, therefore do not name it. The heat at this period is dreadful but I am in hopes it will not last much longer. We expect soon to go into cantonments. I am almost tired of being like gipsies. When I come home I will cook you as good a dinner as ever you sat down to in your life. I hope William will not forget to send my friends the Smiths some moor-game. They were extremely kind to me before I left England, Mr Smith offering me some letters of introduction to some families in Spain and Portugal, and Mrs Smith and the young ladies presented me with a small box of medecines which I regret I refused, for we are in great want of them, it being necessary to leave a considerable quantity with the poor fellows left at Talavera, which I am grieved to say amounted to nearly three thousand. However, we have one consolation, the French behave to them in the kindest manner possible.

Our brigade have at present the post of honour being considerably in advance, a part of the army being at Elvas, which is in Portugal, headquarters at Badajoz. I suppose the

Flushing expedition is returned, and I trust they will send the transports to the Tagus for our troops. I should be extremely happy to find myself on board the *Britannia* again. I was as much pleased when we were advancing and had some prospects of seeing Madrid, but our hopes were destroyed. Our army was reducing every day by sickness, this certainly damped our ardour, but had Ministers landed the Flushing expedition in the north of Spain in time to have co-operated with our army, I still think we should have been successful, at least we should have driven Master Joseph[7] from Madrid and hurled him from his throne, and had the Spaniards been good for anything, we should have destroyed the whole of the French army on the 28th. Four thousand of them set off on the commencement of the action as if the old gentleman had got them without firing a single shot. In the beginning of the engaging of the enemy Sir A. Wellesley sent to demand 15 or 16 thousand of them in the hope of turning the enemy's left, but they would not budge an inch. The Spaniards lost only 100 men which fell on the left of our regiment. They behaved well. Cuesta five days after hung a lot of them for running away.

I must now draw to a conclusion, first telling you George is in excellent condition and appears to enjoy the fun very much. A run at Loversall next summer will do him good. My other horse is in equal spirits but he is one of the lean kind. It is quite ridiculous to see the troop horses. You never saw such a miserable set of devils in your life. Each troop have lost about twenty.

I suppose the new house will be nearly finished before I arrive at home without it is upon a large scale. Col. Dalbiac is in perfect health and desires to be most kindly remembered to all. Give my kindest love to my mother and everyone. Believe me, my dear Father, Your most affectionate son,

Thos. C. Fenton.

I hope to hear a good account of Mary Anne.

---

7 i.e., King Joseph Bonaparte.

Mérida, Oct. 20th 1809.

My dearest Mother,

I have this moment received yours in answer to the one I sent from Talavera. You can have no idea of the joy it gives me to hear that you were all well. It is the first letter I have got since my entering Spain. It has been read over and over again and I am not yet satisfied with it. I thank Dr. Bessy and George for their affectionate note. I am delighted to hear Mr. A and Harriet are recovered, though I regret my profile should have occasioned one pang. I hope the original will arrive safe and sound in England again. It is only the idea of returning home that keeps us in spirits. I have, since I last wrote, had a slight touch of the fever, which I am sorry to say many thousands of the Army have at this time. By my prudence in putting on a flannel waistcoat and my feet into warm water I in a few days, thank God, got well again. I was then at an out-quarter by myself. I am sure ministers must know the sickly state of the army. At present more than half are in the hospitals. I cannot therefore think we shall remain much longer either in Spain or Portugal. I wish we were in the latter place. It is nearer home.

I mentioned in my last letter George Luard's having been ill. He now rides out every day. An application has been made to the Commander-in-Chief for him to return to England. We hope to have him therefore leave us very soon and trust that his native air will soon restore his health and spirits.

In your last you enquired whether the words I used to make use of to frighten you (about my head rolling off) occurred to me during the action of Talavera. I cannot say they did. I am confident during that period self never occupies my mind. My men took all my attention. When we were galloping up to the charge and within two hundred yards of 12 thousand Frenchmen with their muskets ready to fire upon us if we advanced, I gave old George a clap on the neck, grasped my sword tight in my hand, and recommended myself to the care of the Almighty. Immediately a cannon ball passed me within a foot or two, so near that old George had nearly fallen from terror, not perfectly understanding the nature of these things. My right-hand man and covering sergeant's horses were both touched with splinters from a shell. I had also one man and four horses killed in the troop I commanded. I (thank God) got out of the business safe, and I must say I am not anxious for another, and willingly will I let it rest till my next campaign with the old Fourth.

By January I hope we shall be allowed to return. What a happy moment it will be when I enter the door at Loversall. You may be assured of this, that idea often occupies my mind and I feel a heart felt satisfaction morning and night with the thought that we are putting up prayers for each other at the same time. You, I am sure, will feel this equally.

George Dalbiac has joined the regiment. He is looking extremely well. They all desire to be kindly remembered to you. Give my love to Dixon and tell him I certainly should have written to him had he not been my brother, and therefore of course at liberty to see all my letters. I congratulate both myself and him on the recovery of one we both love so well. Tell poor Polly she will also cry when she sees the original of the profile, but it will be with fright for I have got a most tremendous pair of whiskers; they nearly meet. I suppose they will all be at me to cut them off when I get home. I keep them on here to frighten the natives, but I promise a shaving of them the first night I get home.

You tell me you cannot feel interested for such a country as this, a country that has not a spark of patriotism for themselves. The French, when they conquer it, will make them clean and industrious. It is what they want most dreadfully. Since my last we have come in to cantonments in this town, I have fortunately got into a good billet. You would be delighted with my landlady. She is a sincere good woman and she has taken a particular liking to me and Richard. She brings me a present of something every day. I read your letter this morning and she was nearly as well pleased as myself.

I am glad to hear my Uncle Lee's affairs are likely to get into good train. I owe him and my aunt a good deal for their kindness to me in my long illness. I hope I shall always feel grateful. Pray remember me particularly to my aunt. I hope Miss K. is not yet run away with, for I intend on my return seriously to look out for a wife that I may settle and lead a country life. What do you think of this plan? I must have you to put in a word for me or I fear I shall stick fast.

22nd. I have just been reading the English papers. I see Anna Maria Plumer is married to an officer of the 15th. I am sorry to find nothing about transports. I fear ministers are so busy quarrelling among themselves that they forget us. The report here is current that Bonaparte is come into Spain. I wish it may be true. In that case Lord Wellington will think of home.

With kind love to my Father and all at Loversall. Believe me, My dearest Mother, Your most affectionate son,

Thomas C. Fenton.

Mérida, 22 Oct. 1809.

My dear William,

As I know your regard for Col. Dalbiac you will, I am sure, be sorry to hear he has been extremely unwell, but I hope by care and good management he will soon get well. Had he been one that lived hard and had led a dissipated life, I do not believe he would have lived. What a loss we should have had. The regiment would have gone to the dogs. Major A[inslie] would have had the command of it, Ld. Ed. [Somerset] being generally on the staff or employed on parliamentary business. Our friend Col. Dalbiac is beloved by all from the manner he has behaved to everyone during Lord Edward's confinement with the gout.

I mentioned in my last the death of poor Baker. He was a short time ill, you may remember. He had reduced himself so much by walking it is thought the cause of his not recovering. The 3rd Dragoon [Guards] (our Brigade regiment) have lost one Major and a Captain. The state of the army is truly distressing, no less than 10,000 being sick. However, I hope we shall soon return home. Our General has bet a guinea we are not here ten days hence. Heartily do I wish he may win it. We send sixty men of our regiment tomorrow to the General Hospital at Elvas. I am sorry to add Richard is one of them. He is, however, getting much better. He has been everything to me since we left Lisbon. I cannot praise him too much.

You will not expect I am saving money here when I tell you we are paying thirty shillings per pound for tea, four eggs for a shilling, and everything else equally dear. The Spaniards impose upon us in the most infamous manner. They make us pay double for everything. If you can avoid it I would not name this to my mother. It may make her uneasy about me. You of course know there are consequences that must attend all armies in a hot climate. I have not seen James Hervey since we left Mérida, therefore can give no account of him. He was completely sick of the business and I believe would be quite contented with a lieutenantcy in his father's regiment.

I hope you had good diversion on the moors and that you did not forget my friends the Smiths. The 23rd Light Dragoons are going home immediately. They give their horses to the 16th and 14th Dragoons. I hope to hear from you soon, and I am truly, Dear William, Your most affectionate Brother,

Thomas C. Fenton.

Norcliffe has this moment come in and desires to be kindly remembered. It is the talk of the day that we are going to loggerheads with the Spaniards. Report says the Junta have desired Ld. Wellington would either advance or leave Spain.

The former is impossible, therefore we expect the latter every day. The rainy season has just begun. It is not near so hot as it was a few days ago. I wish my mother could see my good landlady cooking me a supper. She has completely cured me. God bless you.

WAGRAM, 1809

Marshal Jacques Macdonald, V Corps, Army of Italy

In 1809 Austria, chaffing under the French tutelage that had come as the consequence of defeat at Austerlitz four years before, joined Britain in the Fifth Coalition against Napoleon. Thus bolstered, Archduke Charles promptly invaded Napoleon's ally, Bavaria; since the Hapsburg had cunningly omitted to issue a formal declaration of hostilities, his advance made spectacular progress; only the arrival of Napoleon himself on the Danube front on 17 April stabilized the situation. Three days later, Napoleon launched a major attack against Archduke Charles' over-extended supply lines, splitting the Austrian army in two at Abensberg. The Emperor then sustained the initiative with a victory at Eckmuhl and an occupation of Vienna on 13 May. However, since Napoleon's strategic aim was never the holding of enemy territory but the defeat of its field forces, he was still obliged to deal with the main Austrian army, some 95,000-strong, located north of the Danube. After bridging the Danube four miles below Vienna (all the city's bridges had been destroyed by the Austrian rearguard), Napoleon sent General Massena's IV Corps across to occupy Aspern-Essling on the north bank; however, Austrian "missiles" floated down the swollen river impeded, even halted, the bridging work, severely restricting the number of French troops able to reach the Aspern-Essling bridgehead. On 21 May, the

Austrians attacked Aspern-Essling in great strength, beginning a two-day battle that eventually resulted in Napoleon's withdrawal to the island of Lobau, a severe reverse for the French. Using all his genius and willpower, Napoleon rallied for another engagement and spent the next six weeks in meticulous planning, fortifying Lobau and summoning up distant forces, including 20,000 from Prince Eugene's Army of Italy. By 4 July Napoleon had 190,000 troops and 617 guns gathered around Lobau.

On that stormy night, the French swung a pontoon bridge from Lobau to the north bank of the Danube and poured over – to the bemusement of the Austrians, who had anticipated an attack at Aspern – and by the evening of the 5th July the Grande Armée *controlled a 15-mile salient from Aspern to Wagram. A second day of intense fighting decided the issue, after Napoleon – with impeccable timing – launched V Corps of General Macdonald's Army of Italy against the hinge of the Austrian line. The juggernaut was unstoppable, and eventually the Austrian line broke. Nearly 30,000 French dead and wounded lay over the battlefield (the Austrians lost 40,000 men), but Napoleon had his decisive victory. A few weeks later Emperor Francis I sued for peace, which Napoleon swiftly accepted because of troubles on other fronts, notably the British amphibious expedition to Walcheren in Holland.*

Marshal Jacques Macdonald (1765–1840) was the son of a Scottish Jacobite exile. He was made general de division *in 1794, and in 1799 became commander of the Army of Naples. He fell foul of Napoleon for defending General Moreau (who had become involved in a Royalist intrigue), but was allowed to rejoin the Neopolitan army in 1807. Although wounded at Piave in May 1809, he recovered in time to lead the Army of Italy's V Corps in the great attack at Wagram, a decisive act which Napoleon gratefully acknowledged by immediately appointing Macdonald a* Marechal *– the only one to receive his baton on the battlefield. In December 1809 Macdonald was ennobled as duc de Tarente. After Napoleon's first abdication,*

he accepted the Bourbon restoration and refused to serve under
Le Tondu *during the 1815 campaign.*

After our fruitless attempt to destroy the bridge at Komorn, I
received orders to advance towards Ofen, capital of Hungary;
but shortly afterwards was recalled by forced marches to the
chief headquarters at Ebersdorf, opposite the island of Lobau. It was clear that a great operation was being prepared.
We were not the last to arrive, and by nine o'clock in the
evening of 4 July we were at our posts on the Danube at the
crossing-place that had been selected for the surprise of the
enemy. We had marched sixty leagues in three days, and
notwithstanding our excessive fatigue, and the heat of the
season, we had but few laggards, so anxious were the men of
the Army of Italy to take part in the great events that were
preparing, and to fight in presence of their brothers-in-arms
of the Grand Army, and under the very eyes of the Emperor.

That night an appalling storm burst upon us; rain and hail
fell in torrents, driven by a raging north wind, the whistling
of which mingled with the peals of thunder and the roar of
cannon. This tempest was extremely favourable to our passage of the Danube upon bridges built on piles, at which they
had been working since the fatal 22nd of the previous May
[the battle of Aspern-Essling]; their activities were masked
by the thickly-wooded island of Lobau. I landed upon the
island at about six o'clock in the morning; what we most
wanted was a good fire to dry us, but the sun soon came out
and warmed us with his kindly rays. Meanwhile, several
corps of the Grand Army, which had roused the enemy from
their security, were driving back their advance-guard, and
this, being supported from behind, was slowly retreating
towards the intrenched position of the camp.

I moved forward in my turn, and was momentarily placed
in the second rank with the remainder of the Army of Italy.

Scarcely had I deployed, being myself on the extreme right, when I heard cries of "vive l'Empereur!" coming from the left.

The soldiers, as he approached, raised their shakos upon their bayonets in token of joy. He turned his horse towards the direction whence the cheering proceeded, and, recognising the Army of Italy, rode down the line; as he approached the right, I moved forward slightly. He spoke to no one, merely saluting with his hand. In spite of what the Viceroy[1] had told me, that I should be pleased with my first interview, I was not more favoured than the rest. I do not know where Prince Eugène then was, but immediately on hearing that the Emperor had passed, he hastened up and said:

"Well, I hope you were satisfied. No doubt he confirmed by word of mouth all that I have written to you?"

"He did not address a single word to me."

"What?"

"Not a word. He merely nodded, as if to say: 'I can see through you, you rascal!'"

The amiable Prince was miserable, fearing, of course wrongly, lest I should think that he had been a well-meaning but clumsy interpreter; and he gave me his word of honour, of which I had no need, so convinced was I of his friendly and honest truthfulness, that he had only written to me the Emperor's exact words.

It was already late. The troops of the Grand Army, tired with marching and fighting since the morning, formed into columns to let us pass. We thus had the honour of becoming the front rank and of pursuing the enemy, who only turned now and again in order to check our ardour. They eventually regained their positions, and we halted within short cannon-range. I was then in front of the position at Wagram; the

1 Viceroi Eugene de Beauharnais (1781–1824), son of Josephine de Beauharnais, stepson of Napoleon; an able soldier, he was promoted general in 1804. He remained loyal to his stepfather until the first abdication, but did not participate in the 1815 campaign.

village of that name was on the left, and that of Baumersdorf on the right. A violent cannonade continued along the whole line while we were forming.

The Emperor came up to speak to the Viceroy, with whom I was talking; I fell back some yards. He did not speak to me as yet, but I heard him say somewhat carelessly:

"Order General Macdonald to attack and carry the plateau. The enemy are retiring, and we must make some prisoners."

Thereupon he went away. The Prince, joining me, said:

"Do you know what the Emperor has just been saying to me?"

"Yes," I replied; "I heard his orders."

"Well! what is your opinion?"

"I think the Emperor is mistaken; the enemy are not leaving, they are simply retiring to the intrenched position they have selected for the battle. Do you not see, the entire army is there, looking very brave? In order to carry through such an undertaking, although we have but an hour of daylight left, we should need to attack with the whole army. Lose no time – go, or else send these remarks of mine to the Emperor."

But he was afraid of him, and answered:

"Not I! He ordered us to attack; let us do it."

"So be it," I answered; "but you will see how we shall be beaten," which of course happened, as it could not fail to do.

We started, well protected by artillery, but our leading columns soon stopped at the Russbach, a stream with steep banks, which covered the Austrian front. I sprang to the ground, made my staff do the same, and sword in hand we set the example of crossing it, and were followed by the men. This bold stroke drove the enemy back, and we obtained possession of the plateau. We were obliged to halt near their huts, and form into columns, in order to attack the enemy, drawn up not far off, and also to wait till General Grenier, who was crossing the stream with his troops, could come up to our support. We had passed the villages of Wagram and Baumersdorf, which other corps of the Grand Army had failed to take; they had even retreated. The enemy debouched in large numbers, and attacked one flank, while the columns that we had held in check advanced against us.

General Grenier's troops, amazed at this unexpected onslaught, threw themselves in disorder among my men, breaking their lines and scattering them. All my efforts to restrain them were vain, although, sword in hand, with the majority of the officers, I had drawn up a line to check the fugitives. A rout ensued, and we were carried away, crossing the stream in the utmost confusion.

The Prince, who had remained on the other side, tried to stop the runaways. On coming close to him, I pointed out that he could not reform men under such a hot fire, as they were now panic stricken, although a few minutes before they had displayed such resolution; that what he should do was to send some detachments of cavalry out of range, and that the fugitives would naturally stop on reaching them. Fortunately, the enemy was satisfied with having repulsed us, and dared not cross the stream in pursuit, although a few squadrons would have sufficed to disperse us, for night had come on, and we should have imagined ourselves charged by the entire Austrian army, and the result would not be difficult to imagine. The loss of my corps in killed, wounded, and prisoners was enormous, amounting to nearly two thousand men. General Grenier had his hand shattered by a bullet at the beginning of this "brush," as the Emperor called it.

I did not leave the Viceroy. We passed the night out in the open, as did not the army, keeping a sharp look-out while our officers tried to rally the fugitives.

"What will the Emperor think?" asked the Prince anxiously.

"Nothing detrimental to you or me. He will realize, now that it is too late, that his orders were hasty. Where I think you were wrong was in not taking or sending to him the observations that I had made to you before embarking upon this unlucky attempt, the result of which was a foregone conclusion."

At daybreak, on 6 July, a violent cannonade began on our extreme right. We re-established our line, and formed up. The enemy in front of us remained motionless, but soon advanced some troops on the right; they slowly descended the heights as if to cross the stream in front of Bernadotte,[2] who was posted on my left in front of the village of Wagram. On the right was Marshal Davout[3], who, marching against the enemy, was either warned, or else met them coming towards him. The firing was violent, and, as the Marshal believed that he had the entire Austrian force against him, all our reserves were ordered up to support him and effect a diversion. The Emperor came to the spot where I was, and addressed himself directly to me, saying:

"Last night you carried the plateau of Wagram; you know the way up to it; carry it again. Marmont[4] will at the same time attack the village of Baumersdorf; you and he seem to understand each other; I will send him to you."

Marmont soon came, and we mutually agreed to support each other; and, in order not to expose ourselves to a repetition of the previous evening's occurrences, the General quite understood that the village should be carried before I commenced my attack upon the plateau; but while we were commencing operations, other events were taking place behind us on the left.

2 Marshal Jean-Baptiste Bernadotte (1763–1844), commander of the Saxon army. His mishandling of his command at Wagram began a cooling in his relations with the Emperor. On his elevation to Crown Prince of Sweden, Bernadotte drew close to the Tsar and eventually rebelled against his old master.
3 i.e. Marshal Davout (1770–1823), commander of the French right wing at Wagram.
4 General August Marmont (1774–1852); appointed Marshal for winning the action of Znaim in the wake of Wagram.

Massena[5] commanded at the real point of attack. The Marshal could not make a stand against troops much superior to his own. He was driven back with great loss on to the *tete-de-pont*, by which we had passed after crossing the Danube. The Austrians sent forward their right. Davout was kept in check; Bernadotte, repulsed before Wagram, left me uncovered. The movements of the enemy on my left and rear were concealed from me by little hillocks and inequalities in the ground. I slowly advanced towards the plateau, because Marmont had met with considerable resistance at the village of Baumersdorf, when the Emperor came up and changed my destination.

The retreat of Massena, which I then learned for the first time, and the retrograde movement made by Bernadotte, had left the centre of the army exposed. I therefore received orders to change my direction – to turn almost completely round, and go and take up my position near the hillocks. The Emperor betook himself to the highest of these in order to observe, and kept sending officers, one after another, to me to hasten my movements. The manoeuvre that I was carrying out, however, demanded some time, and, besides, I thought it would be imprudent to arrive disordered and straggling.

Vexed and anxious to know the reason for these reiterated orders, I galloped towards the Emperor, when I saw him leaving the hillock as fast as his horse could go, followed by his numerous staff. I continued, however, and gained the top of the hillock he had just quitted, when at once I saw what was the matter. The enemy, who were in great numbers at this point, were marching the more boldly that they encountered no resistance: I then understood (as the Emperor afterwards admitted) that his intention in thus hurrying me was to show that he was not in retreat there, as he was on the left. It was therefore necessary to risk something in order to carry this out with the utmost speed; but little did I

5 Marshal Andre Massena (1758–1817), commander of the French left wing.

think that this spot was to become shortly afterwards the principal point of attack, against which the numerous forces of the enemy would come to shatter themselves.

I therefore ordered four battalions, followed by four others which I deployed in two lines, to advance at the double; and while my artillery opened fire, and that of the Guard took up position (which the Emperor called the hundred gun battery), my two divisions formed themselves into attacking columns. The enemy, who were still advancing, halted; and redoubling their fire, caused us terrible loss. However, in proportion as my ranks became thinned, I drew them up closer together and made them dress up as at drill.

While I was doing this, I saw the enemy's cavalry preparing to charge, and had barely time to close my second line on the first one; they were flanked by the two divisions still in column, and the square was completed by a portion of General Nansouty's cavalry that had been put under my orders that morning. I ordered both ranks to open fire, my famous battery mowing down the cavalry. This hot fire broke them just as they were preparing to charge; many men and horses fell pierced by our bayonets. The smoke rising disclosed to me the enemy in the utmost disorder, which was increased by their attempt to retreat. I ordered an advance at the point of the bayonet, after previously commanding Nansouty to charge, at the same time desiring the cavalry officers whom I saw behind me to do likewise. Unfortunately, they were not under my orders, and the Emperor was not there to give any.

The enemy were in extreme disorder; but still their fire during their retreat did us much harm. I was in despair at the slowness of General Nansouty. Not far from us I saw a large number of abandoned pieces of cannon; the Austrian officers were bringing up men, by dint of blows with the flat of their swords, to remove them. At last Nansouty moved, but too late to profit by the gap that I had made in the Austrian centre. I halted to allow his division to pass; I was, moreover, so weakened that I dared not venture into the plain to pursue the enemy (the more so as Nansouty's cavalry was repulsed, but not followed) until the Emperor sent me reinforcements. Unfortunately, the favourable moment had been allowed to slip. The results would have been enormous had Nansouty charged immediately, supported by the cavalry which was in the rear.

I had no staff-officers round me – one of my aides-de-camp had been killed, as well as my orderlies; the others were either incapacitated or away on a mission. While I was thus awaiting reinforcements, a general officer in full uniform rode up to me. I did not know him. After the usual greetings, he paid me great compliments upon the action that had just occurred, and finished by inquiring my name, which I gave him.

I knew you by reputation, he said; and am happy to make your acquaintance on a field of battle so glorious for you. After replying to his compliment, I, in my turn, asked him his name: he was General Walther, of the Guard; I had never heard of him.

"Do you," I asked, "command that fine and large body of cavalry which I perceive in the rear?"

"I do."

"Then why on earth did you not charge the enemy at the decisive moment, after I had thrown them into such disorder, and after I had begged you to several times? The Emperor ought to, and will, be very angry with his Guard for remaining motionless when so glorious a share was offered to them, which might have brought about such enormous and decisive results!"

"In the Guard," replied he, "we require orders direct from the Emperor himself, or from our chief, Marshal Bessieres. Now, as the latter was wounded, there only remained the Emperor, and he sent us no orders."

He added that at the Battle of Essling several Generals had made use of regiments of Guards, and that they had suffered very much; wherefore, since then, Marshal Bessieres had obtained instructions that they should only act altogether and under his orders, or under the direct command of the Emperor.

"But," I retorted, "there are circumstances in which such a rule cannot be considered as absolute – such a case as this, for example. The Emperor could not have failed to approve your action, as it would have secured the destruction of a considerable portion of the Austrian army. And, supposing that we had been repulsed instead of gaining a success, would you not have protected us? and would you have retired from the field without a blow because you had received no orders?"

These questions embarrassed him, he saluted, and returned to his troop. I afterwards learned that the Emperor had reprimanded him and the other Generals of the Guard very severely; but the fault really lay with the Emperor himself. He should not have forgotten the restriction he had imposed, and should have remained in person at the principal centre of the action to direct everything. Later on, in talking over these occurrences with me, he was still very bitter against his Guard.

"Why did you not make them act?" he said. "I put them under your orders!"

"I knew nothing about that," I replied. "I limited myself to repeated, but fruitless, requests. And how could I have made them charge, when I had endless trouble even to get General Nansouty to move? He wanted so much time to form his men!"

"That is true," said the Emperor; "he is rather slow."

The reinforcement I had asked for came at last; it was composed of General Wrede's Bavarian division, and of General Guyot's brigade of light cavalry of the Guard. The enemy's retrograde movement had commenced, and I began mine to follow them. I thought the whole *corps d'armee* were doing the same.

Towards evening I caught up the rear-guard close by a village called Sussenbrunn, which was fortified with earthworks. I made a feint of attacking in front, while I made an oblique movement to outflank it; but the Austrian General, discovering my intentions, immediately beat a retreat. I called back the outflanking party, and warned General Guyot to hold himself in readiness to charge. He sent me back word that his Guards were always ready, a boast that he justified a moment later; for scarcely had I given orders to attack, than both his men and the Bavarians charged together. The two troops stormed the camp, and cut off the column, bringing me back 5,000 or 6,000 prisoners and ten guns. Scarcely were these prisoners removed, when a reserve, posted on a height commanding the village, assailed us with bullets, grapeshot, and a well sustained musketry-fire. I saw General Wrede fall, and hastened to his assistance; his men raised him up, and he then said to me:

"Tell the Emperor that I die for him; I commend to him my wife and children."

He was being supported, and, to reassure him, I said, laughing:

"I think that you will be able to make this recommendation to him yourself; and, what is more, that your wife will continue to have children by you."

It proved to be merely a slight wound from a ball that had grazed his side. The wind of the ball had made him giddy.

The firing was then very severe, and the flames of the burning village helped to reveal our weakness, especially as night was coming on, and the enemy could see to shoot straight and I became seriously uneasy on looking round and finding myself isolated; I had been so occupied in pursuing the enemy that I had failed to notice that the rest of the army was not following. I did not know what singular motive had stopped or suspended its movement, for at five o'clock they had taken up position, and I had received no orders countermanding my advance.

The Emperor, on the other hand, was much surprised to hear such persistent firing going on far off at one particular point of the battlefield. He sent several officers to discover the cause. I had no need to give explanations; our position spoke for itself. From these officers I learned that the whole army had been bivouacked since five o'clock.

Massena also was a long way to the rear of my left. He too sent to know which was the adventurous corps engaged so far ahead.

Meanwhile, in the twilight, and by lying at full length on the ground, we could distinguish in the distance some bodies of cavalry coming towards us, or rather towards the fire, and this reassured me; but if the enemy had had any pluck, they could have surrounded me with superior force, seeing that all their reserves were collected on the heights. Fortunately, their sole idea was to cover the retreat and disorder of their wings.

The firing ceased on either side about eleven o'clock, but we remained under arms till daybreak. As I then perceived that the enemy had retired, I sent my cavalry in pursuit while waiting for orders. They kept on sending back numerous prisoners, including those taken the previous evening; these amounted in the aggregate to 10,000, and 15 guns. At the Island of Lobau 20,000 prisoners had been made. I had therefore captured half the total, and the artillery I took was all that was captured.

A few hours later the Viceroy passed; he gave us great praise, and said that the Emperor was very pleased with me, that he had as yet given no orders as to our ulterior movements, that I was to wait, and that he would follow my cavalry. I then noticed for the first time that my horse had received a bullet in the neck, but which had remained between the skin and the flesh; he was taken away in order that it might be extracted. As for me, I went to one of the houses in the town, where I had passed a few hours the previous night, worn out, and suffering from a kick given me by my horse the day before.

I soon fell asleep, but not for long, as I was awakened by cries of "Long live the Emperor!" which redoubled when he entered my camp. I asked for my horse, but he had been taken away. I had no other, as the rest were far behind. As I could not walk, I remained on my straw, when I heard someone inquiring for me. It was an orderly officer, either M. Anatole de Montesquieu, or his brother, who was afterwards killed in Spain. He came by the Emperor's order to look for me. On my remarking that I had no horse and could not walk, he offered me his, which I accepted. I saw the Emperor surrounded by my troops, whom he was congratulating. He approached me, and embracing me cordially, said:

"Let us be friends henceforward."

"Yes," I answered, "till death." And I have kept my word, not only up to the time of his abdication, but even beyond it. He added:

"You have behaved valiantly, and have rendered me the greatest services, as, indeed, throughout the entire campaign. On the battle field of your glory, where I owe you so large a part of yesterday's success, I make you a MARSHAL OF FRANCE" (he used this expression instead of "of the Empire"). "You have long deserved it."

"Sire," I answered, "since you are satisfied with us, let the rewards and recompenses be apportioned and distributed among my army corps, beginning with Generals Lamarque, Broussier, and others, who so ably seconded me."

"Anything you please," he replied; "I have nothing to refuse you."

Thereupon he went away much moved, as I was also. Thus did I avenge myself for all the petty annoyances caused me by General Lamarque, who, although he had heard me mention his name first of all, still continued to worry me.

Scarcely had the Emperor turned his horse's head, when many exalted personages came to congratulate and compliment me. The one who showed me most affection was the

Duke de Bassano, at that time Secretary of State, then Berthier, Prince of Neuchatel, Major-General of the army. Both
these men were in Napoleon's most intimate confidence.

"No doubt you knew what he intended to do?" I said to the
latter.

"No," he replied naively.

Then came embraces and handshakings that I thought
would never end. Many would have passed me by had it not
been for the Emperor's favour.

The Emperor caught up the Viceroy, and related to him
with considerable emotion the scene which had just taken
place and my elevation. The latter promptly despatched an
aide-de-camp to congratulate me, to invite me to breakfast,
and to beg me to bring my troops forward on the highroad
between Vienna and Wolkersdorf. I found the Prince in the
hunting-lodge known as the Rendezvous; he was at table with
the Artillery-Generals Lariboisiere and Sorbier, the former
of whom was killed at Konigsberg, at the end of the campaign
of 1812; the latter is still living in the neighbourhood of
Nevers. As soon as I was announced, he hastened to meet me,
and we embraced each other effusively.

"The good accounts that you have given of me have
procured me this honour," I said to him. "I shall never
forget it."

"It is you, and you alone," he replied, "who have gained
your baton."

The others joined in congratulating me; I only knew
Lariboisiere by reputation.

"I am sure," I continued to the Prince, "that you knew
what the Emperor had in contemplation, though you concealed it from me this morning."

He answered frankly, "No," and added after a moment's
thought, "I remember now that while I was walking and
talking with the Emperor in his tent early this morning we
spoke of the battle. He regretted that so little had resulted
from it, and after a moment's silence said: 'It is not Macdo-

nald's fault, though, for he worked very hard.' I see now," added the Prince, "that he was then thinking of rewarding you, and was determined to give as much *eclat* as possible to your nomination."

Such was the circumstance that raised me to the dignity of which, I am convinced, I had been deprived by intrigue when the first appointments were made. It was necessary to have had the command in chief of armies to obtain it, and I had had temporary command of that of the North, full command of those of Rome, Naples, and the Grisons, while several others had only commanded large divisions or wings. I think that I have already said that my intimacy with a person belonging to the Emperor's family weighed against me and also the Moreau trial, in which an attempt had been made to implicate me, but which attempt signally failed, as I was proved entirely innocent of any complicity, and finally intrigue and jealousy. One Marshal the less, and especially a man who had every claim to the dignity, was a victory for the vain and the ambitious.

After breakfast the Viceroy proposed to me to accompany him to the Emperor's headquarters at Wolkersdorf, but I had no fresh horses, and, moreover, was suffering a good deal from the kick I had received.

"Here we are," I observed, "in hot pursuit of the Austrians. If the Archduke John, who is commanding their other army, and ought to be at Presburg, pursues us in turn, he may be able to seriously interrupt our communications. I suppose that the Emperor has taken steps to provide against this? Can you in any case question him so as to find out if he has any precise information as to the position and objective of this army. If really at Presburg, I fail to understand why it did not take part in yesterday's affair; but it is lucky for us that it did not."

The Prince departed, and on his return told me that he had submitted my observations, to which the Emperor had replied:

"What would the Archduke do on the rear of my army? He must know that the battle has been lost by his brother."

"No doubt," replied the Prince; "but if he meets with no opposition, nothing need prevent him from harassing you."

"Well," replied the Emperor, frowning, "if he dares to do so I will wheel round and crush him!"

The Prince had not recovered his stupefaction even when he related the answer to me.

Nevertheless, the Emperor thought over what I had said. Shortly afterwards he learnt that the Archduke John was making a movement to follow us. We immediately received orders to face about, and the whole Army of Italy went to meet the Austrian Prince, who in his turn retired as soon as he learnt that we had come to fight him and to join General Reynier's force. This General had replaced Marshal Bernadotte, who had been dismissed by the Emperor for publishing a general order, wherein he attributed the victory of the previous day to his Saxons, although they had vanished from the field and I had taken their place. That had been the object with which I was changing my direction, when the Emperor himself came to me to order it, and made me hasten so much by sending constant messages to be quick: speed was necessary, as I have related. The Emperor, very angry with Bernadotte, issued, to the Marshals only, an order wherein he expressed his displeasure, and said that the praise given by the Commander of the Saxon force belonged to me and to my troops.

As we were approaching the River March, a staff-officer from the Emperor's headquarters galloped up with a despatch from the Major-General.

"What has happened?" I asked.

"Upon my word, I don't know. I hear some talk of an armistice, but I am not acquainted with the contents of the despatches I have brought you."

It was indeed the armistice that was officially announced to me, with orders to halt.

"The armistice is signed," I said to the officer.

"Quite likely," he replied carelessly and indifferently.

The next morning I received orders to recross the Danube, return into Styria, and take up my headquarters at Gratz.

The results of the battle had been so scanty that I could not conceive how it was that the Austrians were compelled to beg for an armistice; but I heard afterwards that their army was in such a state of disorganization that it was equivalent to a rout. Neither was it known then that the Emperor only granted the truce because he also needed opportunity to repair his enormous losses, and because we should infallibly have run short of ammunition. Rewards even were offered to those who collected the balls of either army. On our side we had fired close upon 100,000 rounds![6]

6 Wagram was the greatest artillery battle to that date.

DIARY OF A CAVALRY OFFICER IN THE PENINSULA, 1810

Lieutenant William Tomkinson,
16th Light Dragoons

Born in 1790, Tomkinson was gazetted to a cornetcy in the 16th Light Dragoons in December 1807. A year and half later he arrived in the Iberian Peninsula with his horse Bob, and was almost immediately in action as part of Sir Arthur Wellesley's attack on Marshal Soult at Oporto, on the River Douro, May 1809. A skirmish at Grijo, outside Oporto, in which Tomkinson's cavalry troop charged a 3,000-strong French infantry position, saw Tomkinson badly wounded, his injuries exacerbated when Bob panicked and fled to the rear, en route selecting "a low branch under a vine tree [and] knocked my head into it." After being plundered by German infantry from his own side, Tomkinson was eventually attended by an army surgeon:

"On taking off my clothes, I was found to be wounded by a musket-shot in the neck. It had entered above the left shoulder and come out in front. A second through the right arm, above the elbow, and a third musket-shot through the left, below the elbow, with a bayonet-wound close by the latter."

After several days delirium in a nearby Spanish hovel, Tomkinson was evacuated to Oporto and thence to England.

A little over a year later, Tomkinson arrived back in Portugal to continue his war, about which he kept an assiduous chronicle. The extract presented below, from Tomkinson's re-arrival in March 1810 to the end of that year, covers the River Coa, Bussaco and Torres Vedras campaigns, a defensive phase in the Peninsular War with Wellington concerned to secure the safety of Portugal from a French attack under the great Marshal Massena. Although Massena penetrated as far as Lisbon, he was unable to assail Wellington's fortified Lines of Torres Vedras and was obliged to withdraw, even abandon the invasion of Portugal. Though no-one yet knew it, the turning point in the Peninsular War had been reached.

As archetypal light cavalry, the 16th Light Dragoons tended to be occupied in the Peninsula, above the brief hurrahs of battlefield charges, with skirmishing, patrol and piquet duties – arduous, dangerous toil which took its toll on men and horses alike. During five and half years of Peninsular campaigning, the 14th Light Dragoons lost 1,564 horses, and there is no reason to believe that the 16th was any less demanding on its mounts. Posterity has adjudged the light cavalry to be the most dashing of warriors; that the 16th saw themselves in similar romantic light is clearly proved by Tomkinson's frequent use of the adjective "gallant" to describe his unit's actions, although he was too astute an observer to be blind to those weaknesses of the British light cavalry – a "hot-headedness" that sometimes subordinated the military needs of the moment to a reckless, uncontrolled desire for personal glory – that so infuriated Wellington.

Despite his grievous injuries at Grijo, Tomkinson remarkably passed through the rest of his service almost unscathed, although under fire some 100 times. He was gazetted a captain in the 60th Regiment in 1812, from which he exchanged back, in the common fashion, to his own regiment without ever leaving it.

March 20th, 1810.

I embarked this day on board the *Norge*, a seventy-four, for Lisbon; and sailed the same day, our party consisting of Lieutenant-General Sir Stapleton Cotton; Lord Tweedale, his quarter-master general; Lieutenant Dudley, 16th Light Dragoons, his aide-de-camp.

We arrived in Lisbon on the 29th, having made the Tagus late on the 28th. The vessel struck against a rock when off Fort San Julian, and was obliged to be sent round to Gibraltar to repair. From the gloomy state of affairs in England before we left, we expected to hear at Lisbon of the retreat of the army. Headquarters were at Vizeu, with our outposts on the Agueda, where the 95th Infantry had had an affair with the enemy at Barba del Puerco, they having attempted to surprise them at night, in which they failed, being driven back with considerable loss.

During our stay at Lisbon, Sir Stapleton[1] occupied Quintella's house, one of the best in Lisbon. I bought an English mare and two Portuguese ponies: the two latter for baggage.

Quintella is very opulent; he has the monopoly of all the snuff sold in Portugal.

There are two passages into the Tagus: one close to Fort St Julian, which is narrow and not very deep, and the other farther south, wider and most usually selected on entering the Tagus. The *Norge* is one of the largest seventy-fours in the navy; and the master having been in her and off the Tagus with Sir John Duckworth, at the time of the Convention of Cintra,[2] when it was in agitation to have entered the Tagus and bombard and get possession of Fort San Julian, for which purpose he had been employed in taking soundings, and particularly of the inner passage, thought himself cap-

1 General Sir Stapleton Cotton (1773–1865), cavalry commander. Invalided home in 1812, but returned for the Pyrenees campaign. Promoted Field Marshal 1855.
2 The 1808 agreement between France and Britain, in which the former evacuated Portugal.

able of taking in the ship without a pilot, in which case half
the pilotage goes to the master. The captain of the vessel had
never been in the Tagus; it was his first voyage in the *Norge,*
and, much against his inclination, a pilot was not taken. We
were very close in shore, with every sail set, going twelve or
fourteen knots an hour, a man heaving the lead, and the wind
blowing very fresh off shore on our larboard quarter. The
vessel struck twice on a rock, the masts quite bent; but
fortunately going so quick she got off. It was at the dinner
hour of the men, and all excepting 100 or 150 were below,
and on feeling her hit, in an instant from 500 to 600 hands
were on deck. The vessel made from three to four feet of
water immediately, and the pumps were set going before we
came to an anchor. The master considered it very unreason-
able in the captain to wish for a pilot, his own knowledge of
the harbour being so correct, and the captain distinctly stated
that the master took the whole responsibility on himself. The
captain in my opinion ought to have insisted on one.

April 15th.

We this day arrived at Coimbra, having moved by the
usual stages, and here halted one day.

The 6th Portuguese Regiment of the line was here, under
Colonel Ashworth, brother to Captain Ashworth of the 16th.
The men were very fine and steady under arms, and from all
appearances should make excellent troops.

We made two short days' marches from Coimbra to Santa
Combadaõ, where we found the headquarters of the 16th,
seven leagues from Coimbra. The following day Sir Stapleton moved on to Vizeu. The regiment was by no means
recovered from the effects of the Talavera campaign[3]; but
from the quantity of green forage in the neighbourhood of
every quarter, great changes were evident in a short time.

Headquarters with right squadron, Santa Combadaõ, with
the remainder of the regiment in the adjacent villages.

3 see p 151.

The day after I joined, I was ordered to Frieshada, a small village on the right of the main Vizeu road, to take care of the horses sent there for grazing.

The regiment was brigaded with the first Hussars, K.G.L.,[4] who were up in the front, doing the outpost duty, under Brigadier-General Crawford,[5] on the Agueda.
April 27th.

Headquarters of the army moved this day from Vizeu up to Celorico, eight leagues in advance, and two squadrons of the 16th marched to Vizeu.
April 28th.

This day joined Captain Cocks'[6] troop, and marched with the other two squadrons to Vizeu.
April 29th.

Marched to Villa Cova; called by the peasants four leagues from Vizeu, though from the badness of the road it was near night before we got in, raining nearly the whole way.
April 30th.

The regiment this morning occupied the following villages in the rear of Celorico:–

Mello, Right squadron and headquarters: Ashworth and Lyon, E. and G.

Left centre, Mesquitella: Hay and Swetenham, D.K.

Left, Gouvea: Murray and Pelly, F. and A.

Right centre, divided: Captain Belli's troop at Nabias; Captain Cocks' at Villa Franca.

Headquarters of the army, Celorico: –

1st Division, Celorico: Lieutenant-General Sir Brent Spencer.

3rd Division, Pinhel: Major-General Picton.

4th Division, Guarda: Major-General Cole.

4 King's German Legion.
5 Major-General Robert "Black Bob" Crauford (1764–1812).
6 Lieutenant-Colonel Edward Charles Cocks (1785–1812). Commissioned into the 16th Light Dragoons in 1803, Cocks became famed for his reconnaissance work behind enemy lines.

The 5th Division, as General Leith's corps was then called, was in the neighbourhood of Guarda.

The Light Division upon the Agueda.

Cavalry: Lieutenant-General Sir Stapleton Cotton.

Lieutenant-General Hill, with the 2nd Division, was at Castello Branco, having moved from the south at the same time headquarters advanced from Vizeu.

The houses here are far inferior to those in Estremadura, without chimneys, the people living in the midst of smoke and filth. This makes the inhabitants look twenty years older; and being naturally not the finest race in the world, I can't say much for their appearance.

The regiment was supplied in everything from the country; we got the corn in by cars, passing our receipts for it on the commissary at Celorico, which were paid when presented. Cocks rather did this in a summary manner, and a commissary was sent to Villa Franca to inquire into the complaints of the peasants. We asked him to dinner, and gave him as much wine as he wished, when he said the complaints were groundless.

We heard about the 12th of this month that Massena, the Prince of Essling, had arrived at Valladolid with a considerable reinforcement, and had assumed the command of the army of Portugal.

June 1st.

An order arrived last night for the 16th to move to some villages in front of Celorico, and orders were at the same time given to the first division to hold itself in readiness. The regiment occupied the following villages: –

Headquarters, Right squadron: Marçal de Chaõ.

Right centre: Minuchal.

Left centre: Carnicais.

Left: Frasches.

Headquarters of the cavalry came to Minuchal.

This move was in consequence of the enemy having pushed a considerable force down to Ciudad de Rodrigo,

and having thrown some bridges over the river, all preparatory to the siege of the place and not with any idea of an attack
on us before they take it. Deserters come in daily, and all
report the enemy as short of supplies. They must say something, and this is perhaps the only good reason they can give
for an act, under almost any circumstances, highly disgraceful to a soldier.

Every one, almost, thought Rodrigo would not hold out
forty-eight hours after the enemy's guns opened.

On the 19th of June, Lord Wellington reviewed the 16th,
which looked as well as at a review on Hounslow Heath.[7]
General Anson arrived from England, and as it was necessary
to relieve part of the Hussars with General Crawford, two
squadrons of the 16th were ordered up. This I heard on
dining at headquarters on the 20th, and that the whole
brigade would have gone up, had General Anson been junior
to Crawford.

June 23rd.

The whole regiment moved up this day about two leagues
to the front. Headquarters went to Povoa del Rey with the
right squadron, and the remainder to adjacents. Captain
Cocks' troop to Moimenteria.

June 24th.

The two right squadrons of the 16th this day proceeded on
their march to relieve the Hussars. We marched through
Pinhel, halting at Valverde, in all four leagues. Major Stanhope had the command; Major Archer, with the headquarters of the regiment, remaining behind.

June 25th.

We marched at daylight, passing the Coã at the bridge of
Almeida. The banks are the most rugged and inaccessible I
ever saw: a handful of men might defend the bridge against
any force. Almeida is an irregular work, in tolerable repair. It

7 The appearance of the 16th was good in comparison to what it had
been; but looking in the condition of horses in England, this is perhaps
saying too much – our appearance was good. [WT]

is garrisoned by one regiment of the Portuguese line, the 24th, and two of Militia, with Colonel Cox, a British officer in the Portuguese service, for its governor.

Our route took us to La Alameida, the first village in Spain, two leagues from Almeida and three from Valverde. On our entering the village an order arrived to hasten on to Gallegos, the enemy having driven in our outposts from the other side the Azava, in front of Gallegos. On our arrival at Gallegos, as they had retired and all was quiet, we remained all day on the hill in front of Gallegos, and at night returned to La Alameida. The enemy established their piquets on one side the Azava and Agueda, with ours on the opposite bank. One of the enemy's powder waggons blew up through a shell from the town falling into it; the explosion was seen by us as far back on the march as between Almeida and La Alameida. The enemy's guns opened against the town.

June 26th.

We marched from La Alameida so as to arrive at Gallegos by daybreak, and when the piquets were relieved, occupied the quarters which the two squadrons of Hussars had left in the village of Gallegos.

Brigadier-General Crawford had the command of this advanced corps, consisting as follows: –

43rd Regiment.
52nd Regiment.
95th Regiment.
1st $\Big\}$ Portuguese Cačadores.
3rd
Captain Ross' brigade of Horse Artillery.
2 squadrons 16th Light Dragoons.
2 squadrons 1st Hussars, K.G.L.

There were besides about 4,000 Spanish Infantry in the village on the right, with Don Juliano de Sanchez's Guerrillas, about 200.

Piquets of infantry and cavalry occupied the line of the Azava from the right as far as Carpio, to its junction with the

Agueda, and on that river at the ford of Molleno de Floris. General Crawford's headquarters with his infantry were in Gallegos; the Caçadores encamped on the hill on the right of Gallegos, opposite Carpio. Two squadrons of the 16th, with one of the Hussars, in Gallegos; the other detached to Villa de Puerca, a league to the left, watching the passes of Barba de Puerca, and the others up to our chain of posts.[8]

From the Azava to Gallegos is one short league, and two from that river to Ciudad Rodrigo. The enemy have about 8,000 men over the Agueda, which makes us particularly on the alert. We never unsaddle excepting in the evening, merely to clean the horses; and at night the men sleep in their appointments, with their bridle reins in their hands, ready to turn out in an instant. At two in the morning, the whole turn out and remain on their alarm ground until the piquets relieved, come in, and all is quiet.

The firing both from the town and enemy's batteries was very brisk. It begins before daylight, ceases in the heat of the day, and then again at night.

I was much struck with the difference between the Spaniards and Portuguese; and though from Val de la Meda to La Alameida (the two frontier villages of Spain and Portugal) is only one league, the difference in manners, customs, dress, and language is as great as in nations thousands of leagues distant. The Spaniards are particularly clean in their dress as to outward appearance and houses, each cottage affording one good room, with a small recess or two, large enough for a bed. Their floors are generally of a hard earth, with one small window, generally to the north or west, which in summer is particularly adapted for so warm a climate. The chairs, or rather stools, are as clean as hands can make them, and the walls kept constantly white-washed. In their persons they are not so clean, but in this respect far before the Portuguese.

8 This was the best conducted, most regular chain of posts I saw during the whole war; 1814 this written. [WT]

June 27th.

The 16th, this day, took their share of the duty. The three squadrons found four officers' piquets along the chain of posts. Right piquet at Carpio Ford, an officer, serjeant, and two corporals, and eighteen men supported by infantry at night.

The Mill Ford, an officer and eighteen, sergeant and corporal.

Marialva Bridge; the same, with infantry.

Molleno de Floris (on the Agueda), an officer and twelve of cavalry, with an officer and twenty of infantry.

There was a captain of the cavalry piquets who remained at night at the Mill Ford, with a field officer of the day, who visited the chain of posts without remaining out at night. Two guns were out night and day, ready to support the piquets.

June 28th.

I, this morning, mounted my first piquet, relieving an officer of the Hussars, on the right at Carpio Ford.

The enemy had kept a large force of cavalry in and near the village of Carpio from the time they drove us over the Azava until yesterday, when it was removed. They wished, by this appearance, to make us abandon our line of posts; and on our not doing so, thought us stronger than we were.

June 29th.

The fire at Rodrigo was very heavy this morning. I was relieved at daylight. All remained as usual. We had one alert in the course of this day, but soon turned in, as it was nothing more than one of the enemy's generals visiting their outposts, which may be a pleasant ride for them, though if they would not move their troops it would save us much unnecessary trouble.

June 30th.

General Crawford, with the infantry and four guns, retired to La Alameida, leaving Lieutenant-Colonel Arenschildt of the Hussars, with the three squadrons and two guns, in Gallegos.

The enemy, soon after daylight, brought two regiments of infantry and two guns to the village of Marialva, not a quarter of a mile from the bridge. This turned us out, and it was long before it was known they intended to leave them there. This, with the infantry having left us, makes our situation particularly nice, though perhaps we can get away the better alone; and as we must run whenever they come, we have less to risk.

Our baggage went with the infantry.

The besieging army consists of the 6th Corps d'Armée under Marshal Ney, Duc d'Elchinghen, and of the 8th, under Marshal Junot, Duc d'Abrantés.

The whole amounting to 45,000 men. Massena superintends the whole operation.

The town has a garrison of from four to five thousand Spaniards.

July 1st.

Mounted piquet at Molleno de Floris, relieving Lieutenant Alexander of the 16th. The piquet consisted of twelve men, finding at night three double videttes; so that when the relief was out, he had only the sergeant left with himself. The relief missed its way, and he, conceiving they were taken, came and *reported himself* that the enemy had passed the Agueda. This created much confusion, and on Captain Cocks' going up to the piquet (as the officer on duty), he found the corporal returned with his six men and all quiet. Alexander was put under arrest by General Crawford. In consequence of this I had six more men sent me. Considerable fire of small arms nearly the whole night at Rodrigo.

July 2nd.

I was this morning relieved as usual, all quiet. On my arrival at Gallegos I found the troops formed in rear of the town in consequence of the enemy having pushed a force close to the Azava, apparently with a view to crossing. They remained there for two hours, and retired again, when we turned in to our quarters. We were on duty almost every other night.

July 3rd.

Mounted piquet this morning at the bridge of Marialva. The enemy approached close to the bridge, and by passing some light infantry down the opposite banks, attempted to remove the cars from off the bridge. At the same time their cavalry mounted for foraging, and their infantry got under arms; through this, I reported that the enemy had an intention of passing, and the troops in Gallegos turned out. At night all remained quiet. It was feared I had at first made a hasty report; but I was fully justified in sending word.

July 4th.

The enemy this morning half an hour before daylight passed the ford close to Marialva with two hundred cavalry as an advance, driving in my piquet at a gallop; they were close at our heels for two miles, we firing as much as we could to give the other piquets notice, and cutting at them as they came up to us. I saw a light go down their line as if they were counting men in their ranks on the opposite side the river. I mounted my men (which was fortunate), as they came on at a gallop, and I had some difficulty in getting all away. It was just grey in the morning when they came on. Sergeant Little was the sergeant of the piquet; and in order to keep himself and the men on the alert, he sang nearly the whole night, and behaved very well in retiring.

The troops at Gallegos were turned out on their alarm ground, which checked the enemy on the hill above, where they waited for their force to come up; by that means allowing time for our piquets on the right to come in. The enemy showed four regiments of cavalry on the heights, which caused us to retire in rear of Gallegos, placing our skirmishers on the brook and ravine lineable with the village. The enemy were kept in check some time by this, assisted by the two guns left with us, and allowed time for us to get everything clear away and retire gradually on the La Alameida road, forming behind the bridge and defile, a mile from Gallegos. Here the enemy, perceiving it our intention to withdraw over the brook, and that the greater part was already over, made a dash at our rear skirmishers, who were withdrawn in good order by Captain Krauchenburgh of the Hussars; and we, having allowed a certain number to pass the bridge, charged them back with great success. Two French officers, leading their men, behaved most gallantly, and were killed on the bridge. This success did not retard their advance one moment, for on our right they kept advancing with two regiments, and we remained rather too long. For the last half-mile we were obliged to gallop, with the French dragoons close at our heels, and formed in rear of the infantry, which was drawn up in line in front of the village La Alameida, and received the enemy with a volley which completely checked them, and six guns opening, allowed the infantry to retire quietly over the Duos Casas on Port Conception, leaving the cavalry on the plain near La Alameida. Thus ended the day's business. The enemy lost at the affair at the bridge, and from the well-directed fire of our guns, nearly fifty; our loss, Hussars, one man killed, three wounded – two horses wounded. The 16th lost one man, two horses wounded; had they brought guns, we should probably have suffered equally. This was the first time the Portuguese troops were engaged, and they behaved well. Like all, when first engaged, they were too quick with their fire.

The Light Division encamped near Val de la Mula, the 16th and Hussars on the plain between that and La Alameida, with our piquets extending from Fuentes de Onoro on the right to Aldea del Obispo on the left. The 14th Light Dragoons here joined General Crawford, taking the duty on the left.

The weather was extremely hot, and we were placed in the open plain without a tree to shade us.

The whole day's work took place in the midst of the most beautiful wheat ever seen, with which the plain about Gallegos is covered. We have now left that abundant country, and see nothing but rye. It reached nearly to our knees as we rode through it, and the grain flew out at every step.

The duty at Gallegos was very severe. Every morning before 3 a.m. on the alarm ground, and the subalterns were nearly every other night on piquet. When off duty in the daytime, we had so many alerts that little rest could be had. The evenings, from the heat of the weather, were the pleasantest part of the day, and at first we did not lie down so soon as we ought, considering the early hour we turned out. We soon learnt to sleep in the day or at any time – never undressed – and at night all the horses were bridled up, the men sleeping at their heads, and the officers of each troop close to their horses altogether.

On the commissary of the Light Division complaining to Lord Wellington that General Crawford had told him he would have him hung if the supplies for the Division were not produced by a certain time, Lord Wellington replied, "Then I advise you to produce them, for he is quite certain to do it!"

July 5th.

Retired this day over the Touron, the river which separates the two countries, encamping in a small wood to the right of Val de la Mula. Three squadrons of the 14th came into our camp; their fourth occupied Aldea del Obispo. We found three officers' piquets – one near Fuentes de Onoro, one at the bridge near La Alameida, and the third on the main road in the wood leading from that village to Fort Concepcion, of the same strength as on the Azava.

Very little firing for the two last days at Rodrigo; the enemy are said to be short of ammunition.

July 7th.

Mounted on the Ford piquet, the one on the main road to La Alameida. In the evening General Crawford went with the cavalry to take some of the enemy's dragoons near Barquilla. They had been in the morning, but retired before he got there. The troops returned to their camp ground after dark. On the 9th the firing at Rodrigo was continued through the whole of the day, and so on the 10th until 4 p.m., when it entirely ceased.

At 10 on the night of the 10th, three squadrons of the 14th, two of the 16th, and one of the Hussars, marched from their camp to La Alameida, then turning to the left assembled in a hollow a mile from Villa de Puerca, about half an hour before daylight. We were concealed in a hollow, and were not perceived by the enemy on our march. At daylight the general went forward alone, and shortly returned, moving us at a trot in an open column of divisions, on the village; left in front. We were a little delayed and broken in crossing a defile close to the village, and the squadron of Hussars in front charged a square of the enemy's infantry of about 300. The infantry remained firm, and the Hussars having received their fire from the front side, opened out, passing right and left. The 16th were ordered to form line to the left, and pursue some cavalry near Barquilla. This we did, and secured them all, they laying down their arms on our approach. We made two officers and thirty dragoons prisoners. During this, General Crawford halted a squadron of the 14th, and ordered them to charge the infantry. They were led by Colonel Talbot in the most gallant manner; the dragoons rode up to the bayonets, and Talbot fell in the enemy's ranks, shot through the body. The charge, however, failed; and our general, in the room of carrying it at all risks, ordered the troops to retire. The detached squadron of Hussars that had been in Villa de Cerva made its appearance in the direction the enemy were expected in; and the 14th, also coming from Villa de Puerca to Barquilla, were likewise mistaken for the enemy. In short, never was a business so badly managed. In the first place, had we shown our force, their infantry would have laid down their arms; but from the hurry and confusion in which we attacked, had they surrendered, we must have ridden over them. They beat us off once; and then, in the place of attacking each face with a squadron, we sent on one squadron by itself, which did all it could, but without success, and the enemy's infantry got clear away to Cismiero. We lost: –

14th Light Dragoons: 1 lieutenant-colonel, 1 quarter-master, 6 men, 13 horses, killed.

16th Light Dragoons: 1 man killed, one man wounded, 2 horses killed.

1st Hussars: 13 men wounded, 13 horses killed.

The charge was made in a scrambling manner. There were likewise two guns within a mile of the place, which ought to have been brought up. The French very justly made a flaming despatch. Their detachment should never have been allowed to go back to tell the story.

We followed the Hussars in their charge. I heard the fire from the enemy's infantry; but such was the haste with which the attack was conducted, that had it not been for the whizzing of the shot, I should not have known we were under fire, not seeing where the enemy stood.

To each of the cavalry piquets one of infantry had been added, and the enemy patrolled down to the bridge of La Alameida; finding our posts as usual they retired. We got to our encampment about 8 a.m., and the troops having been out all night, the piquets did not relieve before three in the afternoon, when I mounted on the right. It was with great difficulty I could keep awake.

Ciudad Rodrigo surrendered last night at 6 p.m., with the honours of war, after a most gallant defence of fifteen days from the enemy's batteries opening, and twenty-five from the opening of the trenches. The garrison were marched off prisoners of war to France. The enemy pushed their approaches to the crest of the glacis, when the governor was summoned, and the town surrendered.

July 12th.

I was this morning relieved at the usual hour by a sergeant and twelve; this was a new arrangement. Through the Spanish cavalry having left Fuentes de Onoro, an officer was ordered there.

July 13th.

The enemy showed a considerable force of cavalry on the right, between La Alameida and Fuentes. We assembled on our alarm ground in consequence, but soon returned again to our bivouac. We had been so long in this bivouac that we made huts for ourselves, many of the men doing the same.

July 14th.

Mounted piquet this morning on the ford; all quiet. The enemy, as yet, had not shown the least disposition to advance. Since the town has surrendered, they have almost been quieter than before.

July 17th.

The 16th and Hussars retired to San Padro, leaving the 14th at Val de la Mula, and our piquets keeping their former line. The enemy having pushed on toward Nava del Rey and close to our right piquet, it became necessary to protect the main road running to Almeida through San Padro.

July 18th.

Mounted on the Ford piquet. The enemy during the day sent many patrols down in front of La Alameida, close to my videttes.

July 19th.

At 4 this morning I was relieved by Lieutenant Hay[9] of the 16th, for the purpose of going on a detached party with Captain Cocks. The right piquet was driven in from Fuentes to Villa Formosa, which delayed our march. The enemy retired about 9 a.m.; and at 10 we marched, our party consisting of thirty men from our own troop. We halted for the night in Villa Mayor, three leagues from San Padro, and one from the Coã. We here found Lieutenant Gwin of the 14th, who, in the morning, joined his regiment. Twelve men were detached to the right to Cornet Whych of the 1st

9 Of Dunse Castle, Berwick. [WT]

Hussars, who had been out for some time, and now under Captain Cocks. The enemy have not made any movement of consequence, confining themselves to patrolling into Naver de Aver and the adjacent villages.

July 22nd.

The distance was so great to communicate with General Crawford that the party moved to Mallihuda Sorda, one league to the left. The enemy's patrols came close to the village, and at night we bivouacked in its rear.

The enemy yesterday drove in our piquets from the line of the Dos Casas; and Fort Conception was blown up at three explosions. It was effectually done. Small parties like the one we are now on are of great service by way of gaining information. They should never attempt any operation by way of attacking the enemy's parties.

The enemy this day pushed our advance, under General Crawford, over the Coã. He had been a long time at this advanced duty, and was well aware that, on the army uniting, so great a command would fall from him. He was anxious to do something, and determined on a fight at the Coã. The enemy showed themselves in force early in the morning in front of San Padro, and on the plain near Fort Concepcion. There was time enough to have got the cavalry clear away; they waited till 10 a.m., when the enemy advanced in such force with their cavalry that ours were obliged to pass the bridge of Almeida in a hurry, their light troops, infantry, having come up, and being engaged with our light infantry.

Considerable confusion took place at the bridge, and half of the 43rd, under Major M'Leod, charged the enemy's advance in the most gallant manner, and by that means secured the safe retreat of the remainder.

The infantry having got all clear over the bridge, took up a position on the left bank of the river, and the enemy attempted twice to force its passage. In each attempt they failed, the division keeping its ground. The enemy brought fresh troops down every half-hour, and from their numbers suffered a good deal from our artillery, etc. The affair was a very sharp one, the fire not ceasing till 4 p.m., when, on our ceasing, the enemy did the same. We lost Lieutenant-Colonel Hull of the 43rd, who had joined from England the day before, with fifteen other officers, killed and wounded. The infantry then retired nearly as far back as Celorico, the 3rd Division being withdrawn from Pinhel. Sir Stapleton with the cavalry took the outposts.

Lord W. was much displeased with Crawford for the last affair, though I consider him the best outpost officer in the army.

July 24th.

The party moved back to Villa Mayor. The enemy having driven our advanced corps over the Coã, pushed troops over the river by the bridges at Almeida and Castello Bom. This rendered our situation not safe; and from reports of the advance of troops on our right, Captain Cocks, on the night of the 25th, crossed the Coã at the Ponte Sequeiros, a league from Villa Mayor, and occupied the village of Sardiera, a league on the other side. The enemy's patrols coming near, we did not remain long quiet, and occupied a high hill close to the village, on the top of which there is the convent of Nossa Senhora do Monte, where we were perfectly safe, having a view of the whole country. From the orderlies sent with reports to General Crawford, and patrols out, the party was reduced to four men, and a piquet from the 1st (Royal) Dragoons, belonging to General Slade's brigade, being sent to the point we occupied, it allowed us to go quietly into the village of Richoso, half a league in the rear.

Two patrols, of each two men, from our party were attacked by peasants – one in the village of Marmeliero, on the right, and the other in Richoso, close to our front. In Marmeliero they shot Williams with slugs in seven places, obliging his comrade to make away for his own safety. On Captain Cocks' going there he found the dragoon in the hands of the principal people of the village, who had taken care of him, and though wounded so severely, not in immediate danger; he was brought into the camp. At Richoso they shot Thompson through the body, and kept the dragoon of the Royals with them, tied the whole day to a tree, releasing him in the evening, when he returned to us, reporting what had happened. Captain Cocks, with the party, went out, found Thompson lying amongst the rocks dreadfully bruised with stones, and shot through the lungs. He was brought home, and will never again be fit for service.

Williams recovered; Thompson was invalided, and sent to England. The affairs were reported to General Cole in Guarda, and so on to Lord Wellington, who said he would burn the villages, though nothing was ever done.

The enemy have established their posts for the siege of Almeida, and have broken ground before the place. They subsist very much (the corps in advance) by the plunder they get in the villages between us and their posts, which are all nearly deserted by the inhabitants. The people, finding their parties do not consist of above one hundred men, have collected all their arms and assembled in bodies of 150 round about us. The country is particularly adapted for this, affording perfect shelter in the rocks, always a retreat from cavalry, and with people knowing the country it is impossible for troops to get at them. On the 14th, Captain Cocks called in his party under Weych, he being ordered to join his regiment.

August 16th.

All the peasants collected this day for the purpose of destroying the mills on the Coã, which the enemy made use of to grind their bread. We took the party to prevent any small patrol of the enemy's annoying them, and went to Misquitella on the banks of the river. The peasantry did not like going near the mills, where there were a few of the enemy. They commenced a fire from the rocks, when three French infantry ran out and got away; then the boldest ventured down, and said they had completely destroyed the mill. Five deserters this day came to us on the banks of the Coã. They say they are badly supplied, and that if the peasants would not hurt them, desertion would be more general. We hear a few shots daily from Almeida at the enemy in their trenches. From the nature of the ground the French do not make much progress, being obliged to carry on their whole work above ground, by means of fascines and gabions. Our communication by telegraphs is kept up from Freixedas.

August 23rd.

Captain Cocks marched at night to surprise a French piquet near Misquitella. We were not able to find their lights, and returned at daybreak to our camp. Cocks is anxious to do something, though night expeditions seldom answer; and should we fall in with infantry, and lose two or three men, a whole piquet taken would not repay the loss. We had been the night before and saw their fires, and had they been lighted should have seen them, as I conceive we advanced in a right direction. We had only a couple of men with us the night before.

August 26th.

The party again moved on the same ground after a plundering party of the enemy's, which had been in the habit of passing through the villages in front of their piquets; they had been earlier than usual, and had retired. We patrolled up to their piquet, which left its post and all their bread, which we got; we caused them to light their beacon, and then returned to our camp. We saw the enemy's guns firing on the town, which was the first certain information we had of their batteries having opened, which they did yesterday.

August 27th.

The party this day moved up from the old encampment to the hill of Nossa Senhora do Monte. The sergeant of Hussars coming off piquet reported having heard in the night an explosion towards Almeida.

August 28th.

General Cole ordered us back to our former ground, as the explosion heard was the blowing up of the magazine in Almeida, and the town in consequence having capitulated with the honours of war. The two Militia regiments were sent back to their homes, having taken their oaths not to fight again against the French. The 24th of the line, with the governor, was marched to France. General Cole, with his light companies, remained in Guarda. The division moved back to Prados, two leagues in the mountains, headquarters retired to Gouvea, and the whole of the infantry to the rear of Celorico. It rained hard the whole night; we put up in some houses close to the camp.

August 29th.

General Cole ordered us to Joe Bugal to watch the main road from Almeida to Guarda. This day month we marched to the ground we now left. It was a most excellent camp, the trees affording capital shade; and from the length of time we had been there, each man had a good hut, and the encampment wore the appearance of a small village. We were much safer from any sudden attack; the men and horses both continued healthy from having plenty to eat and something to employ themselves with. The men got as much rye-bread, mutton, potatoes, and wheatflour from the adjacent mills as they wanted, and the horses as much rye in the ear and thrashed as they could eat, and now and then some wheat nearly ripe. Cocks and myself had nothing with us but a change of linen, a pot to boil potatoes, and the same to make coffee in, with a frying pan, which were carried on his lead horse. We never wanted for a single article excepting wheat-bread, which failed us occasionally, and with a person not accustomed to rye, it does not agree. We could always march in five minutes, never slept out of our clothes, and never enjoyed better health; half-past two in the morning was the hour we got up.

August 30th.

We were ordered from Joe Bugal to the right on the

Sabugal road, the enemy having pushed their troops to that place. The 2nd corps of the army of Portugal had moved from their cantonments on the Tagus up to Pena Maçor, and it was not known whether the troops in Sabugal had come from thence or from either of the other two corps employed against Almeida. We rather thought from the second.
Sept. 2nd.

At 2 this day, the beacon at Guarda was set on fire, and our party, with two squadrons of the Royals, all marched up the hill into the town. The light companies and Royals left Guarda under General Cole for Prados, leaving us in the town. We slept in the streets, not thinking it safe to put under cover. From lighting the beacon, several houses had taken fire; and there not being an inhabitant in the town, two or three were burnt down. I was too tired to get up and see the fire.
Sept. 3rd.

We occupied the Bishop's Palace this morning, from which few things had been removed and many left to the mercy of the enemy; we saved a considerable quantity of wine, and a few other useful things to a soldier. The move from Guarda had been occasioned by the enemy's pushing back our piquets near Freixedas, which was only a reconnoissance. General Cole ordered us from Guarda to Prados, where we halted, and for the first time since we went up to Gallegos, slept without the fear of being turned out.

We left a sergeant of the Hussars with four men, who patrolled into Guarda every morning from the small village he was in, one league from the place.
Sept. 5th.

General Cole went to the neighbourhood of Gouvea, and our party was under Sir Stapleton, whose headquarters were at Celorico. He ordered Cocks back to Guarda with fourteen men, leaving me at Prados with the remainder. On the 6th I sent ten men to reinforce Cocks, and Lieutenant Badcock of the 14th having joined him, I marched to my regiment at

Misquitella and adjacents. Captain Cocks' troop was alone in Carvelera.

The enemy remain quiet, preparing for their advance; and the report is, we are to fight at the Ponte Murcella, five leagues on this side Coimbra. The Hussars and the 14th are doing the outpost duty in front of Celorico.

Since our first going up, five men of the 16th have gone over to the enemy; and though each has got into a scrape or lost his character before, yet, to people ignorant of the circumstances, it looks ill. Two of them had broken open a chapel, and feared a general court-martial. One was a man of the name of Jones, from Cocks' troop, and had formerly been of noted bad character.

Sept. 16th.

We all assembled this morning at Villa Cortes. The enemy pushed back the advance a league on our side of Celorico, a little skirmishing took place, and in the evening the whole was withdrawn to Penhañcos, six leagues from Celorico. Captain Persse of the 14th was taken this day.

Sept. 17th.

The 16th marched a short league to the rear, occupying St. Comba and San Miguel. Our squadron with the left went to San Miguel, the headquarters, with the remainder to Santa Comba. Headquarters of the army last night at Coã, and this day moved a short distance further to the rear.

The enemy's three corps all joined at Celorico, amounting to from 60,000 to 70,000. It was calculated at 65,000 infantry and 4,000 cavalry in three Corps d'Armée, the whole commanded by Massena, Marshal in the French service, and Prince d'Essling.

6th Corps d'Armée: Marshal Ney, Duc d'Elchingen.

8th   "   Marshal Junot, Duc d'Abrantés.

2nd   "   General Regnier.

The enemy have broken the Vizeu road from Celorico, and merely sent patrols after us, as far as San Padro. Captain Cocks remains out with his party, in the neighbourhood of

Mello, watching the enemy, and had they moved on the Gallicis road, he would have had a fine opportunity of counting their force; as it was, he ascertained to a certainty that they were moving on Vizeu, and sent Lord Wellington the only information he could receive to be relied on from his own outposts.

We here received our new helmets from England, and not before they were wanted. The old ones were completely worn out, and so warped by the sun that the men could scarcely wear them. They are bad things for a soldier, only looking well for a few months; the first rain puts them out of shape. All the silver to the edging comes off with both men and officers, and the sooner we adopt some other headdress the better.

Sept. 18th.

We marched this morning four leagues on the Ponte Murcella road, and encamped.

I here mounted my bay horse (Bob), which I left in charge of Owen of the 16th, and from his neglect I thought I should have lost him.

Sept. 19th and 20th.

Each of these days we did not march above two leagues, and on the 20th encamped in rear of Gallicis, where a remount of fifty-four horses joined us from England. The Hussars remain in our rear near Coã. The whole force of the enemy has gone the Vizeu road.

Lord W. has assembled the army near the Ponte Murcella, which is destroyed. The villages are all deserted by the inhabitants. We want no commissary, finding corn and meat in every village. It rained the whole night of the 20th, and the greatest part of the day.

Sept. 21st.

By this time the whole of the enemy's force had passed the Mondego, and was assembled in the neighbourhood of Vizeu. Lord Wellington crossed with the whole excepting the 2nd Division, which, on Regnier's joining with the 2nd

Corps d'Armée at Celorico, General Hill had marched by the route of Thomar and joined us at Ponte Murcella; he was left at the Ponte. The brigade moved at daylight, the Hussars two or three leagues in our rear. We crossed the Mondego by a good, though rather deep ford, and halted at dark, within a league of Mortiagua. I was on baggage-guard. The march was not more than five leagues, but through crossing the ford and halting for the Heavy Brigade in our front, we were on horseback the whole day.

Sept. 22nd.

We assembled at daylight on the Mortiagua plain, where we found the Light Division with General Pack's Portuguese brigade. The heavy cavalry had been doing the outpost duty for the last three days since the approach of the enemy from Vizeu, and part of Park's brigade had an affair in the town of Santa Combadaõ, in which they behaved very well.

The three light regiments – 14th, 16th, and 1st Hussars – were ordered to relieve them. Our squadron of the 16th went on duty. Our piquets were along the banks of the Cris, and the bridges destroyed. I remained with the inlying piquet in front of Mortiagua. The enemy made several movements towards our piquets, but not across the river. We were on the alert the whole day. At night all was quiet.

Sept. 23rd.

Every one expected the enemy to move on this morning. At daylight all was quiet, and the piquets being relieved, we returned to our camp ground on the plain. About 3, the enemy drove back our piquets near to the village of Mortiagua, which General Crawford wished to dispute. Sir Stapleton ordered him out to the rear of the plain, forming the three light regiments as a covering party to him. The enemy contented themselves with the heights above the village, and at night we retired, leaving a squadron from each regiment with the Light Division.

Sept. 24th.

We were the whole of last night in passing the Sierra of

Bosoac[10] about two leagues, through the artillery waggons overturning on our front. There are two divisions near us, occupying the heights, and the remaining ones not far off. Every one talks of our not standing, some of the army (viz., the 1st Division) having gone back as far as Coimbra. The brigade went in the evening to some villages near Bosoac, the headquarters of brigade and regiment, to Moito; Captain Cocks' troop to Val de Mo, a little in advance. Lord Wellington has his headquarters in the convent of Bosoac, where he has been since the 21st.

Sept. 26th.

At 2 p.m. we returned to the ground we had before occupied at the foot of Bosoac. The whole army was in position along the Sierra, and General Hill moved across this day from his ground at the Ponte Murcella. The enemy have closed up their whole force to the hills in front of the position, and a general action is expected. From the nature of our position, I cannot think the enemy will make any serious attack. The descent in places is so steep and great that a person alone cannot, without holding and choosing his ground, get down. I cannot think they will be so imprudent as to make it a general affair. We have 52,000 men, and their superiority is by no means equal to the advantage we have from position. They may calculate that the Portuguese troops, of which the greater part of the army is composed, will run away. I think we have rather above 20,000 English, the remainder Portuguese. The army ran from right to left as follows:–

    2nd Division: Lieutenant-General Hill.

    5th   "   Major-General Leith's Corps.

---

10 Or Sierra do Bussaco. Having captured Ciudad Rodrigo and Almeida, Massena's 66,000-strong army had advanced into the heart of Portugal towards Coimbra. To halt the French line of attack, Wellington gathered the Allied army, totalling some 52,000 men, upon the Sierra do Bussaco, an eight-mile long ridge. The battle of Bussaco was fought on 27th September.

3rd	"	Major-General Picton.
1st	"	Lieutenant-General Sir Brent Spencer.
Light	"	Brigadier-General Crawford.
4th	"	Major-General Cole.

General Anson found one squadron for duty with the Light Division, and the Heavy Brigade one in rear of the 1st Division. All were ordered to stand to their arms before daylight, the troops bivouacked as they stood in position, with their generals at the heads of divisions and brigades. Lord Wellington remained in the wood near the convent in the centre of the line. Every one expected and wished a general attack at daylight. The army is in most beautiful order, and the Portuguese as fine-looking men and as steady under arms as any in the world. The only doubt rests with them; if they do their duty, and the business becomes general there can be no doubt of success.

The 16th, at night, retired a short way for forage, no baggage allowed on the hill, but sent to the rear near Malhada.

Sept. 27th.

The troops at daylight were all under arms, anxiously waiting the enemy's attack. All was quiet for some time, and as there was nothing to delay the enemy that we were aware of, Lord W. ordered patrols to our left, from General Anson's brigade. I was sent on one, and about 9 a.m. got on the hills lineable with our position. I there saw the attack on the Light Division; and on ascertaining that no troops had moved to the left, I returned to the regiment, which I found on the old ground where I had left it.

The enemy made two attacks – one on the left on the Light Division, and the other on the right on the 3rd. That on the left consisted of an advance of about 5,000 men, with a large support in its rear.

The troops came up the hill in the best order possible, suffering a great deal from our light infantry. On their gaining the top, the Light Division stood up, and the 43rd and 52nd moved forward to the charge. The enemy did not stand one moment, and were pushed down in the greatest confusion. The general of brigade, Simon, who led the attack, was taken with 150 men. Their columns suffered much from our artillery during their advance and retreat. Massena saw the attack could not succeed, and halted the support at the foot of the hill.

During this the enemy made another on the 3rd Division; their troops here gained the hill in considerable numbers, and were charged by General Mackinnon's brigade, consisting of the 74th and 88th. As in the other attack they fled in all directions, but from having gained the hill they suffered more in retreat. Very few prisoners were taken, and 700 buried on the spot. The Portuguese brigade of the division was, at first, rather unsteady; but seeing the British move forward, they advanced too, and behaved extremely well. With the Light Division the Caçadores did well, and the day gave the Portuguese confidence in themselves and with the army in general.

These were their two attacks, which completely failed, and in which their loss from our artillery, and their columns being exposed on their advance to our tirailleurs, was great. The remainder of the day was employed by a sharp fire, kept up from the light troops on each side. The enemy said the troops they were engaged with, dressed in blue, were British troops in Portuguese clothing. I have some hopes they will have to continue this notion, and will find the colour of the jacket make no difference in the courage of the soldier. The Portuguese wore blue of the same make as British soldiers. *Sept. 28th.*

The enemy renewed his attack with light troops only at 12 o'clock; their columns were seen moving to our left. At 2 p.m. the army was ordered to cook, and General Anson's brigade to the left to watch the Boialva road. The Heavies were still farther to the left; we bivouacked at night in front of Moito.

The Heavies were on the Boialva road, and we on the one crossing the Sierra to Moito.

Sept. 29th.

We returned at daylight to the ground we had left yesterday near Bosoac; the whole army had moved away in the night, and not a straggler to be seen. General Crawford remained on the hill with a few piquets from his division. The whole of the enemy's force had moved on Boialva, and not a man excepting their wounded to be seen.

From the numbers killed and not buried, and their wounded left on the field, their loss was calculated at 8,000, and by some as many as 10,000. Crawford thought the latter; but from what we afterwards learnt, I conceive 4,000 the outside of their losses. 2,000 wounded were left on the field to the mercy of the peasants. Some were brought by General Crawford to the convent of Bosoac, and the remainder left to the mercy of the inhabitants, and no doubt would be murdered when we left; 2,000 were left dead on the field, the greatest number from artillery.

The enemy pushed on by Boialva, driving back the Heavy Brigade. We retired in consequence near to Mulliada, where the Boialva road and Bosoac join.

The retreat of the Heavy Brigade was made in dreadful confusion; Captain Cocks was present when the enemy advanced.

Return of killed and wounded at Bosoac: —

	Officers.	Men.	
BRITISH LOSS.	5	104	killed.
	35	458	wounded.
	1	30	missing.
PORTUGUESE LOSS.	6	84	killed.
	25	487	wounded.
		20	missing.
	72	1183	
		72	
		1255	Total loss.

After Bosoac (or Busaco) the Portuguese said the English were for the sea, but the Portuguese for land. *Los Ingleses por mar, los Portugeses por terra.*
Sept. 30th.

The Heavy Brigade on the Boialva road mistook some bushes for the enemy, and fired at them for half an hour. We marched through Malliada, and formed with General Slade's brigade in its rear. Here we halted some time, and then moved on to Fornos, in front of which we bivouacked for the night; the two other brigades moved to the rear, and bivouacked on the large plain near Coimbra. The infantry this day passed the Mondego, marching on Leiria. General Hill with his corps passed the Mondego by the ford near Bosoac, and retired on Thomar. The enemy pushed a strong advanced guard close to us; we remained bridled up the whole night in a very unpleasant situation. We ought to have been in its rear, and then men might have rested, and horses been feeding the whole night.

We were in a very improper position, and might easily have been surprised.
Oct. 1st.

We formed at daylight in front of Fornos, and Sir Stapleton ordered General Anson to keep his post until attacked by infantry. I was sent to report to him that it was the case; he delayed some time before he came up, and when he did he found us in such a situation as to order our retreat instantly. The country is as much enclosed as possible, only one road to retire by; the enemy's cavalry and infantry close up engaged with our skirmishers. We first walked, then trotted, and at last galloped, and at this rate went through the village of Fornos, and half a mile further, on to the plain of Coimbra. Our rear was much pressed, and obliged to halt and charge in the lane. We lost two or three men from the fire of their infantry, and Captain Krauchenburgh of the Hussars wounded above the hip, though not dangerously. Nothing ever appeared worse, both to ourselves and the enemy, as they must have seen our confusion.

We then formed on the great Coimbra plain. Our brigade advanced, supported by the other two; viz., Colonel de Grey's and General Slade's. In our front ran a large drain cut across the plain, and impassable, excepting at the bridge in our front. The horse artillery, under Captain Bull, fired at their advance; but on perceiving our situation, they did not move from the enclosures. At 10 a.m., the whole moved off – the Heavy Brigade by a ford a league below ours, General Slade's and ours (which remained to the last) by a ford a league below Coimbra. On seeing us move off, the enemy followed, and their advance came up to the ford just after we got over. They attempted to cross, and were charged back by a squadron of the 16th, with the skirmishers; they then kept up a sharp fire from their dismounted dragoons from the other side, and all of ours having got off, the troops retired to Soure, four leagues from Coimbra. I remained with a troop in the rear, and marched in two hours after the brigade to Soure.

We were a little surprised, at passing the Mondego, to find all our baggage in a village close to its banks, and nearly taken by the enemy. The fact was, it had been forgot; and though sent out of the way fifty times unnecessarily, and when wanted by officers, yet here, when it was known in the morning that we were to retire on Soure, the baggage was delayed so long that it scarcely got there before the troops, and was nearly taken.

From the short notice the people had received from Lord Wellington's proclamation, which was only issued after the retreat from Bosoac was determined on, and could not have been sooner made known, they had not time to remove one half, and many not any of their property. Many cars had been pressed by us for the conveyance of sick and stores, and those people were in consequence left without any mode of conveyance. The whole road was covered with families of the first rank in Coimbra, walking on foot with bundles on their heads. I went into one or two houses, which the people had only left in the morning. We found sheep, turkeys, geese, and fowls in greatest abundance, and table linen, shirts, with every other kind of thing, were left in the houses for the enemy. Not an inhabitant remained behind. A person in Coimbra went back to fetch some gold chains left behind in mistake, and never again saw her family. The enemy did not pass the Mondego, excepting with a few patrols; they occupied and plundered Coimbra. Headquarters this night in Pombal; considerable stores were destroyed in Condatia and some in Coimbra.

This could not have been avoided; for without them, had we thoroughly beat them at Bosoac, and advanced, we should have starved, and there was not time to get them away. They were not collected to any great extent. Those at Condatia were stores, etc., for the artillery, and might have been issued to the passing troops. In Coimbra, biscuit, etc., for the troops, but not three days in the whole.

Oct. 2nd.

Soure, like all other places, is deserted by its inhabitants. The manufactory of hats is left full. Tea, sugar, wine, rum, etc., all left in the houses. It was said the Heavy Brigade got a new set out of Portuguese chapeös (hats). Singularity of Foxall in packing tea in a pair of nankeen small clothes, tying up the legs, and carrying them filled round his neck to bring it to the bivouac. (He was one of the best men in action in the regiment, and killed in my troop in charging infantry at Vitoria, 1813.)

We marched two leagues towards Leiria, encamping; the enemy are a long way in our rear, and have remained near Coimbra, plundering and collecting supplies. Headquarters moved to Leiria.

Oct. 3rd.

Marched three leagues, bivouacking on the Rio de Manda Nilla, two short leagues in front of Leiria, on the main road. The infantry were only passing when we got to our ground, and the Light Division remained near us till evening, when they moved off, leaving the cavalry on the river.

Oct. 4th.

We halted on the ground we occupied yesterday. The infantry continued their march to the rear. A man of the 11th Infantry and Portuguese Infantry, also two of 4th Dragoons, were this day hung in Leiria for plundering. In the evening the enemy advanced to Pombal, and the troops in consequence turned out, though not necessary, and through Major Archer having mistaken the orders sent him. The two men of the 4th Dragoons who were hung in Leiria this day were caught in a chapel plundering by Lord Wellington.

Oct. 5th.

Our piquets were this morning driven in, and a good deal of skirmishing took place on the open ground between our camp ground and Pombal. The enemy came on very rapidly, and gave our piquets and the left squadron of the 16th, under Captain Murray, frequent opportunities of charging. We attacked them several times, taking two officers and ten men. Lieutenant Penrice of the 16th behaved particularly well. He rode close up to a French officer, and so much in advance of his men that the Frenchman thought he was going to surrender, and dropped his sword, when Penrice gave him a wipe over his head. The brigade, on turning out, formed in front of the Rio de Manda Nilla, and, on the enemy's advance, retired through a defile on the other side, leaving the left centre squadron, under Captain Swetenham, to cover our retreat. The enemy pressed hard on our rear, and Captain Swetenham received a slight wound in the thigh. Our squadron, with one of the Hussars, was sent to the left of the road to secure that flank, and were obliged to make good our own retreat out of the road. We came to a defile which was almost impracticable, with the enemy close at hand, firing as we passed. Fortunately all got over, and the enemy being checked by the guns, did not advance through the country towards Leiria without infantry, and we retired to the town by a road to our left. Before our troops passed the Rio de Manda Nilla, the enemy brought up two light guns and killed two men of the 16th. In the course of the day we lost twenty men (our whole loss) in killed, wounded, and prisoners. Amongst the last was Lieutenant Carden of the Royals, who had got into a scrape when near Celorico through admitting flags of truce into our lines, and was anxious to do away with any stigma on his character by his conduct on this day. He was the first in one of the charges, and his horse being shot, was taken. We withdrew everything through Leiria, which was completely plundered by our soldiers, and deserted by its inhabitants. I only saw one person, and that an old woman. (Circumstance of Lieutenant Weyland, 16th, thrashing his farrier, Mic. Mullen, for getting drunk, with the flat of his sword.)

Two Portuguese stragglers this day fell into the enemy's hands; they are the first I have seen on the whole retreat.

The brigade was halted close to the town, and the enemy occupying it with his advanced guard, pushed strong piquets of both infantry and cavalry so close to us, that we were obliged to move. We had been hard at it the whole day, and at night our squadron went on piquet. Headquarters this day left Leiria for Alcobassa. The army here marched by two routes, part moving by the Alcobassa and Chaldas roads, and the other by Rio Mayor direct on the Tagus. The Heavy Brigade moved with the Alcobassa column, General Anson's and Slade's by Rio Mayor, Sir Stapleton with the latter. (General Slade providing wine for the Royal Dragoons, saying, "You must not touch this; it is all for the Royals," – there being enough for half the army.)

Oct. 6th.

Soon after daylight our piquets retired, and being relieved marched three leagues to the rear, encamping to the left of the main road, a league in rear of Cavalhos. Towards evening the enemy drove in our piquets with some skirmishing, and wounded two men of the 16th, one severely. The Royals were sent to support, and the enemy contenting themselves with Cavalhos, all remained quiet for the night.

We formed up in squadrons round our fires, bridled up and ready to mount.

Hay was the officer on piquet on the 3rd; and when he turned out, the enemy coming on, his second man had a turkey on one side of his cloak, two chickens on the other, haversack full of other provisions, and so he attempted to skirmish he soon found he must part with his livestock.

Oct. 7th.

Major-General Slade took the rear guard, and General Anson's brigade marched to the rear of Rio Mayor.

We had a false alarm in the evening; the men threw away their dinners, and baggage was sent off. They had not cooked anything regularly for two days.

Oct. 8th.

It rained nearly the whole night. In the morning the troops moved off for Alquentre in the heaviest rain I ever experienced. The left squadron of the 16th was left in Rio Mayor as a rear guard. We marched and encamped in the rear of Alquentre, two leagues. Generals Cotton, Slade, and Anson, with the troop of horse artillery, were in the village, with the two brigades in its rear. About 2 we heard some shots fired near the village, and Captain Cocks' squadron, being the first for duty, moved down as quickly as possible with the first mounted dragoons we could collect, in all not fifty men. On our way down we met five of the guns coming up in the greatest confusion, some with four, some with six horses to them, having got away how they could. On the other side the village ran a considerable brook, which was not passable excepting at the bridge on the entrance into the town. The enemy had two regiments of cavalry close up, and Captain Murray's people were all withdrawn over the bridge. Our party formed up ready to charge down the street. There was a howitzer and two ammunition waggons without a horse to them, commissariat mules and men in the street in the greatest confusion. The enemy did not long remain idle, and detached two squadrons from the 14th Dragoons into the village; they passed the bridge, driving in Captain Murray's people, and came half-way up the street to where we were formed. The enemy's two squadrons were close to each other, in sixes, completely filling up the street. From the bridge to where we were formed, the street makes a right angle; the head of the column passed the turning, the other squadron in the rear, not seeing how we were formed. In this situation they halted, when we charged them; they instantly went about and wished to retire. There was the greatest noise and confusion with the enemy, their front wishing to get away, and their rear, not seeing what was going on, stood still. They got so close together that it was impossible to get well at them. We took twelve and killed six, driving them over the bridge again, and by this means allowing time for what remained in the town to get clear away. The enemy dismounted their dragoons, and we retired through the town, forming on the heights on the other side. The cavalry retired to Quinta de Toro. Our squadron remained skirmishing with the enemy till dark, and then retired half a league in front of Quinta de Toro, where it remained on piquet, with Captain Linsingen's of the Hussars in our front.

We lost one horse and man wounded in skirmishing after the enemy passed Alquentre, though not one in the affair in the town. The enemy expected to find nothing in the town, and when attacked, made not the least resistance, each striving to get the fastest out of the way.

Much was said on the day's work, and Sir Stapleton was to blame for not attending to the reports sent in by Captain Murray of the enemy's advance, as he had ordered him to retire watching the enemy, but not to skirmish.

It was a dead surprise; and had the French dashed into the town without waiting a moment, they would certainly have got the two guns and some part of the general's baggage.

Lord Tweedale (quarter-master general to the cavalry) put us in rear of the town, and Sir Stapleton (or some of his staff) allowed the artillery to take their harness to pieces to clean it.

Rather a new style of war to place guns in a village, and the troops protecting them a mile in its rear.

Oct. 9th.

It rained nearly incessantly from the time we yesterday left Rio Mayor. We lay down in the middle of the road, it raining nearly the whole night. The enemy did not move till late this day. Nearly the whole way from the Quinta de Toro to Alquentre, the country is open with ravines and bogs running at right angles to the road.

Captain Cocks' squadron was on piquet behind me, and Captain Linsingen's two miles in our front. At 2 p.m. they attacked Captain Linsingen with two regiments of cavalry; they were aware that we had nothing up to support the piquet, and it was their intention to take it. In his rear he had a bit of very bad road to pass, and charged two or three times their advance on the road, to secure his retreat. In these charges he lost nineteen men taken, and several wounded, he himself cut in the arm in different parts, though not severely. They drove him in on our squadron, which was formed behind the bridge nearest the Quinta, and seeing it was his intention to pass, pressed him hard in hopes of taking more of his men. We just allowed the Hussars to pass and then charged, driving them back over the bridge. Farther we could not go, as on getting in the open ground the enemy had people on each of our flanks. We then retired, expecting the Hussars would have been ready to have covered us, as we did them. They could not form in the time, having been so scattered, and on our retiring, the enemy followed in very good style close at our heels; we again charged them, and drove them on the bridge. Again we retired close to the bridge immediately below the Quinta de Toro, and passed the defile over the bridge, forming on the plain beyond, with the remainder of the brigade. In both the charges we took some prisoners, but could only get one away. We lost one man of Captain Belli's troop killed, with four horses from the squadron. The regiment with which we were engaged was the 3rd Hussars, and I never saw their cavalry behave so well.

In retiring the second time I caught my bradoon rein in the appointments of a French Hussar who was dismounted lying on the ground, and cut it just as they were about to make me prisoner. My horse's head was held down to the ground, being caught in his appointments; they were not five yards from me when I cut it. I spurred my horse two or three times in hopes he would break it; this he did not, and I was fortunate in catching the rein fair the first cut, and going through it. I will take care not to go into action with a loose bradoon rein.

On the ground near Quinta de Toro, Sir Stapleton intended to check the enemy, there being only one pass up to it by the bridge and causeway on the main road. This he did for some time with the guns firing a few shots at their cavalry; but their infantry coming up, and getting through the bog up the bank near where we were formed, he was obliged to retire. Had this not been the case, an order which he received from Lord Wellington would have brought us back at night. Our squadron was so much knocked up from the two days' duty, that we were sent to the rear, the horses scarcely able to get along.

On our troops retiring, the enemy passed the Quinta and were about posting their piquets for the night, when Sir Stapleton ordered Captain Cocks (who had remained behind) to attack an advanced party of about forty chasseurs, which was supported by a squadron in its rear. His attack was supported by Captain Ally's squadron of the Hussars.

The enemy did not expect it, and on seeing our troops move forward, their advance retired on the squadron; and the squadron, seeing ours advance, retired likewise, each down the road in no small confusion. The advanced party under Cocks only consisted of twenty men. In his pursuit he secured one lieutenant and twenty-five chasseurs.

The squadron of Hussars that supported him were bringing back the prisoners, and was mistaken by the Royals for the enemy pursuing our men; they charged, and going too far, got into the fire of the enemy's infantry, losing three men killed, and one of the 16th wounded. In the confusion eight men of the Royals got thrown from their horses, and they being loose went to the last camp they had occupied, and therefore fell into the enemy's hands.

The whole was withdrawn at night to Carrigada, which was occupied by Sir Stapleton and Hussars with two squadrons on duty in front. The 16th went about a mile to its rear, and encamped in an olive grove up to the horses' knees in mud; it raining incessantly the whole night, most of the officers got into a wine vault.

One of the men of the Royals, in getting some wine out of the vat, fell in. The grapes were just pressed, and left in that state. In this state the men drank it. The dragoon got into it in the night, was half smothered, and caused great confusion. He, or some other, stole a ham from Colonel Archer, which when the colonel perceived, he made a great row; and what with loss of ham, and dragoon in the vat, we had not a very tranquil night.

On arriving at our bivouac, I saw some Portuguese officers and soldiers in a shed at the back of the wine vault. I gave the alarm that the French were expected, when they turned out in an instant, marched away, and I put myself and horses into the place. My old dragoon (Robinson) had got me a turkey out of a house he passed on the march. We had plucked it coming along, and on my return from seeing the men I found him holding it in the flame of the fire, by legs and wings at a time. He had no wood at hand, and broke up and burnt some cane-bottomed chairs, for the purpose of making a fire, which the Portuguese had brought from an adjacent Quinta to sit upon. I rather reproached him, and the only answer I got was that I should find the turkey very good; we soon finished it.

The rain continued, and from the dreadful night and bad

camp the regiment was in a sad state. We got under cover in Carrigada, and at 12 noon there arrived an order for us to retire within the infantry. We marched to Povoa, passing the right of our position at Alhandra. One squadron, the left centre, remained piquet outside the lines. It rained incessantly the whole day; and thus, for the first time since we left Rio Mayor, was there an opportunity of getting on dry clothes.

Oct. 11th.

Marched this morning to Mafra, three long leagues to the left nearer the sea. From the constant fag on our retreat, the horses were in a low state, and the regiment much in want of shoeing and a little rest.

The whole of the infantry were now in our lines for the protection of Lisbon.[11] They extend from Alhandra on the right to Torres Vedras on the left, and so on to the sea. Headquarters are at Pero Negro. In the rear of the first line there are two others, one in rear of Mafra, and the third close on Lisbon. The greatest part of the army are under canvas, and the weakest point at Sobral is protected by a regular fort in which there is General Pack's brigade of 2,500 Portuguese. Should the enemy carry the first line, he is to keep his fort; the men have cover and a certain stock of provisions. The heavy guns from Fort San Julian have been all brought up with many others (which were at Lisbon) of British. The whole line from left to right is as strong as possible, and all wish for an attack.

The whole brigade with headquarters of the cavalry were in Mafra, which held the whole well. The greatest part of the 16th were put up in the stables and cloisters of the convent. It is an immense pile of building, and erected to surpass in size the Escurial near Madrid. That is the only thing thought of by the Portuguese in all their buildings, and the convent of

11 i.e. the Lines of Torres Vedras, a triple line of fortifications around Lisbon, constructed in great secrecy by Colonel Fletcher, Royal Engineers (RE).

Mafra fully exemplifies it. There is a good library well stocked with books; and though the French army retired through the town after the battle of Vimiera [*sic*], the building was not in the least injured. The monks say they are indebted to Louison for this, who would not allow the soldiery to injure anything.

On the 18th I went with Bence to Lisbon, remained there one day, and returned back on the 20th. The town was as full as possible with the inhabitants from the part which the enemy now possess, and many have passed over to Estremadura Portuguese, south of the Tagus. They all seem to think they have done the best for themselves in leaving their houses; and though most of them are ruined, yet they prefer this to remaining for the enemy. It is a great sacrifice, and much good should result from so great a loss.

The Spaniards from the neighbourhood of Badajos this day passed the Tagus into Lisbon; they are under the Marquis Romana, and come to assist us in the defence of the lines. They are about 12,000 men, regularly armed with English muskets and clothed by us.

Many of the first people in Lisbon have sent away their property to the Brazils, some have gone themselves, and more are going. All wish to get their valuables on board, and should the first line be carried, they will get themselves on board and leave Portugal with the English; the French have their party, but at present they keep quite unknown. I question if their party was ever to be feared, indeed much doubt if they ever had any.

Oct. 22nd.

The route arrived yesterday for the brigade to march and relieve the Heavy Brigade stationed in front of the lines near Torres Vedras. We marched to that place, passed the lines to Ramalhial and Amiel, one league in front. The Heavy Brigade moved to some villages to the left of Torres Vedras, and we took the duty, occupying the two villages.

The enemy's whole force is on the right and centre of our

position, and our army opposite. Torres Vedras is very strong with a Portuguese brigade in the town and port. On the right of the town to the ground occupied by our army the country is nearly inaccessible, and Lord W. calculates that from the notice we shall give him, he can move before they can get troops sufficient to gain any considerable advantage. Should they pass a detachment for the purpose of getting in the pass and town of Torres Vedras before troops could arrive, I conceive the brigade now in the place sufficient to defend it until reinforcements arrive to occupy the place, as it should be for its permanent defence.[12]

Between our outposts and the enemy there is a large Sierra, very steep and the roads bad. To pass artillery over will be no small undertaking; and before any considerable body can march from their present camps to our left, we shall have time sufficient to move how and where we like.

We had one officer's piquet from the brigade on the Cadaval Road, one sergeant looking to the road up the Sierra (or hills), and one more to our left on the Obidos road. The enemy's plundering parties come constantly over the Sierra to the villages near us. Our patrols go up the hills, and for a league on their tops, to ascertain that their camps are in the place they have for some time occupied, and that no considerable body passes our way.

The headquarters of the French are at Alenquer, a town nearly in front of Sobral. The deserters say Massena was employed for the first three days he came down in reconnoitring our position, and considered us too strong to attack. He may think so, and yet not like to give the thing up until he can hear from the Emperor.

A day or two after we got to Ramalhial, I went with four men on the patrol over the Sierra. I had not got half a league on its top, when I met a plundering party of 200 infantry with

12 The 16th are looking better than they have done the whole campaign, and turn out near 400 effective men and horses. – *Captain Cocks' Journal.*

about four file of cavalry. The infantry had half of them arms, the other without to carry provisions. They followed me down to the village of Mashul at the foot of the Sierra, three miles from Ramalhial, where they remained for plunder.

A regiment of the Spanish army had been placed under General Anson; he sent 200 of them to drive the enemy from the village, and the cavalry piquet at the same time went down the road, whilst they moved through the enclosures to the right. Had they not shown themselves so soon, we might have got some prisoners; but they gave the enemy notice, and allowed them time to get away. A few shots were exchanged as the enemy left the village and on ascending the hills. The Spaniards killed one and took another wounded. All the Spanish officers excepting one boy remained behind; and had the men been properly commanded, more might have been done. The Spaniards were the next day relieved by two companies of Portuguese Caçadores and the Militia of Torres Vedras. We were glad of the change.

One troop from each of the regiments were sent to Obidos, four leagues from Ramalhial. They were to assist the recruits at Peneche and Obidos in checking the enemy's plundering parties. The two troops were under Captain Linsingen of the Hussars.

The enemy's parties now not only come to the village at the foot of the Sierra, but likewise pass over the plain in our front towards the sea. We have deserters in occasionally, all agreeing that their troops begin to feel the want of supplies, and are becoming sickly from being encamped without tents in the dreadful weather we have lately had. I am sorry to say desertion is not confined to the French, and since we have been in the lines, many of our infantry have passed over. Whether they think the enemy will gain Lisbon, and that they shall have their share in the plunder, or what is the reason, scarcely any one knows. Seven from the Fuzileers went off in one night, and these from one of the best regiments in the service.

Nov. 6th.

Captain Linsingen of the Hussars being obliged to go to the rear through ill-health, Captain Cocks was sent to relieve him this day with his troop, the one of the 16th detached from the first being the troop in his squadron. He found the detachment in Moito, a village two leagues on this side Obidos, and it was optional in him whether to occupy one place or the other; and finding Moito unsafe for one squadron to occupy, he moved the following day to Obidos.

I was detained at Ramalhial on a court-martial until the 12th, when I joined my troop at Obidos. The town is surrounded by an old wall, extremely high, without a ditch, and perfectly safe against any of the enemy's parties that come for plunder. Major Fenwick (a lieutenant in the 3rd Buffs) has the command of the place, with 250 recruits from the depôt at Peneche, as its garrison. On the advance of the enemy to the lines, the place was destroyed and the guns spiked.

With no small degree of labour he has got the guns up, unspiked them, made platforms, and put the place in a state of defence against any plundering party. We, at night, shut the gates, and have not a dragoon on duty. Major Fenwick has been very successful in taking many of the enemy's plundering parties, and with the French arms has armed many of the peasantry. Through these things he gets most capital information of all that passes, and not a party can come anywhere near Obidos without his knowing of it. The country is full of grain and almost every other supply, which we get in for two or three days at a time.

Nov. 14th.

With 50 dragoons and 200 infantry we went after a plundering party of the enemy's. It had left the village before we got there, and we returned to Obidos in the evening. On the night of the 15th we received an order to be in readiness, and during the night another order arrived to march on the

Quinta de Toro. The enemy left the lines on the night of the 12th, and the whole army is on the move up.

Nov. 16th.

Marched this morning from Obidos to Alquentre, four leagues. The brigade came up to Quinta de Toro, and the enemy having left Alquentre, we put up in the sheds of a tanyard for the night, and were glad of this, as it rained almost incessantly. We took five French infantry, who told us the enemy have retired on Santarem. The parties out had not notice of the move, and numbers are straggling all over the country. (Circumstance of Major Archer and some officers of the 16th sleeping in a room at the Quinta de Toro with a dead Frenchman.)

Nov. 17th.

The brigade came up soon after daylight, marching on the Santarem road from Alquentre, our squadron forming the advance guard. In two leagues we fell in with a sergeant and eight French infantry, who laid down their arms. On passing the village of Almustal we were ordered to halt, and sent out parties right and left after the plundering parties of the enemy. I went with twelve men to the left, and Captain Cocks with as many nearly in the same direction. I fell in at first with five infantry, with a flock of goats and nine asses. On our coming up they surrendered, and I forwarded them with two men to the brigade. I then fell in with thirteen infantry under a sergeant, escorting two mules with some asses laden with Indian corn. They at first seemed inclined to fire, cocking their muskets; but on our riding up, laid them down without a shot. Captain Cocks took twenty.

Sergeant Liddle of Captain Belli's troop, belonging to Cocks' squadron, was sent from Alquentre with four men on patrol round by Rio Mayor. He fell in with an officer and fifteen French infantry, and having followed them for some way, attacked them, when they all surrendered.

Sergeant Baxter was sent on patrol from the brigade with four men to the left. He met with an infantry piquet of the enemy's, stationed in a house with their arms piled in front, and got so near unobserved that he thought he might get to the arms before they could take them up. He galloped forward; they had time to turn out, gave him a volley, wounding one of his men. It was too late to turn back; he persisted in his charge, rode up to the enemy, who laid down their arms, he killing one man. In all, forty-one men and an officer, which number he marched in. It was a most gallant thing; but though he succeeded, he was not justified in attacking them.

Sergeant Nichols, of Captain Cocks' troop, took sixteen infantry with six men, on the right, – though I think they were glad to find an English party to save them from the peasantry.

Sergeant Blood, of Captain Cocks' troop, was sent on patrol to our front, in the direction of Santarem. He got within the enemy's line of piquets, and was surrounded by a troop of dragoons; he cut his way through them, losing Storer, of Captain Cocks' troop, who was made prisoner. We were ordered to march to Santarem, and, should the enemy have left it, to occupy the town. These were the orders in the morning, and on coming up to Almustal we found the enemy in considerable force a little in advance.

On the main Lisbon road to Santarem on the banks of the Tagus, the enemy were followed by the Light Division, and General Slade's brigade. On the division's coming in front of Cortaxo, General Crawford found three regiments of infantry with two of cavalry formed up in front of the bridge, or rather with the bridge to their rear, over the river to Santarem, covering the retreat of their baggage. He waited a short time for our coming up on his left, having given his directions to the troops. During this, Lord Wellington came up and countermanded the whole; and it was said, had the thing taken place, most of those five regiments would have been prisoners, and that Lord W. did not remember the bridge and long causeway in their rear.

We bivouacked on the ground near Almustal. The officers got under cover; the men in camp in most dreadful rainy weather.

Nov. 18th.

Turned out at daylight, waiting in front of the village nearly the whole day. The enemy have withdrawn all their force over the river, defending the bridge with its long causeway with sixteen field pieces. The day was employed in bringing up the infantry on the main road. We bivouacked on the same ground. The weather was very bad.

Nov. 19th.

An order arrived during the night for the brigade to move at 4 a.m. this morning to our left. We passed the Santarem river at a bridge near Coyembrogia, and on coming into the Rio Mayor road to Santarem, turned to our right, passing a branch of the same river at the bridge of Calares, and on passing the high ground and defiles on the other side, formed up about a mile and half in front of the bridge. We were now within six miles of Santarem, and not one from the enemy's outposts.

The orders sent to General Anson were to make with his brigade and General Pack's brigade of Portuguese infantry, which was on its march to join us, a sharp demonstration on the Rio Mayor road, at the same time that the infantry attacked the bridge on the main road. A gun was to be the signal for the troops to move.

We waited until 2 p.m., when an officer from the Heavy Brigade was sent to say the attack on the right was all ready, and that we should move on immediately. General Pack was ready to cross the river; but since morning so much rain had fallen that even the bridge was impassable by which we had crossed in the morning. The 1st Division was to have attacked the main causeway, which had been barricaded, so that only one man could have got over at a time. The hills opposite were lined by troops and artillery, and the division formed up, ready to move on. The gun was fired, and before the troops could move off their ground, all was countermanded. It was said at the time to be through the delay of a brigade of Portuguese guns – there must have been other reasons; and from what one could afterwards learn, it was fortunate the business did not take place. The prisoners and deserters taken said Massena was extremely vexed when he saw it was not our intention to attack. His headquarters were in Santarem with the whole of the 2nd Corps d'Armée.

We took two or three small plundering parties of the enemy's, and with one, three horses and two mules belonging to General de Brigade Savary. No orders reached us of the attack being put off, and we waited on the same ground till dark, when we retired across the bridge of Calares, encamping for the night in an olive grove close to the bridge. It rained the whole of the day.

Nov. 20th.

General Pack, with his brigade, passed the river higher up, and occupied the village of Cozembrigera with a strong piquet in front of the Calares bridge and one in its rear. One squadron of the brigade was on duty on the heights in front. This was a mistake, as the troops were only intended to support the infantry, and should not have passed the bridge.

In the evening the left squadron, 16th, and centre moved to the left into the village of Malhiaquaso for the night, the other two remaining encamped at the bridge. The men had been without bread for three days, and procuring as much wine as they wished in the villages, many got drunk. We, this evening, got half a pound per man. It rained incessantly.

Nov. 21st.

The enemy drove in our piquets in front of the Calares bridge. We barricaded the bridge, establishing our line of posts on the river. General Anson, with two squadrons of the brigade, moved to San Juan de Rebiera.

Nov. 22nd.

All idea of any further attack on the enemy was given up, and orders came for the cantonment of the brigade.

Headquarters brigade, with one squadron from each regiment, San Juan de Rebiera.

Captain Ally's squadron, Hussars

Cocks', 16th } Malhiaquaso.

Captain Murray's, 16th: Rio Mayor.

Captain Ashworth's, 16th: Entre Portas.

Captain Gruben's, Hussars: Village on Calares bridge.

The fourth squadron of Hussars was detached near Cortaxo with the Light Division.

Headquarters of the army are established at Cortaxo, with the whole army (excepting the 5th Division left at Torres Vedras) in the adjacent villages. From the reinforcements which joined the army in the lines, a 6th Division has been added and given to Major-General Campbell.

When at the Ponte de Calares, the men, in an adjacent Quinta, found out some wine, and after drinking nearly to the bottom of one of the large casks, holding three or four pipes of wine, they looked into it and saw a dead peasant, who had been put in by the French. The large casks are cleaned by a person getting into them through a large bung-hole left for that purpose, through which he had been put. We all had some of the wine.

Massena placed his headquarters at Gallega, on the Tagus, but shortly moved them to Torres Novas. Santarem, the key to his position, is occupied by nearly the whole of the 2nd Corps d'Armée. Regnier has his headquarters in Santarem.

The 8th Corps, with Junot's headquarters at Pernes, extends from that to Alkanadie. The 6th is in the rear at Torres Novas and Thomar. The 2nd in Santarem.

The enemy entirely subsist from the country they are in, which obliges them to cover as much space as possible. They have no regular communication with Spain, and their only means of sending despatches is through strong escorts of from 400 to 500 men. These must subsist on the country, and will find each village deserted by its inhabitants.

Colonel Trant, with the Militia of the North, attacked the

enemy in Coimbra, where they had left a small guard under the idea of preserving that place as a depôt for their sick. The enemy had no notice of his approach until he appeared before the town. Their piquet fired a few shots and ran back to the town, when a small body of Portuguese cavalry (twenty to thirty) galloped through, forming on the bridge over the Mondego. The enemy finding their retreat cut off, their effective men laid down their arms. In all, 5,400 prisoners were marched to Oporto. The 5,000 were all sick, and those fit for duty were no more than convalescents. By this we gain the whole country north of Mondego; and with the force Trant has, I should hope he will prevent any parties crossing that river. Those for plunder he may prevent, but not anybody marching as an advance to the army or to any station. *Dec. 15th.*

The enemy, this day, drove in our piquets in front of Rio Mayor, and having plundered the villages, withdrew in the evening. The following day they showed about 1,000 infantry on the heights near Calares bridge. The French officers took off their swords and came down to speak to us, saying their object was only foraging, and that we need not put ourselves to any inconvenience, as they should soon withdraw. They complained much of the way they were going on, and hoped to put an end to the business one way or other. They did not appear to think things went on well for them. They invited us to a play in Santarem they had got up, and we them to horse-races, football, and dog-hunts. The communication was put a stop to by a general order.

The Marquis Romana (commanding the Spanish force with this army) died at Cortaxo. He was a true friend to the cause and to his country; should the time ever come for our again joining the Spaniards, his loss will be much felt.

I went with twenty men from the squadron for forage in front of our piquets, and fell in with a party of the enemy's infantry that was come out for the same purpose.

On seeing my party they made off, and after a chase of two

miles we came up with them, when they surrendered without the least resistance – in all, twenty men, belonging to the 15th Volegeurs. They were native French, and the finest men I have seen. They were so blown with running as scarcely to be able to move.

Dec. 17th.

The squadron of Hussars that had been with General Crawford had joined the brigade, and was stationed at Rio Mayor, and this day Captain Ally's squadron was sent from Malhiaquaso to that post. Two companies of Portuguese Caçadores were likewise sent to Rio Mayor from Alquentre, to which place the 5th Division had moved from Torres Vedras.

Rio Mayor was never safe without infantry, being only two short leagues from Alhinadie, which the enemy occupied in force (when an army does nothing on a large scale, we should always guard against their petty warfare, as the account fills up a despatch), the troops at the time lying idle; and from the time posts have been taken up in these cantonments, the enemy may, and no doubt have gained certain information of everything. Posts should always be moved, as by remaining exactly in the same place the facility of taking them is much increased.

In consequence of the squadron going away, Captain Hay's troop, under Lieutenant Persse, was sent to Malhia-quaso.

Captain Cocks went with thirty men to cut off a party of the enemy's cavalry that had been in the habit of coming for straw to a quinta near As Cabus. They discovered him in time to get away, and he returned unsuccessful.

THE STORMING OF CIUDAD RODRIGO AND BADAJOZ, 1812

Lieutenant William Grattan,
Connaught Rangers (88th Foot)

The Spanish fortress of Ciudad Rodrigo guarded one exit of the "Northern Corridor" between Spain and Portugal, and was disputed several times during the Peninsular War. In July 1810 it fell to the French. A year and half later, on 8 January 1812, Wellington began a siege of the fortress, the taking of which was a necessary preliminary if he was to begin the liberation of Spain. Five divisions took part in the operation, and although General Barrie's French garrison of 1,937 men fought a spirited defence by the 19th the Allies had blasted two breaches in the walls. That evening, the breaches were stormed and the town captured and looted.

With Ciudad Rodrigo taken, Wellington then turned towards the heavily fortified town of Badajoz which guarded the Spanish side of the "Southern Corridor." Some 32,000 Allied troops were deployed in the investment, begun on 16 March. The French garrison commander, General Armand Phillipon, could muster only 4,078 combatants (including some 400 invalids), though these included excellent battalions from the 9th Leger, 38th, 58th, 88th, and 103rd Line, plus two battalions of the

Hesse-Darmstadt regiment. After an Allied volunteer force captured the eastern outpost of Fort Picurina, Wellington was able to concentrate his firepower on the weak south-east wall, which by 6 April was breached in three places. That night, the 4th and Light Division stormed the breaches and Major General Picton's 3rd Division escaladed the castle, while the 5th Division mounted a diversion. Assault after assault failed, with bodies piling up around the walls, but at around 11.30 p.m. Picton managed to capture the castle and at midnight General Leith entered the town from the north-west side. An hour later Phillipon ordered the garrison to retreat across the River Guadiana to Fort San Christobal. He surrendered on terms on 8 April, having lost 1,350 killed and wounded.

Allied losses during the assault were 3,400, plus 1,410 casualties sustained in the preparations for the storming. Ten thousand British troops vented their fury by ransacking the town in a drunken, bloody orgy, and for 29 hours Wellington was unable to gain control of "the scum of the earth." Nevertheless, he now controlled both corridors into Spain and could begin on the road which would lead to Salamanca.

Thomas Grattan joined the Connaught Rangers (the 88th Foot) as ensign on 6 July 1809, and went out to the 1st Battalion in the Peninsula later that year. He fought at Bussaco, Fuentes D'Onoro, El Bodon, before participating in the sieges of both Ciudad Rodrigo and Badajoz, between which he won his lieutenancy. After Badajoz, Grattan fought at Salamanca and Burgos and finally, after four years of near continuous fighting, went home on leave in Spring 1813. His military service ended in 1817, in consequence of the reduction of armed forces in that year. He was a distant relative of the statesman Henry Grattan, "the Irish Demosthenes."

Ciudad Rodrigo stands upon an eminence, on the right bank of the river Agueda, and is difficult of access; it had been, since its occupation by the French, much strengthened by the construction of a redoubt on the hill above St Francisco; some old convents in the suburbs were also turned into defences, and these places no longer presented their original peaceful appearance, but were, in fact, very respectable outworks, and tended much to our annoyance and loss at the commencement of the siege.

To be safe against a *coup-de-main*, Rodrigo would require a force of from five to six thousand troops, and its present garrison did not reckon anything like three thousand bayonets; it was therefore manifest that, notwithstanding the unfavourable time of the year, it must fall if not speedily succoured; yet it would seem that Marshal Marmont[1] took no measures to make a diversion in its favour. Strongly impressed with this state of the matter, our commander saw the advantage he would have over his opponent, by acting with as little delay as possible. Protected by a strong escort, Lord Wellington carefully reconnoitred the town on the 8th; and shortly after dark, three hundred men of the Light Division, headed by Colonel Colborne[2] of the 52nd, were formed for the attack of St Francisco. They were followed by a working party, composed also of men of the Light Division. The storming party, led on by Colonel Colborne, advanced under cover of the night, and were not discovered until they had reached to within a few yards of the redoubt, and our troops rushed on with such impetuosity that the outwork was

1 Marshal Auguste Marmont (1774–1852), duc de Raguse; he succeeded Ney as commander of VI Corps in the Peninsula, and then replaced Massena as commander "Army of Portugal" in May 1811. A wily tactician, he manoeuvred against Wellington's 1812 offensive with great ability, but was decisively beaten at Salamanca, at which he was himself severely wounded. In 1814 he negotiated a truce with the Allies, an act never quite forgiven him. The French colloquial verb to betray, *raguser*, is derived from his title.
2 John Colborne (1778–1863), promoted to lieutenant-colonel in 1809 by Sir John Moore's dying wish at Corunna; KCB 1815; field marshal in 1860.

carried, and the soldiers that defended it put to the sword, before the garrison of Rodrigo thought it in danger; and profiting by the panic with which the enemy were seized, Colonel Colborne caused the works of the redoubt to be razed, completed the first parallel, and rendered our future approaches secure.

The duty in the trenches was carried on by the 1st, 3rd, 4th, and Light Divisions, each taking its separate tour every twenty-four hours. We had no tents or huts of any description, and the ground was covered with snow, nevertheless the soldiers were cheerful, and everything went on well. The fortified convents in the suburbs were respectively carried, and each sortie made by the garrison was immediately repulsed; in some instances our men pursued them to the very *glacis*, and many a fine fellow, carried away by his enthusiasm, died at the muzzles of their cannon.

Every exertion was made to forward the work, so fully were all impressed with its necessity; but notwithstanding the animated exertions of the engineers, and the ready co-operation of the infantry, their progress was at times unavoidably slower than was anticipated. In some instances the soil was so unfavourable, it was next to an impossibility to make head against it; instead of clay or gravel, we frequently met with a vein of rock, and invariably when this occurred our losses were severe, for the pick-axes, coming in contact with the stone, caused sparks to issue that plainly told the enemy where we were, and, as a matter of course, they redoubled their efforts on these points; nevertheless, on the 14th, in the afternoon, we were enabled to open our fire from twenty-two pieces of cannon, superior to those which armed our batteries at Badajoz the year before, inasmuch as the former guns were of brass, while those which we now used were of metal. On this night we established the second parallel, distant only one hundred and fifty yards from the body of the place.

On the 15th the second parallel was in a forward state, and

the approach by sap to the glacis was considerably advanced; the effect also of our fire was such as made us perceive a material alteration in the enemy's mode of replying to it; and it was apparent, that although but seven days before the place, our labours were soon likely to be brought to a termination. The cannonade of the enemy, however, if not as great as at first, was more effective, and our casualties more numerous, for their guns and mortars were directed with a scientific precision that did credit to the men who served them. But every hour proved the visible superiority of our fire over that of the enemy, which at times seemed to be altogether extinguished; and whenever it shone forth with anything like brilliancy, it was but momentary, and might be well likened to some spark of combustible matter, issuing from the interior of a nearly consumed ruin. Wherever danger was greatest, there were our engineers, and it was painful to see their devotedness; on horseback or on foot, under cover or exposed to fire, was to them the same, and their example was followed by the soldiers with an enthusiasm unequalled; in short, it was plain that a few hours would suffice to decide the fate of Ciudad Rodrigo. At this period (the 18th) the 4th Division occupied and performed the duty in the trenches.

Early on the morning of the 19th, the 3rd Division (although not for duty that day) received orders to march to the Convent of La Caridad; and as Lord Wellington was not in the habit of giving us unnecessary marches, we concluded that he intended us the honour of forming one of the corps destined to carry the place. On our march we perceived our old friends and companions, the Light Division, debouching from their cantonments, and the joy expressed by our men when they saw them is not to be described; we were long acquainted, and like horses accustomed to the same harness, we pulled well together. At two o'clock in the afternoon we left La Caridad, and, passing to the rear of the first parallel, formed in column about two gun-shots distant from the main breach. The 4th Division still occupied the works, and it was the general opinion that ours (the 3rd) were to be in reserve. The number of Spaniards, Portuguese, and soldiers' wives in the character of sutlers, was immense, and the neighbourhood, which but a few days before was only an empty plain, now presented the appearance of a vast camp. Wretches of the poorest description hovered round us, in hopes of getting a morsel of food, or of plundering some dead or wounded soldier: their cadaverous countenances expressed a living picture of the greatest want; and it required all our precaution to prevent these miscreants from robbing us the instant we turned our backs from our scanty store of baggage or provisions.

Our bivouac, as may be supposed, presented an animated appearance – groups of soldiers cooking in one place; in another, some dozens collected together, listening to accounts brought from the works by some of their companions whom curiosity had led thither; others relating their past battles to any of the young soldiers who had not as yet come hand-to-hand with a Frenchman; others dancing and singing; officers' servants preparing dinner for their masters; and officers themselves, dressed in whatever way best suited their taste or convenience, mixed with the men, without any distinguishing mark of uniform to denote their rank. The only thing uniform to be discovered amongst a group of between four and five thousand was good conduct and confidence in themselves and their general.

It was now five o'clock in the afternoon, and darkness was approaching fast, yet no order had arrived intimating that we were to take a part in the contest about to be decided. We were in this state of suspense when our attention was attracted by the sound of music; we all stood up, and pressed forward to a ridge, a little in our front, and which separated us from the cause of our movement, but it would be impossible for me to convey an adequate idea of our feelings when we beheld the 43rd Regiment, preceded by their band, going to storm the left breach; they were in the highest spirits, but without the slightest appearance of levity in their demeanour – on the contrary, there was a cast of determined severity thrown over their countenances that expressed in legible characters that they knew the sort of service they were about to perform, and had made up their minds to the issue. They had no knapsacks – their firelocks were slung over their shoulders – their shirt-collars were open, and there was an indescribable *something* about them that at one and the same moment impressed the lookers-on with admiration and awe. In passing us, each officer and soldier stepped out of the ranks for an instant, as he recognised a friend, to press his hand – many for the last time; yet, notwithstanding this animating scene, there was no shouting or huzzaing, no boisterous bravadoing, no unbecoming language; in short, every one seemed to be impressed with the seriousness of the affair entrusted to his charge, and any interchange of words was to this effect: "Well, lads, mind what you're about to-night"; or, "We'll meet in the town by and by"; and other little familiar phrases, all expressive of confidence. The regiment at length passed us, and we stood gazing after it as long as the rear platoon continued in sight: the music grew fainter every moment, until at last it died away altogether; they had no drums, and there was a melting sweetness in the sounds that touched the heart.

The first syllable uttered after this scene was, "And are we to be left behind?" The interrogatory was scarcely put, when the word "Stand to your arms!" answered it. The order was promptly obeyed, and a breathless silence prevailed when our commanding officer, in a few words, announced to us that Lord Wellington had directed our division to carry the grand breach. The soldiers listened to the communication with silent earnestness, and immediately began to disencumber themselves of their knapsacks, which were placed in order by companies and a guard set over them. Each man then began to arrange himself for the combat in such manner as his fancy or the moment would admit of – some by lowering their cartridge-boxes, others by turning theirs to the front in order that they might the more conveniently make use of them; others unclasping their stocks or opening their shirt-collars, and others oiling their bayonets; and more taking leave of their wives and children. This last was an affecting sight, but not so much so as might be expected, because the women, from long habit, were accustomed to scenes of danger, and the order for their husbands to march against the enemy was in their eyes tantamount to a victory; and as the soldier seldom returned without plunder of some sort, the painful suspense which his absence caused was made up by the gaiety which his return was certain to be productive of; or if, unfortunately, he happened to fall, his place was sure to be supplied by some one of the company to which he belonged, so that the women of our army had little cause of alarm on this head. The worst that could happen to them was the chance of being in a state of widowhood for a week.

It was by this time half-past six o'clock, the evening was piercingly cold, and the frost was crisp on the grass; there was a keenness in the air that braced our nerves at least as high as *concert pitch*. We stood quietly to our arms, and told our companies off by files, sections, and sub-divisions; the sergeants called over the rolls – not a man was absent.

It appears it was the wish of General Mackinnon to confer a mark of distinction upon the 88th Regiment, and as it was one of the last acts of his life, I shall mention it. He sent for Major Thompson, who commanded the battalion, and told him it was his wish to have the forlorn hope[3] of the grand breach led on by a subaltern of the 88th Regiment, adding at the same time that, in the event of his surviving, he should be recommended for a company. The Major acknowledged this

3 The van of the storming party, the expression being Anglicized from the Dutch *verloren hope*, "lost party." As Grattan relates, there was no shortgage of volunteers for the "forlorn hope" – effectively a suicide mission – at Ciudad Rodrigo or Badajoz.

mark of the General's favour, and left him folding up some letters he had been writing to his friends in England – this was about twenty minutes before the attack of the breaches. Major Thompson, having called his officers together, briefly told them the wishes of their General; he was about to proceed, when Lieutenant William Mackie (*then senior Lieutenant*) immediately stepped forward, and dropping his sword said, "Major Thompson, I am ready for that service." For once in his life poor old Thompson was affected – Mackie was his own townsman, they had fought together for many years, and when he took hold of his hand and pronounced the words, "God bless you, my boy," his eye filled, his lip quivered, and there was a faltering in his voice which was evidently perceptible to himself, for he instantly resumed his former composure, drew himself up, and gave the word, "Gentlemen, fall in," and at this moment Generals Picton[4] and Mackinnon, accompanied by their respective staffs, made their appearance amongst us.

Long harangues are not necessary to British soldiers, and on this occasion but few words were made use of. Picton said something animating to the different regiments as he passed them, and those of my readers who recollect his deliberate and strong utterance will say with me, that his mode of speaking was indeed very impressive. The address to each was nearly the same, but that delivered by him to the 88th was so characteristic of the General, and so applicable to the men he spoke to, that I shall give it word for word; it was this:–

"Rangers of Connaught! it is not my intention to expend any powder this evening. We'll do this business with the could iron."

I before said the soldiers were silent – so they were, but the man who could be silent after such an address, made in such a

4 Lieutenant-General Sir Thomas Picton (1758–1815); one of Wellington's most able – and moodiest subordinates – he took command of the Third Division in 1810. Killed leading his men at Waterloo.

way, and in such a place, had better have stayed at home. It may be asked what did they do? Why, what would they do, or would any one do, but give the loudest hurrah he was able.

The burst of enthusiasm caused by Picton's address to the Connaught Rangers had scarcely ceased, when the signal-gun announced that the attack was to commence. Generals Picton and Mackinnon dismounted from their horses, and placing themselves at the head of the right brigade, the troops rapidly entered the trenches by sections right in front; the storming party under the command of Major Russell Manners of the 74th heading it, while the forlorn hope, commanded by Lieutenant William Mackie of the 88th, and composed of twenty volunteers from the Connaught Rangers, led the van, followed closely by the 45th, 88th, and 74th British, and the 9th and 21st Portuguese; the 77th and 83rd British, belonging to the left brigade, brought up the rear and completed the dispositions.

While these arrangements were effecting opposite the grand breach, the 5th and 94th, belonging to the left brigade of the 3rd Division, were directed to clear the ramparts and Fausse Braye wall, and the 2nd Regiment of Portuguese Caçadores, commanded by an Irish colonel of the name of O'Toole, was to escalade the curtain to the left of the lesser breach, which was attacked by the Light Division under the command of General Robert Craufurd.

It wanted ten minutes to seven o'clock when these dispositions were completed; the moon occasionally, as the clouds which overcast it passed away, shed a faint ray of light upon the battlements of the fortress, and presented to our view the glittering of the enemy's bayonets as their soldiers stood arrayed upon the ramparts and breach, awaiting our attack; yet, nevertheless, their batteries were silent, and might warrant the supposition to an unobservant spectator that the defence would be but feeble.

The two divisions got clear of the covered way at the same

moment, and each advanced to the attack of their respective points with the utmost regularity. The obstacles which presented themselves to both were nearly the same, but every difficulty, no matter how great, merged into insignificance when placed in the scale of the prize about to be contested. The soldiers were full of ardour, but altogether devoid of that blustering and bravadoing which is truly unworthy of men at such a moment; and it would be difficult to convey an adequate idea of the enthusiastic bravery which animated the troops. A cloud that had for some time before obscured the moon, which was at its full, disappeared altogether, and the countenances of the soldiers were for the first time, since Picton addressed them, visible – they presented a material change. In place of that joyous animation which his fervid and impressive address called forth, a look of severity, bordering on ferocity, had taken its place; and although ferocity is by no means one of the characteristics of the British soldier, there was, most unquestionably, a savage expression in the faces of the men that I had never before witnessed. Such is the difference between the storm of a breach and the fighting a pitched battle.

Once clear of the covered way, and fairly on the plain that separated it from the fortress, the enemy had a full view of all that was passing; their batteries, charged to the muzzle with case-shot, opened a murderous fire upon the columns as they advanced, but nothing could shake the intrepid bravery of the troops. The Light Division soon descended the ditch and gained, although not without a serious struggle, the top of the narrow and difficult breach allotted to them; their gallant General, Robert Craufurd, fell at the head of the 43rd, and his second in command, General Vandeleur, was severely wounded, but there were not wanting others to supply their place; yet these losses, trying as they were to the feelings of the soldiers, in no way damped their ardour, and the brave Light Division carried the left breach at the point of the bayonet. Once established upon the ramparts, they made all the dispositions necessary to ensure their own conquest, as also to render every assistance in their power to the 3rd Division in their attack. They cleared the rampart which separated the lesser from the grand breach, and relieved Picton's division from any anxiety it might have as to its safety on its left flank.

The right brigade, consisting of the 45th, 88th, and 74th, forming the van of the 3rd Division, upon reaching the ditch, to its astonishment, found Major Ridge and Colonel Campbell at the head of the 5th and 94th mounting the Fausse Braye wall. These two regiments, after having performed their task of silencing the fire of the French troops upon the ramparts, with a noble emulation resolved to precede their comrades in the attack of the grand breach. Both parties greeted each other with a cheer, only to be understood by those who have been placed in a similar situation; yet the enemy were in no way daunted by the shout raised by our soldiers – they crowded the breach, and defended it with a bravery that would have made any but troops accustomed to conquer, waver. But the "fighting division" were not the men to be easily turned from their purpose; the breach was speedily mounted, yet, nevertheless, a serious affray took place ere it was gained. A considerable mass of infantry crowned its summit, while in the rear and at each side were stationed men, so placed that they could render every assistance to their comrades at the breach without any great risk to themselves; besides this, two guns of heavy calibre, separated from the breach by a ditch of considerable depth and width, enfiladed it, and as soon as the French infantry were forced from the summit, these guns opened their fire on our troops.

The head of the column had scarcely gained the top, when a discharge of grape cleared the ranks of the three leading battalions, and caused a momentary wavering; at the same instant a frightful explosion near the gun to the left of the breach, which shook the bastion to its foundation, completed the disorder. Mackinnon, at the head of his brigade, was blown into the air. His aide-de-camp, Lieutenant Beresford of the 88th, shared the same fate, and every man on the breach at the moment of the explosion perished. This was unavoidable, because those of the advance, being either killed or wounded, were necessarily flung back upon the troops that followed close upon their footsteps, and there was not a sufficient space for the men who were ready to sustain those placed *hors de combat* to rally. For an instant all was confusion; the blaze of light caused by the explosion resembled a huge meteor, and presented to our sight the havoc which the enemy's fire had caused in our ranks; while from afar the astonished Spaniard viewed for an instant, with horror and dismay, the soldiers of the two nations grappling with each other on the top of the rugged breach which trembled beneath their feet, while the fire of the French artillery played upon our columns with irresistible fury, sweeping from the spot the living and the dead. Amongst the latter was Captain Robert Hardyman and Lieutenant Pearse of the 45th, and many more whose names I cannot recollect. Others were so stunned by the shock, or wounded by the stones which were hurled forth by the explosion, that they were insensible to their situation; of this number I was one, for being close to the magazine when it blew up, I was quite overpowered, and I owed my life to the Sergeant-Major of my regiment, Thorp, who saved me from being trampled to death by our soldiers in their advance, ere I could recover strength sufficient to move forward or protect myself.

The French, animated by this accidental success, hastened once more to the breach which they had abandoned, but the leading regiments of Picton's division, which had been disorganised for the moment by the explosion, rallied, and soon regained its summit, when another discharge from the two flank guns swept away the foremost of those battalions.

There was at this time but one officer alive upon the breach (Major Thomson, of the 74th, acting engineer); he called out to those next to him to seize the gun to the left, which had been so fatal to his companions – but this was a desperate service. The gun was completely cut off from the breach by a deep trench, and soldiers, encumbered with their firelocks, could not pass it in sufficient time to anticipate the next discharge – yet to deliberate was certain death. The French cannoniers, five in number, stood to, and served their gun with as much *sang froid* us if on a parade, and the light which their torches threw forth showed to our men the peril they would have to encounter if they dared to attack a gun so defended; but this was of no avail. Men going to storm a breach generally make up their minds that there is no great probability of their ever returning from it to tell their adventures to their friends; and whether they die at the bottom or top of it, or at the muzzle, or upon the breech of a cannon, is to them pretty nearly the same!

The first who reached the top, after the last discharge, were three of the 88th. Sergeant Pat Brazil – the brave Brazil of the Grenadier company, who saved his captain's life at Busaco – called out to his two companions, Swan and Kelly, to unscrew their bayonets and follow him; the three men passed the trench in a moment, and engaged the French cannoniers hand to hand; a terrific but short combat was the consequence. Swan was the first, and was met by the two gunners on the right of the gun, but, no way daunted, he engaged them, and plunged his bayonet into the breast of one; he was about to repeat the blow upon the other, but before he could disentangle the weapon from his bleeding adversary, the second Frenchman closed upon him, and by a *coup de sabre* severed his left arm from his body a little above the elbow; he fell from the shock, and was on the eve of being massacred, when Kelly, after having scrambled under the gun, rushed onward to succour his comrade. He bayoneted two Frenchmen on the spot, and at this instant Brazil came up; three of the five gunners lay lifeless, while Swan, resting against an ammunition chest, was bleeding to death. It was now equal numbers, two against two, but Brazil in his over-anxiety to engage was near losing his life at the onset; in making a lunge at the man next to him, his foot slipped upon the bloody platform, and he fell forward against his antagonist, but as both rolled under the gun, Brazil felt the socket of his bayonet strike hard against the buttons of the Frenchman's coat. The remaining gunner, in attempting to escape under the carriage from Kelly, was killed by some soldiers of the 5th, who just now reached the top of the breach, and seeing the serious dispute at the gun, pressed forward to the assistance of the three men of the Connaught Rangers.

While this was taking place on the left, the head of the column remounted the breach, and regardless of the cries of their wounded companions, whom they indiscriminately trampled to death, pressed forward in one irregular but heroic mass, and putting every man to death who opposed their progress, forced the enemy from the ramparts at the bayonet's point. Yet the garrison still rallied, and defended the several streets with the most unflinching bravery; nor was it until the musketry of the Light Division was heard in the direction of the Plaza Mayor, that they gave up the contest! but from this moment all regular resistance ceased, and they fled in disorder to the Citadel. There were, nevertheless, several minor combats in the streets, and in many instances the inhabitants fired from the windows, but whether their efforts were directed against us or the French is a point that I do not feel myself competent to decide; be this as it may, many lives were lost on both sides by this circumstance, for the Spaniards, firing without much attention to regularity, killed or wounded indiscriminately all who came within their range.

During a contest of such a nature, kept up in the night, as may be supposed, much was of necessity left to the guidance of the subordinate officers, if not to the soldiers themselves. Each affray in the streets was conducted in the best manner the moment would admit of, and decided more by personal valour than discipline, and in some instances officers as well as privates had to combat with the imperial troops. In one of these encounters Lieutenant George Faris, of the 88th, by an accident so likely to occur in an affair of this kind, separated a little too far from a dozen or so of his regiment, and found himself opposed to a French soldier who, apparently, was similarly placed. It was a curious coincidence, and it would seem as if each felt that he individually was the representative of the country to which he belonged; and had the fate of the two nations hung upon the issue of the combat I am about to describe, it could not have been more heroically contested. The Frenchman fired at and wounded Faris in the thigh, and made a desperate push with his bayonet at his body, but Faris parried the thrust, and the bayonet only lodged in his leg. He saw at a glance the peril of his situation, and that nothing short of a miracle could save him; the odds against him were too great, and if he continued a scientific fight he must inevitably be vanquished. He sprang forward, and, seizing hold of the Frenchman by the collar, a struggle of a most nervous kind took place; in their mutual efforts to gain an advantage they lost their caps, and as they were men of nearly equal strength, it was doubtful what the issue would be. They were so entangled with each other their weapons were of no avail, but Faris at length disengaged himself from the grasp which held him, and he was able to use his sabre; he pushed the Frenchman from him, and ere he could recover himself he laid his head open nearly to the chin. His sword-blade, a heavy, soft, ill-made Portuguese one, was doubled up with the force of the blow, and retained some pieces of the skull and clotted hair! At this moment I reached the spot with about twenty men, composed of different regiments, all being by this time mixed *pell mell* with each other. I ran up to Faris – he was nearly exhausted, but he was safe. The French grenadier lay upon the pavement, while Faris, though tottering from fatigue, held his sword firmly in his grasp, and it was crimson to the hilt. The appearance of the two combatants was frightful! – one lying dead on the ground, the other faint from agitation and loss of blood; but the soldiers loudly applauded him, and the feeling uppermost with them was, that our man had the best of it! It was a shocking sight, but it would be rather a hazardous experiment to begin moralising at such a moment and in such a place.

Those of the garrison who escaped death were made prisoners, and the necessary guards being placed, and everything secured, the troops not selected for duty commenced a very diligent search for those articles which they most fancied, and which they considered themselves entitled to by "right of conquest." I believe on a service such as the present, there is a sort of tacit acknowledgment of this "right"; but be this as it may, a good deal of property most indubitably changed owners on the night of the 19th of January 1812. The conduct of the soldiers, too, within the last hour, had undergone a complete change; before, it was all order and regularity, now it was nothing but licentiousness and confusion – subordination was at an end; plunder and blood was the order of the day, and many an officer on this night was compelled to show that he carried a sabre.

The doors of the houses in a large Spanish town are remarkable for their strength, and resemble those of a prison more than anything else; their locks are of huge dimensions, and it is a most difficult task to force them. The mode adopted by the men of my regiment (the 88th) in this dilemma was as effective as it was novel; the muzzles of a couple of muskets were applied to each side of the keyhole, while a third soldier, fulfilling the functions of an officer, deliberately gave the word, "make ready" – "present" – "fire!" and in an instant the ponderous lock gave way before the combined operations of the three individuals, and doors that rarely opened to the knock of a stranger in Rodrigo, now flew off their hinges to receive the Rangers of Connaught.

The chapels and chandlers' houses were the first captured, in both of which was found a most essential ingredient in the shape of large wax candles; these the soldiers lighted, and commenced their perambulations in search of plunder, and the glare of light which they threw across the faces of the men, as they carried them through the streets, displayed their countenances, which were of that cast that might well terrify the unfortunate inhabitants. Many of the soldiers with their faces scorched by the explosion of the magazine at the grand breach; others with their lips blackened from biting off the ends of their cartridges, more covered with blood, and all looking ferocious, presented a combination sufficient to appeal the stoutest heart.

Scenes of the greatest outrage now took place, and it was pitiable to see groups of the inhabitants half naked in the streets – the females clinging to the officers for protection – while their respective houses were undergoing the strictest scrutiny. Some of the soldiers turned to the wine and spirit houses, where, having drunk sufficiently, they again sallied out in quest of more plunder; others got so intoxicated that they lay in a helpless state in different parts of the town, and lost what they had previously gained, either by the hands of any passing Spaniard, who could venture unobserved to stoop down, or by those of their own companions, who in their wandering surveys happened to recognise a comrade lying with half a dozen silk gowns, or some such thing, wrapped about him. Others wished to attack the different stores, and as there is something marvellously attractive in the very name of a brandy one, it is not to be wondered at that many of our heroes turned not only their thoughts, but their steps also, in the direction in which these houses lay; and from the unsparing hand with which they supplied themselves, it might be imagined they intended to change their habits of life and turn spirit-venders, and that too in the wholesale line!

It was astonishing to see with what rapidity and accuracy these fellows traversed the different parts of the town, and found out the shops and storehouses. A stranger would have supposed they were natives of the place, and it was not until the following morning that I discovered the cause of what was to me before incomprehensible.

In all military movements in a country which an army is not thoroughly acquainted with, (and why not in a large town?) there are no more useful appendages than good guides. Lord Wellington was most particular on this point, and had attached to his army a corps of this description. I suppose it was this knowledge of tactics which suggested to the soldiers the necessity of so wise a precaution; accordingly, every group of individuals was preceded by a Spaniard, who, upon learning the species of plunder wished for by his employers, instantly conducted them to the most favourable ground for their operations. By this means the houses were unfurnished with less confusion than can be supposed; and had it not been for the state of intoxication that some of the young soldiers – mere tyros in the art of sacking a town – had indulged themselves in, it is inconceivable with what facility the city of Ciudad Rodrigo would have been eased of its superfluities. And the *conducteur* himself was not always an idle spectator. Many of these fellows realised something considerable from their more wealthy neighbours, and being also right well paid by the soldiers, who were liberal enough, they found themselves in the morning in far better circumstances than they had been the preceding night, so that all things considered, there were about as many cheerful faces as sad ones. But although the inhabitants were, by this sort of transfer, put more on an equality with each other, the town itself was greatly impoverished. Many things of value were destroyed, but in the hurry so natural to the occasion, many also escaped; besides, our men were as yet young hands in the arcana of plundering a town in that *au fait* manner with which a French army would have done a business of the sort: but they most unquestionably made up for their want of tact by the great inclination they showed to profit by any occasion that offered itself for their improvement.

By some mistake, a large spirit store situated in the Plaza Mayor took fire, and the flames spreading with incredible fury, despite of the exertions of the troops, the building was totally destroyed; but in this instance, like many others which we are obliged to struggle against through life, there was a something that neutralised the disappointment which the loss of so much brandy occasioned the soldiers: the light which shone forth from the building was of material service to them, inasmuch as it tended to facilitate their movements in their excursions for plunder; the heat also was far from disagreeable, for the night was piercingly cold, yet, nevertheless, the soldiers exerted themselves to the utmost to put a stop to this calamity. General Picton was to be seen in the midst of them, encouraging them by his example and presence to make still greater efforts; but all would not do, and floor after floor fell in, until at last it was nothing but a burning heap of ruins.

Some houses were altogether saved from plunder by the interference of the officers, for in several instances the women ran out into the streets, and seizing hold of three or four of us, would force us away to their houses, and by this stroke of political hospitality saved their property. A good supper was then provided, and while all outside was noise and pillage, affairs within went on agreeably enough. These instances were, however, but few.

In the house where I and four other officers remained, we fared remarkably well, and were passing the night greatly to our satisfaction, when we were aroused by a noise like a crash of something heavy falling in the apartment above us. As may be supposed, we did not remain long without seeking to ascertain the cause of this disturbance; the whole party sprang up at once – the family of the house secreting themselves behind the different pieces of furniture, while we, *sabre à la main*, and some with lights, advanced towards the apartment from whence the noise proceeded; but all was silent within. Captain Seton of my corps proposed that the door should be forced, but he had scarcely pronounced the words, when a voice from within called out, not in Spanish or French, but in plain English, with a rich Irish brogue, "Oh, Jasus, is it you, Captain?" On entering we found a man of the Connaught Rangers, belonging to Seton's company, standing before us, so disfigured by soot and filth that it was impossible to recognise his uniform, much less his face – his voice was the only thing recognisable about him, and that only to his Captain; and had it not been for that, he might have passed for one just arrived from the infernal regions, and it may be questioned whether or not the place he had quitted might not be so denominated. It appeared, from the account he gave of himself, that he had been upon a plundering excursion in one of the adjoining houses, the roof of which, like most of those in Rodrigo, was flat; and wishing to have a distinct view of all that was passing in the streets, he took up his position upon the top of the house he had entered, and not paying due attention to where he put his foot, he contrived to get it into the chimney of the house we occupied, and, ere he could resume his centre of gravity, he tumbled headlong down the chimney and caused us all the uneasiness I have been describing. His *tout ensemble* was as extraordinary as his adventure. He had eighteen or twenty pairs of shoes round his waist, and amongst other things a case of trepanning instruments, which he immediately offered as a present to his Captain! Had the grate of this fireplace been what is called in England the "Rumford grate," this poor fellow must have been irretrievably lost to the service, because it is manifest, encumbered as he was, he would have stuck fast, and must inevitably have been suffocated before assistance could be afforded him; but, fortunately for him, the chimney was of sufficient dimensions to admit an elephant to pass down it, and, in truth, one not so constructed would have been altogether too confined for him.

Morning at length began to dawn, and with it the horrors of the previous night's assault were visible. The troops not on guard were directed to quit the town, but this was not a command they obeyed with the same cheerfulness or expedition which they evinced when ordered to enter it; in their eyes it had many attractions still, and, besides, the soldiers had become so unwieldy from the immense burdens they carried, it was scarcely possible for many of them to stir, much less march. However, by degrees the evacuation of the fortress took place, and towards noon it was effected altogether.

The breaches presented a horrid spectacle. The one forced by the Light Division was narrower than the other, and the dead, lying in a smaller compass, looked more numerous than they really were. I walked along the ramparts towards the grand breach, and was examining the effects our fire had produced on the different defences and the buildings in their immediate vicinity, but I had not proceeded far when I was shocked at beholding about a hundred and thirty or forty wounded Frenchmen, lying under one of the bastions and some short distance up a narrow street adjoining it. I descended, and learned that these men had been performing some particular duty in the magazine which blew up and killed General Mackinnon and so many of the 3rd Division. These miserable beings were so burnt that I fear, notwithstanding the considerate attention which was paid to them by our medical officers, none of their lives were preserved. Their uniforms were barely distinguishable, and their swollen heads and limbs gave them a gigantic appearance that was truly terrific; added to this, the gunpowder had so blackened their faces that they looked more like a number of huge negroes than soldiers of an European army. Many of our men hastened to the spot, and with that compassion which truly brave men always feel, rendered them every assistance in their power; some were carried on doors, others in blankets, to the hospitals, and these poor creatures showed by their gestures, for they could not articulate, how truly they appreciated our tender care of them.

At length I reached the grand breach – it was covered with many officers and soldiers; of the former, amongst others, was my old friend Hardyman of the 45th, and Lieutenant William Pearse of the same regiment; there were also two of the 5th whose names I forget, and others whose faces were familiar to me. Hardyman, the once cheerful, gay Bob Hardyman, lay on his back; half of his head was carried away by one of those discharges of grape from the flank guns at the breach which were so destructive to us in our advance; his face was perfect, and even in death presented its wonted cheerfulness. Poor fellow! he died without pain, and regretted by all who knew him; his gaiety of spirit never for an instant forsook him. Up to the moment of the assault he was the same pleasant Bob Hardyman who delighted every one by his anecdotes, and none more than my old corps, although many of his jokes were at our expense. When we were within a short distance of the breach, as we met, he stopped for an instant to shake hands. "What's that you have hanging over your shoulder?" said he, as he espied a canteen of rum which I carried. "A little rum, Bob," said I. "Well," he replied, "I'll change my breath; and take my word for it, that in less than five minutes some of the 'subs' will be scratching a Captain's—, for there will be wigs on the green." He took a mouthful of rum, and taking me by the hand squeezed it affectionately, and in ten minutes afterwards he was a corpse!

The appearance of Pearse was quite different from his companion; ten or a dozen grape-shot pierced his breast, and he lay, or rather sat, beside his friend like one asleep, and his appearance was that of a man upwards of sixty, though his years did not number twenty-five. Hardyman was stripped to his trousers, but Pearse had his uniform on; his epaulettes alone had been plundered. I did not see the body of General Mackinnon, but the place where he fell was easily distinguishable; the vast chasm which the spot presented resembled an excavation in the midst of a quarry. The limbs of those who lost their lives by that fatal explosion, thrown here and there, presented a melancholy picture of the remnants of those brave men whose hearts but a few short hours before beat high in the hope of conquest. It was that kind of scene which arrested the attention of the soldier, and riveted him to the spot; and there were few who, even in the moment of exultation, did not feel deeply as they surveyed the mangled remains of their comrades.

I next turned to the captured gun, so chivalrously taken by the three men of the 88th. The five cannoniers lying across the carriage, or between the spokes of the wheels, showed how bravely they had defended it; yet they lay like men whose death had not been caused by violence; they were naked and bloodless, and the puncture of the bayonet left so small a mark over their hearts, it was discernible only to those who examined the bodies closely.

I turned away from the breach, and scrambled over its rugged face, and the dead which covered it. On reaching the bivouac we had occupied the preceding evening, I learned, with surprise, that our women had been engaged in a contest, if not as dangerous as ours, at least one of no trivial sort. The men left as a guard over the baggage, on hearing the first shot at the trenches, could not withstand the inclination they felt to join their companions; and although this act was creditable to the bravery of the individuals that composed the baggage-guard, it was nigh being fatal to those who survived, or, at least, to such as had anything to lose except their lives, for the wretches that infested our camp attempted to plunder it of all that it possessed, but the women, with a bravery that would not have disgraced those of ancient Rome, defended the post with such valour that those miscreants were obliged to desist, and our baggage was saved in consequence.

We were about to resume our arms when General Picton approached us. Some of the soldiers, who were more than usually elevated in spirits, on his passing them, called out, "Well, General, we gave you a cheer last night; it's your turn now!" The General, smiling, took off his hat, and said, "Here, then, you drunken set of brave rascals, hurrah! we'll soon be at Badajoz!" A shout of confidence followed; we slung our firelocks, the bands played, and we commenced our march for the village of Atalaya in the highest spirits, and in a short time lost sight of a place the capture of which appeared to us like a dream.

The fortress of Ciudad Rodrigo fell on the eleventh day after its investment; and taking into account the season of the year, the difficulty of the means to carry on the operations, and the masterly manner in which Lord Wellington baffled the vigilance of the Duke of Ragusa, the capture of Rodrigo must ever rank as one of the most finished military exploits upon record, and a *chef d'oeuvre* of the art of war. Our loss was equal to that of the enemy; it amounted to about one thousand *hors de combat*, together with three generals; of the garrison but seventeen hundred were made prisoners, the rest being put to the sword.

So soon as my regiment reached the village, I obtained leave to return to Rodrigo, for I was anxious to see in what situation the family were with whom I, in common with my companions, had passed the preceding night. Upon entering the town, I found all in confusion. The troops ordered to occupy it were not any of those which had composed the storming divisions; and although the task of digging graves, and clearing away the rubbish about the breaches, was not an agreeable one, they nevertheless performed it with much cheerfulness; yet, in some instances, the soldiers levied contributions upon the unfortunate inhabitants, – light ones it is true, and for the reason that little remained with them to give, or, more properly speaking, withhold. But the Provost-Marshal was so active in his vocation that this calamity was soon put a stop to, and the miserable people, who were in many instances in a state of nudity, could without risk venture to send to their more fortunate neighbours for a supply of those articles of dress which decency required. Upon reaching the house I had rested in the evening before, I was rejoiced to find it uninjured, and the poor people, upon once more seeing me, almost suffocated me with their caresses, and their expressions of gratitude knew no bounds for our having preserved their house from pillage.

Having satisfied myself that my *padrona* and her daughters had escaped molestation, I took my leave of them, and once more visited the large breach. On my way thither I saw the French garrison preparing to march, under an escort of Portuguese troops, to the fortress of Almeida; they were a fine-looking body of men, and seemed right well pleased to get off so quietly; they counted about eighteen hundred, and were all that escaped unhurt of the garrison. At the breach there were still several wounded men, who had not been removed to the hospitals; amongst them was a fellow of my own corps, of the name of Doogan; he was badly wounded in the thigh, the bone of which was so shattered as to protrude through the skin. Near him lay a French soldier, shot through the body, quite frantic from pain, and in the agonies of death. The moment Doogan observed me, he called out most lustily, "Och! for the love of Jasus, Mr. Grattan, don't lave me here near this villain that's afther cursing me to no end." I observed to Doogan that the poor fellow was in a much worse state than even himself, and that I doubted whether he would be alive in five minutes. At this moment the eyes of the Frenchman met mine, "*Oh! monsieur,*" exclaimed he, "*je meurs pour une goutte d'eau! Oh, mon Dieu! mon Dieu!*" – "Now," ejaculated Doogan, addressing me, "will you believe me (that never tould a lie in my life!) another time? Did you hear him, then, how he got on with his *mon dew*?" I caused Doogan to be carried to an hospital, but the French soldier died as we endeavoured to place him in a blanket.

I quitted the breach, and took a parting glance at the town; the smell from the still burning houses, the groups of dead and wounded, and the broken fragments of different weapons, marked strongly the character of the preceding night's dispute; and even at this late hour, there were many drunken marauders endeavouring to regain, by some fresh act of atrocity, an equivalent for the plunder their brutal state of intoxication had caused them to lose by the hands of their own companions, who robbed indiscriminately man, woman, or child, friend or foe, the dead or the dying! Then, again, were to be seen groups of deserters from our army, who, having taken shelter in Rodrigo during the winter, were now either dragged from their hiding-places by their merciless comrades, or given up by the Spaniards, in whose houses they had sought shelter, to the first officer or soldier who would be troubled, at the moment, with the responsibility of taking charge of them.

In the midst of a group of a dozen men deserters from different regiments, stood two of the Connaught Rangers. No matter what their other faults might be, desertion was not a species of delinquency they were addicted to; and as the fate of one of these men – indeed both of them, for that matter – was a little tragical, I purpose giving it a nook in my adventures. The two culprits to whom I have made allusion were as different in their characters as persons; one of them (Mangin) was a quiet well-disposed man, short in stature, a native of England, and, as a matter of course, a heavy feeder, one that could but ill put up with "short allowance," and in consequence left the army when food became as scarce as it did in the winter of 1811. The other, a fellow of the name of Curtis, an Irishman, tall and lank, was, like the rest of the "boys" from that part of the world, mighty aisy about what he ate, provided he got a reasonable supply of drink; but as neither the one nor the other were "convenient" during the period in question, they both left an advanced post one fine night, and resolved to try the difference between the French commissariats and ours. This was their justification of themselves to me, and I believe, for I was not present at it, the *summum bonum* upon which the basis of their defence at their trial rested. There were also six Germans of the 60th Rifles in the group, but they seemed so unnerved by their unexpected capture that they were unable to say anything for themselves.

Towards evening I reached the village which my regiment occupied. An altered scene presented itself. The soldiers busied in arranging their different articles of plunder; many of them clad in the robes of some priest, while others wore gowns of the most costly silk or velvet; others, again, nearly naked; some without pantaloons, having been plundered, while drunk, of so essential, a part of their dress; but all, or almost all, were occupied in laying out for sale their different articles of plunder, in that order which was essential to their being disposed of to the crowds of Spaniards which had already assembled to be the purchasers; and if one could judge by their looks, they most unquestionably committed a breach in their creed by "coveting their neighbours' goods." And had the scene which now presented itself to our sight been one caused by an event the most joyous, much less by the calamity that had befallen the unfortunate inhabitants of Rodrigo, to say nothing of the human blood that had been spilt ere that event had taken place, the scene could not have been more gay. Brawny-shouldered Castilians, carrying pigskins of wine on their backs, which they sold to our soldiers for a trifling sum; bolero-dancers, rattling their castanets like the clappers of so many mills; our fellows drinking like fishes, while their less fortunate companions at Rodrigo – either hastily flung into an ill-formed grave, writhing under the knife of the surgeon, or in the agonies of death – were unthought of, or unfelt for. *Sic transit gloria mundi*! The soldiers were allowed three days *congé* for the disposal of their booty; but long before the time had expired, they had scarcely a rag to dispose of, or a *real* of the produce in their pockets.

A few days sufficed for the reorganisation of the soldiers after they had disposed of their hard-earned plunder, and we were once more ready and willing for any fresh enterprise, no matter how difficult or dangerous. Badajoz was talked of, but nothing certain was known, and the quiet which reigned throughout all our cantonments was such as not to warrant the least suspicion that any immediate attack against that fortress was contemplated by the Commander-in-Chief.

On the sixth day after our arrival at Atalaya, we were again in motion; the village of Albergaria was allotted for our quarters, and a court-martial was ordered to assemble for the trial of the deserters from our army found in Rodrigo. The men of the 60th, and the two men of the 88th (Mangin and Curtis) were amongst the number. The court held its sitting – the prisoners were arraigned, found guilty, and sentenced to be shot! All were bad characters, save one, and that one was Mangin. He received testimonials from the Captain of his company (Captain Seton – ever the soldier's friend) highly creditable to him, and Lord Wellington, with his accustomed love of justice, resolved that his pardon should be promulgated at the time of the reading the proceedings and sentence of the court-martial. Three days after the trial it was made known to the prisoners, and the army generally, that they were to die the following morning.

At eight o'clock the division was under arms, and formed in a hollow square of small dimensions; in the centre of it was the Provost-Marshal, accompanied by his followers, with pick-axes, spades, shovels, and all the necessary etceteras for marking out and forming the graves into which the unfortunate delinquents were to be deposited as soon as they received the last and most imposing of military honours – that of being shot to death! In a few moments afterwards the rolling of muffled drums – the usual accompaniment of the death-march – was heard, and the soldiers who guarded the prisoners were soon in sight. The division observed a death-like silence as the prisoners defiled round the inside of the square; every eye was turned towards them; but Mangin, from his well-known good character, was an object of general solicitude. The solitary sound of the muffled drums at last died away into silence; the guard drew up in the centre of the square, and the prisoners had, for the last time, a view of their companions from whom they had deserted, and of their colours which they had forsaken; but if their countenances were a just index of their minds, they seemed to repent greatly the act they had committed! The three men of the 60th were in their shirts, as was also Mangin of the 88th, but Curtis wore the "old red rag," most likely from necessity, having, in all human probability, *no shirt to die in* – a circumstance by no means rare with the soldiers of the Peninsular army.

The necessary preliminaries, such as reading the crime and finding the sentence, had finished, when the Adjutant-General announced the pardon granted to Mangin, who was immediately conducted away, and placed at a short distance in rear of the division; the rest staggered onward to the spot where their graves had been dug, and having been placed on their knees, their legs hanging over the edge of the grave, a bandage was tied over their eyes. The Provost-Marshal then, with a party of twenty musketeers, their firelocks cocked, and at the recover, silently moved in front of the prisoners until he reached to within five paces of them, and then giving two motions of his hand – the one to present, the other to fire – the four men fell into the pit prepared to receive them. The three Germans were dead – indeed they were nearly so before they were fired at! and if the state of their nerves was a criterion to go by, a moderate-sized popgun would have been sufficiently destructive to have finished their earthly career; but Curtis sprang up, and, with one of his jaws shattered and hanging down upon his breast, presented a horrid spectacle. Every one seemed to be electrified, the Provost-Marshal excepted; he, I suppose, was well accustomed to such sights, for, without any ceremony, he walked up to Curtis, and with the most perfect composure levelled a huge instrument (in size between a horse-pistol and blunderbuss) at his head, which blew it nearly off his shoulders, and he fell upon the bodies of the Germans without moving a muscle.

This ceremony over, the division defiled round the grave, and as each company passed it the word "eyes right" was given by the officer in command, by which means every man had a clear view of the corpses as they lay in a heap. This is a good and wholesome practice, for nothing so much awakes in the mind of the soldier, endowed with proper feeling, the dishonour of committing an action which is almost certain to bring him to a disgraceful end, while it deters the bad man from doing that which will cost him all that he has to lose – for such persons have no character – his life. It was ten o'clock before the parade broke up, and we returned to our quarters, leaving to the Provost-Marshal and his guard the task of filling up the grave. Several Portuguese peasants crowded near the fatal spot, and so soon as all danger was passed, they flocked to wi-ness-he interment, making, all the time, divers appeals to the Virgin Mary; but whether these were intended for the preservation of the souls departed, or their own bodies corporate, I neither knew nor inquired.

Mangin, the man who had received his pardon, was still in a state of stupor. After the lapse of an hour or so his Captain went to see him; but the shock he had received was too severe; he had not nerve to bear up against it; he replied in an incoherent manner, soon fell asleep, and awoke an idiot! Every effort that could be made by the medical men, and every assurance of favour from his Captain, proved vain – he became a palpable, irreclaimable idiot, and shortly afterwards died of convulsions.

Rodrigo having fallen, it was soon rumoured that we were to move off to the south, to assault Badajoz. The soldiers were full of ardour; they anxiously counted the hours as they passed; and when at length, on the 8th of March, the order arrived for the advance of the army to the Alemtejo, their joy was indescribable. Badajoz had ever been looked upon by them as unfriendly to our troops, and they contemplated with delight the prospect of having it in their power to retaliate upon the inhabitants their treatment of our men. On the 9th, the army was in movement; the Light Division opened the march, followed by the 3rd and 4th; they crossed the Tagus by a bridge of boats, thrown over that river at Villa Velha, and pressed rapidly forward towards Elvas. One division of infantry and a brigade of cavalry remained on the Agueda. On the 14th, the Light and 3rd Divisions were concentrated in the neighbourhood of Elvas; they were joined by the 4th Division on the following day, while the remainder of the army, under Hill and Graham, were pushed forward to Llerenn, Merida, and Almendralejo, to observe the motions of Soult, who by this time was informed of the preparations, though not to their full extent, that had been formed against Badajoz.

On the 16th of March, everything being in readiness, a pontoon bridge was thrown across the Guadiana; fifteen thousand men broke up from their bivouac at Elvas, and advanced towards the river; the enemy disputed the ground, and here – even here, with only a handful of cavalry opposed to us – the French horsemen had actually the best of it, and kept us at bay during a march of three hours. At length we gained the river's edge, passed the bridge, drove back the enemy's outposts, and completed the investment. The following day, the 17th, Lord Wellington, accompanied by his engineers, carefully reconnoitered the place. The point of attack which his lordship decided upon, notwithstanding the advantages which were on the side of the enemy, was quite at variance with that of the preceding year, so it must be naturally presumed that the former was found to be faulty. Then the outworks were by no means so formidable as now on the side about to be assailed, while on the San Christoval side, the scene of the former attack, little progress had been made towards its amelioration.

The evening of the 17th of March had scarcely closed

when three thousand men broke ground before the fort of La Picurina, at the distance of one hundred and fifty yards. The night was unusually dark, the wind was high, and the rain fell in torrents – all of which favoured the enterprise. The soldiers, accustomed to fatigues, and knowing by experience, if for nothing but their own safety, the necessity of getting on rapidly with their work, exerted themselves to their utmost, and when the grey dawn of morning made its appearance, the enemy beheld with surprise, through the mist that surrounded them, the first parallel of our works completed, without their having anticipated it, or having thrown one shot in the direction of our workmen; but as the fog cleared away, it was too palpable to be misunderstood that, despite of the sagacity of General Count Phillipon[5] and his devoted garrison, a line of circumvallation had been cut close to one of the best of their outworks, without their having the remotest idea of the attempt. The different alarm-bells in the town rang a loud peal, and in less than half an hour a tremendous cannonade was opened upon us from the guns of the fort as well as the town itself. Some men were killed and several wounded, but excepting this, no loss was sustained; the works were uninjured, their progress unimpeded, and this, our first attempt, for the third time, was crowned with that unlooked-for success which was a good omen for the future.

The entire of the 18th the rain continued to fall, and the trenches were already nearly knee-deep with water, but by the great exertions of the engineers, and the persevering resolution of the soldiers, the works were pushed on with extraordinary vigour, the earth not being as yet sufficiently saturated to lose its consistency. On the night of the 18th it rained still more heavily; nevertheless some guns were

5 General Armand Philippon (1761–1836); enlisted in the Bourbon army as a soldier in 1778; promoted to *general de brigade* 1810, made a baron in the same year. Governor of Badajoz from 1811. Later escaped captivity in England to take part in the Russian and German campaigns, retired in 1813.

dragged through the slough by the soldiers, into the batteries marked out to act against La Picurina, and the following morning the works were in that forward state as to cause the French Governor much alarm for the fate of this outwork. Towards mid-day on the 19th, a dense vapour, issuing from the Guadiana and Rivillas, caused by the heavy rains that had fallen, made Phillipon consider the moment a favourable one to make a rush into our works; he accordingly placed two thousand chosen troops at the different gates and sally-ports with fixed bayonets, ready to storm the batteries at a given signal. At this time our soldiers were working in the trenches, nearly up to their hips in water; the covering party were too distant to afford immediate relief if required to do so, because they were kept out of the wet ground as far as was consistent with the safety of our lines; and the soldiers that composed the working party were in a helpless and defenceless state, their arms and appointments being thrown aside.

I happened to be in the works on this day, and having a little more experience than the officer who commanded the party, I observed with distrust the bustle which was apparent, not only in the fort of Picurina, but also along the ramparts of the town. Without waiting the formality of telling the commanding officer what I thought, I, on the instant, ordered the men to throw by their spades and shovels, put on their appointments, and load their firelocks. This did not occupy more than three minutes, and in a few seconds afterwards the entire trenches to our right were filled with Frenchmen, the workmen massacred, and the works materially damaged; while at the same moment several hundred men attempted to throw themselves into the battery we occupied. But the workmen were armed and ready to receive them; they had just been placed – I must say it, for it is the truth – by me in a posture not only to save their own lives, but the battery also. The Frenchmen advanced with that impetuous burst so well known to those who have witnessed it, and so difficult to stand before by any. They had a double motive to urge them on this occasion: honour had a forcible auxiliary in the shape of a dollar, which they were to receive for every pick-axe or shovel they carried out of our trenches; and, well as I know the French character, it is difficult for me to say which of the two, honour or avarice, most predominated upon the present occasion; I shall only say that it is my firm conviction – and I judge from the spirit of the attack – that both had their share in stimulating those heroic and veteran plunderers to seek for a footing within our trenches, for I never saw a set of fellows that sought with greater avidity than they did the spades and shovels that were thrown aside by our men. Lieutenant D'Arcy of the 88th and Lieutenant White of the 45th pursued them almost to the glacis of the town; and had the movement been foreseen, there can be little hazard in saying that, with a sufficient supply of ladders at the moment, the fort of Picurina could have been carried by the workmen alone, so great was their enthusiasm, with a less loss of lives than it cost us (after six days' labour) on the 25th!

The sortie had been well repulsed at this point, but higher up, on the right, we were not so fortunate; the workmen were surprised, and, in addition to the injury inflicted upon the works, a great loss of men and officers was sustained before the covering party reached the spot. General Picton soon after arrived in the battery where I was stationed, and seemed to be much alarmed for its safety, not knowing in the confusion of the moment, which was great, that the enemy had attacked it, and had been driven back; but when he learned from me that the workmen alone had achieved this act, he was lavish in his praise of them, and spoke to myself in flattering terms – for him; but there was an austerity of demeanour which, even while he gave praise – a thing he seldom did to the Connaught Rangers at least! – kept a fast hold of him, and the caustic sententiousness with which he spoke rather chilled than animated. He was on foot, but his aide-de-camp, Captain Cuthbert of the Fusiliers, was mounted, and while in the act of giving directions to some of the troops (for by this time the whole of the besieging force, attracted by the cannonade, was in motion towards the works) he was struck in the hip by a round shot, which killed his horse on the spot, leaving him dreadfully mangled and bleeding to death. This officer was a serious loss to Picton, and was much regretted by the division; he possessed all the requisites for a staff-officer, without that silly arrogance – the sure sign of an empty mind, as well as head – which we sometimes meet with amongst the gentlemen who compose the *état major* of our army.

We lost in this affair about two hundred men, many of whom were cut down in the works, and several in the depots far in the rear, by a body of the enemy's light cavalry that galloped out of the town at the moment the sortie commenced. Absurd as this may read, it is nevertheless true: the garrison of Badajoz, cooped up within its walls, without a foot of ground that they could call their own beyond the glacis, and, in a manner, begirt by an army of fifteen thousand men, were – by their admirable arrangement of their forces, or by the superlative neglect of our people, enabled to ride through our lines – unopposed by a single dragoon! – from right to left! Brilliant, however, as was this exploit, it was of no such service to the garrison; their loss exceeded four hundred men, and the capture of a few dozen spades and shovels but ill repaid them for so great a sacrifice of lives, at any time valuable, but in their present position doubly so.

The sortie being at length repulsed, and order once more restored, the works in the trenches were continued under a torrent of rain and fire of artillery. Lieutenant White of the 45th, who had been much distinguished in the batteries, was struck by a shell (without a fuse) on the head, which killed him on the spot; he was reading a book at the moment, and Lieutenant Cotton of the 88th, who was sitting beside him, was so covered with his blood, that it was thought at first he had been frightfully wounded.

Up to this time the fall of rain had been so violent as to threaten the total failure of the operation; it had never ceased since the 17th, and the trenches were a perfect river. The soldiers were working up to their knees in water, and the fatigue and hardships they endured were great indeed, but there was no complaint – not even a murmur to be heard! The next day, the 22nd, the pontoon bridge over the Guadiana was carried away by the floods which the late rains had caused in the river, and the stream became so rapid that the flying bridges could not be made use of, and, in short, all supplies from the other side were cut off. In the trenches matters were in as bad a state, for the earth no longer retained its consistency, and it was impossible to get it into any shape. On the 24th, however, the weather happily settled fine, and much progress was made towards forwarding the works; but this and the following day were perhaps two of the most dreadful recorded in the annals of sieges. The soldiers laboured with a degree of hardihood bordering on desperation, while the engineers braved every danger with as much composure as if they either set no value upon their lives, or thought their bodies impregnable to shot or shell. In proportion as our works advanced, the enemy redoubled his fire, and the attempt made by us to drag the heavy guns through the mud, or to form magazines for the gunpowder, was almost certain death; but not content with the destruction which his fire carried throughout our ranks, Phillipon brought to his aid a battery from San Christoval, which he placed close to the edge of the river; the fire of this battery completely enfiladed our works, and rendered it difficult and hazardous for the workmen to keep their ground.

Half a battalion was ordered down to the water's edge, and the effect of their fire against these guns was soon appreciated by the soldiers in the batteries; the cannonade of the enemy lost its effect, their fire became irregular, their shot passed over our heads, and finally they were compelled to limber up their park of artillery, and retrace their steps, at a gallop, up the Christoval height. Nevertheless, this battery did an incalculable hurt to us; many men were struck down by its fire, but, above all, our engineers suffered the most. This was a loss that could be but ill spared, for we were so scantily supplied with this description of force, that it was found necessary to substitute officers of the infantry to act as such during the siege. These officers were very zealous in the performance of the dangerous duties they had to fulfil: some had a tolerable knowledge of the theory, but none, if I except Major Thomson of the 74th, and one or two that had served at Rodrigo, knew anything of the practical part; they strove, however, by great intrepidity, to make up for their other defects; they exposed themselves to every danger, with a bravery bordering on foolhardihood, and consequently, under such a fire as we were exposed to, scarcely one escaped death. Lieutenant Fairclough of the 5th, and Rammage of the 74th, both acting engineers, were cut asunder by a round shot from the San Christoval battery; others, whose names I forget, shared the same fate, and several were wounded.

Towards three o'clock in the afternoon our works had been materially advanced, several small magazines were in progress, the batteries destined to act against La Picurina were armed, and the losses which we sustained amongst our engineers repaired by the arrival of others to replace their fallen companions. It was at this time, while I was seriously occupied with thirty men, in covering with boards and sandbags a magazine which had been, with great labour, formed during the forenoon, that a shell of huge dimensions exploded at the entrance of it. There were, at the moment, above a dozen or so of the Staff Corps and Engineers, with some of the line, placing a quantity of gunpowder in the vault which had been prepared to receive it. The roof of the magazine was, in defiance of the dreadful fire which was incessant upon this point, crowned by a few soldiers of the party under my command; some kegs of gunpowder, which were at the entrance of the cave, unfortunately blew up, destroying all at that side of the magazine, and hurling the planks which were but in part secured upon its top, together with the men that were upon them, into the air: it caused us great loss of lives and labour, but fortunately the great store of powder which was inside escaped. The planks were shivered to pieces, and the brave fellows who occupied them either blown into atoms, or so dreadfully wounded as to cause their immediate death; some had their uniforms burned to a cinder, while others were coiled up in a heap, without the vestige of anything left to denote that they were human beings.

An 88th soldier, of the name of Cooney, barber to the company he belonged to, escaped the effects of the explosion unhurt, except a slight scratch in the face, caused by a splinter from a rock that had been rent in pieces by the blowing up of the magazine; he was an old and ugly man, but yet so vain of his personal appearance as to be nearly in despair at the idea, as he said, "of his good looks being spoiled." While he was in the midst of his lamentation, a round shot struck his head and carried it off. In his coat pocket was found his soap and razor, which were instantly drawn lots for, but to whose "lot" they fell I know not.

The French cannoniers were loud in cheering when they discovered the effects of their fire upon Cooney's sconce; our men cheered in turn, and continued to crown the top of the already half-dismantled magazine, but as fast as they mounted it, they were swept off its face by the overwhelming fire from the town; yet notwithstanding the great loss of lives that had already taken place, and the almost certain death which awaited all who attempted to remain on the magazine, it was never for five minutes unoccupied, and by four o'clock in the afternoon it might be said to be perfectly finished. Baffled in his endeavours to stop our progress, Phillipon was determined to make it cost us as dear as he could. Twelve additional guns were brought from the unemployed batteries and placed along the curtain *en barbette*. These, at half-range distance, without the means on our side to reply to them, were fired with a fearful precision; it was next to impossible to stand under it, but the soldiers, on this day, surpassed all their former efforts. The fire of threescore pieces of artillery was employed in vain against them; the works were repaired so soon as injured, and everything warranted the opinion that, should the night prove fine, our batteries would open the following day.

Captain Mulcaster, of the Engineers, by his heroic conduct, stimulated the soldiers wonderfully; no danger could unnerve him, or prevent his exposing himself to the hottest of the French fire, and for a time he escaped unhurt, but at length, while standing on a rising ground, in front of the battery No. 1, a twenty-four pound shot struck him in the neck, and carried away his head and part of his back and shoulders. The headless trunk was knocked several yards from the spot, but was speedily carried to the engineer camp by some of the brave men who, but a few short moments before, looked upon what was now an inanimate lump of clay, with that admiration naturally inspired by one of the finest as well as the most intrepid young men in the army; for he had endeared himself to the soldiers as much by his kind manner to them as by his total disregard of danger to himself. It is well known that infantry soldiers had a great dislike to being placed under the control of the engineer officers, who exacted, or at least they thought so, too much from them; but Captain Mulcaster had a manner, peculiar to himself, that gained him the goodwill of all.

Major Thompson of the 88th soon after fell. He was observing a party of the enemy who were rowing a *bateau* across the inundation of the Rivillas with a reinforcement of men intended to succour the troops that occupied the ravelin of San Roque. This operation, although embracing but a small portion of the garrison, was one of a very delicate nature, inasmuch as the distance between our works and the inundation was so short as to enable us to command with musketry its entire span; but the Governor, ever ready in strategy, provided against even this chance of his plans for defence being marred. He caused to be constructed a large *bateau*, or, perhaps, more properly speaking, a raft. The side of it which faced our lines was raised by light poles to the height of four feet, through which were intertwined wattles of osier; by this means, a support sufficiently strong, without being too cumbrous to impede the movement of the raft, was completed, and the inside was carefully padded with hay, or such light matter; it made a sufficient defence against musketry without any danger of the machine's losing its centre of gravity. To stop as much as possible this operation, several hundred riflemen were placed in advance, and so soon as the machine was discovered in motion on the water, a heavy fire was opened; a corresponding demonstration was made by the enemy, sustained by several batteries, and those mutual efforts were always productive of a heavy loss of lives on both sides, but particularly on ours, because the enemy's line of musketry commanded us at a distance of three hundred and fifty yards, and up to this time we had not one gun to answer their powerful salvos.

Major Thompson, who was in command of the riflemen, was in conversation with an aide-de-camp belonging to the staff of Marshal Beresford at the moment he fell; a musket ball struck him in the right temple, and passing through the brain, killed him on the spot. He had been but just *gazetted* to his majority, by purchase, and had served with the army from the campaign in Holland in 1794 to the moment of his death, without ever having been absent from his regiment in any of the battles in which it had been engaged, a few of which have been recorded by me. Captain Seton, an officer of precisely the same standing and services, succeeded him in the command of the 88th, and led his regiment up the ladders on the night of the storming of Badajoz, but he gained no promotion, except in his regular turn! and he was the *only* commanding officer of a battalion in the 3rd Division that did not get a brevet step.

Towards evening the fire against La Picurina was so effective that Lord Wellington resolved to storm it after dark.

At about three o'clock in the afternoon of the 25th of March, almost all the batteries on the front of La Picurina were disorganised, its palisades beaten down, and the fort itself, having more the semblance of a wreck than a fortification of any pretensions, presented to the eye nothing but a heap of ruins. But never was there a more fallacious appearance: the work, although dismantled of its cannon, its parapets crumbling to pieces at each successive discharge from our guns, and its garrison diminished, without a chance of being succoured, was still much more formidable than appeared to the eye of a superficial observer. It had yet many means of resistance at its disposal. The gorge, protected by three rows of palisades, was still unhurt; and although several feet of the scrap had been thrown down by the fire from our battering-park, it was, notwithstanding, of a height sufficient to inspire its garrison with a well-grounded confidence as to the result of any effort of ours against it; it was defended by three hundred of the *élite* of Phillipon's force, under the command of a colonel of Soult's[6] staff, named Gaspard Thiery, who volunteered his services on the occasion. On this day a deserter came over to us from the fort, and gave an exact account of how it was circumstanced.

Colonel Fletcher,[7] the chief engineer, having carefully examined the damage created by our fire, disregarding the perfect state of many of the defences, and being well aware that expedition was of paramount import to our final success, advised that the fort should be attacked after nightfall.

At half-past seven o'clock the storming party, consisting of

6 Marshal Nicolas Soult (1769–1851), King Joseph Bonaparte's chief-of-staff; nicknamed "Old Salt" by the British, later led the French defence in the Pyrenees.
7 Lieutenant-Colonel Sir Richard Fletcher (1768–1813), Royal Engineers; killed during the storming of San Sebastian.

fifteen officers and five hundred privates, stood to their arms. General Kempt, who commanded in the trenches, explained to them the duty they had to perform; he did so in his usual clear manner, and every one knew the part he was to fulfil. All now waited with anxiety for the expected signal, which was to be the fire of one gun from No. 4 battery. The evening was settled and calm; no rain had fallen since the 23rd; the rustling of a leaf might be heard; and the silence of the moment was uninterrupted, except by the French sentinels, as they challenged while pacing the battlements of the outwork; the answers of their comrades, although in a lower tone of voice, were distinguishable – "*Tout va bien dans le fort de la Picurina*" was heard by the very men who only awaited the signal from a gun to prove that the *réponse*, although true to the letter, might soon be falsified.

The great cathedral bell of the city at length tolled the hour of eight, and its last sounds had scarcely died away when the signal from the battery summoned the men to their perilous task; the three detachments sprang out of the works at the same moment, and ran forwards to the glacis, but the great noise which the evolution unavoidably created gave warning to the enemy, already on the alert, and a violent fire of musketry opened upon the assailing columns. One hundred men fell before they reached the outwork; but the rest, undismayed by the loss, and unshaken in their purpose, threw themselves into the ditch, or against the palisades at the gorge. The sappers, armed with axes and crow-bars, attempted to cut away or force down this defence; but the palisades were of such thickness, and so firmly placed in the ground, that before any impression could be made against even the front row, nearly all the men who had crowded to this point were struck dead. Meanwhile, those in charge of the ladders flung them into the ditch, and those below soon placed them upright against the wall; but in some instances they were not of a sufficient length to reach the top of the parapet. The time was passing rapidly, and had been awfully occupied by the enemy; while as yet our troops had not made any progress that could warrant a hope of success. More than two-thirds of the officers and privates were killed or wounded; two out of the three that commanded detachments had fallen; and Major Shawe, of the 74th, was the only one unhurt. All his ladders were too short; his men, either in the ditch or on the glacis, unable to advance, unwilling to retire, and not knowing what to do, became bewildered. The French cheered vehemently, and each discharge swept away many officers and privates.

Shawe's situation, which had always been one of peril, now became desperate; he called out to his next senior officer (Captain Oates of the 88th) and said, "Oates, what are we to do?" but at the instant he was struck in the neck by a bullet, and fell bathed in blood. It immediately occurred to Oates, who now took the command, that although the ladders were too short to mount the wall, they were long enough to go across the ditch! He at once formed the desperate resolution of throwing three of them over the fosse, by which a sort of bridge was constructed; he led the way, followed by the few of his brave soldiers who were unhurt, and, forcing their passage through an embrasure that had been but bolstered up in the hurry of the moment, carried – after a brief, desperate, but decisive conflict – the point allotted to him. Sixty grenadiers of the Italian guard[8] were the first encountered by Oates and his party; they supplicated for mercy, but, either by accident or design, one of them discharged his firelock, and the ball struck Oates in the thigh; he fell, and his men, who had before been greatly excited, now became furious when they beheld their commanding officer weltering in his blood. Every man of the Italian guard was put to death on the spot.

8 There were no troops of the Italian guard in this part of Spain, though there were some of the "*Velites*" in Catalonia. Italians there were, but only men incorporated in ordinary French line regiments. [Charles Oman]

Meanwhile Captain Powis's detachment had made great progress, and finally entered the fort by the salient angle. It has been said, and, for aught I know to the contrary, with truth, that it was the first which established itself in the outwork; but this is of little import in the detail, or to the reader. All the troops engaged acted with the same spirit and devotion, and each vied with his comrade to keep up the character of the "fighting division." Almost the entire of the privates and non-commissioned officers were killed or wounded; and of fifteen officers, which constituted the number of those engaged, not one escaped unhurt! Of the garrison, but few escaped; the Commandant, and about eighty, were made prisoners; the rest, in endeavouring to escape under the guns of the fortress, or to shelter themselves in San Roque, were either bayoneted or drowned in the Rivillas; but this was not owing to any mismanagement on the part of Count Phillipon. He, with that thorough knowledge of his duty which marked his conduct throughout the siege, had, early in the business, ordered a body of chosen troops to *débouche* from San Roque, and to hold themselves in readiness to sustain the fort; but the movement was foreseen. A strong column, which had been placed in reserve, under the command of Captain Lindsey of the 88th, met this reinforcement at the moment they were about to sustain their defeated companions at La Picurina. Not expecting to be thus attacked, these troops became panic-struck, soon fled in disorder, and, running without heed in every direction, choked up the only passage of escape that was open for the fugitives from the outwork, and, by a well-meant but ill-executed evolution, did more harm than good.

So soon as the result of this last effort to succour the fort was apparent to Phillipon, he caused a violent cannonade to be opened against it, but it was not of long duration; and our engineers, profiting by the quiet which reigned throughout the enemy's batteries, pushed forward the second parallel with great success. A corps of sappers, under my command, were charged with the work of dismantling the fort, and before day we had nearly completed its destruction.

Thus terminated the siege and storming of La Picurina, after a lapse of eight nights and nine days of unprecedented labour and peril. It might be said that its capture opened to us the gates of Badajoz, or at all events put the key of that fortress into our hands; it nevertheless cost us some trouble before we could make use of the key so gained. Never, from the commencement of the war until its termination, was there a more gallant exploit than the storming of this outwork.

On the 30th of March two breaching-batteries, armed with twenty-six guns of heavy calibre, and of the very best description, opened their fire to batter down the face of the two bastions of Santa Maria and the Trinidad; and, notwithstanding every effort which the powerful resources of the enemy enabled him to command, it was abundantly manifest that a few days would suffice to finish the labours of the army before Badajoz.

The breaching-batteries, which opened their fire on the 30th, were effective beyond our expectations against the works, and the sappers had made considerable progress towards completing a good covered way for the troops to *débouche* from in their attack of the breaches. On the 25th thirty-two sappers were placed under my command, but on the night of the 4th of April their numbers were reduced to seven. I lost some of the bravest men I ever commanded; but, considering the perils they encountered, it is only surprising how any escaped. We were frequently obliged to run the flying-sap so close to the battlements of the town that the noise of the pick-axes was heard on the ramparts, and, upon such occasions, the party were almost invariably cut off to a man. But it was then that the courage of the brave fellows under my orders showed itself superior to any reverse, and what was wanted in force was made up by the most heroic bravery of individuals. There were three men of my own regiment, Williamson, Bray, and Macgowan, and I feel happy in being able to mention the names of those heroes. When a fire, so destructive as to sweep away all our gabions, took place, those men would run forward with a fresh supply, and, under a fire in which it was almost impossible to live, place them in order for the rest of the party to shelter themselves, while they threw up a sufficiency of earth to render them proof against musketry. This dangerous duty was carried on for eleven successive nights, that is to say, from the 25th of March to the 5th of April.

On this day the batteries of the enemy were nearly crippled, and their replies to our fire scarcely audible; the spirits of the soldiers, which no fatigue could damp, rose to a frightful height – I say frightful, because it was not of that sort which alone denoted exultation at the prospect of their achieving an exploit which was about to hold them up to the admiration of the world; there was a certain *something* in their bearing that told plainly that they had suffered fatigues, which they did not complain of, and had seen their comrades and officers slain while fighting beside them without repining, but that they smarted under the one, and felt acutely for the other; they smothered both, so long as their minds and bodies were employed; now, however, that they had a momentary license to *think*, every fine feeling vanished, and plunder and revenge took their place. Their labours, up to this period, although unremitting, and carried on with a cheerfulness that was astonishing, hardly promised the success which they looked for; and the change which the last twenty-four hours had wrought in their favour, caused a material alteration in their demeanour; they hailed the present prospect as the mariner does the disappearance of a heavy cloud after a storm, which discovers to his view the clear horizon. In a word, the capture of Badajoz had long been their idol. Many causes led to this wish on their part; the two previous unsuccessful sieges, and the failure of the attack against San Christoval in the latter; but, above all, the well-known hostility of its inhabitants to the British army, and perhaps might be added a desire for plunder, which the sacking of Rodrigo had given them a taste for. Badajoz was, therefore, denounced as a place to be made an example of; and, most unquestionably, no city, Jerusalem excepted, was ever more strictly visited to the letter than was this ill-fated town.

The demeanour of the soldiers on this evening faithfully exemplified what I have just written: a quiet but desperate calm had taken the place of that gayness and buoyancy of spirits which they possessed so short a time before, and nothing now was observable in their manner but a tiger-like expression of anxiety to seize upon their prey, which they considered as already within their grasp.

Towards five o'clock in the afternoon all doubts were at an end, in consequence of some officers arriving in the camp from the trenches: they reported that Lord Wellington had decided upon breaching the curtain that connected the bastions of La Trinidad and Santa Maria, and as this operation would necessarily occupy several hours' fire, it was impossible that the assault could take place before the following day, the 6th, and the inactivity that reigned in the engineer camp, which contained the scaling-ladders, was corroborative of the intelligence. For once I saw the men dejected; yet it was not the dejection of fear, but of disappointment. Some of the most impetuous broke out into violent and unbecoming language; others abused the engineers; and many threw the blame of the delay upon the generals who commanded in the trenches; but all, even the most turbulent, admitted that the delay must be necessary to our success, or Lord Wellington would not allow it.

The night at length passed over, and the dawn of morning ushered in a day pregnant with events that will be recorded in our history as amongst the most brilliant that grace its annals. The batteries against the curtain soon reduced it to a heap of ruins; and the certainty that the trial would be made the same evening re-established good-humour amongst the soldiers. It was known, early in the day, that the breaches were allotted to the Light and 4th Divisions; to the 5th, the task of escalading the town on the side of the St Vincent bastion; and to Picton, with his invincible 3rd, to carry the castle by escalading its stupendous walls, upwards of thirty feet high. The Portuguese brigade, under General Power, were to divert the enemy's attention on the side of San Christoval; while three hundred men, taken from the guard in the trenches, were to carry the outwork of San Roque.

To ensure the success of an enterprise upon which so much was at stake, twenty thousand men were to be brought into action as I have described; by five o'clock all the ladders were portioned out to those destined to mount them. The time fixed for the assemblage of the troops was eight; that for the attack ten. The day passed over heavily, and hour after hour was counted, each succeeding one seeming to double the length of the one that preceded it; but, true as the needle to the pole, the long-expected moment arrived, and the clear but deep note of the town clock was now heard throughout our lines, as it tolled the hour of eight, and ere its last vibration had ceased the vast mass of assailants were in battle array. A thick and dusky vapour, issuing from the Guadiana and Rivillas, hung above the heads of the hostile forces, and hid alike, by its heavy veil, each from the view of its opponent; the batteries on both sides were silent, as if they reserved their efforts for the approaching struggle; and, except the gentle noise which the rippling of the Guadiana created, or the croaking of the countless frogs that filled the marshes on each side of its banks, everything was as still as if the night was to be one of quiet repose; and a passing stranger, unacquainted with the previous events, might easily have supposed that our army were no otherwise occupied than in the ordinary routine of an evening parade; but Phillipon, profiting by this cessation, retrenched and barricaded the breaches in a manner hereafter to be described.

So soon as each division had formed on its ground in open

column of companies, the arms were piled, and the officers and soldiers either walked about in groups of five or six together, or sat down under an olive-tree to observe, at their ease, the arrangements of the different brigades which were to take a part in the contest. Then, again, might be seen some writing to their friends – a hasty scroll, no doubt, and, in my opinion, an ill-timed one. It is a bad time, at the moment of entering a breach, to write to a man's father or mother, much less his wife, to tell them so; and, besides, it has an un-seasonable appearance in the eyes of the soldiers, who are decidedly the most competent judges of what their officers should be, or, at least, what *they* would *wish* them to be, which is tantamount, at such a crisis.

There is a solemnity of feeling which accompanies the expectation of every great event in our lives, and the man who can be altogether dead to such feeling is little, if anything, better than a brute. The present moment was one that was well calculated to fill every bosom throughout the army; for, mixed with expectation, hope, and suspense, it was rendered still more touching to the heart by the music of some of the regiments, which played at the head of each battalion as the soldiers sauntered about to beguile the last hour many of them were destined to live. The band of my corps, the 88th, all Irish, played several airs which exclusively belong to their country, and it is impossible to describe the effect it had upon us all; such an air as "Savourneen Deelish" is sufficient, at any time, to inspire a feeling of melancholy, but on an occasion like the present it acted powerfully on the feelings of the men: they thought of their distant homes, of their friends, and of bygone days. It was Easter Sunday, and the contrast which their present position presented to what it would have been were they in their native land afforded ample food for the occupation of their minds; but they were not allowed time for much longer reflection. The approach of General Kempt, accompanied by his staff, was the signal for the formation of the column of attack; and almost immedi-

ately the men were ordered to stand to their arms. Little, if
any, directions were given; indeed, they were unnecessary,
because the men, from long service, were so conversant with
the duty they had to perform, that it would have been but a
waste of words and time to say what was required of them.

All was now in readiness. It was twenty-five minutes past
nine; the soldiers, unencumbered with their knapsacks –
their stocks off – their shirt-collars unbuttoned – their
trousers tucked up to the knee – their tattered jackets, so
worn out as to render the regiment they belonged to barely
recognisable – their huge whiskers and bronzed faces, which
several hard-fought campaigns had changed from their natural hue – but, above all, their self-confidence, devoid of
boast or bravado, gave them the appearance of what they in
reality were – an invincible host.

The division now moved forward in one solid mass – the
45th leading, followed closely by the 88th and 74th; the
brigade of Portuguese, consisting of the 9th and 21st Regiments of the line, under Colonel de Champlemond, were
next; while the 5th, 77th, 83rd, and 94th, under Colonel
Campbell, brought up the rear. Their advance was undis-
turbed until they reached the Rivillas; but at this spot some
fire-balls, which the enemy threw out, caused a great light,
and the 3rd Division, four thousand strong, was to be seen
from the ramparts of the castle. The soldiers, finding they
were discovered, raised a shout of defiance, which was
responded to by the garrison, and in a moment afterwards
every gun that could be brought to bear against them was in
action; but, no way daunted by the havoc made in his ranks,
Picton, who just then joined his soldiers, forded the Rivillas,
knee-deep, and soon gained the foot of the castle wall, and
here he saw the work that was cut out for him, for he no
longer fought in darkness. The vast quantity of combustible
matter which out-topped this stupendous defence was in a
blaze, and the flames which issued forth on every side lighted
not only the ramparts and the ditch, but the plain that

intervened between them and the Rivillas. A host of veterans crowned the wall, all armed in a manner as imposing as novel; each man had beside him eight loaded firelocks; while at intervals, and proportionably distributed, were pikes of an enormous length, with crooks attached to them, for the purpose of grappling with the ladders. The top of the wall was covered with rocks of ponderous size, only requiring a slight push to hurl them upon the heads of our soldiers, and there was a sufficiency of hand-grenades and small shells at the disposal of the men that defended this point to have destroyed the entire of the besieging army; while on the flanks of each curtain, batteries, charged to the muzzle with grape and case shot, either swept away entire sections or disorganised the ladders as they were about to be placed, and an incessant storm of musketry, at the distance of fifteen yards, completed the resources the enemy brought into play, which, as may be seen, were of vast formidableness.

To oppose this mass of warriors and heterogeneous congregation of missiles Picton had nothing to depend upon for success but his tried and invincible old soldiers – he relied firmly upon their devoted courage, and he was not disappointed. The terrible aspect of the rugged wall, thirty feet in height, in no way intimidated them; and, under a frightful fire of small arms and artillery, the ponderous ladders were dragged into the ditch and, with a degree of hardihood that augured well for the issue, were planted against the lofty battlements that domineered above his soldiers' heads: but this was only the commencement of one of the most terrific struggles recorded during this hardfought night. Each ladder, so soon as placed upright, was speedily mounted and crowded from the top round to the bottom one; but those who escaped the pike-thrusts were shattered to atoms by the heavy cross-fire from the bastions, and the soldiers who occupied them, impaled upon the bayonets of their comrades in the ditch, died at the foot of those ladders which they had carried such a distance and with so much labour.

An hour had now passed over. No impression had been made upon the castle, and the affair began to have a very doubtful appearance, for already well nigh half of the 3rd Division had been cut off. General Kempt, commanding the right brigade, fell wounded, early in the night; and the 88th Regiment alone, the strongest in the division, lost more than half their officers and men, while the other regiments were scarcely in a better condition. Picton, seeing the frightful situation in which he was placed, became uneasy; but the goodwill with which his brave companions exposed and laid down their lives reassured him; he called out to his men – told them they had never been defeated, and that now was the moment to conquer or die. Picton, although not loved by his soldiers, was respected by them; and his appeal, as well as his unshaken front, did wonders in changing the desperate state of the division. Major Ridge of the 5th, by his personal exertions, caused two ladders to be placed upright, and he himself led the way to the top of one, while Canch, a Grenadier officer of the 5th, mounted the other. A few men at last got footing on the top of the wall; at the same time Lieutenant William Mackie of the 88th – he who led the forlorn hope at Rodrigo (unnoticed! – still a lieutenant!!) – and Mr Richard Martin (son of the member for Galway, who acted as a volunteer with the 88th during the siege) succeeding in mounting another. Mackie – ever foremost in the fight – soon established his men on the battlements, himself unhurt; but Martin fell desperately wounded. A general rush to the ladders now took place, and the dead and wounded that lay in the ditch were indiscriminately trampled upon, for humanity was nowhere to be found. A frightful butchery followed this success; and the shouts of our soldiery, mingled with the cries of the Frenchmen, supplicating for mercy or in the agonies of death, were heard at a great distance. But few prisoners were made; and the division occupied, with much regularity, the different points allotted to each regiment. Meanwhile the ravelin of San Roque was carried by the gorge, by a detachment drawn from the trenches, under the command of Major Wilson of the 48th; and the engineers were directed to blow up the dam and sluice that caused the inundation of the Rivillas, by which means the passage of that river between La Picurina and the breaches could be more easily effected. One entire regiment of Germans, called the regiment of Hesse Darmstadt, that defended the ravelin were put to death.

While all this was taking place at the castle and San Roque, a fearful scene was acting at the breaches. The Light and 4th Divisions, ten thousand strong, advanced to the glacis undiscovered – a general silence pervading the whole, as the spirits of the men settled into that deep sobriety which denotes much determination of purpose; but at this spot their footsteps were heard, and, "perhaps since the invention of gunpowder," its effects were never more powerfully brought into action. In a moment the different materials which the enemy had arranged in the neighbourhood of the breaches were lighted up – darkness was converted into light – torches blazed along the battlements – and a spectator, at a short distance from the walls, could distinguish the features of the contending parties. A battery of mortars, doubly loaded with grenades, and a blaze of musketry, unlike anything hitherto witnessed by the oldest soldier, opened a murderous fire against the two divisions; but, unshaken by its effects, they pressed onward and jumped into the ditch. The 4th Division, destined to carry the breach to the right, met with a frightful catastrophe at the onset. The leading platoons, consisting of the fusilier brigade, sprang into that part of the ditch that had been filled by the inundation of the Rivillas, and were seen no more; but the bubbles that rose on the surface of the water were a terrible assurance of the struggles which those devoted soldiers – the men of Albuera – ineffectually made to extricate themselves from the deadly grasp of each other, and from so unworthy an end.

Warned by the fate of their companions, the remainder

turned to the left, and following the footsteps of the Light Division, pressed onwards in one mingled mass to the breaches of the curtain and La Trinidad. Arrived here, they encountered a series of obstacles that it was impossible to surmount, and which I find great difficulty in describing. Planks, of a sufficient length and breadth to embrace the entire face of the breaches, studded with spikes a foot long, were to be surmounted ere they reached the top of the breach; yet some there were – the brave Colonel Macleod, of the 43rd, amongst the number – who succeeded so far, but on gaining the top, *chevaux de frise*, formed of long sword-blades firmly fixed in the trunks of trees of a great size, and chained, boom-like, across the breach, were still to be passed; while at each side, and behind the *chevaux de frise*, trenches were cut, sufficiently extensive for the accommodation of three thousand men, who stood in an amphitheatrical manner – each tier above the other – and armed with eight muskets each, like their companions at the castle, awaited the attack so soon as the planks on the face, and the *chevaux de frise* on the top of the breach were surmounted; but they might have waited until doomsday for that event, because it was morally impossible.

The vast glare of light caused by the different explosions, and the fire of cannon and musketry, gave to the breaches the appearance of a volcano vomiting forth fire in the midst of the army: the ground shook – meteors shone forth in every direction – and when for a moment the roar of battle ceased, it was succeeded by cries of agony, or the furious exultation of the imperial soldiers. To stand before such a storm of fire, much less endeavour to overcome a barrier so impregnable, required men whose minds, as well as frames, were cast in a mould not human; but, nevertheless, so it was. The gallant Light and 4th Divisions boldly braved every danger, and with a good will, rarely to be found, prolonged a struggle, the very failure of which, taking into account the nature of the obstacles opposed to them, and their immense losses, was sufficient to

immortalise them. At length, after a dreadful sacrifice of lives
– all the generals, and most of the colonels, being either killed
or wounded – they were driven from the breaches, while the
Frenchmen, securely entrenched behind them, might be seen
waving their caps in token of defiance. This was too galling for
men who had never known defeat – and they ran back headlong to the attack, and destruction. But for what end? To
judge from the past, when their numbers were more numerous, they had failed; they were now reduced to less than half,
while the resources of the enemy were unimpaired, and the
prospect before them was hideous. Again did they attempt to
pass this terrible gulf of steel and flame – and again were they
driven back – cut down – annihilated. Hundreds of brave
soldiers lay in piles upon each other, weltering in blood, and
trodden down by their own companions. The 43rd left
twenty-two officers and three hundred men on the breach;
four companies of the 52nd were blown to atoms by an
explosion; and the 95th, as indeed every other regiment
engaged, suffered in proportion. Our batteries, from whence
a clear view of all that was passing could be distinguished,
maddened by the havoc at the breaches, poured in a torrent of
shot; and, in the excitement of the moment, killed friends as
well as foes. Finally, the remnant of the two divisions retired;
and, with a valour bordering upon desperation, prepared for a
third trial; but the success of Picton's attack was by this time
whispered amongst them, and the evacuation of the breaches
soon after confirmed the rumour.

While the attack of the castle and breaches was in progress,
the 5th Division, under General Leith, maintained a fierce
and dangerous struggle on the other side of the city beyond
the Pardeleras fort; but the resistance at those points was
feeble, as compared with the other two. In some instances the
French troops deserted the walls before they were carried;
and it is worthy of remark, that while the 38th Regiment were
mounting the ladders, the imperial soldiers were scrambling
down them at the reverse side – in many instances treading

upon the fingers of our own men! The few men of Leith's division, thus established on the ramparts, boldly pressed on in the hope of causing a change in favour of the men at the breaches; but the multitude that had fled before this handful of troops became reassured when they beheld the scantiness of their numbers, and, returning to the fight, forced them up a street leading to the ramparts. Leith's men became panic-struck by this unexpected burst, and retraced their steps in confusion; many were killed ere they reached the wall; and some, infected by the contagion of the moment, jumped over the battlements, and were dashed to pieces in their fall. One, an officer, bearing the flag of his regiment, fearing it might be captured, flung himself from the wall, and falling into a part of the ditch that was filled with the slime of the river, escaped unhurt. At this critical moment General Walker reached the spot with a fresh body of troops, and driving back the French with ruinous disorder, established his men at this point; and from that moment the fate of Badajoz was sealed. The enemy fled in every direction towards the bridge leading to San Christoval; and the remnant of the ill-fated Light and 4th Divisions with difficulty entered the town by the breaches, although unopposed.

It was now half-past two o'clock in the morning, and the fighting had continued, without cessation, from ten the preceding night. More than three hundred and fifty officers and four thousand men had fallen on our side; yet the enemy's loss was but small in proportion; because, with the exception of the castle, where the 3rd Division got fairly amongst them, the French, with that tact for which they are so remarkable, got away the moment they found themselves out-matched.

Shortly after the last attack at the breaches had failed, and long after the castle had been carried (although it was not generally known at the time), I was occupied, with Major Thomson of the 74th (acting engineer), in placing some casks of gunpowder under the dam of the Rivillas, in front of San

Roque; when, while leaning on his shoulder, I was struck by a musket-bullet in the left breast; I staggered back, but did not fall, and Thomson, bandaging my breast and shoulder with his handkerchief, caused me to be removed inside the ravelin; but the firing continued with such violence upon this point, that it was long before I could venture out of it. At length, nearly exhausted from loss of blood, and fearing that I might be unable to reach the camp if I delayed much longer, I quitted it, accompanied by two sappers of my own corps (Bray and Macgowan), who supported me as I walked towards the trenches. Bray was wounded in the leg while he tried to cover me from the enemy's fire; but this brave fellow soon recovered, and afterwards greatly distinguished himself in the battle of the Pyreness, by killing a French colonel at the head of his battalion.

By this time the attack of Badajoz was, in effect, finished. Some irregular firing was still to be heard as the fugitives hurried from street to street towards the Roman bridge leading to San Christoval, but all resistance might be said to have ceased. An attempt to retake the castle was made in vain; but the brave Colonel Ridge of the 5th, who had so distinguished himself, lost his life by almost one of the last shots that was fired in this fruitless effort to recover a place which had cost the army the hearts' blood of the 3rd Division; and the dawn of the morning of the 7th of April showed to the rest of the army, like a speck in the horizon, the shattered remnant of Picton's invincible soldiers, as they stood in a lone group upon the ramparts of a spot that, by its isolated situation, towering height, and vast strength, seemed not to appertain to the rest of the fortifications, and which the enemy, with their entire disposable force, were unable to take from the few brave men who now stood triumphant upon its lofty battlements. Nevertheless, triumphant and stern as was their attitude, it was not without its alloy, for more than five-sixths[9] of their officers and com-

9 An exaggeration: the 3rd Division lost about 1,100 men out of 4,300. [Charles Oman]

rades either lay dead at their feet, or badly wounded in the ditch below them. All their generals, Picton amongst the number, and almost all their colonels, were either killed or wounded; and as they stood to receive the praises of their commander, and the cheers of their equally brave but unfortunate companions in arms, their diminished front and haggard appearance told, with terrible truth, the nature of the conflict in which they had been engaged.

Early on the morning of the 7th of April, Phillipon and his garrison, which had taken refuge in San Christoval, hoisted the white flag in token of submission, and from that moment the beautiful and rich town of Badajoz became a scene of plunder and devastation.

Badajoz, one of the richest and most beautiful towns in the south of Spain, whose inhabitants had witnessed its siege in silent terror for one-and-twenty days, and who had been shocked by the frightful massacre that had just taken place at its walls, was now about to be plunged into all the horrors that are, unfortunately, unavoidable upon an enterprise such as a town taken by storm. Scarcely had Count Phillipon and his garrison commenced their march towards Elvas, when the work of pillage commenced. Some – many indeed – of the good soldiers turned to the ditch of the castle and to the breaches to assist and carry off their wounded companions; but hundreds were neglected in the general and absorbing thirst for plunder.

The appearance of the castle was that of a vast wreck; the various ladders lying shattered at the base of its walls, the broken piles of arms, and the brave men that lay as they had fallen – many holding their firelocks in their grasp – marked strongly the terrible contest in which they had been engaged, and presented to the eye of a spectator ample food for reflection. It was not possible to look at those brave men, all of them dead or frightfully maimed, without recollecting what they had been but a few short hours before; yet those feelings, fortunately perhaps, do not predominate with soldiers, and those sights, far from exciting reflections of a grave nature, more usually call forth some jocular remark, such as "that he will have no further occasion to draw rations"; or "that he has stuck his spoon in the wall and left off messing" – such is the force of habit.

At the breaches, the Light and 4th Division soldiers lay in heaps upon each other – a still warm group; and many of those veterans, from whom the vital spark had not yet fled, expired in the arms of the few of their companions who sought to remove them to a place better suited to their miserable condition. But war, whatever its numerous attractions to a young mind may be, is but ill calculated to inspire it with those softer feelings so essential to soothe us in the moment of our distress; it must not, therefore, be wondered at that a wish for plunder and enjoyment took the place of humanity, and that hundreds of gallant men were left to perish from neglect.

Before six o'clock in the morning of the 7th of April, all organisation amongst the assaulting columns had ceased, and a scene of plunder and cruelty, that it would be difficult to find a parallel for, took its place. The army, so fine and effective on the preceding day, was now transformed into a vast band of brigands, and the rich and beautiful city of Badajoz presented the turbulent aspect that must result from the concourse of numerous and warlike multitudes nearly strangers to each other, or known only by the name of the nation to which they belonged. The horde of vagabonds – Spaniards as well as Portuguese, women as well as men – that now eagerly sought for admission to plunder, nearly augmented the number of brigands to what the assailing army had reckoned the night before; and it may be fairly said that twenty thousand people – armed with full powers to act as they thought fit, and all, or almost all, armed with weapons which could be turned, at the pleasure or caprice of the bearer, for the purpose of enforcing any wish he sought to gratify – were let loose upon the ill-fated inhabitants of this devoted city. These people were under no restraint, had no person to control them, and in a short time got into such an awful state of intoxication that they lost all control over their own actions.

In the first burst, all the wine and spirit stores were forced open and ransacked from top to bottom; and it required but a short time for the men to get into that fearful state that was alike dangerous to all – officers or soldiers, or the inhabitants of the city. Casks of the choicest wines and brandy were dragged into the streets, and when the men had drunk as much as they fancied, the heads of the vessels were stove in, or the casks otherwise so broken that the liquor ran about in streams.

In the town were a number of animals that belonged to the garrison, several hundred sheep, numerous oxen, as likewise many horses; these were amongst the first taken possession of; and the wealthy occupier of many a house was glad to be allowed the employment of conducting them to our camp, as, by doing so, he got away from a place where his life was not worth a minute's purchase. But terrible as was this scene, it was not possible to avoid occasionally laughing, for the *conducteur* was generally not only obliged to drive a herd of cattle, but also to carry the bales of plunder taken by his employers – perhaps from his own house – and the stately gravity with which the Spaniard went through his work, dressed in short breeches, frilled shirt, and a hat and plumes that might vie with our eighth Henry, followed, as he was, by our ragamuffin soldiers with fixed bayonets, presented a scene that would puzzle even Mr Cruikshank himself to justly delineate. The plunder so captured was deposited in our camp, and placed under a guard chiefly composed of the soldiers' wives.

The shops were rifled, first by one group, who despoiled them of their most costly articles, then by another, who thought themselves rich in capturing what had been rejected by their predecessors; then another, and another still, until every vestige of property was swept away. A few hours was sufficient for this; night was fast drawing near, and then a scene took place that has seldom fallen to the lot of any writer to describe. Every insult, every infamy that human invention could torture into practice was committed. The following day, the 8th of April, was also a fearful one for the inhabitants; the soldiers became reckless, and drank to such an excess that no person's life, no matter of what rank, or station, or sex, was safe. If they entered a house that had not been emptied of all its furniture or wine, they proceeded to destroy it; or; if it happened to be empty, which was generally the case, they commenced firing at the doors and windows, and not unfrequently at the inmates, or at each other! They would then sally forth into the streets, and fire at the different church-bells in the steeples, or the pigeons that inhabited the old Moorish turrets of the castle – even the owls were frighted from this place of refuge, and, by their discordant screams, announced to their hearers the great revolution that had taken place near their once peaceful abodes. The soldiers then fired upon their own comrades, and many men were killed, in endeavouring to carry away some species of plunder, by the hands of those who, but a few hours before, would have risked their own lives to protect those they now so wantonly sported with: then would they turn upon the already too deeply injured females, and tear from them the trinkets that adorned their necks, fingers, or ears! and, finally, they would strip them of their wearing apparel. Some 'tis said there were – ruffians of the lowest grade, no doubt – who cut the ear-rings out of the ears of the females who bore them.

Hundreds of those fellows took possession of the best warehouses, and for a time fulfilled the functions of merchants; those, in their turn, were ejected by a stronger party, who, after a fearful strife and loss of lives, displaced them, and occupied their position, and those again were conquered by others, and others more powerful! and thus was Badajoz circumstanced on the morning of the 8th of April 1812. It presented a fearful picture of the horrors that are inevitable upon a city carried by assault; and although it is painful to relate these disgraceful facts, it is essential nevertheless. I feel as much pride as any man can feel in having taken a part in actions that must ever shed lustre upon my country; but no false feeling of delicacy shall ever prevent me from speaking the truth – no matter whether it touches the conduct of one man or ten thousand!

To put a stop to such a frightful scene, it was necessary to use some forbearance, as likewise a portion of severity. In the first instance, parties from those regiments that had least participated in the combat were ordered into the town to collect the hordes of stragglers that filled its streets with crimes too horrible to detail; but the evil had spread to such an extent that this measure was inadequate to the end proposed, and in many instances the parties so sent became infected by the contagion, and in place of remedying the disorder, increased it, by joining once more in revels they had for a time quitted. At length a brigade of troops was marched into the city, and were directed to stand by their arms while any of the marauders remained; the Provost–Marshals attached to each division were directed to use that authority with which they are of necessity invested. Gibbets and triangles were in consequence erected, and many men were flogged, but, although the contrary has been said, none were hanged – yet hundreds deserved it.

A few hours more were sufficient to purge the town of the infamous gang of robbers that still lurked about its streets, and those ruffians – chiefly Spaniards or Portuguese, not in any way attached to the army – were infinitely more dangerous than our fellows, bad as they were. Murder – except indeed in a paroxysm of drunkenness, and in many cases, I regret to say, it did occur in this way – never entered their thoughts, but the miscreants here referred to would commit the foulest deed for less than a dollar.

Towards evening tranquility began to return, and, protected as they now were by a body of troops untainted by the disease which had spread like a contagion, the unfortunate inhabitants took advantage of the quiet that reigned; yet it was a fearful quiet, and might be likened to a ship at sea, which, after having been plundered and dismasted by pirates, is left floating on the ocean without a morsel of food to supply the wants of its crew, or a stitch of canvas to cover its naked masts; by degrees, however, some clothing, such as decency required, was procured for the females, by the return of their friends to the town; and many a father and mother rejoiced to find their children alive, although too often seriously and grossly injured. But there were also many who were denied even this sad consolation, for numbers of the townspeople had fallen in the confusion that prevailed; some of our officers also were killed in this way, and it has been said, I believe truly, that one, a colonel commanding a regiment, lost his life by the hands of his own men.

The plunder with which our camp was now filled was so considerable, and of so varied a description, that numerous as were the purchasers, and different their wants, they all had, nevertheless, an opportunity of suiting themselves to their taste; still the auction had not commenced in form, although, like other markets, "some private sales were effected." From the door of my tent I had a partial view of what was taking place; but for the present I shall leave the *marché*, and describe how I myself was circumstanced from the period I reached my tent, wounded, on the morning of the 7th.

The two faithful soldiers, Bray and Macgowan, that conducted me there, on entering, found my truss of straw, or bed, if the reader will so allow me to designate it, occupied by Mrs Nelly Carsons, the wife of my batman, who, I suppose, by the way of banishing care, had taken to drinking divers potations of rum to such an excess that she lay down in my bed, thinking, perhaps, that I was not likely again to be its occupant; or, more probably, not giving it a thought at all.

Macgowan attempted to wake her, but in vain – a battery of a dozen guns might have been fired close to her ear without danger of disturbing her repose! "Why then, sir," said he, "sure the bed's big enough for yees both, and she'll keep you nate and warm, for, be the powers, you're kilt with the cold and the loss ov blood." I was in no mood to stand on ceremony, or, indeed, to stand at all. I allowed myself to be placed beside my partner, without any further persuasion; and the two soldiers left us to ourselves and returned to the town. Weakness from loss of blood soon caused me to fall asleep, but it was a sleep of short duration. I awoke, unable to move, and, in fact, lay like an infant. The fire of small arms, the screams of the soldiers' wives, and the universal buzz throughout the camp, acted powerfully upon my nervous and worn-out frame; but Somnus conquered Mars, for I soon fell into another doze, in which I might have remained very comfortable had not my companion awoke sooner than I wished; discharging a huge grunt, and putting her hand upon my leg, she exclaimed, "Arrah! Dan, jewel, what makes you so stiff this morning?"

It required but few words from me to undeceive her. Ten and chocolate were soon in readiness, and having tasted some of the former, I sat up in my bed waiting the arrival of the first surgeon to dress my wound. My batman, Dan Carsons, shortly afterwards made his appearance; he led up to the door of my tent three sheep, and had, moreover, a pig-skin of enormous size filled with right good wine which the Spaniards call *la tinta de la Mancha*: "And sure," said he, "I heard of your being kilt, and I brought you this (pointing to the pig-skin of wine), thinking what a nate bolster it i'd be for you while you slept at your aise," and, without waiting for my reply, he thrust the pig-skin under my head. "And look," said he, shewing me a spigot at the mouth of my bolster, "when you're thirsty at-all-at-all, you see nothing is more pleasant or aisy than to clap this into your mouth, and sure won't it be mate and dhrink for you too?"

"Oh, Jasus!" responded Nelly, "he's kilt out and out; see, Dan, how the blood is in strames about the blankets."

A little learning is a dangerous thing, so – under certain circumstances – is a little laughing! and Dan Carsons and his wife made me laugh so immoderately, that a violent discharge of blood from my wound nearly put an end to my career in this world. Had it not been for the arrival of Dr Grant, the staff-surgeon of the division, who just now made his appearance, I doubt much if any of my readers would ever have had the pleasure of reading these my reminiscences. But I must have done with myself, Dan Carsons, and his wife Nelly, and resume my narrative of the sale of the plunder with which our camp was, to use a mercantile phrase, glutted.

Early on the morning of the 9th of April a great concourse of Spaniards had already thronged our lines; the neighbouring villages poured in their quota of persons seeking to be the purchasers of the booty captured by our men, and each succeeding hour increased the supply for their wants, numerous and varied as they were, and our camp presented the appearance of a vast market. The scene after the taking of Rodrigo was nothing in comparison to the present, because the resources of Badajoz might be said to be in the ratio of five to one as compared with her sister fortress, and, besides, our fellows were, in an equal proportion, more dexterous than they had been in their maiden effort to relieve Rodrigo of its valuables. It may, therefore, be well supposed, and the reader may safely take my word for it, that the transfer of property was, on the present occasion, considerable. Some men realised upwards of one thousand dollars (about £250), others less, but all, or almost all, gained handsomely by an enterprise in which they had displayed such unheard-of acts of devotion and bravery; and it is only to be lamented that they tarnished laurels so nobly won by traits of barbarity for which it would be difficult to find a parallel in the annals of any army. The sale of the different commodities went on rapidly, notwithstanding we had no auctioneers; there was no "king's duty," but, most undeniably, if the Spaniards paid no "king's duty," they paid the piper! While the divers articles were carried away by the purchasers, the wounded were removed to the hospitals and camp, and the lamentations of the women for their dead or wounded husbands made a striking contrast to the scene of gaiety which almost everywhere prevailed.

Towards the evening of the 9th our camp was nearly emptied of all its saleable commodities, and the following morning was occupied in getting rid of the many Spaniards who still hovered about us, endeavouring to get a bargain of some of the unsold articles. By noon all traffic had ceased, and the men began to arrange themselves for a fresh combat with Marshal Soult, who was advancing towards Badajoz. The appearance and demeanour of the soldiery in no way warranted the idea that they had been occupied as they were for the last three weeks, but more especially for the last three days. They were the same orderly set of men they had been before the attack on the town, and were just as eager to fight Soult as they were to storm Badajoz: the only change visible was their *thinned ranks*. In my regiment alone, out of seven hundred and fifty privates, four hundred and thirty-four had fallen; and of the officers, who at the commencement of the siege counted twenty-four, but five remained unhurt! Our total loss exceeded five thousand men; and although no officer of a higher rank than colonel was killed, it is a singular circumstance that every general actively engaged was wounded on the night of the assault. Picton, Colville, Kempt, Walker, and Bowes, who headed the assaulting divisions and brigades, were every one of them hurt on that fatal 8th of April.[10]

10 Picton headed the 3rd Division; Kempt its 1st Brigade. Colville commanded the 4th Division; Bowes its 2nd Brigade. Walker the 2nd Brigade of the 5th Division. The total loss of the British during the siege was 72 officers and 963 men killed, and 306 officers and 3,483 men wounded. There were also 100 missing, mostly, it is believed, men whose bodies fell into the Guadiana or the Rivillas and were not found. This gives a total of 4,924, so that Grattan's figure of "over 5000" is hardly exaggerated. [Charles Oman]

On the 15th of April, 1812, the heroes of Badajoz took a last farewell of the scene of their glory and the graves of their fallen companions, and marched towards the banks of the Coa and Agueda, where, but a few months before, they had given proofs of their invincible valour. Indeed it might be said, without any great stretch of historical truth, that every inch of ground upon which they trod was a silent evidence of their right to be its occupant – so far, at least, as right of conquest goes.

Ill as I was, in common with many others, who, like myself, lay wounded, and were unable to accompany our friends, I arose from my truss of straw to take a parting look at the remnant of my regiment as it mustered on the parade; but in place of upwards of seven hundred gallant soldiers, and four-and-twenty officers, of the former there were not three hundred, and of the latter but five! At any time, when in the full enjoyment of health and vigour, this sad diminution would have affected me; but in my then frame of mind it acted powerfully upon my nerves. I asked myself, where are the rest? I suppose I spoke louder than I intended; for my man, Dan Carsons, ran out of his tent to inquire "who I was looking after?" – "Dan," I replied, "I am looking for the men that are absent from parade; where are they?" – "Kilt, sir," replied Dan, "and the greater part of them buried at the fut of the ould castle forenent ye." "Their *bodies* are there, Dan, but where are they themselves?" "Och, Jasus!" cried Dan to his wife, "he's out of his sinces! Nelly! run and fetch the pig-skin of wine; you-know how it sarved him last night when he was raving." Nelly brought the remnant of the Tinta de la Mancha, and a few mouthfuls of it raised my spirits considerably, but the fever with which I was attacked was increasing rapidly.

The drums of the division beat a ruffle; the officers took their stations; the bands played; the soldiers cheered, and, in less than half an hour, the spot which, since the 17th of the preceding month, had been a scene of the greatest excitement, was now a lone and deserted waste, having no other occupants than disabled or dying officers and soldiers, or the corpses of those who had fallen in the strife. The contrast was indeed great, and of that cast that made the most unreflecting think, and the reflecting feel. The sound of the drums died away; the division was no longer visible, except by the glittering of their firelocks; at length we lost sight of even this, and we were left alone, like so many outcasts, to make the best of our way to the hospitals in Badajoz.

It is a task of more difficulty than may appear to the reader to describe the feelings that a separation, such as I have told of, caused in our breasts. More than half of our old companions – dear to us from the intimate terms upon which we had lived together, fought together, and, I might say, died together, for three years – were parted from us, most of them for ever! – the others gone to a distant part of the theatre of war, while we, enervated and worn down, either by loss of limb, or by loss of strength and vigour, were left to seek shelter under the roofs of those very people who had been so barbarously maltreated by our own soldiers. Nevertheless every one betook himself to the method he thought best suited to the occasion. Some caused themselves to be conveyed in waggons; others rode on horseback; and many, from a disinclination to bear the jolting of the carts, or the uneasy posture of sitting astride a horse, hobbled on towards the dismantled walls of the fortress. As we continued our walk, we met, at almost every step, heaps of newly turned-up earth, beneath which lay the bodies of some of our companions; and a little farther in advance was the olive-tree, at the foot of which so many officers of the 3rd Division had been buried. At length we reached the ravelin of San Roque.

The Talavera gate was opened for our admission; it was guarded by a few ill-looking, ill-fed, and ill-appointed Spanish soldiers. As we entered, each man we passed saluted us with respect; but the contrast between these men, who were now our protectors, and the soldiers we had but a short time before commanded, was great indeed; and the circumstance, trifling as it may appear, affected us proportionably. We walked on towards our wretched billets, and as we passed through the streets that led to them, we saw nothing but the terrible traces of what had taken place. Piles of dismantled furniture lay scattered here and there; houses, disfigured by our batteries, in a ruined state; the streets unoccupied except by vagabonds of the lowest grade, who prowled about in search of plunder; while at the windows of some houses were to be seen a few females in disordered dresses; but their appearance was of that caste that served rather to increase the gloom which overhung the city. Nevertheless, as the wounded men and officers passed, they waved their handkerchiefs and saluted us with a *viva*; but it was pitiable to witness the wretched state to which the unfortunate inhabitants had been reduced.

Upon reaching the house allotted to me, I was met at the door by an old woman who showed me my apartment. It was scantily garnished with furniture, most of which was broken; the bed was on the tiles, but that was rather an advantage than the contrary, because the heat was excessive. I stood in no need of any refreshment; my man, Dan, having been so active during the *bouleversement* that he supplied my cellar as well as larder; and it was fortunate that he did so, for the inhabitants of the house, as I afterwards learned, were without a morsel of food or a stitch of clothing, having been plundered of everything.

I lay down upon my mattress, soon fell asleep, and in less than an hour awoke in a high fever. Dan wished that I should attack the pig-skin of the Tinta de la Mancha, but I positively refused to do so: "Why then, sir," said he, "hasn't it been the making ov yee?" – "You mean the killing of me, Dan. Go and seek for a surgeon." He went, and soon returned with a young man in the uniform of the staff surgeons of our army; but from his youthful appearance, and the unworkmanlike manner he went about dressing my wound, I opine he was but an hospital mate. My man Dan was decidedly of my opinion; for after the doctor had examined my breast, and applied some dressing to it, he was about to retire, when Dan said with an air of authority, "You're not going to be afthur going without looking at his hinder part?" meaning my back. The doctor took the hint, and, turning me on my face, found a large piece of the cloth of my coat, which had been carried in by the ball, protruding through the wound. The doctor looked confounded; Dan looked ferocious, and though he spoke with respect to the medical man, I plainly saw the storm which was gathering. I feared that he was about to make use of the *fortiter in re*, in preference to the *suaviter in modo*; so I dismissed the doctor, upon an assurance that he would visit me the following morning.

After a lapse of three days, all the wounded capable of being removed were ordered to Elvas. Spring waggons, carts drawn by oxen, mules harnessed with pack-saddles, and in default of them, asses prepared in like manner, were put in requisition for the purpose of freeing Badajoz of as many of the disabled men, who crowded the hospitals, as possible. I was among the number, but so ill was I as to have no recollection of how I was transported, except that a waggon stopped at my door, and, after some hours, I found myself in the streets of Elvas. From the waggon I was placed in a car, and it was night before my man Dan, with all his tact, was enabled to procure me a billet. During a space of fifteen days I lay in a state of great pain, accompanied by fever, but after that I soon recovered my strength, and being allowed the option of either joining the second battalion of my regiment, to which I then belonged, quartered at home, or going back to the army, I preferred the latter.

My friends, Darcy and Adair, were my companions on my route to the army; and, punctual at the appointed hour, we left Elvas at six o'clock on the morning of the 3rd of June, without any encumbrance, such as a detachment to look after. We had no escort except our three servants, and Dan's wife Nelly; and it is needless to say that they were perfectly competent to take care of themselves, without causing us one moment's uneasiness, either on their account or our own; and never did any three officers in the service of His Britannic Majesty, or in the service of any other sovereign, set out on a route to join their companions with a more fervent intention of making the time pass as agreeably as possible. Our route towards Salamanca, near which city the army was stationed, lay through the old line of march, and we were obliged, unfortunately, once more to encounter that place of dirt and wretchedness, Niza. No matter what change had taken place either amongst ourselves or the different towns through which we passed, Niza was still the same; positively dirt – comparatively dirt – superlatively dirt! – dirt! dirt! dirt! The ditches were filled with reptiles, the houses with bugs and fleas, and Adair, who was already blind of one eye, had the other nearly darkened by the bite of a huge centipede. We poulticed his eye with rye bread and cold water, and in the morning carried him, with *a wry* face, to his saddle.

Once clear of Niza, we traversed the country towards the Spanish frontier; at length we got clear of Portugal, and once more reached the village of Fuentes d'Oñoro; every house, I might almost say every face, was familiar to me. The heaps of embanked earth, which denoted the places where many of our old companions had been interred, were covered with grass, which grew luxuriantly over the graves of the men who had once stood there victorious, but who were now lifeless clay. We traversed the churchyard where so many of the Imperial Guard and our Highlanders had fallen; and we marked well the street where three hundred of the former had been put to death by the 88th Regiment. Many of the doors still retained the marks of the contest; and the chimneys, up which the Guard had sought shelter, bore the traces of what had taken place. The torn apertures in the large twigged chimneys, broken down by the Guard in attempting to get up them, were in the same state we had left them –

untouched, unmended. Even the children could trace with accuracy the footsteps of those fallen heroes.

We walked on to the chapel wall, where the 79th had suffered so severely, and through which the French had forced their passage, under a torrent of shot, against the bayonets of the brave Highlanders. The chapel door was riddled through and through with bullets, and the walls bore the marks of the round shot fired from the French batteries. Several mounds of earth, covered as they were with herbage, still pointed out the grave of some one who had fallen; yet, to a passing stranger, the inequality of the ground would scarcely have been noticed, so little attention had been paid to the arrangement of the graves, which were dug in the hurry of the moment; but with us it was different. We could point out every spot, and lay our finger on the place where a grave ought to be found.

It so happened that the house I was quartered in for the night was one of those in which some of the Imperial Guard had sought shelter. I asked my patron why he had not mended the broken chimney? His reply was, that he preferred the inconvenience of the smoke which the aperture caused, for the pleasure he derived from viewing the grave, as he termed it, of the base French who had so scandalously ravaged his country. I cannot say that I much admired his feeling.

From Fuentes d'Oñoro we reached Rodrigo, which we had left only five months before. The breaches were repaired, the trenches levelled, and were it not for the different spots that had been assigned to many of our fallen companions, which we found untouched, there was no trace of those works which had caused us so much time and labour to construct. But those places, well known to us, brought back to our recollection the ground upon which we had stood a short time before, under circumstances so different; and the change that had taken place during the short interval – the thousands that had fallen in the two sieges, – and the difference of our attitude as compared to what it was when we before trod the spot we were then standing upon, afforded ample food for reflection. From the period of our investment of Rodrigo to the capture of Badajoz, that is to say, eighty-eight days, we lost in my regiment alone twenty-five officers and five hundred and fifty-six men; and it cannot be wondered at that we, who were alive and in health, should have a feeling of regret for our less fortunate companions, as also a feeling of thankfulness for our own escape.

There may be some who will think that such ideas are out of place, but, in my opinion, they are not so. No truly brave man ever looked upon the graves of his fallen companions without a feeling of regret. A man falling in the heat of battle is quite a different thing, because *there* all are alike, and subject to the same chance; and it is, moreover, wrong to mourn over the death of a comrade while the strife is going on; but the strife once ended, then will the feelings be brought into play, and the man who is incapable of a pang of regret for his fallen companion is unworthy of the name of a British soldier.

My man, Dan, had scarcely arranged my billet, ere I bent my steps to the house where I had slept on the night of the storming of the town. I had scarcely made my appearance at the portal, when the old lady to whom the house belonged recognised my voice. She ran forward to meet and welcome me; her daughters accompanied her, and it was in vain that I said I had a billet in a distant part of the town. The excuse would not be taken, and I was forced, absolutely forced, to have my baggage conveyed to the house where I had so short a time before entered under far different circumstances. The old lady asked how long I was to remain at Rodrigo. I replied, for that night only. "*J'en suis fâché,*" she replied in French, which language she spoke tolerably well, – "*mais j'essayerai de faire votre séjour ici plus agréable qu'elle ne l'était la dernière fois*" – and she immediately sent an invitation to her friends to assemble at her house the same evening.

Profiting by the confusion which of necessity took place in arrangements for the *soirée*, I left the house and took a survey of the town and breaches. The houses which were destroyed in the Great Square, by the fire which had taken place on the night of the assault, as also those near the breaches, remained in the same ruined state we had left them; but excepting this, and a few gabions which outtopped the large breach, whose reconstruction had not been quite completed, we could find nothing to denote the toil and labour we had sustained during our operations. An hour sufficed for me to make my "reminiscence" of past events. It was eight o'clock before Darcy and Adair joined me, and when we reached my billet, we found the saloon filled by a large and varied company.

Upon entering the room, all eyes were turned towards us, for the good hostess had said a thousand kind things in my praise, and the height and imposing look of Darcy were in themselves sufficient to cause a *stare*; but the elegance of Adair's manners, who had passed the greater part of his life on the Continent – his perfect knowledge of the Portuguese, Spanish, Italian, and French languages – captivated all. And although he was some fifteen or twenty years our senior, he decidedly bore away the palm; and in less than an hour after our *entré*, he made, to my own knowledge, five conquests; while Darcy and myself could boast of but two each! I never felt so humiliated – and from that moment I resolved that if ever I had a son I would make him a linguist.

The ball was opened by Avandano de Alcantara, a young Portuguese captain, belonging to the garrison of Almeida, and Señora Dolores de Inza, a Spanish lady, a relative of the Governor. The dance was the bolero, of which I had heard so much, but had never seen danced before. All eyes were turned towards the spot which the youthful couple occupied. I was an attentive spectator. Avandano danced well, and kept his elbows – a material point by the way – in that position which no bolero dancer should depart from (I obtained this information at Madrid), not to raise them higher than his ear;

but he danced mechanically, like one that had been taught, and had his lesson by rule more than by heart. Although he moved his arms with much grace, and kept the proper measure with his feet, there was nothing inspiring in his mode of dance, or in the manner he used his castanettes. His partner, on the contrary, had all the fire of the true Andalusian breed. Her movements, though not perhaps as correct as his, were spirited, and drew down thunders of applause from the spectators; and each plaudit, as was natural, caused her to increase her exertions. She danced beautifully, and every one expressed by their approbation the gratification they felt by her display; but the dance had scarcely ended when she fainted away, in consequence, no doubt, of the exertions she had made. She soon recovered, and would have once more joined the dance, had not her friends dissuaded her from so foolish an act, and she was reluctantly obliged to be a spectator for the remainder of the night. Waltzing was continued to a late hour; but there was no lady hardy enough to attempt the bolero after the success of Señora Dolores in this most difficult and graceful dance. The company at length retired to their different homes; I bade an affectionate good-night to my hostess and her daughters; and long before they were awake in the morning, I was several miles on the road leading to Salamanca.

TRIUMPH AND TRAGEDY: SALAMANCA AND BURGOS, 1812

Captain William Bragge,
3rd (King's Own) Dragoons

The Allied capture of the Ciudad Rodrigo and Badajoz fortresses opened the two corridors into Spain, and in early June 1812 Wellington advanced on Marshal Marmont's Army of Portugal, already depleted of troops for the Russian campaign. For nearly a month outside Salamanca the two armies tried to outmanoeuvre each other without committing to a decisive engagement, a "phoney war" which at least allowed Wellington to capture, on 27 June, three forts in the town. The deadlock continued until Marmont suddenly took the initiative by launching a feint to the west on 15 July, then crossing the Douro on the night of 16–17 July to establish contact with the rear of Wellington's army. During the 18th the Allies were in headlong retreat, Marmont's cavalry on one occasion breaking through the Allied rearguard to nearly capture the British commander himself. Nonetheless, when the day was finished, Marmont's strategic move had availed him little, although he consoled himself by believing he now had the measure of his opponent. Accordingly, Marmont – now heading upwards of 50,000 men and 78 guns – wheeled south to outflank the Allies and crossed the River Tormes during the rainy evening of the 21st, hoping to outstrip Wellington by hard marching. By the late morning of the 22nd, Marmont was convinced that Wellington was in full retreat and ordered his eight divisions to swing around what he judged to be Wellington's right flank. It was a fatal mistake. The bulk of the Allied army of 48,569 men and 60 guns was actually covertly deployed on the reverse slopes of Las Torres, holding an east–west line. In truth, Marmont was moving parallel to the main face of the Allied army and, worse, there were great gaps in his strung-out column. The French divisions were inviting piecemeal destruction.

After casting a cursory glance through his telescope, Wellington announced, "This will do at last, I think" and ordered d'Urban's Portuguese cavalry and Pakenham's 3rd Division to attack the lead French division under Thomieres. Unsuspecting and isolated, Thomieres' division was scattered, its fugitives running into Macune's division a mile to its rear. Some 15 minutes later, at 5 p.m., Wellington let loose the 5th Division and Le Marchant's 1,000 horsemen on Macune, who was likewise broken. Seeking more victims, Le Marchant then engaged the next French division, under Brennier, who went the way of his colleagues, although Le Marchant himself was slain in the repeated charges. And so Wellington reduced "40,000 French in 40 minutes," the French rot only stopping when General Clausel – who took command when Marmont was badly wounded by a shell – calmly ordered a counterattack on the Allied 4th Division, and drove a deep salient in the Allied position. So intense was the resultant firefight that General Clinton lost a third of his effectives in five minutes. However, Wellington's skilful deployment of his massive reserves eventually restored the Allied line and Clausel's shattered division retired in confusion, with Clinton in pursuit. The timely arrival of Ferey checked the British, the French general deploying seven of his nine battalions in classic, drill-book three-deep lines and the remainder in squares to cover the wings. After provid-

ing nearly an hour of respite to the remainder of the French forces, Ferey fell back to the edge of the forest and formed another line, before artillery and the intervention of the British 5th Division compelled his battalions to withdraw through the forest and join their comrades in flight towards the bridge at Alba de Tormes.

Salamanca was Wellington's greatest victory yet. For the loss of 4,800 men, the British had inflicted 13,000 casualties on the Army of Portugal, the fatalities including Ferey and Thomiere. More than that, Wellington had broken the French hold over northern and central Spain.

For political reasons, Wellington then decided to march on Madrid, the seat of King Joseph (Bonaparte) of Spain, entering the city on 12 August 1812. A month later he appeared before his next military goal, the fortified town of Burgos, which controlled a vital section of the Madrid–France highway, Wellington calculating that an offensive against the town would surely oblige the French into a major battle. Alas, the 2,000-strong French garrison under the inspired General Jean Louis Dubreton put up a stalwart defence and, although the Allies captured the Great Hornwork and some lower levels of the fortress they never reached the citadel. Torrential rain, which flooded the siege trenches, and a shortage of siege artillery only hindered matters. On 21 October, after four weeks of siege and 2,000 casualties, Wellington gave the order to retreat. The French had lost only 300 men. After the glory of Salamanca, Burgos was a tragic farce and the Allies went into retreat once more.

William Bragge, a scion of minor Dorset gentry, went to the Peninsula as a junior lieutenant in the 3rd (King's Own) Dragoons. He served in the Salamanca and Burgos campaigns, and was present for the French defeat at Vitoria in 1813. That same year he was gazetted captain.

Village of Villares,
3 miles from Salamanca.
June 28th 1812.

My dear Father,

The Idea of having a tedious Business in the South of Spain, without any opportunity of writing or sending Letters to England induced me to send a short and hasty Epistle from Vaiamonte on the 20th of May, which I afterwards regretted, as we again returned to our old Quarters on the 27th without having performed any Thing of consequence except re-establishing all our sore Backs, which were before in a fair way towards recovery.

The cause of this little excursion of about 100 Miles has never been fully explained to us, but I firmly believe it was occasioned by General Slade's *retiring* from a Patrole of about 50 Men and immediately reporting that the Enemy were advancing towards Merida in considerable Force, and as the aforesaid General has since run his whole Brigade (in the eagerness of Pursuit) into an Ambuscade losing all his Prisoners and nearly 200 of his own Men, I should not be much surprised to hear that Ld Wellington had recommended him to the Secretary of State for the Home Department, as an Officer whose consumate Skill and Abilities could nowhere be so well employed as in checking the unbridled efforts of King Ludd and his murderers.[1]

On the 1st June we once more left Cabeço de Vide and on the 11th were encamped on the Banks of the Agueda about 3 Miles from C[d] Rodrigo. On the 12th L[d] Wellington reviewed all the Cavalry and on the 13th his whole Army crossed the Agueda in three Columns, our Brigade with the Left under Gen[l] Picton.[2] On the 16th we arrived in front of Salamanca, where the Cavalry had a smart Skirmish. On the 17th the

1 The Luddite rioters flourished 1812–8, destroying technologies which they believed deprived them of jobs.
2 Lieutenant-General Sir Thomas Picton (1758–1815), commander of the 3rd Division.

French having retired, our Troops entered Salamanca and invested a Fort which contained about 700 French. On the 19th the French Army under Marmont[3] again made their appearance and cannonaded the King's Own Dragoons for some Time, which I am happy to state they stood with the greatest Firmness. Our Loss was confined to the Horses, 7 of which were killed and many of which were wounded. The French hovered about for some Days with the Idea of Relieving their Fort and at length finding themselves baffled in all directions and not liking to risk a Battle, the whole retired on the 26th and the Fort surrendered on the 28th, the Garrison consisting of 600 Men and upwards.

All the Cavalry have more or less experienced the skill of their Artillery Men but none so effectually succeeded in checking the approach of the Army towards Salamanca as Gen[l] Bock's[4] Brigade of Heavy Germans who singly, and unsupported, opposed themselves to Fort, Horse and Artillery and completely succeeded in keeping them in check until our Infantry had crossed the River and taken up their Positions.

The Fort, which at first was supposed to be very weak, stood a Siege of Ten Days and repulsed our Troops once, and had they been inclined to hold out, I do not see how it was possible to storm it. Our Fire had done little or no Damage to the Works but having set the Convent in Flames the Garrison were fearful of their Magazine blowing up.

From Castelo Branco to Salamanca we were encamped every Night and as the Weather was remarkably fine the whole March, we found our Tents full as comfortable as the Portuguese Houses; from Ciudad Rodrigo to within six Miles of Salamanca the Road passes through a most Beautiful Forest of very rich Land with moving Grass up to the

3 Marshal Auguste Marmont (1774–1852), commander of the Army of Portugal from early May 1812.
4 General Eberhardt von Bock, commander of the Heavy Brigade of the King's German Legion.

Horses' Knees, and as our mode of encamping is merely tying up the Horses to the largest Trees, a Camp of Cavalry in this Country is as pretty a Scene as it is ugly in England.

We are now, and have been for some days past, in a very decent Village in Rear of the Position and should be more comfortable were we not roused at Two O'Clock every Morning in order to be at the Alarm Post before Day Break, from whence we return as soon as a Report arrives from the outposts that all is Quiet. We have had a slight touch of the out Post Duty, which is truly Luxurious – no Trumpets, Baggage or Tents, our Backs to lie on and Bellies to cover us, without ever taking Saddles off the Horses even for the Purpose of cleaning, not to mention the Sun at noon Day in a Country as bare of shelter as Salisbury Plain. We are, however, better off than the Infantry who are exposed to the same Weather on a high Hill and consequently farther from both Wood and Water, neither of which is to be had nearer than two miles.

For three Days the Armies were within cannon Shot and the Videttes close to each other, the whole expecting an Engagement daily. The French have now fallen back on Zamora, where, I suppose, we shall follow as soon as Ld Wellington receives a Reinforcement of 4,000 British, the heavy Dragoon remounts and some Portuguese Infantry, all of which will arrive in two Days.

Salamanca is situated in an open Country completely bare of trees but is in some Respects superior to Oxford, notwithstanding the horrid Depredations of the French who have destroyed two Thirds of the Colleges and Convents in order to fortify their Convent. The Cathedral, Square and some of the Colleges are the most Beautiful Buildings I ever saw, and not being exposed to severe Frosts or Smoaky Chimnies, are as fresh and the Sculpture as entire as ever. I should conceive that Three of their Colleges were larger than Christ Church but the Quadrangles much smaller. Their Cathedral is truly magnificent both within and without, not so long as ours usually are, although richer in Sculpture. It had a very narrow escape of being demolished with the other Churches etc., but Marmont was graciously pleased to save it on condition of the Clergy paying a pretty severe contribution. The Cathedral was threatened as often as the French wanted Money.

The People here are in every Respect superior to those we have seen in the South and certainly more zealous in the cause. Dons Julian [Sanchez] and Carlos [de España], the great Guerilla Leaders, joined our Army with their Myrmidons and a more verminous looking set of fellows you never beheld. The Infantry [are] in English Clothing and the Cavalry, both Horse and Man, completely armed and equipped in the Spoils of the Enemy, so that it is next to impossible to distinguish Friend from Foe. The Don himself wears a Pelisse like the 16th Dragoons with an immense Hussar Cap and the Eagle of Napoleon reversed. In this dress, accompanied by two aides de camp equally *genteel* in Appearance, Twelve Lancers, a Trumpeter in scarlet on a grey Horse and three led Horses I saw the renowned Chieftain enter Salamanca amidst the acclamations of the Multitude who received him with every mark of Respect.

The Dammage we have done the Inhabitants by Feeding our Cattle of every Description on Green Wheat is incalculable, but they appear to bear it with the greatest Patience, being perfectly satisfied that Lord Wellington will drive the French out of Spain.

Nava del Rey,
July 4th 1812.

This Afternoon I have an opportunity of forwarding this Letter towards England and shall therefore employ the Morning in endeavouring to fill upon the Sheet my Adventures up to the present Moment, but we have lately led such a wandering Life that I have some difficulty in recollecting dates and Places.

On the 27th – not the 28th – of June the Fort at
Salamanca was taken and on the 29th our Brigade together
with the whole Army advanced towards Toro but in the
course of the day changed our direction and encamped in a
Wood on the Valladolid Road, about one League and a half
from where we started, having loitered about in the Sun 14
Hours. The next day we advanced about 4 Leagues and again
encamped on the Downs, and on the first of July the whole
Army amounting to 40,000 then encamped on the Banks of
the Rio del Nava, about 6 Miles in rear of this Village, and
the next Morning advanced as far as the Banks of the Douro,
where the advanced Troops had some skirmishing and took a
few Prisoners, but the whole of Marmont's Troops passed
the River and blew up the Bridge without farther Molestation. Yesterday the 3rd Division, our Brigade, Don Julian's
Cavalry and some Artillery proceeded to a Ford where our
Artillery and theirs had some shots at each other, part of our
Riflemen [of 60th Ft.] getting across the River and skirmishing but nothing consequential took Place. We were ordered
back to this Town and once more got into decent Houses and
good Beds, from whence I was again unnecessarily roused at
2 O'Clock, eat an enormous Breakfast and finding it to be a
false alarm again retired to my downy Couch. The Third
Division are still at the Ford but nothing will be attempted
this day or we should not be indulged with a Halt.

The Douro is nearly half a Mile Broad and the Fords
completely commanded by their Artillery, which are placed
very advantageously on the opposite Banks so high that our
Cannon cannot dislodge them, therefore some other place
must be found or we shall never get to Valladolid. We are
about equal to them in Numbers and the Deserters say they
are famished for want of Bread.

From Salamanca to the Douro and from hence as far as the
Eye can reach you can scarcely see a Tree, except the wood
where we encamped on the 29th. The whole country is one
extensive Range of Corn or Vines, the Villages are very large

and the Roads remarkably good. The Harvest is now getting [in] fast and as the Commissary General has given an order for nothing to be brought from the Rear but Bread and Spirits, there appears to be every reason for expecting a long Business. The Troops are in the highest possible Spirits and astonishingly healthy.

The current Reports (I suppose Lyes) are that General Hill[5] is advancing on Soult,[6] who is supposed to have raised the Siege of Cadiz and retired towards Madrid. If this is true, Gen[l] Hill will have his own Division of 18,000 Men encreased to 28,000 by the Garrison of Cadiz being released, which, with the addition of Ballasteros' Force, will make him considerably stronger than Soult. Another Report is that ten Thousand British have landed in Catalonia and laid siege to Barcelona, and that the Galician Army, hitherto immovable for want of Transport, have advanced as far as Zamora, which will enable us to cross the Douro immediately. If these Acc[ts] prove true, the Tide of Fortune appears to be turning against the French in every Direction. I am sorry to add that General Graham suffers so much from Weak Eyes, that his return to England is absolutely necessary – an event which L[d] Wellington and the Army at large have great Reason to regret, especially at this Moment. If anything happens to the Peer, the Command of the whole Army devolves on Sir S. Cotton.[7]

I have received yours of the 27th May and Lucy's of 21st, together with Newspapers up to the Ninth of June, by which I am extremely rejoiced to find that in spite of every Effort, the Perceval Administration still continue to conduct the Reins of Government.

My Horses are still in good condition and the little Bay

5 General Sir Rowland Hill (1772–1842); returned to duty in 1811 after the breakdown of his health. Captured the important bridge over the Tagus at Almaraz on May 1812.
6 Marshal Soult (1769–1851), chief-of-staff to King Joseph Bonaparte.
7 General Sir Stapleton Cotton (1773–1865), cavalry commander.

Mare rolling in Fat which cannot be wondered at, as we walk into a Barley or Wheat Field and out as much as we please.

Be kind enough to give my Love to my Mother, Brothers and Sisters and believe me Your dutiful Son, WILLIAM BRAGGE.

P.S. The day before our Army left Salamanca, high Mass was performed and the Te Deum sung in the Cathedral and a splendid Ball given to the Allies in the Evening. Yesterday and today we have had some Rain but I trust it will prove fine tomorrow [or I] shall say nothing more of the Comforts of Campaigning.

Pollos,
July 18th 1812.

My dear Father,

By some unaccountable Delay your Letter of the 8th June did not arrive until the 14th July, although we had received Letters and newspapers up to the 21st, but in the multiplicity of Business transacted solely by a Serg^t in the Post Office at Lisbon, we cannot much wonder at a Letter or two occasionally lying idle.

I am extremely apprehensive from the Acc^t you give of my Vaiamonte Letter [of May 20th], that poor Bean will be disappointed in the Draft which I sent him, and in order to relieve him as soon as possible, I have by this Post written to him explaining the circumstance and requesting that in case other attempts fail, he would immediately apply to you, whom I have assured him will without delay procure him his Money. After having once experienced a Disappointment in procuring Money from England, it appears extraordinary that I should a second Time run my stupid Head into the same Gap, though I am not without a faint hope that my draft was drawn in that sort of way that Mr Stevenson (if I have written it so) will immediately inform the Bearer of the Probability of such a mistake.

In order more effectually to prevent a recurrence of such

Blunders on my part, I should be obliged to you to lodge a small sum in Mr Greenwood's[8] Hands for my use, and request him to acquaint me of the circumstance, as most of the Officers transact money concerns with him, and would rather accept a Draft on him than any other Banker. With regard to the Paymaster General of the Army, [he] is now Four Months in Arrear and I believe has no Money for the Pay of the Troops nearer than Lisbon. Indeed if we were paid regularly as in England, I should have very little occasion for troubling you.

I wrote to you a few Days back from Nava which is comparatively speaking a Heaven to this Village of Pollos, situated immediately on the Banks of the Douro and about half a Mile from the French Camp. The River is about half a Gun shot in breadth and almost a continual succession of Fords, so that we live in a State of alarm all Night and lie in Bed all Day. Our Force consists of our own Reg^t and the third Division of Infantry with about 4,000 Spanish Infantry and Don Julian's Guerillas, who on the outpost Duty are very superior to any British Cavalry, having the Fear of the Halter constantly before their Eyes.

For the first Day or two we lived here very peaceably and had only a small Picquet out at Night, but as the French are expected to cross the River in order to serve it out to Lord Wellington, we are turned out bag and Baggage every Night at Ten, Breakfast on Beef and Onions at 4 in the Morning and afterwards go to Bed until evening. Even this extraordinary sort of Life agrees better with me than perfect inactivity and in an open country without any source of amusement and a scalding hot Sun, you cannot much wonder at a Person being little inclined to take exercise voluntarily.

Marmont boasts of our having lost 3,000 Men in taking the Fort at Salamanca (anglia 300) and says he offer'd us battle for three Days with little more than half our Force, which the

8 Greenwood was a regimental agent.

British Army cowardly refused, notwithstanding our superior position. He now gives out that in a few Days he crosses the River to chastise us for our Temerity in advancing so far into Spain.

Lord Wellington, it is supposed, will not oppose his crossing the River, and has actually fixed on a Position in rear of Nava del Rey, where I sincerely hope Marmont will put the courage and Skill of the British Army to the Proof in the course of a Day or two. Our Forces are nearly equal, therefore after the brilliant Examples of Talavera, Albuera etc., there can be no doubt as to the Result of a General Engagement.

If Lord Wellington keeps his Men in their present Encampments, the being exposed Night and Day together with the Heat of the Sun must destroy hundreds, and if Marmont suffers him to remain there a week longer, the Harvest will be under the Ground and out of reach of him – Marmont – and his Army, who will consequently suffer for the next three years a greater want of Bread than they do at present, which we know to be very great indeed.

Salamanca has suffer'd considerably since we left it by an explosion of Gunpowder, which Report says has destroyed 500 People and three Streets. It is, I fear, a melancholy Business though not so great an extent as reported.

Our Remount arrived yesterday bringing a reinforcement of three subalterns, whose Assistance is greatly required as sickness and Staff Employment had reduced our original Number to five, which is no great Number for two Picquets a Night. The Horses were excellent and I do believe we are as well, if not better mounted than any Reg^t out here.

Like the Devonshire Huntsman, I have neither Butes or Breeches, everything coming from England having been left at Abrantes. If any one *ask* you to bring a Parcel for me, you may load him with a Map and Spy Glass, both of which I suffer from the want of and cannot procure here, unless the French were to retreat rapidly when I expect to make a number of Things. We have an honest depôt Seg^t at Belem who I know would send anything to me, if I could be certain of its ever getting to his Hands. Things sent by the Packet, I believe, come to a very considerable amount.

We have no Butter or Spirits and scarcely any vegetables but onions, therefore our meals are rather extraordinary – especially Breakfasts. Honey is nearly out as well as Cheese, therefore I almost pray for this Fight to be over, which will probably not be more dangerous than riding behind Old Major in your Buggy.

The French are very civil and allow us to water horses and bathe in the River; the latter experiment I have not tried although hundreds do every day.

Be kind enough to give my Love to my Mother and Charlotte and accept the Same from Your dutiful Son,

WILLIAM BRAGGE.

I hope my next will be dated at Valladolid.

Flores d'Avila,
July 25th 1812.

My dear Father,

Knowing the Anxiety you and my Mother will feel upon hearing of a great and sanguinary Battle, in which the Third Dragoons bore no inconsiderable share, I take the earliest possible opportunity of informing you that I escaped perfectly sound, Wind and Limb, together with the Little Bay Mare who carried me through the Day delightfully and I believe to her Speed and Activity I may in a great measure attribute my marvellous escape, as I at one Time had to gallop along the whole Front of a French Brigade retreating in double quick step.

I have often heard you say, after reading the public Dispatches, that you could never make anything of the History of a Battle, therefore I shall not attempt to describe the Fight of Salamanca any farther than what happened on our immediate Left and Right which was simply this. Marmont endeavoured to turn Lord Wellington's right and had taken possession of a Hill. [the great Arapile] in that direction but the British Hero rather counteracted his Intention by having detached the Third Division still farther to the Right under General Packenham, with most of the Cavalry drawn up in Line on the Left of General Packenham, as if to keep up the communication between the Third Division and the rest of the Army. At least this was our situation about 3 O'Clock, the French keeping up a tremendous Cannonade on the cavalry and Infantry, our People not firing a Gun until Four, when I believe Lord Wellington gave the Signal for a general Attack by opening with six eighteen-Inch Howitzers. Immediately upon this, our Right and Left turned theirs, the Enemy were driven from the Hills and the Cavalry advanced upon the Backs of the Infantry. Our Brigade literally rode over the Regiments in their Front [the leading brigade of Packenham's 3rd Division] and dashed through the Wood at a Gallop, the Infantry cheering us in all Directions. We quickly came up with the French Columns [Maucune's 5th Division] and charged their Rear. Hundreds threw down their Arms, their Cavalry ran away, and most of the Artillery jumped upon the Horses and followed the Cavalry. One or two charges mixed up the whole Brigade, it being impossible to see for Dust and Smoak, but this kind of Attack – so novel and unexpected – threw the French into confusion and gave our Infantry Time to get another Battle at them, when they served it out nicely, making them fly in all directions. We lost our General[9] in a square of Infantry [the leading regiment of Brennier's 6th Division] and in him we have experienced a severe Loss. One Lieut. was killed by his side, but in other respects our Loss is trifling considering we were solely

9 i.e. Major-General John Le Marchant (1766–1812), designer of the 1796 British light cavalry sabre and author of *Rules and Regulations for the Sword Exercise of Cavalry*. At Salamanca he was wearing his old blue 7th Dragoon uniform, which was markedly conspicuous among the redcoats of his brigade.

engaged with Infantry and Artillery. The Brigade marched off nine Pieces of Artillery and about 500 Prisoners.

We marched to Alba de Tormes on the 23rd and here on the 24th (yesterday) and this day the whole Army halts. We passed by the Heavy Germans yesterday and saw the Ground where they had gained immortal honour by charging three Squares of Infantry, breaking them and capturing 1,600 Prisoners. Lord Wellington was a Spectator and declares he never saw so gallant an Affair.

Our Loss will, I should suppose, not exceed that at Badajoz. The French estimate theirs at 16,000; Lord Wellington certainly underrates it at 10,000. We know of 19 Pieces of Cannon and five Eagles taken besides Standards and Colours innumerable. French Generals were wounded, one taken Prisoner. Marmont had his arm amputated at Alba de Tormes and was conveyed from thence on a Litter borne by Twelve Grenadiers. Sir Stapleton Cotton was wounded by the Portuguese.

We have frequently been employed lately and on the 18th had the credit of saving the 1st [German] Hussars and the 14th from a perilous Situation, so that the Heavy Dragoons will, I trust, be in greater Repute than formerly. The night before the action, we Bivouac'd close to Salamanca [at Santa Marta] and had scarcely linked Horses when a tremendous Clap of Thunder bursting over their Heads, the whole Brigade broke from their moorings and dashed over the Men, wounding about 50. The Night Dark, Rain in Torrents, French at Hand, and the Horses at Liberty in a Country as open as Salisbury Plain, only conceive our confusion. We recovered all our Nags but the 5th lost 18 Horses. P.S. An acc[t] has just arrived of the Death of Marmont, Bonnet and Marshal Beresford.[10]

You will receive this Letter nearly as soon as the Gazette Account, as it goes with the dispatches which are to be

10 The report was wrong on all 3 counts; Bonnet [Bonet], Marmont and Beresford all lived until the 1850s.

conveyed to England by Lord Clinton. You must excuse the writing for although "sub Tegmine Tenti", I am not exactly "lentus in Umbra" – in other words I lie down under a scorching Sun to write on a Blanket. Until last night I have not had my clothes off for a Fortnight and have seldom been under the cover of a tent but continue quite well.

We are on the high Road for Madrid, probably with a view of taking or making the French destroy their immediate Stores at Segovia.

With Love to all, Believe me Your dutiful Son,

WILLIAM BRAGGE.

P.S. What a Glorious Campaign this has been: –

Garrison of Badajoz	5,000
D° Ciudad	2,000
Fort at Salamanca	700
Taken at Almaraz	250
Llerena	150
	8,100
[SALAMANCA]	12,000
	20,000 approx.

The Spaniards know no bounds to their Joy. All the Medical People in Salamanca came out to dress the wounded and the most respectable Inhabitants carried the Soldiers on their Backs.

Madrid,
August 18th 1812.

My dear Father,

After having halted one Day at the Village of Flores d'Avila; we again proceeded with a burning scent after Marmont's Army but having allowed him too much Law, he got off without farther Molestation except the Loss of 900 Sick and some heavy Spanish Guns at Vallodolid, where our

Advance gave up the Pursuit. Our Brigade marched to the Banks of the Douro and the next Morning turned off for Segovia and Madrid, which latter Place we entered on the 12th August, having I believe loitered on the Road for that Purpose.

I did not obtain a Sight of Valladolid, which I very much regret as I wish to render this Campaign as much like a Tour of Pleasure as possible and by seeing as much as other People to prevent being humbugged hereafter. The Cathedral and Castle at Segovia were well worth seeing, as well as the magnificent Aqueduct built by Trajan. About two Leagues from thence we halted in a very Picturesque Valley amidst the Mountains of the Sierra Guadarrama, over which there is only one Pass but that so admirably contrived you may trot the whole way if your Horses are good enough. About a mile from this Encampment is the Royal Pallace of Ildefonso, a place much resembling our Hampton Court, but inferior to it in the size of the Apartments as well as in the Collection of Paintings with which the Rooms are crowded. The Gardens are magnificent but as we march there to take up our Quarters tomorrow, another Letter will probably give a better account of it.

Our next halt was near Escorial, where we were nearly Surprised by the French in consequence of the Portuguese Cavalry having run away in the most cowardly manner and in doing so upset 3 or 4 of our Light Guns which, together with some Gunners, Captain and 27 Horses were consequently taken by the Enemy. The heavy Germans, however, arrested their progress or they would have been in our Camp and taken half the Brigade. Knight of 15th [Lt. Dr.] had just obtained a majority in the 11th Portuguese Cavalry which he joined two Days before this Affair (in which he narrowly escaped being taken) happened.

Of Lord Wellington's success and our very favourable Reception in Madrid you will have an account in the News-papers. All the Prisoners marched out drunk, made the

Escort drunk and then got wounded and plunder'd themselves in consequence.

The Inhabitants testified their Joy by hanging all their Curtains, Tapestry etc., out of the Windows, which had a very pretty effect and was greatly encreased for 3 Nights by a splendid Illumination with Immense Wax Candles. On the third Night they gave a Ball to the Army, which afforded me an opportunity of seeing more splendid Cloathes than I ever before saw. The Women are beautiful, very fond of the English and all – What d'ye call 'ems in England? Therefore you may suppose we rather regret leaving Madrid, although going to a Pallace.

Madrid is, I should suppose, the most delighted Metropolis in the World and certainly the best calculated for the Town Residence of a Gentleman, as there is in no Part of it those dreadful Nuisances which necessarily accompany many of our Trades in London and elsewhere. They have no Court end, but magnificent Houses scattered indiscriminately over the whole Town, many of them surpassing our best Houses. There is only one Royal Pallace, which although only in an unfinished State, still exceeds any we have in England. In short the Streets, Houses, Fountains and Public Walks are so good, as well as the Roads in the Neighbourhood, that I do think if any thing ever Tempts me out of England, it will be the Idea of spending a Winter at Madrid. There are no suburbs but each entrance to the Town passes under a beautiful Gateway.

The poorer Class have suffered dreadfully from the high Price of Provisions but I hope our Efforts will yet relieve them from their oppression. Bread has already fallen two Thirds in Price. Here, and at Salamanca, the 3 Shilling Loaf of two Pounds weight, being sold for one Shilling.

Adney informs me that Lucy is going to increase her Menagerie which I am sorry to hear. He likewise says his Team of Pointers is not so good in consequence of Phoebus beginning to grow old.

I fear Jack's Examination is a humbug, as being refused your Testimonium is what is in Oxford termed being *plucked*.

I have received two Letters lately, yours of the 27th July arrived yesterday. With regard to the Banker's Account, I am almost as much in the dark as yourself but can assure you I have only drawn two Drafts, one in favour of Mr Bean for 50£, and one in favour of Mr Sealy for 26£ odd. From Bean I have never heard, therefore trust his Draft is paid, and as for Mr Sealy, either he or Capt. Heywood owes me 100 Dollars which I sent by the letter to Lisbon. Heywood is now extremely ill at Celorico, therefore it will be some Time before I hear from him.

Pray give my Love to my Mother and Charlotte and Believe me Your dutiful Son, WILLIAM BRAGGE.

When I live in Madrid I will buy some better Paper.

Valladolid,
8th Septr 1812.

My dear Father,

I have had a Letter ready written for some Days but as the Army has advanced pretty rapidly since I began it. I am induced to write it over again in order to give you the latest Intelligence and I understand the Packet leaves Vallodolid this Afternoon. An English Mail has arrived up to the 21st August but the Letters are not yet delivered.

We left Madrid on the 19th of August and in three Days reached the Royal Palace of Ildefonso, where I got into very excellent Quarters and for once spent a delightful Week in Spain, being constantly in the Company of a very Gentlemanly and entertaining Patron who was Vicar of the Place and had a very accomplished Niece living with him, as good natured as she was pretty, therefore you may suppose I was what the Spaniards call "muy contento" with my situation. [This] was soon changed for one of a very different Nature, for at the end of the Week we were pushed on to the Villages near the Douro doing a sort of half outpost Duty which lasted another Week, when Lord Wellington brought up his Divisions and crossed the Douro at Herrera immediately to the great surprise of the French, who had no idea of his being nearer than Arevalo. They waited for us to attack them, but the Artillery having gone to the wrong Ford, it was found necessary to defer the Attack until the next Morning (yesterday). The Gentlemen, however, retired in the Night and blew up the Bridges [over the Pisuerga on the other side of the town], therefore we entered Valladolid (the most disaffected Town in Spain) without opposition.

Lord Wellington is here with four Divisions and a devilish Temper in consequence of the Artillery not having come up in Time Yesterday, which circumstance saved the French from another beating, as we had as many Men as they. His Lordship had given an order to attack which was afterwards countermanded. The Enemy have retired towards Burgos, but not a Soul of the HeadQuarters Staff knows whether we shall follow them or return towards Madrid to assist Soult, who is advancing from the South spreading all over the country most direful Proclamations. When the latest Accounts left the South of Spain, Soult was at Cordoba and Gen[l] Hill at Almaraz, therefore all is going on well in that Quarter. And if one may venture to augur anything from L[d] Wellington's countenance *previous* to his crossing the Douro, nothing could be more favourable than the present situation of our Affairs.

Amidst the Troubles of Spain some few English have remained in Madrid, amongst whom I got acquainted with a most curious Trio: an Irish Friar, formerly confessor to the Queen, a Scotch Saddler and a mad Widow, all of whom have resided there upwards of 20 Years. I likewise met with several People who spoke English.

The Theatre of Madrid has degenerated in proportion with every thing else since the gay Days of Laura and Arsenia. At present the Company of Comedians are very paltry and the most applauded Actor amused us with using the Pot de Chambre and pulling off his Breeches, previous to going into Bed, which Scene concluded the Play.

Sir Howard Douglas [the British Commissioner at Corunna] has just arrived from Corunna, where I believe he has been a sort of Agent for furnishing Spanish Armies with Arms etc. The Account he gives of the renowned Galician Army is really miserable, therefore we can reckon nothing on any assistance from them, and as for the Guerillas, I'll tell you a Story.

Some Time in May last, 800 of these formidable fellows undertook the Siege of Ildefonso, which was at that Time garrisoned by eighty of the Imperial Guard and two officers. 300 entered the Town and 500 surrounded the Place about Noon, but in less than two Hours the Eighty French drove them out of the Town killing and taking numbers, to the great satisfaction of the Inhabitants who have a greater dread of these Villains than they have of the French. My Patron and his Niece were Eye witnesses and told me this Anecdote.

I have this morning rec^d two Doubloons being a Fortnight's pay, and must of Necessity buy some Cloathes as every thing I have is worn out, and my new Boots are at Abrantes, where – I suppose – they will stay until the War is over. We have lately been in a state of Beggary but I trust we shall now get Money more regularly. Mr Sealy has given Heywood credit for the 100 Dollars I sent him in May so I hope to be rich some Day or other.

I hope to God this will be Lord Wellington's last Campaign in Spain as I get quite weary of Service. You cannot conceive half the Misery of it – we are wretched. What think ye of having choice of Quarters (in a Village where the People were half of them absolutely dying) after 5 Generals and their Staff? This happened to my Squadron the other Night and the consequence was that I slept in the same House with two other Officers, two Portuguese Boys, the Patron and his wife and 9 Guerillas. I wish some of our gay young Men in

England could have changed Beds for the Night. I forgot to observe there were *no Doors* in this elegant Hovel but plenty of Fleas.

We have not seen Lord Wellington's Dispatches in the English Newspapers but if the Portuguese is a literal Translation, our Brigade, and particularly our Reg^t, have no great reason to thank him for his commendation. On the 18th of July, the 3rd were ordered out in a hurry to support the 1st Hussars and 14th [Lt. Dr.] who at that Time were completely clubbed and running away, until a charge from the Third turned the Tide, which was done in sight of Lord Wellington and the whole Army. The Regiment afterwards kept their Ground with Riflemen shooting at them until our Infantry had Time to come up. Upon this occasion Genl Alten and Col. Hervey thanked Major Clowes and they in turn got thanked by his Lordship. On the 22nd [Salamanca] the Dragoons of our Brigade took 7 Guns, Horses and all to the Rear, and Prisoners out of Number – I should suppose certainly not less than 2,000 – therefore we are rather vexed that Lord Wellington did not make mention of us more favourably in his Dispatches, which in England are read as Gospel. 5 of our Men had charge of 700 the whole Night.

I have been nearly loosing the Bay Mare but she is now getting about again and is really an invaluable Creature on Service, being always fat and hearty.

The Artillery Officer taken near Madrid on the 11th Augt has made his Escape. He says the French begin to croak, saying it is all over with them in Spain. This Northern Army only mustered 22,000 yesterday which was six weeks since 45,000. With Maitland and Hill our Army must nearly equal theirs. Marshal Beresford brought up 4 different Brigades on the 22nd and was advancing a 5th Time about 20 yds in front of the Colours when a Ball struck him.

Give my Love to my Mother and Charlotte and believe me, Your dutiful Son, WILLIAM BRAGGE.

Claret is here 3d a Bottle. At Madrid the English drank up a stock for *6 Months* in 3 Nights.

Villayerna,
a Village one League in front of Burgos,
Septr 25th 1812.

My dear Father,

We left Valladolid on the morning of the 10th and arrived in the Vicinity of Burgos about the 20th,[11] the French not allowing us to make more than about Two Leagues a Day. The Armies encamped regularly within sight of each other, but the Enemy appeared not to have the slightest Inclination for a second Engagement, nor did our noble Leader wish to attack them as long as they would keep out of his Way. They took up a very strong Position one morning in order to gain Time but decamped and retired through Burgos, leaving a powerful Garrison in a very strong Castle, which – in my opinion – will cost the British Army dearer than Ciudad Rodrigo.

Our Troops succeeded in taking an outwork of the Castle the first Evening [19th], but not without considerable loss on our part, in consequence of Ld Wellington having employed a Division not used to the noble science of storming. Had the Light or Third Division been there [they were still at Madrid], we should not have lost above 50 Men, but as it was the Troops advanced to the Glacis and there stood to be shot at without endeavouring to gain the Fort, and have since that failed in an attempt on the Castle. I believe the Army would regret their Loss more had they not foolishly complained to Lord Wellington after the 22nd [July – Salamanca] of not having "Justice done them" – anglia: not fighting enough – to which his Lordship replied: "They had been very ill used but he would see them righted at the first opportunity", which unfortunately happened to be the Fort

11 The investment of Burgos began on 19 September 1812.

and Castle of Burgos. The Division is composed of Guards and Highlanders. I am happy to say we marched in rear of the whole Army and had consequently nothing to do the whole Journey, which was upon the whole the most unpleasant we have had, it being extremely cold and the Nights very wet, but the Weather is now warmer and I trust we shall have no more Rain, which is certainly a curse to Soldiers.

By our Batteries not having opened yet, I rather think we are endeavouring to take the Castle by Sap,[12] which is – I believe – rather a tedious process, but as Lord Wellington in all his military Career never missed taking a Fort, I do not imagine he is going to be outdone at Burgos. The French have a strong Position about 8 Leagues from here, but will hardly advance to relieve their Garrison. Their Troops are certainly in a great state of Insubordination and are so strongly impressed with the Idea of *going to France* that another Battle would prove fatal to the army of Portugal. They have one strong Fort between this and the Ebro [at Miranda] and another at Pamplona.

All the Troops, both English and French, are considerably weakened by Sickness; our sick amount to *20,000*, in which are included all men taking Medicine whether with or away from their Regiments, and the Army under Soult are so weakened by it, that he is striving to the utmost to keep out of Gen¹ Hill's Road.

The noted Galician Army have at length joined us under Castaños and look much like an Army of Mendicants with Brown Cloaks on. Their Artillery are very superior to the French and are in general drawn by English Horses with a complement of Men mounted on the best Spanish Nags. They have one squadron of Hussars dressed in the same style with ours but the rest of their cavalry are inferior to Don

12 Wellington commenced a "parallel" (i.e. trench) against the castle's western front on 23 September, from there pushing a mine, or "sap," towards the enemy's position.

Julian's Guerillas. I believe their effective strength does not exceed 10,000.

I was very much delighted to find that my Letter had anticipated the Gazette of the 22nd [July], and care not how soon I have the Pleasure of communicating such another glorious piece of News. I see the opposition Papers do not give Lord Wellington credit for some of his Laconic Speeches previous to the Battle, but although not the Language of the Marlboroughs and Peterboroughs, it is very much this modern Hero's style of addressing his Generals and is found to answer equally well.

The Parcel you sent Cartwright for me is, I have no doubt, perfectly safe, at *Abrantes* where our necessaries are likely to remain, tho' Report says everything is coming up. I think the Contest will end in Spain as our Army is here maintained at nearly one Third the Expense in consequence of the abundance of Corn.

Our present Leader (Col. Ponsonby) is no great Genl. He was ordered the other Day to advance until he was stopped, which he did by moving our Reg^t down an Avenue with a Front of Threes and no advanced Guard until the Enemy thought proper to Fire a Gun, which enfiladed the Road and might have killed 30 Men had it been pointed properly. Another shot took two Light Dragoons Heads off and the next passed under my Mare's legs and the covering Serg$^{ts'}$ horses without doing either any Injury.

Burgos is one of the worst large Towns I have seen in Spain and the Country round it extremely dreary although abounding with Corn. The People [are] horridly ugly and what is rather remarkable for Spaniards excessively dirty, therefore I have no wish to go farther North, except to embark.

I still continue well, but most of our Officers are complaining and some of them very ill of Fevers and Agues which cannot be much wondered at as we have only been under a Roof two Nights since we left Valladolid.

Be kind enough to give my Love to my Mother, Brothers and Sisters and accept the Same from, my dear Father, your dutiful Son, WILLIAM BRAGGE.

Remember me kindly to Froward the first Time you see him, and tell him how much obliged I am to him for forwarding my Salamanca Letter.

I thank you for lodging Money for me with Greenwood, some of which I hope to transfer immediately.

> Villayerna,
> 3 Miles from Burgos,
> Oct^{ber} 18th 1812.

My dear Father,

Since the commencement of the Year 1812, I do not believe you have ever received two Letters from me at the same Village, nor would that event have now happened had not Lord Wellington been under the Necessity of keeping a strong Force in the immediate Neighbourhood of Burgos, in consequence of the Difficulty of reducing the Garrison in its Castle which the Enemy have threatened to relieve more than once, although their Efforts have hitherto been shabby in the Extreme.

From the Moment we first invested this cursed Castle, the Weather has proved particularly unfavourable to our operations, having scarcely ceased raining the whole Time accompanied by occasional High Winds and very severe Nights, notwithstanding which our Divisions of Infantry still remain encamped and may truly be said to resemble "Father Pigs", not having any covering but very indifferent Huts built of Boughs and open at each end, without any Straw, Palliasses or things of that nature to lie on. You can easily conceive the state of such a Camp on low Ground after three Weeks Rain, which has almost filled our Trenches with Mud and Water as well as the Camp. Our Men for the last Fortnight have had a Lodgement on the outer Wall of the Castle from whence they keep up an incessant Fire of Musquetry but I fear without doing the Enemy any farther Mischief than preventing their annoying our Working Parties. The Castle is now mined in several Places and I expect we shall make a desperate attempt either this Evening or Tomorrow Morning as his Lordship's Dispatches ought to go off the next Day. At the beginning of the Fray we had Thunder, Lightning and Nelson (3 eighteen Pounders so-called) to assist us, but the contending elements have long since given way to the superior skill of the immortal Nelson, who now singly, opposes himself to nine Twenty Four Pounders.

I received yours of the 12th September a few Days since and this Morning had a Letter of the 15th from Greenwood acknowledging the receipt of 100£ which you were good enough to lodge in his Hands for my use. I have not seen Newspapers of a much later Date but understand that Lord Wellington has some which announce the Dissolution of Parliament, as well as a Truce between the Russians and French, a Piece of Intelligence which although extremely probable I shall be sorry to see confirmed, as with the Assistance of Russia I am thoroughly convinced we could settle the French in this Part of the world, whereas a strong Reinforcement from France might easily turn the Tables on us.

The Spaniards according to their own accounts have been doing wonders lately, but I am incredulous enough not to believe a single Syllable of their Dispatches. They starved the French out of Astorga and accepted *their own* proposals for a Capitulation, but had no sooner got possession of the French than they disarmed the Escort (1 Frenchman to Five Spaniards) stripped both men and Officers, and marched the whole to *Corunna* to be exchanged at a convenient opportunity. The First and second-in-commands shot themselves the next Day and the Spaniards used the remainder as ill as possible on the Road; but villainous as it is, the French richly deserve this treatment. The Spanish Armies put one in mind of the Foppish Midshipman who marked his ownly Two shirts 59 and 60.

It must be allowed that War, or rather Service, is a famous

thing for promotion. I was twelfth Lieutenant when I landed at Lisbon; am now Fifth and shall probably be first for purchase by the Time I have served the regular Period as more of our Capt^s and Sub^s are heartily sick of the Business. As a preliminary step to promotion, I should like to know how much my Freehold would sell for, as I should wish it to go for that purpose.

The dissolution of Parliament happening so soon after Mr M. Pitt's severe domestic calamity will probably induce him not to offer himself again for the county, in which case I suppose there will be a union of Colours, having myself no hopes for the King of Basan, who Lord Charles [Manners] says: "We (meaning the Brothers Hunt) have considered a Poor Creature since his Marriage and fond of Money."

With the Assistance of borrowed Money and some deceased Officers' Kits, I have been enabled to rigg myself again tolerably well but was a few weeks since almost naked. This Climate certainly has agreed with my constitution wonderfully well hitherto, and will I hope continue to do so. I am become immensely heavy and Fat, and shall have a very respectable Bay Window by the Time I return to England, which I trust we shall do before another Twelve months pass over our heads.

Do you not think it very bad Policy to send Life Guardsmen on service and to keep Hussars in London, who are in no respect half so well calculated to keep Cockneys in order as the Old London Troops? I begin to think with the Editor of the *Examiner* that some Princes were born for Tailors.

My horses are at present in excellent condition and so indeed are most of the Troopers, except the Old ones, who at this Time of Year always look miserably ill. We have had a Field Day, a Review and two false Alarms since we came to this Village. I find, by referring to a Journal, that this is the only Instance of our having remained Three Weeks in the same Place since January. Should this Castle be taken, we shall certainly go back to the South of Spain, which is a much pleasanter Part of the World to be in, as the People in this Neighbourhood are poor and almost all of them Labourers.

I am sorry to have so indifferent an Account of Jack and would willingly write him a Letter did I not know that most of his Friends had taken that trouble in vain. I wish for a week or two he could see the Luxury of being an Infantry Officer on Service, whose Life is many Degrees worse than that of the meanest mechanic in England, but "He that is truly dedicate to War, Hath no self Love".

Ned Phelips suffers very much from the Ague. He has now been ill more or less for three Months; if he gets better one Day, he is out coursing the next – how like Papa.

With this, you ought to have received Five Letters from me since the Battle; one from Flores d'Avila, one from Madrid, Valladolid and Burgos. I have sent as many to the Adneys but do not get so many answers from them as I could wish.

I hear every Gun that is fired against the Castle and believe the Firing to have encreased greatly since Yesterday Morning. The Castle is situated much like that at Corfe, but the Twenty Four Pounders on its Top command the opposite Hill, which could not have been the case at Corfe Castle. There appears to be a Triple Line of Defence.

The Ground is so slippery and dirty that walking is almost impossible. I shall therefore ride out in the rain in order to cure a Heavy cold.

I wish you to remember me to old Fowler, who will I hope live to see me come back again. Do you think he and his Family would stand cannonading well?

With Love to my Mother, Sisters and Brothers, Believe me my Dear Father, Your dutiful Son, WILLIAM BRAGGE.

Aldeia da Ponte,
Novr 26th 1812.

My dear Father,

I perfectly agree with you in thinking it a most secondary Consideration whether a Person dates his Letters from a

Pallace or a Pigstye, provided he enjoys the same State of Health in both Situations, but I very much doubt whether there would not be a visible difference in two Letters written by the same Person from "Butye's" Cabin and the Bedford Coffee House. I am led to make this Remark from an Observation in your last Letter that mine from Valladolid and Madrid contradict each other, a circumstance which I can only attribute to the Badness of my Quarters, Toughness of the Rations or a short Allowance of *Rum*, as I still mean to maintain that Madrid is the most delightful City, and Ilde-fonso the most beautiful Valley, I ever saw in my Life. With regard to the rest of Spain, it is equally ugly and uninterest-ing to the English Traveller, having scarcely any Meadows or Trees except here and there a sombre Forest of Pines.

You will already have seen a circumstantial Account of our late Retreats, which have really been very Disastrous and from want of a little better Arrangement in the Com-missariat and other Departments rendered more terrible than a Sanguinary Action, as besides the Inclemency of the Weather we had the worst of all Enemies to contend with, proving fatal to Hundreds, namely Hunger and want of Spirituous Liqour, no Rations being given to the Troops for Four – and in many Instances Six – Days. The Weather was very Rainy, intensely cold, and the Country we had to retreat over much like part of Oxfordshire, being very deep and intersected by numberless Brooks and Rivers which in our Advance to Salamanca we never perceived. Our Spring Waggons and Mules went by one Road and the Troops by another, so that every knocked up and wounded Man fell into the Enemies Hands and all the Cavalry went with the same column of Infantry, leaving two others completely uncovered. To this circumstance we owe the loss of Sir E. Paget [on 17th Nov[r]] and Quantities of Baggage. Sir Edward was taken between two Columns of our Infantry retiring on the same Road and immediately recognised by a French Dragoon who recollected him in Egypt.

After being kicked about for a Month without any Hopes of Reversing oneself on these Rascals, I cannot say but that I felt considerable Satisfaction at being once more across the Agueda and secure from all Alarms, but I regret excessively having been obliged to have to recourse to this measure, which has dissappointed the Expectations of England and the Hopes of Spain, besides which they will revert into a State of Despondency and never again have any Confidence in the Effort of a British Army. It has likewise given our Enemies an opportunity of exulting, which I could have dispensed with, though they certainly have brought all their Troops from the farthest Points of Spain to effect (by Manoeuvre and not by fighting) this desirable object. I must give the French Credit for having once more outmanoeuvred the English in the passing of a River, over which they threw Ten Thousand Men before we were aware of it. Having got their Troops over, they declined a second Contest on the Arapiles but proceeded in the direction of Ciudad, necessarily compelling us to retire. Had they procrastinated passing the River another Day, Salamanca would still have been ours.

The Situation of Spain is truly pitiable, being constantly exposed to the Ravages of three Roving Armies and the Inhabitants sure to suffer either in Person or in Property, let them enlist under which Banner they will. We deceive them, the French impoverish them and the Spanish Troops, regular and irregular, plunder them of every earthly Thing they possess. Of the Spanish Troops I still entertain the same opinion which is, that they will not stand Fire unless greatly superior in Numbers; but allowances are certainly to be made for Men dragged from their Homes, without confidence in their Officers, without Pay, without regular Rations and but for the Liberality of England, would be without clothing. Amongst their Leaders there are undoubtedly some very Brave Men, but generally speaking they want even that good Quality and either from Jealousy, Peculation or Treason are little worthy of their Situations. Ballasteros, for disrespect of

Lord Wellington, and Don Carlos for Peculation are both in arrest and superceded.

During the late Operations our usual good luck has attended me, and the Brigade I belong to; me in having escaped throughout the Campaign without Pip or Palsy, which is rather to be wondered at, as I never changed my Clothes or washed my Face and Hands for the last 6 Days, and the Brigade in having no Fighting when in the Rear and escaping annihilation in the late March to Valladolid when completely cut off from the rest of the Army by 5,000 French Cavalry with a River in our Rear, through which we accidentally found a Ford in the Night. Nor must I forget a liberal supply of Pigs, Beef and Mutton, which the Heavy Germans had shot and left in the Camp upon being suddenly ordered out when we were without Rations.

We were in this Village last January when it did not afford us a Mouthful of Forage, in which respect it is now considerably bettered, but having since that Period received the Benefit of an *eighth* Visit from the French [it] is in a most Dilapidated State and has very few Houses remaining with Roofs on, notwithstanding which we have at present Two Portuguese Reg^{ts} of Infantry, a Squadron of Dragoons and Troop of R.[oyal] W.[agon] Train or (as I see on the opposite Wall) Newgate Blues. We expect to move to Fundão tomorrow or the next Day.

So great has been the Mortality amongst our Officers, that I have been very apprehensive of having a Junior Lieut. put over my head in consequence of my not having served Three Years; but as one of our Captains has lately changed his mind, I am tolerably secure until May. The Army List should now run: Shakespear [A.D.C. to Sir S. Cotton], *Burn*, Bowater – Adj., Bragge, leaving me fourth on the List and second for purchase. Major Clowes having resigned goes home tomorrow. In him we have a great Loss.

One of your Letters reached me at Dueñas, and two others here, together with one from Adney informing me of Lucy's

Disappointment. Should it be attended with no farther serious consequence than the Loss of a Nephew for a Twelvemonth, I shall be very happy. Adney's Letter is chiefly about his Dogs and Horses which are usually super-excellent.

In consequence of Bean's directing his Letter to a Confidential Serg^t, I did not receive it until two Months after its arrival. He duly received his money from Stephenson and I have lately recovered mine from Sealy, which has made me tolerably rich to begin the Winter Sports. My horses, from the severity of the Weather during the last month and want of Corn, are wasted to nothing, especially the Dun Mare who the last Morning was from the above reason completely knocked up. She is so big and so liable to a *Fever in the Feet*, that I should certainly sell her could I find a Purchaser.

It rained till we reached this Village. Since that, it has been a hard Frost and will apparently Tomorrow be a deep Snow. I and my Captain are in a Room, with a Roof to it and out of pure Charity made room for two Field Officers to sleep by moving the Table and Chairs.

Whilst in position near Salamanca, we heard of Caffarelli's having retired to Burgos. He made a Feint that way, but speedily turned down the Douro, and would have crossed and been in our rear had not our Army retreated.

I do not think the French have too much reason to boast of the Year 1812, in which they have lost 50,000 Men and are at last obliged to bring all their Troops to one point. I trust my Lord will breed more Mischief this Winter.

With Love to my Mother, Brothers and Sister, Believe me Your Dutiful Son, WILLIAM BRAGGE.

FIGHTING THE REDCOATS, 1812–5

Corporal Samuel Stubbs, Kentucky Militia

During the Napoleonic Wars, both the French and British fleets
violated the maritime rights of the United States as a matter of
course, seizing no less than 1,100 American vessels between
1803 and 1812. The French were eventually persuaded from
the practice, but the British refused to renounce the right of
searching vessels suspected of conveying strategic materials to
France. And so it was that in June 1812, the United States
Congress declared war on Great Britain, a declaration also
prompted by American desire to assimilate parts of British
Canada.

The War of 1812 proved an inglorious affair all round.
British forces, in alliance with north-western Native Americans, seized Detroit, occupied north-western Maine and burned
Washington, DC, whilst the Royal Navy blockaded the East
Coast ports. These gains were then offset by the British losing
Detroit and suffering defeat at Lake Champlain and Baltimore.
After a year and half of scrapping with neither side able to gain
the military upper hand, the two nations headed for the diplomatic table, signing the Peace of Ghent in December 1814. But
before the treaty was ratified, General Andrew Jackson's
volunteers defeated the British at New Orleans on 8 January
1815, with 3,500 assorted Americans – 700 regulars, plus

Kentucky and Tennessee militiamen, Afro-Americans, and Creoles – withstanding a charge by 6,000 British regulars, battle-seasoned veterans of the campaigns against "Boney" himself. This victory, in the very moment of the war's end, retrospectively cast the 1812 conflict, for Americans at least, as a second War of Independence, a decisive victory for the American character and the American way of warfare. Yet, if this has truth, so does the legend of the unflinching British infantryman. At New Orleans, the British continued the assault until nearly all officers had been shot down, and 2,000 men had been killed, wounded or captured.

American losses were eight dead.

Samuel Stubbs signed up to fight the redcoats in 1812, aged sixty-three. As a member of the Kentucky Militia, he fought at Queenstown, Lundy's Lane, Fort Erie and New Orleans. The militia formed the bulk of American forces in the war, and although frequently ill-disciplined and parochial (most militiamen refused to join General van Renselaer's 1812 attack on Queenston, Canada, because they were only contracted to serve on US territory) they were steeped in what General Jackson termed "untutored courage."

Brother Ephram,

I just write you to enform you that I'm still alive and in tolerable helth and choice spirits – altho as well as my brother *officers*, I have had some hair bredth escapes. Sposing that you would like to know something about my military life since I quit home, I'll give you the whole story.

When the express first came into our neighborhood, calling upon us all to turn out and march against the Canadians, I was like another [Israel] Putnam, ploughing in my field – but I immediately unharnest the old daples, swung my napsack, shouldered my old gun that had killed me forty-five deer the three months past, and marched away for head quarters.

In four days time I joined the army with a dozen more of my neighbors, near Queenstown. The brave Col. Van Rensselare was our commander in chief, under whose command we the next day (which being the 13th day of October 1812) in boats crossed over to Canada – But, ah, in the end it liked to have proved rather a bad job for us, for the opposite shore was lined with redcoats as thick as bees upon a sugar maple – but after exchanging a few shots our brave Colonel buzzed in among them, while I and the rest followed close to his heels, and drove them all up a steep bank. We now got a fair footing and stuck up the American colours in Canada! We did not obtain this much however without some loss on our part, and what was unfortunate for us all, our Colonel was severely wounded – but he was still able to keep upon his legs and with great courage ordered us to push forward and storm their fort, and that we did, and made them one and all scamper off into the woods.

But we were now in our turn unfortunate, for one half of our army was yet on the other side of the river, nor would the cowardly dogs come over to assist us when they saw the d–d redcoats cutting us up like slain venison![1] The enemy now doubled their numbers while every shot diminished ours; in truth they got the better of us, and again got possession of their batteries, altho we let fly showers of ball and buck shot into their very teeth and eyes! Ah! the poor Yankee lads, this was a sorry moment for ye! They dropped my brave companions like wild pigeons, while their balls whistled like a northwest wind through a dry cane break! Our Commander ordered a retrete, but nature never formed any of our family you know for runners, so I wadled along as well as I could

1 General van Renselaer crossed the Niagara River at Queenston with 900 regulars and some militia; most of his 2,270 militiamen refused to cross on the ground that they were only raised to fight within the US. At the ensuing battle of Queenston Heights, the British General Brock, heading 600 British regulars and 400 Canadian militia, inflicted 250 casualties and took over 700 prisoners.

behind; but the redcoat villains overhaul'd me, and took me prisoner! But not until I had a fare shot at their head commander General Brock, who galloping his horse after my retreting comrads, bellowed out to 'um like a wounded buffalo to surrender; but I leveled my old fatheful Bess, which never disappointed me in so fare a mark, and I heard no more of his croaking afterwards.

Oh one thousand which crossed over, but a few escaped biting the dust! As for poor me, I expected they'd kill and scalp me, but after stareing at me as if I had been born with two heads, and enquiring of what nation I was, and from what part of the world I came, their Colonel ordered me liberated, who said to me, "Old daddy, your age and odd appearance induces me now to set you at liberty; return home to your family and think no more of invading us!" This I promised him I would do, but I didn't mean so, for I was determined I wouldn't give up the chase so, but at 'um again.

So I hastened off and joined General Deerbon's army; and on the 27th day of April [1813] we took Little York, which is the chief town of the Upper Province. We went in boats, and the redcoats peppered a good many of us before we reeched the shore. But when we got footing, they fled before us like an affrighted flock of redwinged boblinkons. We drove 'um, from their battery, and then in a powerful body of pursuing 'um, when on a sudden, as if the whole earth was paring asunder and discharging from its bowels huge rocks and stones, a dreadful exploshon took place from the maggazeen, which the arch dogs had fixed for the purpose! And a serious exploshon it proved for us, I tell ye, for it killed one hundred of our men, including our brave commander General Pike. For my own part, I scaped with just my life as you may say, for a stone as big as your fist struck me on the head, and nocked off a piece of my scalp as broad as your hand! But, faith, this I didn't mind much, but waddled on with the rest, over dead bodies as thick as cowslops, and soon got poses-shon of the town. The cowerdly British chief, General Sheaff, had thought it best to scamper off with his soldiers and Indians before we entered the town, so that I got but one fare shot at one of their copper-colour'd sanups, whose heels I soon made too light for his head, and would have scalped the dog, but my captin would'nt allow it.

As all the work appeared now to be done in this quarter, I marched off. And on the 20th June [1814] joined General Browne's army, which amounting to about three thousand brave boys of us, on the 3d day of July, crossed the Niagara. General Scott commanded the first brigade, Gen. Ripley the second, Gen. Porter the militia, and Farmers' Brother the Indians, who were painted as red as maple blosums. Fort Eree[2] surrendered to us that very day, and on the next we marched to Chippewa, driving the enemy before us like so many fire-frightened antelopes!

On the 5th, the enemy's commander, General Riall, came out upon Chippewa plain, with two thousand two hundred regelers, while my militia boys and the Indians on both sides were engaged in the woods. For my own part, I climed a sturdy oak, where I assure you I did not suffer my old Bess to grow cold, for whenever I saw an Indian creeping like an allegator upon his belly, I gave him the contents in full, and made him hug the ground to sum purpose. I'm sure I killed fifteen of 'um in fifteen minnits, and shood have been glad to have fleeced them; but the New England men don't approve of scalping. At this time our brave troops under Gen. Scott[3] was hotly engaged with Gen. Riall's redcoats, who after an hour's hard fighting, they turn'd tail to and run in all directions, and saved their pork by gaining their works at Chippewa. We killed about five hundred of them, while our loss was three hundred twenty-nine killed wounded and prisoners. And thus ended this engagement.

2 i.e. Fort Erie.
3 General Winfield Scott; the grey coats of his regular brigade became the model for the dress uniform at West Point.

On the 25th, I agin marched with Gen. Scott, who advanced with his brigade, betwixt eight and nine hundred, about a mile in the Queenstown road, where we found the enemies, and engaged 'um about sunset.[4] The enemies were guessed to be four thousand[5] stout, and were cummanded by Gen. Drummond. The tussel lasted til about leven a'clock, when, gad! I believe both parties were willing to quit the field. We took twenty pieces of artilary from 'um; one of 'um I took, faith, myself alone with charg'd bagnut [bayonet]! The loss on both sides was about nine hundred; the redcoats commander, Gen. Riall, and about twenty officers were taken prisoners. Our Gen. Brown and Gen. Scott were wounded. The next day, we return'd to Fort Eree, under command of Gen. Ripley.

August 15th, Gen. Drummond ordered an assalt upon our fort in three columns, consisting of the bestest men of his army, to the amount of three thousand. There was about one thousand five hundred of us, under Gen. Gaines, who took cummand of us about the first of August. We repulsed the redcoats with great loss. We killed, mangled and made prisoners of about one thousand five hundred of 'um. They lay as thick as slartered mutton around. Ha, brother Ephe, a fine picking for skelpers! Our loss was sixty killed and wounded.

I continued with the American troops until they were about to go into winter quarters, when with the thanks of my General, like another Cincinnaty, I started home, to exchange my rifle and bagnut for the ploughshare and pruning hook. But I did not get half way when I was summoned to repair to New Orlenes, where the redcoats had landed and were thretening to over run the whole country! Accordingly, I right-about-face, and with quick step steered my course for New Orlenes, where by land and water tacks I arrived in seven days.

4 This was the battle of Lundy's Lane, perhaps the most vicious firefight of the War.
5 British forces were closer to 3,000.

I found the whole place in alarm. They had had some skermishing with the redcoats, but the desisive battle was yet to be fought, as you shall here. I joined capt. Copp's company, a nice man, who gladly receiv'd me, and in three days promoted me to the office of a CORPORAL! As I never held any office before, you know, it made me feel kinder queer at first; but I soon learnt my duty, and the grate responsibility attached to my office.

On the morning of the 8th [January 1815] before day-light, the enemy silently drew out a large force to storm our lines, where we were entrenched up to our chins. There was a great fog, and their columns advanced unperceived to within about half a mile of our camp, and drove in our piquet [picket] guard. About the break of day, they as bold as hunger wolves advanced to our entrenchments, led on by their foolish officers up to the very muzels of our guns. I could have dropped them as easy as a flock of benumb'd wild turkeys in a frosty morning. But I picked for those who had frog paws upon their shoulders, and the most lace upon their frocks. Aye, the Corporal did his duty that day I'll warrant ye. Some of the foolish redcoats penetrated into our lines, where they were soon baganuted or taken prisoners; many fell mounting the brest works; others upon the works themselves. The roar of artillery from our lines was insessant, while an unremitted rolling fire was kept up from our muskets. Ah, *my men* performed wonders. For an hour and a quarter the enemy obstinately continued the assault; nor did they faulter until almost all their officers had fallen. They then retreted, leaving from one thousand five hundred to two thousand in killed mangled and prisoners. On our side the loss was confined to about twenty men – but I lost but one out of my company!

So I remain, yours, &c.
Corporal Samuel Stubbs

THE RETREAT FROM MOSCOW, 1812–3

General Louis-Francois Lejeune,
I Corps, Grande Armée

If the "running sore" of war in the Peninsula was one cause of Napoleon's downfall, the other was Russia. Defeated at Jena-Auerstadt and Friedland, Tsar Alexander I had sued for peace on a raft at Tilsit in 1807, but no sooner was the ink dry on the treaty than relations between the two powers deteriorated. Russia had no intention of being a mere vassal state and resented the effects of the Continental System, while Napoleon himself was distrustful of the Tsar's intentions towards Constantinople. The Convention of Erfurt, 1808, shored up Franco-Russian relations temporarily, but only temporarily. From 1811 Napoleon began building up a vast army beyond the River Oder, seemingly to intimidate the Tsar into submission. When Tsar Alexander called the French bluff, Napoleon had little option but to send his 600,000 men over the River Niemen into Russia. They crossed in June 1812. Roughly half the infantry and one third of the cavalry came from French satellite states, principally Germans from the Confederation of the Rhine, but including Italians, Poles, Netherlanders, Portuguese, Greeks, Spanish, even former foes from Prussia and Austria. The initial French advance was unusually slow-a-foot, allowing the retreating Russians to destroy everything of use to the invader (the policy of "scorched earth") and to avoid a set-piece battle, until the bloody but indecisive encounters at Smolensk on 17 August and Borodino on 7 September. Napoleon pressed on, believing that the capture of the Russian capital must finally compel the Tsar to sue for peace. In truth, Moscow was easily given up, the departing Russians putting much of the city to the torch to deny the French the advantages of its occupation. For a month, the Grande Armée *waited for the Russian reply to its peace proposal. It never came.*

On 19 October 1812 Napoleon, realizing the impossibility of wintering in Moscow, ordered the retreat. Blocked from following a southerly route through Kaluga at Maloyaroslavetz on 24–25 October, the Emperor fatally chose to withdraw along his invasion route – through territory which had barely supported the advance. It would not sustain the retreat. Meanwhile, the weather turned from balmy to cruel. The Russians under the wily field marshal Mikhail Kutusov held back from full-scale attack, contenting themselves with allowing the Cossacks to harass the French flanks and rear. There was little death-dealing for the Russians to do: exhaustion, hypothermia and starvation was doing it for them. As the fatalities mounted in the Grande Armée, *cohesion and discipline in most regiments broke down and the retreat took on the cast of a refugee flight. By 22 November Napoleon had less than 25,000 troops under arms from the 95,000 who had left Moscow; behind this cohesive body trailed some 40,000 stragglers, including non-combatant women and children. The final crisis came on the River Berezina. With the body of the* Grande Armée *dying before them, the Russians moved in for the kill. Admiral Tshitsagov and 34,000 Russians blocked the line of French retreat on the Berezina, while another Russian army, 30,000 strong, under General Wittgenstein closed in from the north-east, and Kutosov, with some 80,000 troops pursued the French rear. Worse still, the Berezina, usually frozen in winter, was in full spate due to an unseasonal thaw; and Napoleon himself had ordered the destruction of the pontoon train only days before.*

That anything of the Grande Armée *emerged from the trap on the Berezina was due to four factors. Napoleon had three corps in Russia – II, VI and IX – which had not been part of the "Moscow army," and II Corps under the heroic and oft-wounded Marshal Oudinot and IX Corps under Napoleon's old Italian comrade Marshal Victor played key roles in the ensuing battle of River Berezina, 27–28 November 1812. Secondly, General Jean-Baptiste Corbineau, commanding the second brigade of II Corps' cavalry, discovered an unmarked ford over the Berezina near Studienka, north of the bridge at Borisov which had been destroyed by the Russians. Thirdly, General Baron Jean-Baptiste Eble, commander of the pontoon-train, had wilfully disobeyed Napoleon and preserved two field forges, two wagons of charcoal and six of implements – enough equipment, provided wood could be found, to fashion bridges. Fourthly, with his metaphorical back to the wall, Napoleon rediscovered his metal.*

Accordingly, Napoleon ordered Oudinot to make a feint to the south on the 25th to distract Tshitsagov from the unmarked ford, with the Russians obligingly taking the bait. The Studienka crossing uncovered, Eble and 400 pontonniers and engineers tore down the wooden buildings of the nearby village and fashioned two trestle bridges, the men working up to their necks in freezing water, a number of them dying of exertion and slipping under the water to their deaths. The first bridge was completed by 1 p.m. on the 26th, with 11,000 men from II Corps hastening over to join a detachment of Corbineau's cavalry to form a bridgehead on the western bank. By 4 p.m., the second bridge was opened for artillery and vehicles. That part of the "Moscow army" still under discipline crossed over the Berezina through the rest of the 26th and the day of the 27th. By then, Tshitsagov was aware of his duping and Wittgenstein was fighting his way to the bridges from the east, against a fierce rearguard action from Victor's comparatively fresh IX Corps. All through the 28th, battle raged on both banks, with Victor's diminishing forces holding firm and Oudinot and Marshal Ney engaged with superior numbers at the western bridgehead, amid falling snow that reduced visibility to 30 feet. At one juncture II Corps threatened to collapse, but were rallied when General Doumerc's 3rd Heavy Cavalry charged through woodland to inflict some 2,000 Russian casualties. It proved a telling blow and Tshitsagov fell back.

On the eastern bank, Victor's men were similarly saved by the cavalry when the Russians launched a fierce offensive against the centre of their precarious position. The so-called "Charge of Death" by the Baden Hussars and the Hessian Chevauxlegers repelled the Russians, but of the 350 cavalrymen who started from the French line a mere 100 returned. Meanwhile, non-combatants crossed the bridges, several times in mass panics as Russian guns fired on the crossing and the fugitives gathered around the eastern approach. At 9 p.m. on the 28th, Victor received orders to evacuate the east bank, and by 6 a.m. on the 29th the last of the combatant elements of the Grande Armée had crossed the Berezina. However, few of the straggler horde could be persuaded to cross the bridges at night, despite Elbe's most desperate entreaties. At around 9 a.m., faced with the absolute military necessity of destroying the crossings over the river, Elbe ordered the bridges burned. At this, the stragglers still on the eastern bank stampeded towards the river, and scenes of appalling tragedy unfolded as thousands were crushed in the press or drowned in the Berezina. Cossacks slaughtered 10,000 survivors.

All this notwithstanding, Napoleon had extricated that part of the Grande Armée still under arms and shaken off the Russian pursuit. The cost of the battle was 20,000 Grande Armée combatants, and perhaps 40,000 non-combatants. Russian losses were 10,000 killed. There were no more major actions as Napoleon's battered force wended its way to the sanctuary of Poland. By early January 1813, the last Grande Armée survivor was out of Russia, by repute this being Marshal Ney after his valiant holding of the bridge at Kovno. Behind him rested the remains of nearly 550,000 of his comrades.

*General Baron Louis-Francois Lejeune combined a preco-
cious talent as an artist with a military career. He was commissioned in the artillery, transferred to the engineers before
becoming ADC to Marshal Berthier in the Marengo campaign.
Imperial staff duties thereafter alternated with engineering ones,
as Lejeune served* Le Tondu *in a roll-call of battles in Germany
and Spain. After escaping from captivity in England, Lejeune
joined Napoleon for the invasion of Russia, serving as chief-of-
staff to Marshal Louis Davout of I Corps. After surviving the
"terrible retreat", Lejeune commanded a brigade of VII Corps
in the German campaign of 1813. A serious head wound on the
day after the battle of Hanau (30 October 1813) forced him into
retirement from military service.*

On October 18 we received orders to leave Moscow, and to
march by way of the Kalouga road on the 19th. Thus, after a
month's delay at Moscow, which had been of no special
advantage to us, during which our army had received few
reinforcements and our troops had been worn out hunting for
provisions, we left that city and sadly began our retreat
towards France. We were fortunate in having beautiful
autumn weather, and the first few days' march was peaceful
enough, for we only had to drive off a few Cossacks who
hovered on the flank of our columns. But, as on our advance,
we were everywhere harassed by the Russian plan of burning
everything on our approach, and we could do nothing to
prevent it. About ten leagues from Moscow the first corps
halted at the base of a fine castle, the foundations and first
floor of which were of hewn stone. I had several orders to
write, and I went up a grand staircase into a suite of rooms
which seemed to have been but recently deserted, for they
still contained a piano, a harp, and a good many chairs, on
which lay a guitar, several violins, some music, drawings,
embroideries, and lady's unfinished needlework. I had scar-

cely been writing ten minutes, when we all noticed a smell of smoke. This smoke quickly filled the place, becoming so dense that we were obliged to give up work to try and find out whence it came. It seemed to issue chiefly from the wooden framework of one door. I had it broken in, and thick smoke at once poured through the aperture. I then went down into the cellars to see if the fire originated there, but I could discover nothing. I tried having a few buckets of water flung into the opening we had made, but even as my orders were obeyed such masses of flames rushed out upon us that we had only just time to collect our papers and escape. We had scarcely got downstairs when we heard the windows breaking with a crash, and as we looked back on our way to join the bivouac of our corps we saw volumes of flames issuing from all the windows of the castle, which fell at last, bearing witness by its destruction to the patriotic fury with which the Russians, torch in hand, were determined to pursue us.

Of course other fires occurred accidentally, with which the Russians had nothing to do. The little grain or flour found by our soldiers was made into cakes and put in the ovens with which all the peasants' huts were provided. Scarcely was one batch of cakes done before other troops came up, and the oven was heated again till the chimney would suddenly catch fire. This was how most of the fires which were to light up our passage from Moscow to the Niemen came about.

My courage almost fails me when I try to relate the horrors of those awful days and nights of suffering. But in spite of that, I shall put down here all that I find in my notes, for I think that the lessons taught by the past should be brought forcibly before the eyes of those whose genius leads to their being called to command armies.

Kutusoff[1] justly felt that the best way to make war on us was to cut off our communications, so as to isolate us in the

1 Field Marshal Mikhail Golenischev-Kutusov (1745–1813), appointed commander of the Russian armies in the West in late summer 1812. He died of exhaustion following his long campaign against the French.

midst of a hostile population to whom our loss would be gain. He therefore took up a position at Vinkowo commanding the Kalouga road, by which he thought it probable that we should retire. The success he had achieved on the 18th confirmed his belief that the course he had adopted was the best, and the aim of his later manœuvres was to bar our passage.

Under these circumstances it was important that we should push on as rapidly as possible during the first days of our retreat, so as to gain a couple of days' march on the enemy and get possession, without fighting, of the principal passes. But, alas! this was just what we did not do. Although much of the impedimenta of the French army had been sent on some days before, we were still encumbered with a great number of wagons and carriages laden with provisions for the prisoners, and with the booty we had taken, which included warm garments to protect us from the cold we should have to encounter. The amount of baggage was really enormous, and to give some idea of it I will just mention what I, an officer, who realised as much as any one the importance of getting rid of encumbrances, was trying to take with me. I still had: 1. Five saddle horses; 2. a barouche, drawn by three horses, containing my personal effects and the furs in which I meant to wrap myself when bivouacking in the open; 3. the wagon, drawn by four horses, in which were all the papers of the staff, the maps, and the cooking utensils for the officers and their servants; 4. three smaller wagons, each drawn by three little Russian horses, in which rode our servants and the cook, under whose care were the stores of oats, a few precious trusses of hay, with the sugar, coffee, and flour belonging to the staff; 5. my secretary's horse; 6. the three horses I had lent to my sister, which had gone on in front, making altogether six carriages and twenty-five horses, to take along little more than bare necessaries. The traces of the carriages were constantly breaking, the march was retarded whilst they were mended, there were perpetual blocks in the sand, the marshes, or in the passes, and it often took our troops twelve hours to do a distance which a single carriage could have accomplished in two.[2]

The Emperor, who was very much concerned at these delays, ordered that all the carriages not absolutely necessary for the transport of the few provisions we had with us were to be burnt and the horses used to help drag the artillery. So many were, however, interested in eluding this stern but wise sentence, that it was very insufficiently carried out. To set an example the Emperor had one of his own carriages burnt, but no one felt drawn towards imitating him, and the army, which still numbered between 105,000 and 106,000 combatants, and had 500 pieces of cannon, took six days to cover some thirty leagues. Further precious time was lost in getting across country by difficult roads, from the main Kalouga route, which was very bad, to a better one, and the Emperor leaving only Murat's cavalry and Marshal Ney's infantry on the old road to cover us from the attacks of the army under Kutusoff.

The Viceroy's corps marched at the head of the column on the new road, whilst the Delzons division, as advanced guard, occupied Malo-Jaroslavitz,[3] the passage through which was extremely difficult.

Malo-Jaroslavitz was a little town of wooden houses, with tortuous streets, built on the steep sides of a lofty hill, at the base of which wound the little river. Luya in a deep valley it had hollowed out for itself. A narrow bridge spanned the river below the only road by which the town could be reached from Moscow, and this road was here bounded on either side by impassable ravines, down which flowed the rapid torrents of such frequent occurrence in Russia during the rainy season. On the evening of the 23rd the town was occupied

2 Marbot says that the army in retreat was followed by 40,000 vehicles. TRANS.
3 Maloyaroslavetz, on the River Lusha.

without resistance by the first of our battalions to arrive, the inhabitants having all fled at their approach.

That same evening the Emperor halted at the post-house of Malo-Jaroslavitz, a mere peasant's hut, where he passed the night after having sent out officers bearing his orders to the corps écheloned on the road from Moscow to Smolensk, telling them to meet him at the latter town.

On October 24 the Emperor was riding with the first corps and his Guard, as he thought, in perfect security, when a considerable body of cavalry appeared on the right, which we all took at first to be Murat's troops. We were not long left in our error. It appeared that a certain Platoff,[4] a celebrated Cossack hetman or general, had promised Kutusoff to carry off Napoleon, and now with several thousands of his men he suddenly flung himself upon that part of the French army which he fancied included the Imperial staff. He had guessed rightly, and in the twinkling of an eye Napoleon was surrounded by Cossacks and compelled to draw his sword in his own defence. Fortunately, however, his escort was made up of men devoted to his person, and they pressed round him, breaking the shock of the barbarian charge. General Rapp, as he was engaged in trying to get the Emperor away, was overthrown in the mêlée, whilst his horse was pierced by a lance. Several officers near the Emperor were wounded. The mounted grenadiers and chasseurs of the Guard, however, recovering from the momentary surprise caused by the bold attack and wild cries of the hordes of Cossacks, dashed into their midst and put them to rout. In this struggle Emmanuel Lecouteulx, one of Prince Berthier's[5] aides-de-camp, having broken his sword in the body of a Cossack, seized his lance

4 General Matvei Ivanovich Platov (1751–1818), Hetman of the Don Cossacks, whom he led into Paris in 1814.
5 Marshal Louis-Alexandre Berthier, prince de Neuchatel et de Wagram (1753–1815), chief-of-staff of the *Grande Armée en Russie*. After refusing to rejoin Napoleon in 1815, he was overcome by remorse and committed suicide by defenestration.

and brandishing it above his head pursued his other enemies with it. A green furred pelisse, rather like those often worn by Russian officers, hid his uniform, and a French grenadier, taking him for a Cossack, plunged his long sabre into his shoulder, the point coming out through his breast. We all thought this terrible wound would lose us a favourite comrade, but God preserved him, and he is still alive. After being thus quickly dispersed, the Cossacks, leaving many of their numbers behind, dashed away, but they were stopped in their flight by a Dutch battalion, which flung itself upon them and greeted them with volleys of musketry.

Soon after this skirmish news was brought to the Emperor that our advanced guard had been vigorously attacked at Malo-Jaroslavitz, and the army quickened its march to go to the rescue. General Kutusoff, informed of our change of route, had at once sent a body of infantry and artillery more than 60,000 strong, under command of General Doctoroff, with orders to take possession of Malo-Jaroslavitz. These troops easily turned out the few French battalions under General Delzons, and occupied the town in their place. General Delzons, it is true, drove the Russians back to the centre of the town, but a ball fractured his skull, killing him and his brother, who was beside him, on the spot. The French began to give way, and the Russians recovered the ground they had lost. General Guilleminot was sent to replace Delzons, and Prince Eugène[6] supported him with the Broussier division. Again and again Guilleminot drove the Russians beyond the principal square, but fresh efforts on the part of the enemy forced him in his turn to retreat. The formidable Russian artillery placed on the heights overlooking the town and in its gardens poured a murderous fire down upon the road on which the French were coming up, whilst we were unable to reply with an effective fire from below, as

6 i.e. Viceroy Eugene de Beauharnais (1781–1824), son of Josephine de Beauharnais and stepson of Napoleon. He assumed command of the retreat towards its close.

we could only get our guns into position in the meadows by the Luya. Everything had therefore to be done by us with the bayonet in a space so limited that any flank manoeuvres were impossible. The enemy had all the advantages alike of the ground and of superiority of numbers. During the thick of the struggle, Prince Eugène had a second bridge flung across the river beside the first, so as to facilitate the passage of his troops.

Ten times at least we drove the Russians back, only in our turn to lose the ground we had gained; but at last the united efforts of Guilleminot and Broussier, supplemented later by the gallant charge of the Italian grenadiers under Pino, compelled the enemy to retire, leaving us masters of the town, which was now in flames. Our artillery was at last able to scale the hill so as to debouch in the plain, and dashing through the burning streets, crushing the wounded, the burnt, and the dead as they went, they succeeded in getting through the town and taking up their position on the hills, to pour down in their turn a hot cannonade upon the Russian troops posted within range across and behind the road to Kalouga.

The first corps seconded this operation, and spent the evening actually amongst the bodies of the dead all kneaded up by the wheels of the guns. A dark night fortunately shrouded the horrors from our sight, and we were able in the end to take up our position on the plain beyond the mangled remains of our comrades.

In this battle, in which our numbers were but one to four of our adversaries, we lost many men, and we were threatened with a similar struggle at every pass.

The Emperor went over the scene of the awful combat, overwhelmed Prince Eugène and his generals with praise, and then withdrew to a distant hut, where he passed the night. I was told afterwards that he held a council of war with several of the Marshals and King Murat, and that, after having the maps spread out and discussing them, he seemed to be for some time plunged in the greatest uncertainty. He finally dismissed every one at midnight without having come to any decision. This must have been indeed a cruel night for the great man, who now saw his star beginning to set, his power crumbling away, and who must already have begun to wonder if he could ever re-establish it, or even if he would get back to France.

On the morning of the 25th, Marshal Davout, Colonel Kobilinski, and I went the round of our outposts and saw with regret that the Russian army was drawn up in good order not far off, completely blocking the road to Kalouga, which we hoped to take. We made our dispositions for forcing a passage, and as we stood in a close group, bending over our maps, we offered an excellent mark for a Russian artilleryman. A ball from a twelve-pounder passed between the Marshal and me, and carried away one of Colonel Kobilinski's legs. The unfortunate officer fell against me, and we thought he was killed, but he recovered miraculously, and I shall speak of him again later.

The Marshal and I, with hearts torn by this catastrophe, impatiently awaited the signal to advance, when a very different order filled us with surprise and dismay.

I must explain that Kalouga, whither we thought we were bound, was a town of great importance to the Russians, as it was their emporium of provisions and weapons. Built as it was beside a river divided into several branches, it could easily be fortified, and afforded an admirably defended position for the Russian army, which had arrived before us. The Emperor doubted whether we were strong enough to force a passage through it, and he had lost so much time hesitating that he was now reduced to the necessity of ordering the army to abandon the Kalouga road for the one leading to Mojaisk, by which we had come. This was to fling us back upon the desert without provisions, to make us tramp once more over the ashes we had left behind us on our way to Moscow; in a word, it was to deprive us of all hope of finding a scrap of food. Needless to say that this decision afflicted us all most cruelly. The Emperor with his Guard went first, followed by the various corps of the army with all their terrible encumbrances, whilst henceforth Marshal Davout's corps, which of course was also my own, formed the rearguard.

It became momentarily more difficult to reassure our soldiers on the subject of this loss of time and retrograde movement. On the second day of our retreat for the Mojaisk road, that is to say on October 26, a fine cold rain set in, which damped every one's spirits yet more, and greatly increased the difficulties of the march. Once more we saw a fine castle, which looked as if it would provide us with a comfortable shelter, but we had no sooner entered it than fire broke out, and that before our people had lit a match. We found the incendiary apparatus, which had been left in position by the owner, but too late to extinguish the flames. Our troops were already beginning to suffer from dysentery through insufficient and badly cooked food, a few cakes and a little poor soup being all they had even now. The sick who were unable to march with the rest were abandoned on the road. Meanwhile Marshal Mortier[7] rejoined us at Verea with the two divisions of the Young Guard; he had accomplished the melancholy task assigned to him of blowing up the Kremlin, against which his noble soul had revolted.[8] Before leaving Moscow some of Mortier's troops took prisoner one of our bitterest enemies, the Russian Lieutenant-General Vintzingerode, and he was being taken to the Emperor, when he had the good fortune to make his escape.

On the 27th the advanced guard of the army re-entered Mojaisk, still encumbered with the wounded left behind after the battle of Borodino, and on the 28th the rearguard arrived. How painful and touching was the meeting with our

7 Marshal Adolphe Mortier, duc de Trevise (1768–1835).
8 Mortier, in fact, refused to demolish the Kremlin.

unfortunate wounded, to whom we now returned with none of the comforts or the cheering news which they expected us to bring them! All we could offer them was an exhortation to resignation; we dared not tell them that we were about to abandon them once more, this time finally, and we were ourselves slowly beginning to face the fact that their terrible lot would most probably soon be our own. Wherever we passed, every refuge still left standing was crowded with wounded, and at Kolinskoy alone there were more than 2,000. Hitherto we had only been pursued by a few Cossacks, but every day their numbers increased, and they became more aggressive. Just before we left Kolinskoy on the 30th, wishing to reconnoitre the enemy on the plain, I was walking along the terrace of a convent, when I suddenly found myself in the presence of about a hundred Cossacks, who were like myself approaching to reconnoitre. When they caught sight of me they at first took to flight; but seeing that I was alone, they returned, and I had only just time to mount and gallop off to rejoin our troops, who had started and were already some distance off. Here and there we passed carriages left on the road because the starved horses, exhausted with fatigue, had fallen down. The few which could be made to get up again were at once harnessed to the wagons containing some of the wounded, but they all died after dragging their new burdens for a few steps only. Then the wounded were in their turn abandoned, and as we rode away we turned aside our heads that we might not see their despairing gestures, whilst our hearts were torn by their terrible cries, to which we tried in vain to shut our ears. If our own condition was pitiable, how much more so was theirs with nothing before them but death from starvation, from cold, or from the weapons of the Russians! The 30th was a sad and terribly long day, for we had to march nearly all night in intense cold, the severest we had yet had to encounter, it being important that we should arrive at Giatz before the enemy, who were pushing on rapidly by cross roads in the hope of getting there first.

The first corps arrived at Giatz on the 31st, and a few hours afterwards the Russians appeared in great force. The next day, November 1, they tried to force a passage through our troops, and having failed they had to be content with hotly cannonading one of our big convoys which had been considerably delayed, and was defiling near the entrance to the town just in front of the enemy's guns. The balls wrought terrible havoc in this convoy of ours, and amongst the carriages was that in which I had sent my sister on in advance. I was fortunate enough to be able to save her. The coachman assured me that the three horses were still fresh and in first-rate condition, so I said to my sister, "Dare you face the guns?" She replied trembling, "I will do what you tell me." I at once turned to the coachman with the words, "Cross that meadow at a gallop; the balls will go over your head, and you will succeed in getting in front of the rest of the convoy. You will then be able to push on without stopping." He followed my advice and with the best results, for my sister got off unhurt. The convoy consisted of some hundreds of badly harnessed carriages, containing many wounded, with the wives and children of several French merchants of Moscow, who were flying the country after having been robbed of their all by the Russians. The company of the Théâtre Français of Moscow had also joined this party, the unlucky actors little dreaming of the terrible tragedy in which they were to play their part through placing themselves under our protection, so soon, alas! to avail them nothing.

On November 2 snow began to fall, and there were already eight or nine degrees of frost. The various divisions of the first corps took it in turns to act as rearguard, and on that day it was the turn of the Gérard division, with which we had passed the night in a wood beneath the snowflakes. The effects of the great cold were already disastrous; many men were so benumbed at the moment for departure as to be unable to rise, and we were obliged to abandon them.

We reached Viasma on November 3 at the same time as the Russians, whose advanced guard was checked by Marshal Ney's troops drawn up in front of them. It was evident that a battle must take place here, and every preparation was made on both sides. The French troops in a position to take part in it numbered about 30,000 or 40,000, whilst the Russians had two corps consisting together of more than 60,000 men. Marshal Davout's and the Viceroy's corps, with the Poles under Prince Poniatowski,[9] were successively engaged, and for a long time exposed to an overwhelming fire from a strong body of artillery with horses better harnessed and in far better condition than ours, which were too worn out for manoeuvring. The first corps and that under Prince Eugène became separated from each other twice, and were both for a time in very critical positions. Fortunately Marshal Ney was able to send a regiment to the rear of the Russian army, which threw it into confusion, and Generals Kutusoff, Milorado-wich, Platoff, and Suvoroff, who had hoped to make us lay down our arms, stopped the pursuit, though fifty pieces of cannon still poured out their fire upon our luckless convoys, which were defiling past during the battle. Many men were lost on both sides here as elsewhere, for our soldiers were still undaunted, and nearly every shot from us told in the Russian ranks, which were more numerous and more closely serried than ours.

Marshal Ney, whose turn it was to act as rearguard, now protected the Viasma pass, and the French army marched towards Dorogobouj. After having passed the night of the 3rd and the day of the 4th on the road, we halted in the evening in a pine forest on the borders of a frozen lake not far from the Castle of Czarkovo, where the Emperor had been for two days. On the 5th the first corps took up its position at Semlevo, so as to let that of Marshal Ney pass on, it being our

9 Prince Poniatowski, nephew of the King of Poland, commander of the Polish and Saxon troops which formed V Corps. He was drowned in the withdrawal from Leipzig in October 1813.

turn now to be rearguard. The Cossacks harassed us greatly, and many of our stragglers, whose numbers increased every day, fell into their hands. We now also made out on our flanks numerous columns of Russian cavalry and artillery, which were trying to pass us so as to await us at the entrance to the pass on this side of Dorogobouj. Marshal Ney foresaw this danger, and instead of going through the pass he halted near it for us to come up. Thanks to his forethought and support, we only suffered from a slack cannonade and reached Dorogobouj safely.

Leaving that place on the 6th we made a long march, and at nightfall we camped in a large wood, where General Jouffroy had been obliged to halt with the badly harnessed and damaged artillery under his care. We spent the night in packing the wagons which were still in a fit state to proceed, blowing up those we had to abandon, and burning the gun-carriages we could not take with us. These explosions, which were now of very frequent occurrence, were signals of our misfortunes, and affected us much as the tolling of the bell at her child's funeral would some bereaved mother.

General Jouffroy had had a tent pitched, and invited me to share its shelter and his supper. A supper! Good heavens! what a luxurious treat in the midst of our misery!

I had a new experience at that supper. Hitherto a few cows had still remained to the staff, and I had not been reduced to eating horseflesh. But now the General had nothing to offer me but a repast of horseflesh so highly spiced that in spite of its toughness and the coarse veins, which resisted the efforts of the sharpest teeth to masticate them, it really tasted not unlike what the French call *bœf à la mode*. Generally horseflesh is so black, and its gravy is so yellow and insipid, so very like liquid sulphur, that it looks most repulsive, but we quite enjoyed our meal, washed down as it was by a flask of good wine which had belonged to some great man of Moscow.

For a long time the only meat our soldiers ever tasted had been horseflesh, and the poor fellows were so brutalised by misery and famine that they often did not wait till an animal was dead to cut it up and carry off the fleshy portions. When a horse stumbled and fell, no one tried to help it up, but numbers of soldiers at once flung themselves upon it, and cut open its side to get at the liver, which is the least repulsive part. They would not even put it out of its misery first, and I have actually seen them angry at the poor beast's last struggles to escape its butchers, and heard them cry, "Keep quiet, will you, you rogue?"

The numbers of the stragglers increased in a perfectly appalling way; they stopped in crowds to roast a few shreds of horseflesh, and the French, who must always have their joke whatever their misery, called the tattered wretches the *fricoteurs* or revellers.

During the night of the 6th and the day of the 7th, a heavy fall of snow drifting before a strong wind rendered our march extremely arduous. We were often unable to see two paces before us, but all the time the balls from the enemy were ploughing up the ground, and every now and then a few victims fell. No one had the heart to stop to help those who were struck, for the most selfish egotism crushed all kindly feeling in almost every breast. It was in a state of bodily and mental torpor that we reached Pnevo on one of the tributaries of the Dnieper, a very difficult river to cross. To protect its passage during our occupation of the country, we had had a big log hut built surrounded by a weak earthwork. This little redoubt was the only shelter which had not been burnt on the long road we were traversing, and the first corps halted there to pass the night. It was built in the same way as the huts of the peasants, with big squared trunks of trees laid horizontally on each other, forming walls almost impervious to balls, but not more than fifty people could get inside, so that the rest of the troops had to camp around it. The heavy snow and the bitter wind prevented us from going to get fuel, for there were no trees near, and every one suffered terribly from cold during the night.

In our halts we always faced the north. The Viceroy, who was marching on our left, met with the greatest difficulties, for he had counted on finding a bridge over the Wop, but this bridge was broken, so that he had to cross by the ford, and the water was all frozen over. His artillery and baggage stuck fast in the mud on the banks, and he was compelled to abandon them.

General Rapp and several other officers came to share our small quarters, where we were all very closely packed together. At nine o'clock the next morning when we left our shelter we found the ground near the wretched little redoubt encumbered with poor fellows, who, after having with infinite trouble managed to light fires, had been overcome with the cold, and burnt by flying sparks though covered with snow. Many of them were never to rise again from the spot on which they had fallen. Before we left we had the log hut burnt down.

The coating of ice on the roads made them so slippery that men and horses could scarcely keep their feet. My horse fell with me, and I was so much hurt that I could not remount, and I went to share Marshal Davout's *wurst*[10] or ambulance wagon, drawn by a very strong pair of cobs, which galloped along on the ice as easily as others would on turf.

Having burnt the bridge behind us, we imagined ourselves to be in security for the rest of the day. But when we halted for the first time about noon, we heard a brisk firing a short distance off, which evidently came from the twelve-pounders of our own park of artillery. This made the Marshal both uneasy and angry, and he sent for the officer in command of the artillery. He came hurrying up with a smile on his face, as if he were the bearer of good news. Davout, however, frowning at him from his *wurst*, accosted him roughly with the words, "So it's you, you scoundrel, who have dared to fire my reserve guns without orders from me!" Greatly

10 The *wurst* was an open ambulance waggon, now no longer in use. TRANS.

surprised at this address, the officer had the presence of mind to pretend not to know to whom Davout was speaking, and after looking about him, he said as he set spurs to his horse to return to his post, "Surely that language cannot be addressed to me!" A few minutes later we learnt that some 1,200 Cossacks had flung themselves upon the big park of artillery, but when the commanding officer halted he had prudently prepared his guns for action and formed squares to guard against a cavalry charge, so that when that charge was made a volley of grapeshot from thirty guns overthrew one half of the assailants and put the other half to flight. I now once more entreated the Marshal, as I had so often done before, to choose another chief of the staff, pointing out to him that half our aides-de-camp and commissaries were already killed or taken prisoners, and that I really could not do all the work he required alone. He, however, begged me to remain, with a politeness which was so truly remarkable from him, that General Haxo maliciously asked me, "Whatever have you done to the Marshal? He must be very fond of you, for I never saw him pet any one as he does you."

On this same eventful 9th of November we re-entered Smolensk, where the Emperor received news of the Malet and Lahorie conspiracy at Paris,[11] and of the check received by the corps which he had ordered to debouch on his flanks. The tidings from Spain were not of a kind to afford him any consolation, for there was no unity of purpose or of action amongst the French Generals there, a fact by which the enemy was not slow to profit. The Emperor, fearing lest discouragement should spread through the ranks of our retreating army, pretended to be quite unmoved by all this

11 This conspiracy all but succeeded in overthrowing the Imperial Government; Malet, who had escaped from prison, where he was confined for participation in the plot of 1801, having circulated the news of Napoleon's death, and forged a decree of the Senate. He was, however, taken prisoner by Laborde, and shot, with Lahorie and other traitors to the Emperor, on 29 October 1812. TRANS.

distressing news. He wanted to appear superior to every adversity and ready to face calmly every event, however untoward, but his assumed indifference was misinterpreted and had a bad effect.

We no longer had a smithy for rough-shoeing our horses, so that they nearly all fell and were too weak to get up again. Our cavalry was thus completely destroyed, and the dismounted men even flung away their weapons, which their fingers were too frozen to hold. Some 300 officers, who had lost all their men, then proposed forming themselves into a kind of picked corps, ready to fight together on every emergency; but with them, as with the common soldiers, strength and discipline soon gave way, and what might have been a noble band, bound together by misfortune, fell to pieces in a few days without having rendered the slightest service to any one.

We camped for the night of the 10th on the banks of the Dnieper, beside the bridge where General Gudin had been killed. Our bivouac fires were soon surrounded by those of the numerous stragglers who had met here. Their appearance would have torn our hearts if we had not already been reduced to the level of the brutes, without the power of feeling compassion. Many of the poor wretches, who were all without weapons, were wearing silk pelisses trimmed with fur, or women's clothes of all manner of colours, which they had snatched from the flames of Moscow or taken from carriages abandoned by the way. These garments, which were fuller and looser than those of men, were a better protection from the cold. Some also wore the clothes of their comrades who had died on the road.

Numbed with cold and famishing with hunger, those who had been unable to make a fire would creep up to their more fortunate comrades and plead for a little share in the warmth, but no one dreamt of sacrificing any of the hardly won heat for the sake of another. The new arrivals would remain standing behind those seated for a little while, and then, too weak to support themselves longer, they would stagger and fall. Some would sink on to their knees, others into a sitting posture, and this was always the beginning of the end. The next moment they would stretch out their weary limbs, raise their dim and faded eyes to heaven, and as froth issued from their mouths their lips would quiver with a happy smile, as if some divine consolation had soothed their dying agony. Often before the last breath was drawn, and even as the failing limbs stretched themselves out with an appearance of heavenly calm, some other poor wretch, who had been standing by, would seat himself upon the still heaving breast of his dying comrade, to remain resting upon the corpse with his living weight until, generally very little later, his own turn should come, and he also, finding himself too weak to rise, should yield up his breath. The horror of it all was but slightly shrouded by the falling snow, and we had to witness this kind of thing for yet another thirty days!

The first corps entered Smolensk on the 11th, and remained there till the 16th. The interval was employed in distributing to the troops the few provisions and clothes which had been collected in the storehouses by order of the Emperor,[12] and in seeing off for Wilna all the convoys which could still be supplied with horses.

The Imperial Guard, which was always held in reserve, had fought very little and lost fewer men than any of the other corps. The Emperor still owned in that Guard a force of from 3,000 to 4,000 men in good fighting condition, but these troops, though the discipline to which they had to submit was much less severe than that enforced in the rest of the army, really suffered quite as much as we did. The Emperor had their affection for him very much at heart, and in the friendly familiar way which he knew would please them he used sometimes to go amongst them, and pulling the

12 Large quantities of food and clothing had been brought together at Smolensk, but there was some mistake about their distribution, and many men got too much, whilst others received nothing. TRANS.

long moustaches, all stiff with ice, of one or another, he would say, "Ah, old *Grognards*,[13] you may count on me as I count on my Guard to fulfil the high destiny to which they are called." These few words would at once restore the confidence of the brave fellows in their chief, and to the end of the journey the Emperor was always surrounded by them.

We had still more than 120 leagues to cross between Smolensk and the Niemen. There were already from 12 to 15 degrees of frost, and the cold was still increasing. The roads grew worse every day, and there was too little of everything at Smolensk for the four days' halt to have done much to recruit the exhausted strength of the troops, or to restore anything like order in the disorganised army. My chief, the Prince of Eckmühl (Marshal Davout), who, as the Emperor justly remarked, was a man of iron constitution,[14] was very exacting, and expected the Staff accounts to be written up every day just as in times of peace. Now all my assistants but one had disappeared, and I therefore again tendered my resignation. Just as we were leaving Smolensk, the Emperor consented to my leaving Davout, and named Charpentier, a general of division just removed from the Government of Smolensk, to take my place. That general, however, being not at all anxious to take up a task of which he knew the difficulties, evaded appearing at his post for ten or twelve days, so that I had to go on doing the work of the chief of the Staff without the title or pay.

Before he left Smolensk the Emperor ordered Marshal Ney to remain there until the 17th, when he was to blow up the fortifications. He also told him that his corps was to act as rearguard after the departure of the 1st corps, which was to

13 The *Grognards* was the popular name given to the Old Guard of Napoleon I. TRANS.
14 Davout (1770–1823) was one of Napoleon's most cherished Marshals; the Emperor also wrote of his "distinguished bravery and firmness of character, the first qualities in a warrior."

precede him by one day and await him at the Krasnoe ravine. This ravine, which was a very difficult pass, had been encumbered for nine days with carriages, many of which were being burnt to clear the way.

The Viceroy's corps, now reduced to 1,200 or 1,500 men, which was marching in advance of ours, had been greatly harassed ever since leaving Smolensk by some 12,000 or 14,000 Russians, with a strong force of artillery mounted on sledges. The Emperor and his Guard had waited at the entrance to the terrible defile for the Viceroy to come up with his corps and protect his passage through it, and he now determined not to enter it until the arrival of the first corps also, which had not been able to leave Smolensk until two o'clock in the morning of Monday, the 16th. During this halt Napoleon learnt that the enemy was advancing in force upon Orcha to intercept the passage of the Dnieper, and had massed a large number of troops in the village of Kourkovo, not far from us. The Young Guard, commanded by General Roguet, whose gallant audacity was well known to the Emperor, had joined him during the day, and Napoleon now sent him to create a diversion in the night by attacking the enemy's corps which was causing us so much uneasiness.

The 1st corps, which had been the 4th under the Viceroy, was terribly harassed all through the march on the 16th by numerous Cossacks with artillery. When darkness fell the attacks lessened, and we availed ourselves of the reprieve by marching all night towards the Krasnoe pass. With the first gleams of light on the 17th, however, we found ourselves threatened by great masses of Russian infantry and cavalry struggling to surround us and make us lay down our arms; and though they did not venture actually to attack us, the fire from their guns wrought great havoc amongst us. Again and again our little army, reduced to 4,000 men bearing arms, but hampered by numerous stragglers, halted to face the enemy and await Marshal Ney, who was to cover our retreat. On this occasion I had a fresh opportunity of admiring the courage and *sang-froid* of General Compans. Severely wounded in the shoulder, and suffering greatly, he was compelled, like most of us, to march on foot. This, however, did not prevent him from facing the enemy with a smiling face and as unruffled a calm as if he were walking about in his own garden at home. The sight of his happy face and composed demeanour had the best results on his soldiers, giving them a sense of security, and leading them to imitate their general's stoicism.

Our position at Krasnoe was, however, anything but pleasant. Surrounded by enemies ten times as numerous as ourselves, we could not imagine how it was that Marshal Ney, whom we supposed to be just behind us, had not managed to beat off at least some of them. We fought steadily, hoping every moment to see him appear. But the enemy's cannonade became hotter and hotter, making terrible gaps in our ranks, and the snow, which had been falling heavily ever since the evening before, added to our difficulties, rendering our situation all but desperate. The Emperor, who was becoming very anxious about our fate, generously turned back and came to meet us, cutting a passage through our assailants at the head of the Old Guard, and meeting Marshal Davout's advanced guard beyond Krasnoe.

Meanwhile nothing had been heard of Ney and the rearguard with him, but it turned out afterwards that on leaving Smolensk the Marshal, with the few troops still remaining to him, had been immediately pursued by thousands of the enemy, who poured such a hot fire into his already diminished ranks from every side, that after three days' continuous struggle he was compelled to abandon the attempt to cut through the enemy's forces, and to deviate from the main road to Krasnoe, where we were so anxiously awaiting him. When darkness was beginning he found himself far away from us, with the Dnieper between him and safety. He took up a position parallel with the river, and allowed his troops to light their bivouac fires. Kutusoff, who had followed Ney, now looked upon him as his certain prey, for he could see no way of escape for him, and sent an officer with a flag of truce to summon him to surrender.

The envoy, who performed his mission with the greatest politeness, was received with assumed courtesy, and detained on various pretexts whilst the Marshal was having the depth of the river sounded, and the strength of the ice on it tested. He was told that several men had gone over to the other bank and returned safely. He then ordered the throwing of fresh fuel on the fires, as if he had decided to remain where he was, and telling the envoy that he would have to accompany him, he gave the signal for crossing the river, instructing his subordinates to make the men go over in single file, and to keep well away from each other. Everything – artillery, baggage, even wounded – which would have hindered the safe crossing or broken the ice, was abandoned on the banks.[15] The transit was accomplished without accident, and at daybreak on the 18th the Marshal was several leagues from the further bank, but he was now attacked by a considerable body of Cossacks under Platoff, but he managed to fight his way through them,[16] though he had none but infantry with him, and after three days' march along the winding banks of the river, his rear harassed perpetually by Bashkirs and Tartars, who picked off and ill treated all stragglers, Ney at last rejoined the Emperor at Orcha.

In the struggle at Krasnoe, which lasted the whole day and in which we were exposed to a terrible artillery fire, my servant was wounded by grapeshot, and the two saddle

15 This crossing of the Dnieper was one of the most brilliant feats achieved by the French in this or any campaign. The story of its accomplishment is variously told by eye-witnesses, but all agree that but for its successful performance the whole of the rear-guard would have been cut to pieces or taken prisoners by the Russians. TRANS.

16 Marbot says that Platoff was in a drunken sleep when the French came up, and that, discipline in the Russian army being very strict, no one ventured to wake him or to stand to arms without his orders, and that it was to this circumstances that the Marshal owed the final escape of his little body of men. TRANS.

horses he was leading were killed, whilst that on which he was mounted was very badly hurt. I thought the poor animal would certainly die of his awful wound, but, strange to say, he was the only one of all my horses to live to reach the Vistula. He was, in fact, quite well again when he was taken by the enemy at the gates of Thorn, and my poor servant was killed. With the horses I lost the furs they were carrying for my use, and nothing was left to me to protect me from the cold but a silk waterproof cloak, which turned out much more useful than I could have imagined, for it kept out the cold, and prevented my own animal heat, little as it was, from escaping.

As the day wore on at Krasnoe, and Ney did not appear, the anxiety of the Emperor and the army became more and more intense. Napoleon, fearing that his own retreat to Orcha would be cut off, dared not linger longer at Krasnoe, and he and his Guard left us an hour before nightfall, ordering us to wait for Marshal Ney. When the Emperor abandoned Krasnoe, the little town was full of those who had been wounded during the day. Nothing could have been more heart-rending than the sight of all the rooms in every house crowded with fine young fellows, their ages ranging from twenty to twenty-five years, who had but recently joined the army and had been under fire for the first time that day, but who within one short hour were to be left to their fate. Some few, who were able to march after their wounds had been dressed, were eager to be off again, but all the rest to the number of about 3,000 were left without surgeons or any necessaries.

The whole of the Guard was already gone, our much reduced first corps could no longer defend the heights beyond Krasnoe, and General Compans, who had remained till the very last, went down towards the town and crossed the ravine as night fell. He had scarcely done so, when, anxious to find out what the enemy were doing, I managed to creep along behind a hedge at the borders of the pass. The ravine was not more than thirty paces wide, and I very soon found myself almost face to face with a body of Russian artillery, which was being hastily put in position so as to riddle us with grapeshot. Beyond the ten or twelve guns of this battery I could see several considerable infantry corps advancing in line in our direction, leaving me no longer in any doubt of our being completely cut off from Marshal Ney. I hurried back with this distressing news to Marshal Davout, and recognising the hopelessness of waiting for Ney any longer, he did at once all that was left to us under the circumstances, by having a few guns placed in position to prevent the enemy from crossing the ravine, whilst the infantry was ordered to withdraw towards Lidoni, where we arrived a little before daybreak, our retreat having been facilitated by a very dark night. The Russians, thinking that we were still in force at Krasnoe, did not enter it till the next morning.

The army was still deeply grieved at the supposed loss of Marshal Ney, for we were all certain that if he were alive he had been taken prisoner. The thought of his fate caused general discouragement, and all we hoped was to escape captivity ourselves. The numbers of the stragglers, ever on the increase, had now become immense; at every pass or difficult bit of road there was a block of wagons and carriages, and many vehicles broke through the ice on the marshes and remained embedded in the mud beneath. This was how I myself in our march from Lidoni to Koziani lost my baggage wagon and a barouche, which were still properly harnessed, for both of them with their drivers and horses were swallowed up by the mud. Hundreds of others met with similar misfortunes, and as I was going through Dombrowa the day after my loss, I came upon a carriage belonging to a M. de Servan, in which sat my sister. She had lost her carriage in the same marshes as I had mine, and De Servan, who had been more fortunate than either of us, had been good enough to take her on with him. A few hours later, just at the entrance to Orcha, De Servan's carriage was smashed by a cannonball. M. Levasseur, however, whose carriage got through safely, was good enough to allow me to transfer my sister to it, and showed her every possible attention.

On the evening of the 20th, when the moon was shining brightly, our advanced posts on the right bank of the Dnieper saw an officer approaching, whom they at first mistook for a Russian. They soon saw, however, that he was French, and on questioning him they learnt to their great joy that Marshal Ney, who had miraculously escaped from the clutches of Kutusoff, was but a league away from us. It would be difficult to describe our delight at receiving this news, which did much to restore the tone of the army, so lowered by discouragement. The Viceroy and Marshal Mortier hurried off to meet Ney, and the next day he was welcomed by the Emperor, who received him with the greatest enthusiasm, greeting him with the words, "I would have given everything rather than lose you."[17]

The first corps continued to cover the retreat, and we were aroused before daybreak after our arrival at Orcha by the coming up of the Russians in great force, who hoped to shut us into that town. Like every other place we passed through in our retreat, Orcha was encumbered with carriages crowded, as were the houses, with sick and wounded. A young cousin of mine, Alexander Lejeune, had been left at Orcha as manager of a hospital. I saw him as I went through, and he stuffed my pockets full of sugar and coffee ready roasted and ground. I urged him to fly whilst he could, and advised him to start in advance of us. He said he would just go and fetch a cloak and his money, but I never saw him again. He was probably delayed, and perished in the crowd after we left. If blood shed in the service of one's country is a patent of nobility, our family escutcheon ought to receive ten or twelve new chevrons of honour! for many of my nearest relations were wounded or killed in the Emperor's service, including five first cousins, namely, one Gérard, killed in

17 Henceforth Ney was nicknamed "the bravest of the brave."

Egypt; one Vignaux, killed in Spain; one Lejeune, killed in Russia; my brother, wounded at Friedland; the husband of my eldest sister, Baron Plique (General), wounded several times, who died whilst on active service; the brave and witty General Clary, brother of my wife, also wounded several times; and her other brother, who died at the age of twenty-two, as colonel of a regiment he had himself got together in Spain, and who was mourned as a son by his uncle, King Joseph.

I feel very proud at leaving such memories as these behind for my son, and have already too long delayed recording them in my Memoirs.

At Orcha the Dnieper is very wide, and so rapid that the ice was not firm enough to allow of our crossing it easily, although there were twenty-five degrees of frost. The two bridges, which were all we had been able to construct, were very narrow and far from strong, whilst the approaches to them were so slippery as to be very dangerous. We had had a great many carriages burnt in the streets of Orcha, but we were still terribly encumbered with them; the enemy harassed our rear perpetually, and had already gained a position from which they could cannonade our bridges. As soon as our troops were across we were compelled to set fire to these bridges, leaving behind us all who were without arms, or were for any reason unable to follow our rapid march. It was a terrible moment for us when we had thus to abandon so many of our wounded.

We passed the night of Sunday the 22nd with the rear-guard in a little wood on the road, and arrived in the evening of the 23rd at Kokonow, where we learnt, alas! that General Tchichakoff[18] had taken possession with a large force of Borisow,[19] so that we were cut off from that way of retreat. This news was distressing enough, but at three o'clock the

18 Admiral Pavel Tshitsagov (1767–1849); his naval title was purely honorific and he was a land commander throughout his long career.
19 Borisov.

next morning an event occurred which in its horror surpassed almost anything which had yet befallen us.

Opposite the house occupied by Marshal Davout and his
officers, and not more than a couple of paces off, was a huge
barn with four large doors, in which some five or six hundred
persons, including officers, soldiers, stragglers, &c., had
taken refuge as affording some shelter from the cold. Thirty
or forty fires had been lighted, and the inmates of the barn,
broken up into various groups, were all sleeping heavily in
the warm air, which afforded such a contrast to the bitter cold
of their usual bivouac, when the thatched roof caught fire,
and in an instant the whole place was in flames. Suddenly,
with a dull crash, the burning roof fell upon the sleepers,
setting fire to the straw in which they lay, and to their clothes.
Some few, who were near the doors, were able to escape; and
with their clothes all singed they rushed to us screaming for
help for their comrades. We were at the doors in a very few
seconds; but what a terrible sight met our eyes! Masses of
flames many yards thick rushed out from the doors to a
distance of several yards, leaving only the narrow passage of
exit some six feet high beneath a vault of fire which, fanned
by the wind, spread with immense rapidity.

We could not, any of us, get near the poor creatures, whom
we could see struggling wildly or flinging themselves face
downwards on the ground so as to suffer a little less. We
hastily tied ropes, our handkerchiefs, anything we could get
hold of, together, to fling to them, so as to be able to drag
some of them out; but fresh shrieks soon stopped our efforts,
for as we pulled they fell upon and were stabbed by each
other's bayonets. Captain d'Houdetot got nearer to them
than any of the rest of us were able to, but his clothes caught
fire and he had to draw back. The 500 or 600 victims made
several last despairing efforts to rise, but their strength was
soon all gone, and presently the building fell, in upon them,
their muskets became heated, the charges in them exploded,
and their reports were the only funeral salute fired over the

corpses of all the brave fellows. Very few escaped from the terrible conflagration, and those few had to tear off all their clothes. I saw one poor child of twelve or fourteen years old going about stark naked, but none of us could give him anything to put on, for we had lost our carriages, our horses, everything. There were now 13 degrees of frost, but we had to harden our hearts against the sufferers, for to help them was beyond our power.

On November 24 we passed the night at Tokotschin. The evening before Marshal Victor, pursued by Count von Wittgenstein, had joined the Emperor here, and would now protect his retreat. The Marshal had only just arrived from Germany, and had still 5,000 fresh troops in good order, whilst ours were thoroughly disorganised.

A singular episode occurred on the afternoon of the 24th, which had opened so tragically. I will just mention it here to give an idea of the vicissitudes we went through in our terrible retreat. Like the rest of us, I suffered very much from hunger, and for several days I had had nothing to eat but a little biscuit, whilst my only beverage was an occasional draught of cold coffee, which, however, kept me going somehow. I was marching sadly along, pondering on our woes, when an officer whom I scarcely knew by sight ran up to me, and with a pleasant smile asked me to do him a favour. "My position," I answered laughing, "is not such as to enable me to serve any one. But what do you want?" His reply was to hand me a parcel carefully done up in paper, and about the size of my two fists, which he begged me to accept. "But tell me what is in it," I said. "I entreat you not to refuse it." "But at least say what it is," I urged, trying to push it away with my right hand; but he closed my fingers over it and ran off. A good deal puzzled by suddenly receiving a present from a stranger, and quite at a loss to imagine his motive, I smelt the packet to begin with, and the result encouraged me to open it, when lo! and behold! a delicious odour of truffles greeted my nostrils, and I found myself the happy possessor of a quarter of a *pâté de foie gras* from Toulouse or Strasburg. I never saw the officer again, but I think my fervent expressions of gratitude must have found an echo in his heart. May he have escaped the fate which overtook so many of us, and from which his timely gift preserved me for a few days!

Another bit of good fortune marked this same day. As I have already said, I had lost all my furs and winter clothes, and in these deserted districts money was of no avail to buy new ones. I was feeling the want of them dreadfully, when I came across Colonel L. shut up in his carriage, and quite ill from the excessive precautions he was taking against the cold. "What do you want with all those furs?" I asked him. "You will be suffocated in them. Give me one." To which he replied, "Not for all the gold in the world!" "Bah!" I cried, "you will give me that bearskin, which really is in your way, and here are fifty gold napoleons for it." "Go to the devil! go to the devil with your napoleons! you bother me! – but there, General, I can't refuse you anything." He took the napoleons, and I hastily seized the bearskin, for fear he should think better of it. I went off with my treasure with indescribable joy, but the unlucky owner of so many sables and other furs was frozen to death a few days later.

The first corps passed the night of the 24th at Toloczin, and at daybreak the next morning the Russian firing recommenced, and we were pursued during the whole day by them, their balls mowing down our ranks. It was throughout our disastrous retreat the custom of the enemy to harass us all day, and when night fell to withdraw to distant villages, where they had a good rest and plenty of food, neither of which we were able to obtain, returning the next morning stronger than ever to attack us again with fresh vigour, whilst we were ever growing fewer and weaker.

On the 25th we passed the night in a wood close to a burnt village. The snow was very deep, adding greatly to our discomfort, and we made great piles of faggots on which to rest, all of us turning our feet towards one big fire. My bearskin was nearly fourteen feet square, and I let general Haxo roll himself into it with me. We were very warm and comfortable inside, and as we fell asleep we mentally blessed the man who had sold it to me. The next morning, the 26th, we started again before day-break as usual, not daring to count those we had to leave behind.

On the same day we went through Borv, and the first corps halted for the night at Kroupski. A newly formed brigade of light Polish cavalry had just arrived in this village, and were heating the ovens in the cottages. An inn with stabling for twenty horses was assigned to Marshal Davout. In putting the horses which had followed – for, as I have said, we all went on foot now – in the stable, we found three children in a manger, one about a year old, the other two apparently only just born. They were very poorly dressed, and were so numbed with the cold that they were not even crying. I made my men seek their parents for an hour, but they could not be found; all the inhabitants had fled, and the three poor little things were left to our tender mercies. I begged the Marshal's cook to give them a little broth if he succeeded in making any, and thought no more about them. Presently, however, the warmth of the horses' breath woke the little creatures up, and their plaintive cries resounded for a long time in the rooms in which we were all crowded together. Our desire to do something to help them kept us awake for a long time, but at last we were overcome with sleep. At two o'clock in the morning we were roused by the news that the village was on fire; the overheating of the ovens had led to flames breaking out nearly everywhere. Our house, standing somewhat apart, was the only one to escape, and our three children were still crying. At daybreak, however, when we were starting, I could hear them no longer, and I asked the cook what he had done for them. He had, of course, suffered as much as we had, and he answered, with the satisfied air of a man who has done a good action, "Their crying so tore my heart that I could not close an eye. I had no food to give them, so I took a hatchet, broke the ice in the horse trough, and drowned them, to put them out of their misery!" Thus does misfortune harden the heart of man!

During the retreat many of the French were drowned. The wells in the village were all open and level with the ground, so that when troops arrived in the dark several men often fell into them, and rarely did any of their comrades try to save them. I saw more than ten wells, none of them very deep, on the surface of which the dead bodies of such victims were floating. Overcome with misery, other poor fellows committed suicide, and we often heard the discharge of a musket close by, telling of the end of some unfortunate wretch. On the other hand, some of the men who were simply covered with wounds kept up their courage and marched steadily on. One day, weary of walking, I sat down to rest on the trunk of a tree beside a fine young artilleryman who had just been wounded. Two doctors happened to pass us, and I called out to them to come and look at the wound. They did so, and at the first glance exclaimed, "The arm must be amputated!" I asked the soldier if he felt he could bear it. "Anything you like," he answered stoutly. "But," said the doctors, "there are only two of us to do it; so you, General, will be good enough to help us perform the operation." Seeing that I was anything but pleased at the idea, they hastened to add that it would be enough if I just let the artilleryman lean against me. "Sit back to back with him, and you will see nothing of the operation." I agreed, and placed myself in the required position. I think the operation seemed longer to me than it did to the patient. The doctors opened their cases of instruments; the artilleryman did not even heave a single sigh. I heard the slight noise made by the saw as it cut through the bone, and in a few seconds, or rather minutes, they said to me, "It is over! it is a pity we have not a little wine to give him, to help him to rally." I happened still to have half a bottle of Malaga with me, which I was hoarding up, only taking a drop at a time, but I gave it to the poor man, who was very pale, though he said nothing. His eyes brightened up, and he swallowed all my wine at a single gulp. Then, on returning the empty bottle with the words, "It is still a long way to Carcassonne," he walked off with a firm step at a pace I found it difficult to emulate.

Marshal Oudinot, who had recovered from his wound,[20] was now sent forward to Borisoff to try and take possession of the bridge over the Beresina, which had already been for several days in the hands of the Russian forces under Tchichakoff. This general had only just come from Moldavia, and on seeing the boldness with which Oudinot's troops advanced he took it for granted that the whole of the French army was approaching, and thinking his own position with the river behind him a very disadvantageous one, he wished to avoid a regular battle. He therefore only made sufficient defence to cover the retreat of his army, and retired beyond the Beresina. Marshal Oudinot attacked Borisoff with his usual vigour, and entering it took 500 or 600 prisoners and all the baggage belonging to the Russian army. Tchichakoff had, however, burnt the bridge over the Beresina after crossing it, so that this victory gained us nothing.

The Emperor, who had no means of forcing the passage of the Beresina with an army of some 40,000 Russians opposing him, endeavoured to find a favourable point for throwing bridges across, and at the same time evading Wittgenstein, whom Marshal Victor was with infinite difficulty holding at bay, and Kutusoff, who was pursuing us. He was told that there was a ford at the village of Studzianka,[21] which he could reach by ascending the left bank of the river, but though the water was at the most four or five feet deep the approaches were very marshy and would be difficult for our carriages and

20 The redoubtable Oudinot had been severely wounded at the battle of Polotsk, 17 August. He would be wounded again at Berezina, a bullet lodging inside his abdomen; he refused restraint, instead merely bit on a napkin while surgeons probed for the object.
21 Studienka.

artillery. The river, which was very muddy, was covered with ice, but it broke beneath those who tried to walk across it.

The difficulties on the other side, if we succeeded in reaching it, would be even greater, for heights commanding the banks were occupied by a Russian division, and the approach to these heights was a marshy tract without any firm road whatever. The road from Borisoff to Molodetschno by way of Zembino, the only one we could hope to reach, was a very narrow causeway, with many bridges raised to a good height above the marsh, much of which was quite under water. If any one of these little bridges should break, the march of the whole army would be arrested; but the Emperor had really no choice, and was compelled to resign himself to attempting the passage at Studzianka.

The engineers, pontonniers, and artillerymen therefore set to work at once, all the wood found in the village, even that of which the houses were built, being quickly converted into trestles, beams, planks, &c., and on the evening of the 26th, all appearing ready for the throwing across of the bridge, an attempt was made to place it in position. But the bed of the river was so muddy that the supports sank too deeply in it. It was, moreover, wider than had been supposed, and all the work had to be done over again. Two bridges instead of one were now made, and the army began its march for Studzianka. On the 27th the first corps, now forming the rear guard, passed through Borisoff, and arrived at night at the ford chosen, where there was already a terrible block of carriages, those belonging to the corps of Marshal Oudinot and Marshal Victor, who had but recently rejoined us, being added to the others which had escaped from previous accidents, and whose owners had evaded the orders for burning them.

When we arrived at Studzianka about nine o'clock in the evening, the Emperor had already sent over in small rafts several hundred skirmishers to protect the bridges and those making them, whilst the corps of Marshals Ney and Oudinot with 500 or 600 cuirassiers of the Guard had crossed the river and taken up a position on the right in a wood beyond Studzianka. We passed the night in trying to bring something like order into our arrangements for crossing, sending the ammunition wagons first, and repairing the bridges where they had given way under the weight of the artillery. It was a very dark night, and many French, Dutch, Spanish, and Saxon soldiers fell into the wells of the village and were drowned. Their cries of distress reached us, but we had no ropes or ladders with which to rescue them, and they were left to their fate.

At daybreak the crossing of the river by the bridges went on without too much confusion, and I was able to go backwards and forwards several times, seeing to the safety of all that was of the greatest importance for the army; but at about eight o'clock in the morning, when the light revealed the immense crowds which had still to be got over, every one began to hasten to the bridges at once, and everything was soon thrown into the greatest disorder. Things became even worse when an hour later a combined attack was made on us by all the Russian forces, and we found ourselves between two fires. Truly our misfortunes had now reached their height.

Marshal Victor, who had taken up a position on the heights above Studzianka, was trying to beat off Wittgenstein, who had attacked him about ten o'clock with a large force of artillery, and although he had but very few troops with him, he managed to keep the Russians at a distance, but their balls, falling amongst the masses of carriages blocking the approaches to the bridges, flung their occupants and drivers into the most indescribable disorder, killing many and smashing up the vehicles. Some balls even rolled on to the bridges.[22]

22 Marbot relates that Marshal Victor's rearguard took the wrong road on its way to Studzianka, "and walked straight into the middle of Wittgenstein's army. The division was quickly surrounded and compelled to lay down its arms." TRANS.

On the right bank meanwhile Tchichakoff was attacking the French all along the line with some 25,000 or 30,000 Russians, whilst Marshals Ney and Oudinot had to oppose them only 9,000 or 10,000 men, with what was left of the Imperial Guard behind them as a reserve. Their front was but half a league in length, and the ground was very much broken up by woods. The Russians came to the fight well fed and warmed up by plenty of brandy; the French were debilitated by privations, and had moreover a cutting wind driving the snow in their faces. But with the enemy before them, they seemed to regain all their old energy, and Tchichakoff tried in vain to break their ranks, though he flung upon them in succession all the forces under his command. Marshal Oudinot, always in the front amongst the skirmishers, was wounded at the beginning of the action, and Marshal Ney took the command. Seizing a favourable moment he ordered General Doumerc, who had just brought up some 500 cuirassiers, to make a charge. This threw a Russian column into disorder, and won the French 1,500 prisoners. It was during this brilliant charge that a young officer, whom I loved for his many engaging qualities, met his death. Alfred de Noailles, only son of the Duc de Noailles, was struck in the heart by a ball,[23] and his face and body were so disfigured by being trampled beneath the feet of the horses, that he was only recognised by his height and by the mark on his fine white linen.

It was a melancholy consolation to his mourning widow and family to find his portrait in my album, in which I had collected likenesses of many young officers whom I numbered amongst my friends, and all of whom had been cut off in the flower of their age, before they had had time to fulfil the lofty destiny to which their noble names and exalted courage would have called them.

23 Marbot says that De Noailles escaped in the actual charge, but was killed by Cossacks after the engagement, he having ventured too far "to see what the enemy were doing." TRANS.

Towards three o'clock in the afternoon, when it was already beginning to get dark, for night falls very early in the winter in these latitudes, Tchichakoff drew back, and we soon saw the fires of his bivouac, marking the position he had taken up about a league away from us.

Whilst all this was going on, the most awful scenes were being enacted at the entrance to the bridges on the right bank of the Beresina, and we could do absolutely nothing to prevent them.[24] Wittgenstein's artillery poured shells upon the struggling crowds, beneath whose weight the bridges were bending till they were under water. Those who could swim flung themselves into the river, trusting to their skill to save them, but they were overcome by the cold, and hardly any reached the further bank. On either side the hapless fugitives pressed on, driving others into the water, many clutching at the ropes of the bridges in the hope of being able to climb on to them. In the awful struggle none who fell ever rose again, for every one was immediately crushed to death by those behind, whilst all the while shells and balls rained upon the helpless masses. I was blessing God that my sister had escaped this terrible catastrophe, and had crossed some time before, when, to my horror, I saw M. Levasseur carrying her in his arms and endeavouring to make his way up to me. He had managed to extricate her from the crowd, and now brought her to me. "In what an awful moment do we meet again!" I exclaimed; "and what in the world can I do with you in your exhausted condition, now that you have found me? But courage," I added. "I got General Vasserot safely over in his carriage; I will find him, and put you under his care." This I managed to do, and two hours later my sister was kindly received by the General, to whom she said, "Oh, General, you have saved me; now I will take care of you."

24 Many eye-witnesses of this awful disaster relate that the bridges were left almost empty on the night of the 27th, before the Russians came up, when all the non-combatants on the French side might quite easily have crossed. TRANS.

The Beresina disaster was the Pultava with which the Russians had threatened us; it was not our only defeat or the last, but it was by far the most bloody of any which befell us. It involved the loss of the greater part of Marshal Victor's corps, which perished in defending our passage; and the loss of the whole of the Partouneaux[25] division, which had to surrender. In a word, it cost the French and their allies some 20,000 or 30,000 men, killed, wounded, drowned, or taken prisoners. General Eblé, charged with the painful duty of burning the bridges after Marshal Victor's corps had passed over, had the greatest difficulty in cutting his way to them, and many of our own people were piteously struck down by the hatchets of his men before they were able to perform the task assigned to them. When at last the flames arose and the last hope of safety was cut off from those left on the other side, terrible were the cries of anguish which rent the air as thousands of poor wretches flung themselves into the water in a last despairing effort to escape. The ice broke beneath them; all was over, and the Cossacks swept down on the quarry, finding an immense amount of booty abandoned on the banks.[26]

On the evening of this terrible November 28 we halted at Zembino, a little town which had already been pillaged by our predecessors.[27] Marshal Davout and I took up our quarters in a little house crowded with others, which was heated by a stove. By dint of very close packing we managed

25 This was Marshal Victor's rearguard, which mistook the road to the river. TRANS.

26 General Eblé delayed the burning of the bridges till the last possible moment, but the Russians were advancing to fall upon the rear of the fugitives, and, had they been able to use the bridges, the French loss would have been even greater than it was. TRANS.

27 Lejeune passes very lightly over the march from the Beresina to Zembino, but it was a terribly arduous one, owing to the fact that the marshes, generally frozen over at this time of year, were still quite soft, and had the enemy pursued vigorously scarcely a man would have escaped to tell the tale. TRANS.

to be able to lie down on the ground, and most of us slept profoundly till the time came to start again, which was before daybreak. I had been roused a few minutes before the clock struck the hour for departure by hearing stifled sobs, and by the dying light of a lamp I now made out the form of a tall and beautiful woman leaning against the stove, her face hidden by her hands, whilst the tears trickled through her fingers. It was a long time since I had seen any human creatures who had not lost all pretensions to good looks through their privations, and I was struck by the graceful attitude of this weeping figure, with the masses of light hair shading her ideal features. She reminded me of Canova's "Muse leaning on a Sepulchral Urn, and lost in Meditation." Whilst every one, wrapped in selfish egotism, left the room without taking any notice of the lady in distress, I approached her and asked her in a gentle voice what she was weeping about. She turned to me, revealing her beautiful face, wet with tears, and pointing to a pretty child asleep at her feet, she said, "I am the wife of M. Lavaux, a Frenchman, who had a library at Moscow. The Governor Rostopschin has sent him to Siberia, and I took refuge with my boy in the French army. The Duc de Plaisance and two other generals let us share their carriages till they were destroyed, and I have carried my child from the Beresina here, but my strength is exhausted. I can go no further, and I am in despair." "Could you keep your seat on horseback?" I asked at once. "I could try," she replied. "Well, do not lose courage; let us make haste. I will take your boy and place him on my sister's knee; she is in General Vasserot's carriage, and I will put you on a horse which a faithful servant shall lead. You will thus be able to follow your boy." A smile of hope lit up her expressive features. I fetched a wolf's skin, which was on the horse I meant to give her, and wrapped it about her to protect her from the intense cold which had now set in, took off several silk handkerchiefs I had about me, and tied them together to make sashes to fasten her on to her steed. I then placed her on her horse, put her under the care of one of my mounted servants, and they started together. I never saw lady, servant, or horses again; but Vasserot and my sister took care of the child, and gave him back to his mother, who came to claim him in the evening. I shall refer again to what I was able to learn of the adventurous career of this lady, who two years later was found by the Emperor Alexander I teaching the Demoiselles of the Légion d'Honneur at St Denis.

Beyond Zembino we had to cross a number of little bridges which the enemy had neglected to burn, and we felt that God had not entirely deserted us when He left us this means of getting over the marshes. We had not a scrap of food to give the 2,000 or 3,000 prisoners we were taking with us, and I purposely shut my eyes when they availed themselves of every chance of escape in the woods through which we passed. I could not bring myself to enforce their remaining with us by the cruel measures which alone could have availed, and I knew well enough that at any moment our fate might be worse than theirs.

Sunday, the 29th, was occupied by a dreary march to Kamen, which we reached about midnight. Our men, as tired out as ourselves, and longing for sleep, took a few bits of meat from the one wagon we still retained, in which tobacco and everything else were mixed together helter skelter. They did not notice in the darkness that some tobacco was sticking to the meat, and put it all into the pot on the fire together. At four o'clock in the morning, just before we started, the soup was given out, but it tasted most horribly of tobacco, and nobody but myself would take any of it. I was so hungry that I was not so prudent as the others, and I swallowed the whole of my portion. I had not marched far before a terrible headache came on; I felt sick, and soon began to vomit. I fainted away, and it was easy to see that I was poisoned. The news spread; even the Emperor heard of it, and in his despatches for Paris of that day he mentioned the matter, so that every one there thought I was dead. When we halted during the day, General Haxo and others, who had still a little humanity left, made me some tea, and drinking it saved my life. I remained with Marshal Davout in his *wurst*, and we arrived at Kotovitchi in the evening, where we put up at the house of the priest, a good old man, who spoke French very well, and who had declined to leave with the rest of the inhabitants because, though he had nothing with which to supply our bodily needs, he hoped to be able to minister to our spiritual necessities. Under his affectionate care I completely recovered, and when we set off again at four o'clock the next morning we were full of real gratitude to him.

During the whole of December 1 we were marching through dense forests, in which at every turn we came to difficult passes. We lost nearly all our prisoners here.

On December 2 we crossed the Ilia before daybreak, and entered yet other vast forests with no well-defined roads, and the snow added to the difficulties of our march, so that it was late before we got to Molodetschno. Whilst arranging for the camping of our troops in the dark, I fell into a swamp, and was only with great difficulty extricated. The cold was so intense that the mud froze about me immediately, so that it was hard work to get me out. On the very same day and at the same hour seven years before I had been seated on the snow beneath a tree, but it was after the battle of Austerlitz, and I was in a very happy frame of mind. The Emperor arrived at Molodetschno the same day, but instead of celebrating the anniversary of the greatest victory of his life, he had to dictate that terrible twenty-ninth bulletin describing succinctly the disasters his army had met with, though he disguised their true extent.

At four o'clock on the morning of the 3rd we started once more, without daring to count those who were unable to rise. Our route was strewn with the dead; and the wheels of the carriages, which were scarcely able to turn, went over the ice-covered corpses, often dragging them along for a little distance.

Haxo and I walked arm in arm, so as to save each other from slipping, and a soldier and an officer were walking one on either side of us. Presently the soldier drew a hunk of black Russian bread about the size of a fist out of his pocket, and began to gnaw at it greedily. The officer, surprised to see such a thing as bread, offered the grenadier a five-franc piece for it. "No, no!" said the man, tearing at his bread like a lion jealous of his prey. "Oh, do sell it to me," pleaded the officer; "here are ten francs." "No, no, no, no!" and the bread rapidly disappeared, till quite half was gone. "I am dying! I entreat you to save my life! Here are twenty francs!" Then with a savage look the grenadier bit off one more big mouthful, and, handing what was left to the officer, took the twenty francs, evidently feeling that he had made anything but a good bargain.

We were all covered with ice. Our breath, looking like thick smoke, froze as it left our mouths, and hung in icicles from our hair, eyebrows, moustaches, and beards, sometimes quite blinding us. Once Haxo, in breaking off the icicles which were bothering me, noticed that my cheeks and nose were discoloured. They looked like wax, and he informed me that they were frozen. He was right, for all sensation was gone from them. He at once began to rub them hard with snow, and a couple of minutes' friction restored circulation, but the pain was terrible, and it needed all my resolution not to resist having the rubbing continued. Colonel Emi, of the engineers, was frozen in exactly the same way a few minutes later, and in his despair he flung himself down and rolled about on the ground. We did not want to abandon him to his fate, but we had to strike him again and again before we could make him get up. Dysentery also worked terrible ravages amongst us, and its victims, with their dry and livid skin and emaciated limbs, looked like living skeletons. The poor creatures had had nothing to eat but a little crushed corn made into a kind of mash, for they had no means of grinding or of cooking it properly, and this indigestible food passed through the intestines without nourishing the body. Truly the unhappy wretches, many of them stark naked, presented, as they fell out by the way, a picture of death in its most revolting aspect.

Providence, however, had still a few moments in reserve for some of us, in which we found consolation for our woes, and gathered up fresh strength for the further trials awaiting us.

This was the case on December 4, as I will now relate. We had started before daybreak to escape a cannonade from some Cossacks, and we were already some distance from our bivouac when a second troop of Cossacks, bolder and more numerous than the first, flung itself across our path, and carried off two carriages belonging to the Commissary-General. Fortunately he was on foot, and managed to escape. A few miles beyond our party the same horde of Tartars drew up at the entrance to a ravine through which a body of some 300 or 400 Polish cavalry was endeavouring to pass so as to rejoin us. The Cossacks seemed likely to completely crush the Poles, when the noise of the firing attracted our attention, and we realised the danger of the brave fellows. General Gérard, with his usual chivalry, at once offered his services to Marshal Davout, and asked for volunteers to go to the aid of our allies. Though his men were worn out with fatigue, they were still full of confidence in him, and they one and all shouted, "I am ready! I am ready!" General Gérard dashed across the plain at their head, and when the Cossacks saw the little body of infantry approaching, they feared they were about to be caught between two fires and galloped off. The Poles thus rescued soon joined us, and a bit of really good fortune rewarded us all for our mutual help.

Some carriages belonging to a convoy from Germany had succeeded in reaching Markovo, a little village we were just about to enter. These carriages were packed full of fresh provisions of many different kinds, and the delight of our brave soldiers may be imagined when they found awaiting them a good meal of bread and cheese and butter, with plenty of wine to wash them down. What a feast it seemed after forty days of such scanty and miserable diet as theirs had been! We of the first corps shared in this rare good fortune.

General Guilleminot with his division had been the first to arrive at Markovo, and he had taken care that the precious carriages should not be pillaged. He was at the window of a little château when we were passing, and he called to us to join him. After having taken the necessary precaution of rubbing our faces with snow, but for which we should certainly have lost some of our features, we went into a warm room, where a very unexpected sight awaited us. Tea services of beautiful china were set out on handsome mahogany tables, whilst here and there were great piles of white bread and hampers of Brittany butter. At the sight of this wonderful spread, after our many weeks of privations, our eyes brightened and our nostrils became expanded like those of some Arab steed at the sound of the trumpet. Needless to say how eagerly and gladly we accepted the invitation to share in this delightful breakfast. We each did the part not of four, but of ten – our appetites were simply insatiable. Never did any breakfast party do greater justice to the fare provided than we did to the great bowls of tea poured out, and the thick slices of bread and butter cut for us by our host. It was hard work to tear ourselves away from this warm room with all its comforts to go and camp beneath the cold light of the stars near Smorgoni, where there were twenty-five degrees of frost.

The name of Smorgoni roused our curiosity, for we knew that the inhabitants of that village, situated as it was in the heart of a vast forest, devoted themselves to the chase of bears, selling the furs of the older animals, and training the young ones as gymnastic performers, often taking them the round of Europe to show off their tricks. The people of Smorgoni had not expected us, and took flight at our approach, carrying their furs and young bears with them, but for all that we expected to find the village interesting.

It was at Smorgoni on December 5 that the Emperor, yielding to the earnest entreaties of his most faithful servants, decided to leave the army and return to France, where his presence was most urgently needed. Before leaving, he signed the order for the promotion and reward of many officers and generals, which had been drawn up by Major-General Prince Berthier. He called his marshals together, frankly expressed to them his great regret at having lingered too long at Moscow, and announced to them his approaching departure, appointing King Murat of Naples to the command of the army.

It was eleven o'clock at night, and there were twenty-five degrees of frost when the Emperor left Smorgoni, accompanied by the Dukes of Vicenza and Friuli (Marshal Duroc) and the Count of Lobau (Marshal Mouton), and made his way to Osmiana, miraculously escaping from the 1,200 Cossacks whom he had to pass, and who would certainly have taken him prisoner if they had known he was so near them with an escort of scarcely 100 men. A little before dark these same Cossacks had been beaten by General Loison, and driven out of Osmiana, where they had hoped to arrest our retreat. Whilst waiting for daylight the enemy were sleeping a little distance from the road, and the Emperor passed them unnoticed. Napoleon's departure threw the whole army into the greatest discouragement.

General Charpentier still declined to take my place, and I was compelled as before to perform the duties of Chief of the Staff. Fortunately, Marshal Davout now seemed to understand my position better, and was no longer so exacting. This made me willing to remain with him a few days longer.

On December 6 we passed through the little village of Pletchinzy just as a very interesting scene was taking place in it. Marshal Oudinot and General Pino, both wounded, had passed the night there with twenty-five or thirty officers and men belonging to their suite. A Cossack officer had heard of their presence, and thinking to take a great prize, he with some 200 men had surrounded the house in which they were. Speaking in good French, he politely summoned them to surrender. "We never surrender," was the reply, and a few well-aimed shots struck down some of the Cossacks. The hovel, for it was little more, was now regularly besieged, the French firing at close quarters into the ranks of the assailants, which they thinned considerably. Marshal Oudinot himself, though suffering greatly from a ball in the loins and unable to rise from the pallet on which he lay, made some holes in the walls between the planks, and firing through them picked off a good many Cossacks, for he never once missed his aim. Meanwhile, however, the enemy received reinforcements, and a gun was brought up to their aid. Four balls had already made a breach in the hut, but no one had been hurt. The French, after the manner of the Spanish, at once turned the opening to account by firing through it at their besiegers. A fifth ball broke the pallet on which the Marshal lay, and at the same time brought down the side of an oven in which five or six little children belonging to the peasant who had owned the hut, were discovered huddled together. The poor little things rushed out into the smoke and confusion in a great state of terror, much to the surprise of our men. There was something very touching in the way the little creatures clung to each other in the midst of the struggle. Fortunately our party came up just when things were going hardly with the besieged, for we had quickened our pace when we heard the firing, and the Cossacks, who had lost some fifty men killed and wounded, took to flight at our approach. We escorted the Marshal to Osmiana, where we halted for the night.

Here we found a division, consisting of some 12,000 fine young recruits, who had just arrived from France as reserves, under General Loison. Alas! twenty-four hours of our temperature was enough to kill off half of them, for they were in summer clothing, and not yet acclimatised; and three days later, when we reached Wilna, not one survived of the poor fellows whose weeping mothers had watched them start so short a time ago. I have been told since by several Russians that if the wind had blown from the north with the temperature at from 25 to 30 degrees, not one of us would have escaped alive. When the murderous north wind is blowing, the Russians generally remain in doors all day and night in rooms heated by stoves, and if they ever do venture forth it is only after a good meal, cased in woollen garments and thick furs, with which in our inexperience few of us had provided ourselves. The French died off, but the Cossacks fared splendidly.

The nearer we got to Wilna the more intense was the cold, especially at night, and every morning those still capable of bearing arms became fewer and fewer. The first corps now numbered scarcely 300 men, and the colonels and generals had to carry the colours of their regiments themselves. The enemy continued to cannonade us without venturing to come to close quarters. At last on December 8 we arrived on the heights of Wilna, where the little remnant of General Loison's corps perished of cold whilst a brisk cannonade from the Russians was going on. The approach to Wilna by the Minsk gate was so blocked with carriages piled up on each other and inextricably locked together, that I gave up trying to get in that way, but made my entrance through a garden by means of two ladders conveniently placed one on each side of a wall.

The first object I noticed in the street I entered, which was also much encumbered by broken vehicles, was the over-turned carriage of the paymaster of the army; the cash boxes had been broken open, and most of the contents stolen, but some 200,000 to 300,000 francs were scattered about on the ground for the first comer to pick up. The frozen metal, however, blistered the fingers of those who tried to carry it off, and the emaciated passers-by, scarcely able to drag themselves along, had not the courage to stoop or to burden themselves with heavy money.

What was my surprise at meeting in this street Colonel Kobilinski, who, as related above, had had his thigh smashed at Malo-Jaroslavitz and had fallen against me! He had been found by some soldiers, who carried him on their shoulders to a hospital. He slipped from their hold some twenty times in his insensibility, but when his wound had been dressed for the first time, four Jews carried him to the house of a nobleman of Wilna, where he was kindly received. He had suffered greatly for no less than fifty days from cold, hunger, and dysentery, yet his iron constitution brought him safely through all, and he is now in the service of Russia as governor of a fortress.

As I hurried about the town trying to make arrangements for my return to France, I came upon General Vasserot's carriage, which had safely arrived the evening before with its owner and my sister in it. They had escaped all the dangers of the road, and were just about to start for Danzig, where they were to wait for me. They had still perhaps the most difficult and dangerous part of the journey to perform, for between Wilna and Kovno were two very steep hills, now completely covered with ice. Always almost impassable, the presence of the enemy now added greatly to the difficulties of this part of the route, and here was left behind the last remnant of our war material. General Vasserot, however, who was a soldier to the backbone, managed to get safely over every obstacle, and was amongst the very few who did so.

I went back by way of my two ladders to tell Marshal Davout, Generals Haxo and Gérard, of this way of getting into the town, as they would probably not have discovered it for themselves. On my way to them I found a young artillery officer, who had had his arm amputated, exactly where I had left him some hours before. I had told him then that he had better follow me, as I could lend him a hand in climbing over impediments. He had thanked me, but said he had promised to wait at the entrance to the suburb for his servant. I said no more then, but when I came upon him again I represented to him the risk of remaining stationary in such murderous cold. 'I know all about that,'' was his reply; "but my faithful soldier George is my foster brother, and he has given me a thousand proofs of his devotion ever since I joined the army. My own mother could not have taken better care of me since I was wounded. He is ill and suffering, and I would rather die than break my word to him." Touched by this devotion at a time when hardly any one had a thought but for his own preservation, I did not dare to suggest to him that his beloved foster brother might be dead of cold, or a prisoner in the hands of the Russians. I merely asked him his name, his age, and his country. "My name is Arthur de Birassaye, I am twenty-two years old, and I come from Bayonne," was the reply. I never saw the officer again, but when I was in Bayonne some years later, I made inquiries about him, and learnt that he had never returned thither.

The people of Wilna, who during our absence had received immense convoys of stores and provisions, which were collected in magazines, received us kindly, and were full of hospitality and pity for our sufferings; but gradually, as fresh crowds of starving, debilitated wretches arrived, and it became impossible to maintain order in the distribution of food, pillage set in, all discipline was at an end, and scarcely anybody profited by the supplies. Fortunately, however, when the town itself was about to be pillaged, a strong force of police was organised, and the destruction was arrested. Meanwhile Major-General Prince Berthier, the Duke of Bassano, and Count Daru, Commissary-General, did their best to restore order in the ranks of the army, but they could achieve little. King Murat recognised that the task the Emperor had left him was beyond his powers, and his efforts were restricted to escaping being taken alive by the Cossacks, whom he had so often defied and so many of whom he had cut down, or from falling into the hands of the dreaded Tchichakoff, of whom we all stood in great awe, though so far he had not done us very much harm.

The Emperor had left orders for us to hold Wilna, and General von Wrede, with the few troops remaining to him, had joined us there with a view to supporting us. He fought valiantly all day long under a ceaseless cannonade from the enemy, but it was hopeless to attempt to stop the movement of retreat now, and all idea of making a stand at Wilna was soon abandoned. King Murat was himself the first to leave for Kovno with the remainder of the Guard, for he was eager to place the Niemen between himself and the enemy, but that river was frozen hard, and could no longer be said to divide the districts on either side of its course.

I now held no post in the army, and had taken leave of Marshal Davout, so that I was free to get back to France as best I could. I bought a sledge, and as the Polish General Kovitzki offered to act as my guide and interpreter, we left Wilna together at three o'clock on the morning of December 10. We crossed the ice covering the Wilia, and took the least frequented route on the right bank of that river for Kovno. The next morning at Assanovo we met Prince Radzivil, said to be the richest nobleman in Poland. Several of his ancestors had been chosen to wear the crown, so long hereditary in the Jagellon family. The Prince joined us and was good enough to let us have some of the horses he had ordered for himself at every posting house, so that we reached Kovno at the same time as Marshal Davout, who had taken the shorter route.

The weather was very bad, and snow was falling so heavily on the day of our arrival that we could hardly see ten paces before us. Half of Kovno was on fire, whilst the other half had been given up to pillage, and the wagons containing the Imperial treasure had only with great difficulty been saved.

The King of Naples was preparing to leave, having heard that the Prince von Schwarzenberg, who had already withdrawn to Bialistock, was continuing his retreat towards Warsaw. Marshal Macdonald meanwhile, abandoned by the Prussian corps under General York, was retiring on Memel.[28] Nothing could have exceeded the melancholy

28 General York's treachery to Napoleon ought to have been foreseen by him from the first, and it was the height of imprudence to employ the Prussian corps under him as the left wing of the *Grande Armée*. – TRANS.

appearance presented by Kovno, with snow falling so thickly as to darken the air, and scarcely any light but that from the flames consuming the town. It was indeed a gloomy augury for the future. The little remnant which had returned to Kovno represented to me the army whose fortunes I had shared so long; and when I turned my back on it, it was with feelings such as those of some brother abandoning the dead bodies of those belonging to him in a home smitten by the plague.

As I cautiously made my way across the bridge in my sledge, I could not keep back the tears at the thought of the contrast between the scene I gazed on now, on this melancholy 12th of December, and that I had so proudly looked down upon on June 24. True, the storm which had broken upon us then might have warned us of what was in store for us. It had really been, though we did not realise it, premonitory of the disasters awaiting us, from which none but the strongest escaped, and I thanked God for having brought me safely through them all. I now took the shortest route to Königsberg, and was soon out of hearing of the cannonade from the Cossacks, and the yet more melancholy reports, so long of daily occurrence, of the blowing up of our ammunition wagons to save them from falling into the hands of the enemy. I did not stop at Königsberg, but pushed on for Danzig, where I arrived on December 10. My sister and General Vasserot joined me there the next day. The General still needed rest for his complete recovery from his wound, and we too were worn out, so we stopped quietly at Danzig for ten days, which we spent in providing ourselves with new clothes. As soon as I arrived I burnt the clothes I had travelled in, for they literally swarmed with vermin, and for the first time for two months and a half I enjoyed the luxury of a bath and a shave, for during our retreat I had never been able to give the slightest attention to my toilette, and my face was literally blackened with smoke and exposure. I now resumed my usual habits, and my spirits rose greatly.

On December 30 my sister and I took leave of our good

friend General Vasserot, and we left Danzig together in my sledge. A tremendous storm overtook us by the way, and our vehicle was several times overturned. Each time we fell, we left the impression of our faces in the snow. If only that snow had been clay or some other enduring material, those impressions would have been preserved as curiosities by the people of the district, which is rich in fossils, many being embedded in the stones of which the houses are built. These small accidents, which were rather comic than tragic, only made us laugh, and restored to us the gaiety to which we had so long been strangers. The storm had melted the snow, and the sledge was no longer of any use, so we had to stop at Neustadt to buy a carriage. I got one of the little *chars à bancs* in Germany which are as light as they are pretty, and on the third day, the snow having disappeared, we were able to resume our route.[29]

29 Lejeune reached Paris on 5 February 1813.

VITORIA, 1813

Ensign George Hennell,
43rd (Monmouthshire) Regiment of Foot

After the fiasco of Burgos, Wellington wintered in Portugal, where he absorbed reinforcements from England and planned a campaign that would drive the French from the Peninsula altogether. By Spring 1813 the strategic position could scarcely be bettered, for Napoleon's desperate struggle against the German nations had siphoned off droves of men and and guns from Iberia. "I shall never be stronger . . . and the enemy will not be weaker," Wellington wrote home. Not underestimating the fighting power of his opponent, however, Wellington launched an offensive of consummate professionalism, combining frontal pressure towards Salamanca with a long, enveloping "hook" to the north undertaken by General Graham. Desperate to avoid envelopment, the French retreated and retreated until King Joseph and Marshal Jourdan retired behind the River Ebro, convinced that Wellington would be unable to surmount the surrounding difficult terrain. Unfortunately for the hapless Joseph, the Allies had developed a commissariat network, based on the depots at Santander, that allowed them to move forward at a staggering rate. In less than three weeks, Wellington traversed half of mountainous northern Spain and by the middle of June his main force was descending on the French at Vitoria. By 20 June Wellington had 80,000 troops poised for assault, against Joseph's 58,000. The climactic battle of Vitoria, the end play in the Peninsular War, opened at 8 a.m. the next day along a 12-mile front, with Wellington sending four huge columns against the French lines. By 6 p.m. the situation was irretrievably lost for the Imperial forces, and Joseph ordered the remnants of the "Army of Portugal," "Army of the Centre," and "Army of the South" on an all-out retreat. The French had suffered 7,500 casualties (to Wellington's 5,000). The powder-stained Allied soldiers might have upped their tally in a vigorous pursuit, but most stopped in the rain to loot the fabulous hordes of treasure the French had abandoned in their haste. "The soldiers of the army have got about them about a million sterling," complained Wellington.

There was still fighting to come in the Peninsular War, at San Sebastian, at Pamplona, in the Pyrenees and in Southern France, but courtesy of the victory at Vitoria French power in Iberia was broken forever.

George Hennell went to the Peninsula as a Volunteer, or probationary officer. He so distinguished himself in the storming of Badajoz that he was gazetted as an ensign – without purchase – in the 43rd (Monmouthshire) Regiment of Foot (Light Infantry), more commonly known as the 43rd Light Infantry, one of the best regiments of the line.

Camp on the banks of the river Aragon, near Caseda,
2 lea [gues] S. of Sanguessa.
June 29th 1813.

DEAR BROTHERS,

This is the first hour I have had to write since my last of the 20th inst. We halt today. One reason is [that] if we did march we should leave half behind us – they are completely knocked up. Every hour since my last is so full of incident that I shall give you it as much at length as I can.

On the 21st our own division marched. I was in orders for the charge of the baggage which was to march at 7 o'clock.

We did so & went round that mountain from which we had heard firing the night before. After marching ½ a league the baggage halted for the reserve artillery & Household troops to pass. We then mov'd up the hill & I there learned that a general engagement was begun. I gave the sergeant charge of the baggage & immediately galloped on & at the top of the hill saw the whole of the French army in a plain with Vitoria in their rear & a smart skirmish on my right. Ours was the first brigade.

On arriving I found the 43rd in front & came up to them as it was going round a hill to a wood on the top, the river running just below. We remained there about an hour & then marched round by No. 2 bridge which was *not* defended, to a hill overlooking the whole plain with a wall in front breast high & we formed behind it. They gave us a salute with one or two guns from bridge No. 3 which did no damage. This was to begin with.

I have called this spot a plain because it is so in comparison with this mountainous country surrounding. It is an oval form (No. 1) but it is crowded with little hills 3 or 400 yards asunder, very disadvantageous for a retiring army. The hill (No. 2) in front was the highest. No. 3 was a line of artillery and infantry well formed to defend bridge No. 1.

The 2nd Division began the battle on our right. In the meantime our main force, viz: 1st, 7th, 3rd & 4th divisions moved round to their right.[1] We had between 70 & 80,000 men: French 60,000. We all expected they would have defended the bridges obstinately and their positions more so but they most shamefully and very unlike Frenchmen gave up both with scarcely a shadow of defence.

About 10 o'clock the 1st 95th moved along the river side, the 2nd brigade moving round to attack bridge No. 3. The river is fordable in some parts. The bridge was lined with skirmishers, 2 or 3 troops of cavalry & 2 guns. The 2nd

1 A mistake of the pen; the 4th Division was to the right of the Light Division.

brigade sent skirmishers below the bridge. They opened a fire just as Graham's columns came in sight. At a distance of ¼ a mile the 95th was running down to flank them [the French]. They had a large body in squares (No. 4). All now began to return to them as fast as they could run. We then moved down the hill in open column of companies and, at No. 5, formed line and, with a few skirmishers in front, were ordered to attack the hill. A sergeant was in the centre with [one] Colour and myself with the other. We were to make for the centre of the middle & highest hill, the 17th Portuguese supporting us. When we were ½ way up the hill, they [the French] disappeared without firing a shot. During this time the 2nd brigade were moving round the hill and our columns were crossing the river. Their [French] line (No. 2) moved off before them. We moved round the hill & heard a heavy fire on our left & very near. We moved on to a hill 300 yards farther & there the cannon balls began to hiss over our heads. We mov'd on to a hill 100 yards from the village, No. 1, a very heavy fire continuing on our left. We formed line about 20 yards from the bank (2 yds high). Here we had a very strong fire from a battery of theirs, No. 6, of balls & shells, while the 95th & some other troops were attacking the village which they defended well.

The first ball that came was a spent one. It struck the ground about 50 yards from us & was coming straight for me but it rebounded about 10 yards [from me] & went to my left, just over the heads of the men & struck our old colonel [Daniel Hearn] on the arm. He called out but was not much hurt as it came about as swift as a swallow flies. Finding the fire heavy, we moved under a bank & lay down. At that moment a shell came gently hopping direct for me but it was polite enough to halt on top of the bank about 6 yards from us. We lay down & in about 1 minute it burst doing no harm. In another minute a ball struck the close column of the 17th Portuguese not a yard from the place the 43rd colours had just left & about 16 yards from us. It killed a sergeant & took off the leg of each of the ensigns with the colours. This was about 2 o'clock.

We halted there a $\frac{1}{4}$ of an hour until the village was taken by the 95th, who captured their cannon. We then moved in open column to our right, the battery, No. 6, firing as fast as possible all the time. During this time some Spanish troops were skirmishing with a flock (for they were all scattered) of French on the side of the mountain and a body of French between us & them, which the 4th Division was chasing, kept retiring and taking up good positions & most cowardly abandoning them till we came to the village, No. 2. This is to be said for them that their principal force was on our left & was retiring hotly engaged. The 3rd Division had most of it (the attack) & were nearly a mile before them so that they were afraid of being cut off. At the same time they had to support their skirmishers on the mountain as they were more behind still. We were about even [i.e. level] with them & against village No. 2, on the right of which there was a wood. We moved to our right hoping to cut them off but they ran too fast for us.

Just after we came out of the wood we found a little valley & they had regularly taken up an excellent position. We formed line on the hill while the one opposite us was taken. The 45th was in line in the hollow ready to charge up the hill, No. 8, more in the rear, on which were 18 or 20 pieces of cannon playing upon our regiment & [village No.] 2. They were $\frac{1}{2}$ a mile distant. We kept driving in their skirmishers to a line formed on a hill to our right, No. 7. (No. 8 their cannon; No. 9 our line). After this a Portuguese regiment moved round their left &, appearing on their flank, they all set off from that, & the next, No. 9, leaving all their artillery.

(*Note*. The French had no idea of our attacking them today. If we had done so they would have had batteries all along the hill, & if they had been obliged to retire, would have returned to this position & suddenly opened upon us a most destructive fire. It was their intention to attack us, but Lord Wellington had a better head than any of their miserable generals who commanded them on that day.)[2]

All this time Genl. Graham was pressing their main force on the [ir] right. It was near here that two of our officers [Major John Duffy & Lieutenant George Houlton] were wounded. They did not maintain their position more than $\frac{1}{2}$ an hour. Several of our officers remarked, & I think it just, that cannon make more noise and alarm than they do mischief. Many shots were fired at us but we suffered little from them. A young soldier is much more alarmed at a nine pounder shot passing within 4 yds. of his head than he is of a bullet at a distance of as many inches, although one would settle him as effectively as the other. Artillery makes great havoc when in close column. The French are very correct in aiming their artillery. [At] $\frac{1}{2}$ past 3, in passing the line the 45th occupied in the valley, I saw 10 or 12 killed or wounded in the space of as many yards owing to the fire kept up on them from the hill.

Upon their cannons ceasing to fire, our guns galloped after them as fast as they could move. They began to run faster than we could follow. We chased them by Vitoria in grand style, leaving them no time to save their immense baggage. They took up a position $1\frac{1}{2}$ miles beyond Vitoria which they abandoned as soon as some 9 pounders from a hill close to Vitoria played upon them. As they went up the hill in the greatest disorder, scattering like a flock of sheep, we kept moving forward leaving Vitoria $\frac{1}{2}$ a mile to our right. After this the Household troops, viz: the [Life] Guards & Blues, came galloping by us. I do not know what good they did, if any I am sure you would hear of it.

At 6 o'clock we came up to a village where were 8 or 10 wagons overturned with all kinds of valuable baggage

2 King Joseph had no intention of an attack, and was merely holding Vitoria to buy time for the huge army trains to clear the area heading for France.

attended by dragoons, Spaniards & stragglers plundering them. The smell of French brandy was very strong, I am sorry I cannot tell the taste. The soldiers were not allowed to touch a drop. If they attempted it the officers knocked it out of their hands. However, as they had to march over a great quantity it could not be entirely prevented. We saw the French no more this day. We continued marching till dark, 9 o'clock, passing more wagons overturned & baggage of every description, including flocks of sheep, goats, bullocks, asses, mules, horses & c.

At last we halted at the side of a narrow lane stopped up with wagons, our artillery in front of us firing as long as they could see. We here found a flock of sheep, mostly killed & tumbled one upon another into a deep ditch. In the same ditch were 2 or 3 pieces of cannon, overturned, horses & mules with them. You can hardly form any conception of the scene here – everyone busy & most employed in getting the sheep out of the ditch, while others were skinning them, the whole, as you may suppose, knocked up. In the morning I was fortunate in being on the baggage so [had] had an excellent breakfast & took the precaution to put some bread & meat in my pocket. Many of the officers had nothing all day. From bridge No. 1 to Vitoria is 2 leagues & we marched $1\frac{1}{2}$ leagues beyond it. The division then formed upon a hill close by. The baggage, of course, could not get up.

I shall now conclude this with a short description of the scene presented on halting. The wood of the wagons supplied fuel & about every 2 yds. square was a fire & a circle round it. One will describe the whole – one making dough boys (flour & water mixed) swearing all the time at one for not producing a frying pan, at another for getting in his light; another giving a young soldier a thump for crossing between him & the fire while he plastered his blistered feet. The poor creature is turning round to beg his pardon, when he treads upon another, who threatens to upset him if he does not sit down. A woman who is undressing by his side (perhaps the wife of one of the party) raises her shrill voice & blasts him for not being quick. An old soldier sits smoking his pipe & frying the mutton or skimming the pot, while a dirty fist seizes the mutton, and another equally so lays hold of it & it is torn asunder by a knife with edge & back alike. The whole is shortly devoured & they lie down to sleep in their blankets. It was a cloudy but fine day. I had not the slightest touch of shot or shell.

YOURS & c.
G.H.

"THE ONLY REGIMENT OF ENGLISH": FIGHTING THE NORTH GERMAN CAMPAIGN, 1813

Sergeant Thomas Morris, 73rd Regiment

Napoleon's disastrous invasion of Russia led directly to the War of German Liberation, as Prussia opportunistically threw off the French yoke for alliance with the Tsar and Great Britain in the so-called "Sixth Coalition." By zealous application of the conscription laws, Napoleon raised another half million men for the resultant German campaign, beating the Coalition in battles at Lutzen, then Bautzen, in May 1813. Even so, Napoleon was unable to deter Austria, Sweden (this latter country ruled by le petit caporal's *sometime marshal, Jean-Baptiste Bernadotte) and a number of German states from joining the Coalition, which bolstered its forces in northern Germany with the dispatch of 3,000 men from Britain, comprising the 25th, 33rd, 54th, 73rd, 91st, and first Royals, commanded by Major-General Sir Samuel Gibbs.*

Thus it was that seventeen-year-old Sergeant Thomas Morris, a Londoner in the 73rd Regiment, found himself taking part in his first campaign. Along with his regiment, he arrived on the Baltic island of Rugen in early August 1813. Two weeks later

Napoleon drubbed the Allies at the Battle of Dresden, 26–27 August. Yet, French forces were dangerously dispersed along the front, and were successively isolated and crushed. In the north-west of Germany, the Coalition ordered General Walmoden of Hanover to move against Marshal Davout's corps on the lower Elbe; among the resulting engagements was the Battle of Gohrde, 50 miles south-east of Hamburg, on 16 September, an almost forgotten combat at which Morris's 73rd, plus half a rocket battery, was the only British participant. It was Morris's personal regret that he was not present at Leipzig a month later in the "Battle of the Nations," which effectively cost Napoleon control of Germany and allowed his enemies to advance to France's borders, but he found recompense in being with his regiment at Waterloo for the final hurrah in the war with Bonaparte.

We now left Yarmouth with a perfectly fair wind, and without any further delays reached the coast of Denmark when one of our transports, the *Robert Harrison*, having part of the 91st regiment on board ran aground, and fears were entertained for their safety; but on the return of the tide, they were relieved from their perilous position with but little damage.

We were at this time under convoy of the *Amphion* frigate; and on entering the Belt to get to the Baltic Sea, we joined a fleet of merchantmen and kept company with them some distance. We were detained for some time in the Belt, by continual calms, and the prevalence of the thickest fog I ever saw; taking advantage of which a number of Danish gun-boats came out and fired on us, without however doing much injury. On one occasion we were progressing slowly and rather too near the Danish batteries, which opened on us, but were soon silenced by a few broadsides from the *Lion* seventy-four.

While we were becalmed here, the vessels were occasionally so close together that we could converse with each other; and having every bit of canvas spread, there being no wind, and the several regimental bands playing of an afternoon, the scene at such times was of the most imposing nature. The officers too, used to encourage games among the men, sometimes forming them in parties for dancing on deck; and having several boxes of oranges on board, they would throw them among the men, to produce a scramble. These various pastimes had the effect of keeping up a good understanding among the officers and men. There was one private soldier, named Ealy, on board, who, from his extraordinary likeness to Wellington, was called "Lord Wellington", and in these sports he generally headed one of the parties, producing a great deal of amusement. From this trifling circumstance, I have no doubt had he afterwards conducted himself well, he would have been rapidly promoted; but in the first action we entered, he proved himself a rank coward, and the officers then turned their backs on him.

The monotony of the voyage was one morning rather unpleasantly relieved, by the infliction of corporal punishment. The officers had, by some means, obtained some fresh vegetables, and what was not consumed, was placed on the deck aft, under the charge of the sentry; the prisoner, who made free with a couple of carrots, was detected in the act, tried by a court-martial, and sentenced to receive one hundred and fifty lashes.

The morning the punishment took place, there was a stiff breeze, and the motion of the vessel prevented the drummers from always hitting one spot, so that the lashes fell sometimes on the back of the neck, then on the shoulders, and also over the back, which gave the man the appearance of having been very dreadfully punished, whereas in reality, he did not suffer so much as if he had been struck always on one place. However, as it was, it was considered quite unnecessary, and rather too severe for the offence; had they stopped his grog for a few days, it would have been quite sufficient.

These delays in our progress gave us ample time to reflect on our probable destiny. I have sat for hours together, meditating on my own folly or temerity, in thus rushing on to certain danger – perhaps to death. Of our regiment, consisting of about 30 officers and 550 men, how many of them were destined never to return? how many of them were to be disabled by severe wounds? and the question would arise – should I be among the first? or second? or should I return in safety?

The shots fired at us, on passing the Belt, had created rather uneasy sensations among us, being all young soldiers – not more than a dozen of us having ever before seen a shot fired in anger; and I must here confess that I felt the enthusiasm which had hitherto urged me on oozing out very fast: though I determined still to do my duty whatever dangers I might be exposed to.

Our officers on the whole seemed to be very soldierly. The colonel was the son of General Harris, who gained so much celebrity and renown as commander of the Anglo-Indian forces at the storming of the important fortress of Seringa-patam.[1] The son had yet to be tried; but he had every appearance of being likely to do his duty. He had as fine a regiment under his command as any in the service, consisting chiefly of young men, from eighteen to thirty years of age, fit for any sort of duty.

Our light company was for the number, the finest set of men I ever saw, being a mixture of English, Irish and Scotch, commanded by a captain who had risen from the ranks. Report said, that he was indebted for his promotion, to his beautiful black eyes and whiskers, which had attracted the notice of his colonel's lady; who had sufficient influence to obtain for him a commission as ensign. He was now captain; and though his whiskers were tinged with grey, his eyes possessed all their former fire and brilliancy.

1 1799.

He was very eccentric in his ways; and his men scarcely knew how to please him. On one occasion, as we were going into action, one of the men excited his anger, and he ordered him to have an extra guard; and calling to his lieutenant, said, "Reynolds[2] if I am killed, see that Gorman has an extra guard." – "Sergeant Pennyton!" – "Sir." – "If Reynolds and I are killed, see that Gorman has an extra guard." – "Yes, Sir." – "None of your ready-made answers, Sir; but mind you do it, Sir!" – "Yes, Sir."

On another occasion, he found a Bible in possession of one of the men, and ordered him to burn it; and made use of the following blasphemous expression: "D–n you, Sir, I'll let you know that your firelock is your Bible, and I am your G – a –!" With all his faults, however, he was a brave and well-disciplined officer.

His lieutenant, Reynolds, was a good little fellow; but was very unfortunate. If there was a shot fired at all, he was sure to get hit; while some men pass through so many fights without receiving a scratch.

The ensign of the light company, was a fine manly fellow named Loyd,[3] now a major in the service. He had sometimes to put up with the arbitrary conduct of his captain. Once, the latter said to him, "D – n you, Sir, I'll let you know that I am your captain!" The ensign replied, "And, Sir, you will please to recollect, at the same time, that I am Ensign Loyd, and a gentleman!"

By this time, we were acquainted with our destination, Swedish Pomerania, the Crown Prince having entered into a treaty with the British Government, whereby, on receiving one million of money, he engaged to join the Allied Sovereigns, with 80,000 Swedes; and it was intended that we should co-operate with him.

Our force consisted of the following regiments – the 25th; 33rd, 54th, 73rd, first Royals and 91st, amounting

2 Lieutenant Thomas Reynolds.
3 Ensign John Lloyd; major, 1828.

altogether to about 3,000 men; under the command of General Gibbs.[4]

In the latter part of August, we arrived at the island of Rugas [*Rügen*]; where we disembarked, and marched across the island to Stralsund – the place which acquired so much celebrity under the romantic Charles XII of Sweden. Our baggage, which took some time getting on shore – the ships not being able to come within half-a-mile of the beach – was afterwards conveyed by some small vessels up the river, and did not reach Stralsund till next day.

> Sound, sound the clarion! fill the fife,
> To all the sensual world proclaim –
> One crowded hour of glorious life
> Is worth an age without a name!

The first morning after our arrival in Stralsund *7 August 1813*, we discovered that our duties were likely to be of the most onerous, if not of the most dangerous, nature. The French General Morrand, had taken possession of it some few months before; and being called away suddenly, he destroyed most of the batteries and fortifications; and as there was a probability of its being now again attacked, it was necessary to place it in a state of defence. The Crown Prince who paid us a visit, drew off all the men capable of bearing arms, the tradesmen and wealthy burghers mounted guard at the town hall as private soldiers, and every man capable of labour was obliged to assist in repairing the batteries; we also were compelled to assist them; and there still being a deficiency of labourers, about a thousand young women, of the lower classes, were engaged, and dressed in male attire, were set to work, and were found very efficient; the women in that country being inured to field labour. Some ludicrous mistakes took place with some of our men, who in carrying on

4 Major-General Sir Samuel Gibbs; killed at New Orleans, 1815.

affairs of gallantry, were not always able to distinguish the women from the men.

Our duty now became very severe, as may be seen from the following statement for one week. Namely, Monday forenoon, attend parade at ten o'clock, eleven o'clock mount guard. Tuesday morning (at eleven) relieved from guard, go to quarters, change dress, and work for the rest of the day at the fortification. Wednesday, fall in two hours before daybreak, or as they say on service, "until we can see a grey horse a mile": this was to prevent our being taken by surprise. Attend regimental parade at eleven; at eight o'clock in the evening fall in for picket; and patrol the streets till twelve. Go to quarters, get an hour or two rest; fall in two hours before daybreak on Thursday, get back to quarters by seven, attend regimental parade at ten, mount guard at eleven. Friday, relieved from guard at eleven, change dress and go to work. Saturday, fall in two hours before daybreak, attend parade at ten, work the rest of the day, picket at night. Sunday morning, fall in before daybreak as usual, parade at ten, mount guard at eleven.

Thus, it will be seen that we had very little time for rest; and we were so completely worn out, that one night, when I was placed as sentinel on a post of very considerable importance – although I knew the safety of the town depended on my vigilance – I could not resist the inclination to sleep; so, deliberately laying myself down on the ground, resting my firelock by my side, and placing a stone for my pillow, I fell asleep. Time passed quick; and I was awakened by a most terrific dream. An immense lion, I fancied was about springing on me. In the utmost terror I started to my feet, instinctively grasping my firelock, and heard footsteps approaching. I had sufficient presence of mind to give the usual challenge – "Who comes there?" and "The Grand Round" was the reply. I demanded, "Stand fast, Grand Round; advance sergeant, and give the countersign." The sergeant advanced a few paces, pronounced the mystic word, and I called out, "Pass on, Grand Round; all's well."

It would not have been "well" for me, had they caught me asleep; the inevitable punishment for such a crime under such circumstances would have been death. In a few minutes afterwards, the relieving sentinels came round, so that I had been asleep nearly two hours. I did not feel any more an inclination for sleep that night. I thanked God for my deliverance; and vowed never again to indulge in a nap while on sentry.

As the batteries were assuming a state of efficiency; and no tidings of the enemy, General Gibbs detached the 54th Regiment, to reconnoitre the country; and they had not been gone more than three or four days, when they returned in the utmost disorder; stating they had met with the enemy in considerable numbers, which induced them to make the best of their way back to Stralsund: and we, of course, expected the French would now pay us a visit. As there were still no signs of them, the General left Stralsund himself, taking only our regiment with him.

We left Swedish Pomerania, and proceeded through Germany, by forced marches, of about thirty miles a day; and as we had no Commissary with us, we were obliged to trust entirely to chance for our daily supplies. In the various towns through which we passed, more particularly at Güstrow, the inhabitants behaved towards us with the greatest kindness, striving with each other which should have the honour of entertaining us.

Our journey, after leaving the last-named town, was through a country purely agricultural; and yet, though it was in the beginning of September, there were no signs of harvest. The country had been overrun with troops, alternately friendly and hostile; but (whether one or the other) draining them of their resources, driving away their cattle, and producing the utmost desolation; so that though the inhabitants of the villages were extremely kind of us, it was not in their power to furnish us with any provision, even for money. The only inhabitants indeed remaining in the villages, were old men and women, and young children, no cattle, no horses, sheep, pigs or poultry; the trees, indeed, were yielding abundance of fruit, and there were a few tobacco fields in cultivation: with these exceptions, it is impossible to describe the state of desolation to which the country had been reduced.

Though General Gibbs left Stralsund with us, he did not accompany us always. He was desirous of falling in with some of the allied troops. Napoleon was at this time at Dresden, with upwards of 100,000 men. Murat, Ney, Davout and some others of the French marshals were occupying strong positions between Dresden and Leipsic, ready to act singly, or co-operate with their master, as circumstances might require. Against these, were the combined forces of Austria, Russia and Prussia and the Crown Prince, with 30,000 Swedes. The utmost reliance was now placed in the fidelity and ability of Bernadotte; and he was created Generalissimo of the Allied Troops.

Our regiment continued to advance, though with what object was not known. The weather was very hot; and for a whole week we had nothing to subsist on but such potatoes or fruit as we could pick up on the march; generally bivouacking in a wood, at night.

On 15 September, towards the close of the day when our colonel was looking out for some suitable spot on which to pass the night, and pointing to a wood in the distance as seeming to promise the necessary accommodation; having nearly reached the spot – whether through the ignorance or treachery of our guide, I know not – but we found ourselves within two miles of the French camp, of 20,000 men. Had they been aware of our approach, they could have detached two or three regiments of cavalry and have taken the whole of us prisoners. As soon as we found out our mistake, we lost but little time in placing ourselves at a more respectful distance. Having gone about five miles in another direction, we fell in with General Walmoden, with about 20,000 Germans and Hanoverians; and though night was drawing on, he was breaking up his camp to attack the enemy, whom we were so close upon.

We were now fortunate enough to get a supply of bread, and two cows, alive; they were soon dispatched however, and cut up after a manner – some of the men roasting their portions at the wood fires, and some actually devouring it raw – warm, as it came from the beast, after the Abyssinian fashion.

After two or three hours' rest, we also were ordered to advance, but not exactly in the track of our allies. They crossed the Elbe, at Dormitz[5], and we proceeded to Dannenberg, where the enemy had broken down the bridge, and it was midnight before a bridge of boats could be constructed to enable us to pass. How we got over I cannot tell; for we were so thoroughly fatigued, that we actually slept as we walked along. Towards morning we were indulged with about two hours' repose, on the grass; when we were again urged forward.

General Count Walmoden had overtaken and engaged the enemy, on the plains of Gordo [*Göhrde*][6], in Hanover, about fifteen miles from our last town. As soon as we heard firing we were hurried on to assist, and went double-quick through the wood – in which we passed a delightful country seat, the property of George III, as Elector of Hanover; and soon afterwards, emerging from the wood a most extraordinary sight presented itself to us.

On our left was the French army, drawn up with their right near the wood. On their right centre was a hill on which some cannon with a strong body of infantry, were placed. On their extreme left was a solid square of French infantry; and as we entered the field, the latter were attacked by some of our

5 Domitz.
6 Gohrde.

cavalry, consisting of the 2nd and 3rd German Hussars[7]. The attack was not successful; the cavalry were repulsed with considerable loss.

As soon as Walmoden perceived us, he rode up with a couple of aides-de-camp. His appearance, for a general – especially for a general commanding in a field of battle – was the most extraordinary I have ever seen. He was actually smoking one of the long German pipes, the flexible tube passing round his body, and the bowl deposited in a pouch, by his horse's side. Addressing our commanding officer, he said, "Colonel, I am glad you are come; I want that hill taken!" pointing to the one with the two pieces of cannon, and about a thousand men on it. "Will you charge them, Colonel?" "Yes, Sir," was the answer. "Well," said the German, "I shall send a Hanoverian regiment to assist you." On which our colonel observed, "Let us try it ourselves, General, first; and if we fail, then assist us." Then, addressing the regiment, he said, "Now, my lads, you see what we have to do; we are the only regiment of English in the field: don't let us disgrace ourselves!" A hearty cheer from the men was the assurance that they would do their duty. The colonel, calling the quartermaster, told him to endeavour to get us a supply of schnaps, by the time we had done the job; and then he led us on to the foot of the hill. As we began to ascend, the enemy fired one volley, which being ill-directed, passed over us harmless, or nearly so; and then they abandoned their position, and retreated, on perceiving the English colours, which our officers had just unfurled; previously, they were rolled up in oilskin cases.

In order to account for this apparent cowardice on the part of the French, their general, himself, informed us afterwards, when taken prisoner, that when he was attacked by the Hanoverians, the whole being in British uniform, he had a difficulty in persuading his men that they were not English;

7 i.e. of the King's German Legion.

and when our regiment began to ascend the hill, they, of course, took us to be part of the Hanoverians; but when the British colours were exhibited, the French troops fancied that not only we, but the majority of the red coats were English, and this circumstance caused such a panic among his men, that he could no longer keep them to their duty.

The French right, on seeing the hill abandoned, fled also. The square of French infantry on the left, which I have before alluded to, were still firm; but there happened to be two or three of the Rocket Brigade in the field, and the first rocket fired, fell directly in the square, putting them in the greatest confusion; and while they were so, the German Hussars, who had been previously repulsed, charged them again, and influenced by feelings of revenge, cut among them, right and left, giving no quarter.

The French were now defeated at all points, and the result was about 800 French killed, 1,200 wounded, and 1,500 prisoners; our loss in killed and wounded, was about 800.[8] This battle is very slightly mentioned in history, and no notice whatever has been taken of our presence. If it had been a battalion of the Guards so engaged, the circumstance would have found a prominent place in history; but as it was only a paltry regiment of the line, of course it was not worth recording, as there was nothing in the shape of patronage to be secured by it.

I have stated that the French General was taken prisoner, and there was a circumstance connected with his capture worth recording. Finding his efforts to rally his men ineffectual, being wounded, he endeavoured to make good his own retreat but was closely pursued by one of the 2nd German Hussars. The General, in order to check him in the pursuit, threw on the ground a well-filled purse. The hussar noticed the spot where the purse fell, but continued the pursuit, when the General surrendered, and on retracing

8 Morris's own regiment suffered no casualties. Eight guns were also taken by the Allies.

their steps the German dismounted, took up the purse and gave it to the General: who, when he met our General, reported the brave and disinterested conduct of the man. General Gibbs, who arrived in the field during the action, was so struck with the conduct of the hussar, that he attached him to his own person as an orderly, and when that general was killed afterwards at New Orleans, in America, the man was found dead by his side.

In the course of this engagement, we were joined by a Regiment of Russian Cossacks; a set of barbarians, inspiring as much terror in our own ranks as in those of the enemy. There was nothing like discipline preserved by them, and their principal object seemed to be plunder, no matter how obtained, whether from friend or foe. One of them having killed a man, was in the act of stripping him, when another came up to assist him, "No, no! my good friend", said the first one, "go and kill a man for yourself." They did not confine themselves to taking watches, money, or other valuables, but stripped the dead and dying of every particle of clothing, taking with them such as they thought worth carrying, and scattering the rest about the ground.

Having collected the prisoners, to the amount of 1,500, who were placed under our charge, we paid such attention to the wounded as circumstances would admit of, and there being no town nearer than the one we last left, and the weather extremely wet, we made the best arrangement we could for the night; and miserable indeed was our position. The rain continued the whole night, increasing tenfold the sufferings of the wounded, and rendering our situation anything but pleasant.

Notwithstanding these unpleasant circumstances however, such was our state of exhaustion that no sooner were the prisoners arranged, being surrounded by sentinels with orders to shoot any of them who should endeavour to escape, than the rest of us laid down and slept on the ground, exposed to the "pelting of the pitiless storm". At day-break next morning the weather cleared up, and we were engaged for an hour or two in lighting fires and drying ourselves. A number of wagons arrived from Dannenberg for the removal of the wounded, and we had to escort the prisoners to that place. Some of them had been in English prisons, and seemed pleased when it was intimated to them that they would be sent to England, by which we may suppose they had been tolerably well treated there. On our arrival at Dannenberg, the prisoners were placed under a guard in the Town Hall, and the wounded French, as they arrived, were deposited on straw in the pews of the church.

General Gibbs was here with us, and we were billeted on the inhabitants. I obtained tolerably good quarters; but just as I had got something to eat, and was about to retire to rest on some clean straw, (there being so many of us, beds were out of the question) I was called out on what is called "fatigue duty", and our employment during the whole of the night was assisting the surgeons in the church, who had taken their station near the altar; and we carried to them such of the wounded as were marked for amputation, holding them while the operation was performed, and then depositing them on the floor with straw to lie on, and an allowance of bread and water to each; and occasionally, carrying away such of them as had died, to the holes prepared in the yard for them. In the morning there was a stack of amputated limbs beside the altar, which we had afterwards to remove and bury.

On leaving this place we were relieved from the charge of the prisoners, where they were taken to I never could learn. We returned by the same road through Germany, and were exposed to the same privations until we had passed Güstrow, when, as on our advance, we subsisted on the inhabitants; instead of going back to Stralsund, we diverged to the left, and went to Rostock in Mecklenburgh, where we obtained very comfortable quarters.

During our stay at Rostock, the reigning Prince of Mecklenburgh returned to his palace, a splendid building, situated at the end of the principal street; and a series of entertainments were given to celebrate the release of Germany from the thraldom of the ambitious Napoleon.

Notwithstanding the desolation of the surrounding country, the town of Rostock seemed to be amply supplied with provisions, of every sort; and to us they appeared remarkably cheap. At an eating-house near the Town Hall, I have frequently got an excellent dinner, consisting of poultry, fish, and flesh, with abundance of vegetables, and a glass of schnaps included, for threepence halfpenny. Geese, here, are remarkably good and plentiful; a good sized one could be had at the cook-shop, ready dressed, for 1s. 3d. A great many of the inhabitants of this and other towns in Germany keep geese, which I suppose by some municipal regulation, are taken out every morning to feed on the commons. The man who takes charge of them, goes through the town in the morning blowing a horn, on hearing which the keepers of geese turn them out. When all are collected, they are taken to the common: and at night the man brings them back to the owners. A similar practice prevails in regard to the pigs which are summoned by the cracking of a whip, and taken in like manner to the common. The abundance of geese enables the people to indulge in the luxury of the finest feather beds, one under, and one over them, with a pair of sheets only between them.

I had the good fortune to be quartered here upon a very respectable Lutheran minister, whose house was adjoining the church. He could speak a little English; and I understood, by this time, something of the German; and every morning, when I was off duty, he would invite me into his library: when the servant used invariably to bring us in two buns, and two glasses of rum, and he would question me about England, its customs, politics, religion, and so on, occasionally referring to some of his books. After passing an hour thus, he would dress and go to the church, to perform his religious duties. The short time I passed in the house of this worthy pastor, was about the most agreeable that I have ever experienced.

The latter end of October the frost set in with the great severity, and the weather-wise then predicted that we should have a long and severe winter.

On the arrival of the transports, we left Rostock amidst the strongest manifestations of goodwill and friendship from the inhabitants; and after a march of a few miles, we reached the shores of the Baltic, in the Gulf of Lubec. This was on the 2nd of November 1813; the sea was uncommonly rough, and the process of embarkation was both difficult and dangerous. Having none but the ships' boats, it was late at night before the various regiments got on board; and then some of the officers were obliged to leave their horses behind them.

The two vessels in which our regiment embarked were the *Ajax* and *Mountaineer*, rickety things, of about 400 tons each. The wind increased in violence, and we were buffeted about at the mercy of the waves for two days and nights; every wave dashing over the vessel, compelling us to keep the hatchways closed, and the watch, on deck, obliged to lash themselves to some part of the vessel, to prevent them from being washed overboard.

As it was found impossible to proceed, in such weather, we sought shelter in the harbour of Gottenburg; where we were detained for fourteen days. This delay was very distressing, as the majority of our men were attacked with dysentery; and the effluvia between deck was so horribly offensive and insupportable, that those who were free from the disorder (and I was fortunately one of them) chose rather to remain, day and night, on deck, sleeping in or under the long-boat, in the forecastle, or anywhere that we could stow ourselves away; the frost at the time being so intense, that the ships were actually frozen in. A Lieutenant Dowling,[9] and another

9 This officer is now Barrack-master at the Wellington Barracks, London. [Morris]

officer, belonging to us, were sent up the river to Gottenburg, where they were detained for a fortnight; and spent –
for their own subsistence – the money with which they had
been provided to purchase some necessary things for the
men.

When released from this place, we had a favourable,
though rather brisk, wind; and in four days we reached
Yarmouth Roads, where we were exposed to another tremendous storm, which continued, with fearful violence,
through the night. When daylight appeared, seventeen vessels were discovered on shore, some of them complete
wrecks.

We hoped, having so much sickness on board, that we
should be permitted to land directly; but had to await the
arrival of instructions from the Government, which, when
they came, were a sad disappointment to many. The order
was – the whole of the women and children should be left on
shore, at Yarmouth, and the troops sent directly to Holland;
and it was expected our landing there would be strongly
contested by the French. These orders were a sad disappointment to most of us; but it was particularly distressing to the
married people, to be separated thus suddenly – the women
and children landed in a strange place, perhaps hundreds of
miles from their home, and no resources; the men, most of
them ill, on board, with the prevailing disorder. But the
orders were imperative, and so, after getting in a supply of
fresh provisions, we left Yarmouth with a fair wind, and in a
few hours made the coast of Holland.

On 12 December, we reached Helvoetsluys, which had just
been evacuated by the French. We proceeded up the river to
Williamstadt which was also just abandoned by the enemy;
and we had the opportunity of landing without any interruption. It was fortunate for us, that such was the case, as
most of our men were so dreadfully weakened by the disorder, that it was with the utmost difficulty they were got on
shore; and they were instantly sent into the hospital. How-

ever, a few days' judicious treatment, with proper diet, and medicines, put them to rights, and we soon began again to assume an appearance of efficiency. The illness I have alluded to was confined to our regiment, and was supposed to have been produced by our excessive fatigue, and bad living, throughout Germany. The other portion of the troops had remained all the time in quarters, at Stralsund; where, after we left, the duty was tolerable, as the works were completed; and having correct information of the operations of the contending armies, they were no longer under any apprehensions of an attack.

Our regiment cut rather a miserable figure beside the other regiments in another respect. They having been in a state of comparative inactivity, had preserved their regimental dresses in good order; while ours, from our bivouacking in the woods, and marching a distance of upwards of 300 miles, were in such a shattered condition, that many of the men had their red coats mended with the grey trouser cloth, there being no possibility of obtaining any red cloth for the purpose. But though the others could boast of a superiority in appearance, all the honour rested with us.

In again alluding to the battle of Gorde, it will be perceived, that the enemy we defeated, had been detached on a most important duty; namely, to open the passage for the French troops to Magdeburg. The consequence of our victory was, that the French General, Davout, was not able to carry into effect his plan of reaching that place; and without arrogating too much to ourselves, I think our regiment may consider the panic caused by the appearance of their colours, was the means of rendering the victory more decisive than it would otherwise have been.

Should it be supposed that I have exaggerated the fears of the French, on the appearance of the English colours, I could adduce two more instances, in which the French have contended well with us, before they discovered that we were English, when they instantly fled. But the fact I have already alluded to, can be attested by respectable parties now living. There are two officers now resident in this metropolis, who were present; the one is Major Mead, who then belonged to us, and was aide-de-camp to General Gibbs; he exchanged from us into the 21st Fusiliers, and very sorry we were to lose him, for he was, in every sense of the word, an officer and a gentleman. He holds now an appointment in the Adjutant-General's office, at the Horse Guards. Captain Dowling was present; and would, I have no doubt, bear testimony to the truth of my observations.

I believe, the reason why our presence in that engagement was not noticed at the time, was, that the general (Gibbs) had exceeded his instructions in carrying us so far. I am sorry he did not take us a little farther, as I should much like to have witnessed the grand operations before Leipsic; – not that I am, by any means, fond of slaughter; but there was something so very interesting in the capture of Leipsic, that I have often wished I had been there.

"THE BATTLE OF THE NATIONS": LEIPZIG, 1813

General Jean-Baptiste Marbot,
23rd *Chasseurs à Cheval*

After a flurry of minor defeats in the German campaign of 1813,
Napoleon began to regroup his forces west of the Elbe, determin-
ing to use Leipzig on the River Elster as a forward base of
operations. This plan went quickly awry, when both the armies
of Blücher of Prussia and Bernadotte of Sweden forced crossings
over the Elbe and moved on Leipzig from the north; Prince
Schwarzenburg, at the head of another vast Allied army,
marched up from the south. By 15 October, Napoleon's
122,000 troops concentrated around the city were surrounded
on three sides. Early on 16 October, the battle of Leipzig opened,
when Schwarzenburg launched 78,000 men on the city's southern approaches and Blücher's 54,000 Prussians attacked Marshal Auguste Marmont's forces in the north. VI Corps, however,
held their ground against double their number. By the end of the
first day, the French had successfully repelled the Allies, but the
latter were buoyed by the approach of tens of thousands of fresh
troops; in contrast French reinforcements were severely limited.
During the 17th, Napoleon reorganized his defensive perimeter,
while the Allies attended the arrival of a further 150,000 men.
On the 18th, 355,000 Allies unleashed an offensive against all
sectors of the French line. After nine hours of fierce, even heroic,

fighting by his forces (grown to a maximum of 195,000 men and 700 guns), Napoleon ordered a phased withdrawal through Leipzig and over the Elster. Defeat in the biggest battle of the Napoleonic wars effectively meant the end of the Emperor's German possessions, save for Hamburg alone.

General Jean-Baptiste Marbot joined the army in 1799 as an aide to his father (a general), before becoming ADC to Marshal Augeau in the campaign of 1806–7. Celebratedly, he tried to rescue the Eagle of the 14th Line at Eylau. Later Marbot served on the staffs of Murat and Lannes, before becoming commander of the 23rd à Chausseurs Cheval in 1812. At Waterloo, he commanded the 7th Hussars. A famous literary defence of the exiled Napoleon earned Marbot a bequest of 100,000 francs in the ex-Emperor's will.

On October 14 a brisk cavalry engagement took place between our advance-guard and that of the Russians and Austrians, without decisive result; ending in that most absurd of warlike operations, a cannonade going on till nightfall, with no effect beyond the destruction of a good many men. Early next morning the Emperor reached Leipzig, leaving 25,000 men at Dresden under Saint-Cyr.

The exact facts about the battle of Leipzig will never be known. The fighting, which lasted several days, took place on a vast and complicated field, and the immense number of troops which took part in it belonged to different nations. It is on the French side that documents are chiefly lacking; so many commanders of army corps and divisions, as well as staff-officers, fell in the battle or were taken prisoners that their reports were never completed, and those which came to hand showed the hurry and disorder amid which they had been drawn up. In my own case, being colonel of a regiment, and compelled to follow all the movements of my division, I could not know what others were doing, as in the days when I was an aide-de-camp, and by carrying orders to different parts of the field was enabled to know something of the general plan of operations. I must therefore more than ever abridge my story, and confine myself to what is absolutely necessary in order to give a notion of the most important events in a battle which so powerfully influenced the destinies of Napoleon, France, and all Europe.

The ring of steel in which the enemy was preparing to enclose the French army was not yet completed round Leipzig, when the King of Wurtemberg thought it his duty to warn Napoleon that all Germany was, at the instigation of the English, about to rise against him; and that as the troops of the Confederation would shortly desert him he would not have more than time to retire behind the [River] Main. He added that he himself would be unable to avoid following their example, for he must at length yield to the pressure of his subjects and follow the torrent of public feeling in Germany.

Strongly affected by the advice of the ablest and most loyal of his allies, the Emperor had, it is said, the idea of retreating towards the hilly district of Thuringen and Hesse, and, covered by the Saale, allowing the Coalition to attack him in a difficult country. Had this plan been carried out, it might have saved Napoleon; but for that prompt action was needed before the enemy's armies were wholly joined and near enough to attack us on the retreat. The Emperor, however, could not make up his mind to abandon any part of his conquests, nor yet to let it be believed that he considered himself beaten. The great captain's excess of courage was our ruin: he overlooked the fact that his army, weakened by its heavy losses, numbered among its ranks many strangers who were only waiting the opportunity to betray him, and that in the broad plains of Leipzig he ran every chance of being overwhelmed by numbers. If, on the other hand, he had assumed a defensive position in the mountains, the approach of winter and the need of feeding their numerous forces would soon have compelled the enemy to break up, while the French army, protected in front and on the flanks by the natural difficulties of the country, would have had the fertile valleys of the Rhine and Neckar in its rear. At the very least, we should have gained time, and perhaps wearied out the Allies till they desired peace. But Napoleon's confidence in himself and in his troops prevailed, and he decided to accept battle in the plains of Leipzig.

Hardly had this fatal decision been taken when a second letter came from the King of Wurtemberg, with the news that the King of Bavaria had come to terms with the Coalition, and that the united Austrian and Bavarian armies under General von Wrede, were marching on the Rhine. With much regret Wurtemberg had been compelled by the strength of this army to unite here with it; and the Emperor might therefore expect that before long 100,000 men would be investing Mainz and threatening the French frontier.

This unforeseen news led Napoleon to think that he had better return to his plan of retiring behind the Saale; but it was too late. The main force of the Allies was by this time in the presence of the French army, and too near for retreat to be possible without being attacked during the operation. He therefore determined to fight, though his whole force, French and allied, amounted only to 157,000 men, including 29,000 cavalry, while Schwarzenberg could dispose of 350,000 Russians, Austrians, Prussians, and Swedes, his cavalry being 54,000.

The town of Leipzig, one of the busiest and wealthiest in Germany, stands near the middle of the vast plain which extends from the Elbe to the Harz Mountains. The situation of this district has made it the principal theatre of war in Germany. The small stream of the Elster, almost insignificant enough to be called a brook, flows from south to north through a shallow valley amid marshy meadows. Being divided into many branches, it offers a serious obstacle to the operations of war, and requires a great many bridges for communication among the villages. The Pleisse, a still smaller stream than the Elster, flows about a league and a half from it, and joins it under the walls of Leipzig, while north of the town the Partha flows into it. Being thus at the confluence of these three streams, and almost surrounded on the north and west by their many arms, Leipzig is the key of the position. The town, which at that time was not very extensive, was surrounded by an old wall having four large and three small gates. The road to Lutzen, by Lindenau, formed the only communication open to the rear of the French army. It was on that part of the ground between the Pleisse and the Partha that the hardest fighting took place. A noticeable point is the Kolmberg, known as the Swedish redoubt, because in the Thirty Years' War Gustavus Adolphus had raised fortifications at that point.

The battle of Leipzig began on October 16, 1813, and lasted three days. Without going into the details of this memorable action, I think I ought to specify the principal positions occupied by the French army, which will also give a general idea of those of the enemy. Murat commanded our right wing, the extremity of which rested on the Pleisse near the villages of Connewitz, Dölitz, and Mark-Kleeberg, which were occupied by Prince Poniatowsky and his Poles. Next to these, behind the village of Wachau, was Marshal Victor; Augereau's troops occupied Dosen. These corps of infantry were supported by cavalry under Kellermann and Michaud. The centre, under the immediate command of the Emperor, was at Liebertvolkwitz. It consisted of Lauriston's and Macdonald's corps of infantry with the cavalry of Latour-Maubourg and Sébastiani[1]; my regiment, forming part of the latter general's corps, was posted facing the Kolmberg. The left wing, under Marshal Ney, was formed of

[1] General Horace Sebastiani (1772–1851), cavalry commander; his ineptitude at reconnaissance led to the nickname "General Surprise"; became Foreign Minister under the Bourbons and later appointed Marshal of France.

Marmont's, Reynier's, and Souham's corps, supported by the Duke of Padua's cavalry. It occupied Taucha, Plaussig, and the banks of the Partha. A corps of observation, 15,000 strong, under General Bertrand, was sent to the further side of Leipzig to hold Lindenau and the road to Lutzen. At Probstheida, in rear of the centre, was the reserve, under Oudinot, consisting of the Old and Young Guard, and Nansouty's cavalry. The King of Saxony remained in the town of Leipzig with his own guard and a few French regiments.

During the night of the 15th, Marshal Macdonald had made a movement to concentrate on Liebertvolkwitz, but as it was not wished to let the Kolmberg fall into the enemy's hands before morning I was ordered to watch it till daybreak. It was a ticklish duty, since it involved advancing with my regiment to the foot of the hill while the army retired half a league in the opposite direction. I ran the risk of being surrounded and carried off with my whole regiment by the enemy's advance-guard. Their scouts could not fail to ascend the hill as soon as the first light of dawn should permit them to see what was going on in the plain. It was splendid weather, and one could see very well by the starlight; but, as in such a case one can much more easily perceive from below men coming on to high ground than those above can see those below, I brought my squadrons as near as possible to the hill, and, after ordering perfect silence and stillness, awaited events. Chance very nearly produced one which would have been very fortunate for France and for the Emperor, and would have made me for ever famous. It happened thus.

Half an hour before the first light of dawn, three horsemen, coming from the enemy's side, slowly ascended the Kolmberg. They could not see us, while we plainly made out their outlines and heard their conversation. They were talking French; one was a Russian, the other two Prussians. The first, who appeared to be in authority, told one of the others to let their majesties know that there were no French at that point, and that they could come up, for in a few minutes all the plain would be visible, but that they must make the most of the time lest the French should send skirmishers in that direction. The officer to whom these words were addressed remarked that the escorts were still some way off. "What matter?" was the answer, "since there is no one but us here." At this my troops and I redoubled our attention, and soon perceived on the top of the hill a score of officers, one of whom dismounted.

Although I certainly had had no expectation of capturing a great prize, I had warned my officers that if we saw any of the enemy on the Swedish redoubt, two squadrons should, at a signal which I would give with my handkerchief, work round the hill to right and left, so as to cut off anyone who should have ventured so near to our army. I was, therefore, very hopeful, but just then the over-eagerness of one of my troopers wrecked my plan. The man, having accidentally let his sword drop, instantly took his carbine, and, fearing to be left behind when I gave the signal for attack, fired into the group and killed a Prussian major. As you may suppose, in the twinkling of an eye all the enemy's officers, having no escort but a few orderlies, and seeing themselves on the point of being surrounded by us, galloped away. Our people could not follow them far for fear of themselves falling into the hands of the escort, whom we could hear coming up. My men, however, captured two officers, from whom we could get no information, but afterwards I learnt from my friend, Baron von Stoch, that the Emperor Alexander of Russia and the King of Prussia were among the officers who had so nearly fallen into the hands of the French near the Swedish redoubt. If this had happened the destinies of Europe would have been changed. As, however, luck had decided otherwise, there was nothing left for one but to withdraw quickly towards the French army.

On October 16, at eight in the morning, the Allied batteries gave the signal for attack. A brisk cannonade opened along all the line, and the Allied army marched on us at all points. The action began on our right, where the Poles were driven back by the Prussians and abandoned the village of Mark-Klee-berg. On our centre, the Russians and Austrians six times attacked Wachau and Liebertvolkwitz, and each time were beaten with heavy loss. The Emperor, doubtless regretting the abandonment of the Swedish redoubt, whence the enemy was pouring a hail of grape upon us, gave orders to recapture the hill, which was promptly effected by the 22nd Light Infantry supported by my regiment.

After this success, the Emperor, being unable to produce any impression on the enemy's wing owing to the great extent of their front, resolved merely to keep them employed while he endeavoured to pierce their centre. To this end he sent Mortier with two divisions of infantry, and Oudinot with the Young Guard, towards Wachau, Dronot supporting the attack, which to some extent succeeded, with 60 guns.

On his side, Marshal Victor routed the Russian corps under Prince Eugene of Wurtemberg; but the latter rallied his troops at Jossa. At the same moment Lauriston and Macdonald debouched from Liebertvolkwitz, the enemy was put to flight, and the French took possession of the wood of Gross Possna. In vain did the Austrian cavalry under Klenau, supported by a "pulk" of Cossacks, endeavour to restore the fight; it was charged and thrown into disorder by Sébastiani's corps, after desperate fighting, in which my regiment took part. I lost some men, and my senior major, M. Pozac, was wounded by a lance in the breast, in consequence of having omitted to adopt the customary protection of his rolled-up cloak.

Meanwhile, Prince Schwarzenberg, seeing his line badly shaken, brought up his reserves, upon which the Emperor determined to order a grand cavalry charge. Kellermann, Latour-Maubourg, and the dragoons of the guard took part in this, and the first overthrew a division of Russian cuirassiers, but, being taken in the flank by another division, he had to retire to the high ground near Wachau, after capturing several stand of colours. Then Murat brought up the French infantry and fresh fighting took place. The Prince of Wurtemberg's corps was broken again, and lost 26 guns. After this rough handling, the enemy's centre began to bend, and was on the point of being pierced, but the Emperor of Russia quickly brought up the cavalry of his guard, and they, catching Latour-Maubourg's squadrons in the disorder which always results from a charge pushed home, drove them back in their turn, and recaptured 24 of the guns. In this charge, General Latour-Maubourg had his leg shot off.

As neither side had so far gained any marked advantages, Napoleon, by way of a decisive stroke, launched on the enemy's centre his reserve, composed of all the Old Guard and a corps of fresh troops from Leipzig. But at that moment a regiment of the enemy's cavalry, which had made its way by design or accident to the rear of the French, caused some uneasiness among our troops. They halted and formed square to avoid a surprise, and before the cause of the alarm could be discovered night came on, and suspended operations at that point.

On our extreme right, General Merfeldt had during the whole day been vainly trying to get possession of the passage over the Pleisse, which Poniatowski's Poles defended. Towards evening, however, he succeeded in making himself master of the village of Dölitz, thus putting our right wing in danger. But the chasseurs of the Old Guard, under General Curial, came up at the double, hurled the Austrians back over the river, taking several hundred prisoners, General Merfeldt himself falling, for the third time in his life, into the hands of the French. Although the Poles had allowed Dölitz to be taken from them, the Emperor thought it well, in order to inspirit them, to give a marshal's baton to their chief, Prince Poniatowski: he did not long enjoy the honour of bearing it.

On the other side of the Elster the Austrian general,

Gyulai, had carried the village of Lindenau after seven hours' hard fighting. On hearing of this serious event, which endangered the retreat of the greater part of his troops, the Emperor ordered General Bertrand to attack Lindenau, and the position was recaptured with the bayonet.

On our left Ney's impatience nearly brought about a great disaster. That marshal, who was commanding the left wing posted according to the Emperor's orders, finding that by ten o'clock no troops were to be seen in front of him, of his own accord sent one of his army corps under General Souham to Wachau, where the fighting appeared to be hot. But during this ill-judged movement Marshal Blücher, who had been delayed, came up with the Army of Silesia, and captured the village of Möckern. Thereupon Ney was obliged, owing to the reduction of his force, to retire towards evening within the walls of Leipzig, and to confine himself to defending the suburb of Halle. In this engagement the French lost heavily, and a bad effect was produced on those of our men who in other parts of the field could hear the firing in their rear. Towards eight in the evening all firing ceased on both sides and the night was quiet.

This first day left victory undecided, but still it was in favour of the French, since, with forces far inferior, they had not only made headway against the Coalition, but had driven them from some of the positions which they had occupied the day before. On both sides preparations were made to renew the combat next morning, but, contrary to expectation, the 17th passed without any hostile movement taking place. The Allies were awaiting the arrival of the Russian army from Poland, and also the troops which Bernadotte, the Crown Prince of Sweden, was bringing up. Napoleon, on his side, regretted that he had rejected the proposals for peace made two months ago, but hoped for some result from a pacific message which he had sent the night before to the Allied sovereigns by his prisoner, the Austrian general, Count Merfeldt. The sequence of events is sometimes very strange;

this Count Merfeldt was the same man who, 16 years before, had come to General Bonaparte, then commanding the Army of Italy, to sue for the famous armistice of Leoben. It was he who had brought back to Vienna the treaty of peace concluded between the Austrian Government and the Directory, represented by General Bonaparte. It was he who, during the night after the battle of Austerlitz, had carried from the Emperor of Austria to the Emperor of the French proposals for an armistice; and now that General Merfeldt's destiny brought him once more to Napoleon at the moment when Napoleon needed an armistice and a peace, there seemed an encouraging hope that the same emissary would again bring about the desired result. But things had advanced too far for the Allied sovereigns to treat with Napoleon; the mere fact of his proposing it showed that he was in difficulties. Thus, although they had not been able to beat us on the 16th, they had still a hope of overwhelming us by a renewed effort with greater forces. They reckoned also on the defection of the German troops which were still among us, whose chiefs, all members of the Tugendbund, took advantage of the quasi-armistice of the 17th to agree upon the manner in which they should carry out their notable treachery. No reply was ever given to the message brought by Count Merfeldt.

Early on the 18th the army of the Coalition opened the attack. The 2nd cavalry corps, to which my regiment belonged, was posted as before between Liebertvolkwitz and the Kolmberg. The fighting was hottest towards our centre, where the village of Probstheida was attacked simultaneously by a Russian and a Prussian force. Both were repulsed with heavy loss. But the combat went on at all points, and the Russians attacked Holzhausen, which Macdonald successfully defended. Towards eleven o'clock firing was heard beyond Leipzig, in the direction of Lindenau; and we heard that our troops had at that point broken the circle in which the enemy flattered himself that he had shut up the French army, and that General Bertrand was making his way in the direction of the Rhine. The Emperor then gave orders that the baggage should be withdrawn towards Lutzen.

Meantime the plain was the scene of a fierce engagement about Connewitz and Lössnig; and the earth shook with the thunder of a thousand guns. The enemy tried to force the passage of the Pleisse, but were repulsed, though the Poles spoilt some of our finest cavalry charges. Then the 1st Cavalry Corps, seeing the Austrian and Prussian squadrons coming up to the aid of their allies, issued from behind Probstheida, broke the enemy and drove them back on their reserves, which were commanded by the Grand Duke Constantine. The Allies at once brought up immense forces and tried to carry Probstheida, but the formidable masses were so well received by our infantry that they promptly recoiled. At this point we lost Generals Vial and Rochambeau; the latter had just been created marshal by the Emperor.

Up to this time Bernadotte had not fought against the French, and was said to be wavering.[1] But at length, under the exhortations and even threats of Marshal Blücher, he decided to cross the Partha above the village of Mockau with his Swedes and one Russian corps. A brigade of Saxon hussars and lancers was posted at this point, and, on seeing Bernadotte's leading Cossacks approach, made as though to charge them; but they suddenly wheeled round, and forgetting the risk to which they were exposing their King, who was still in the midst of Napoleon's army, these scoundrelly Saxons turned their muskets and cannons against the French.

1 A sometime French Republican zealot, Marshal Bernadotte (who had "Death to tyrants" tattooed on his arms) elected Crown Prince of Sweden on 21 August 1810, changing his name to Charles-Jean. He took Sweden into the Sixth Coalition against Napoleon in 1813. His shillyshallying at Leipzig was largely because he wished to appear considerate to his former countrymen; he seems to have harboured delusions of succeeding Napoleon as Emperor.

The head of Bernadotte's army marched along the left bank of the Partha towards Sellershausen, which Reynier was defending. That general, whose troops were almost entirely drawn from the German contingents, after witnessing the desertion of the Saxon cavalry had lost confidence in the infantry of the same nation and placed Durutte's cavalry near them to keep them in hand. But Ney, with over-confidence, bade him deploy the Saxons, and send them in support of a French regiment which was holding the village of Paunsdorf. Hardly, however, had the Saxons got away from the French troops, when, seeing the Prussian standards near Paunsdorf, they made off at full speed in that direction, led by General Russel, their unworthy chief. Some French officers, unable to imagine such treachery, thought that the Saxons were going to attack the Prussians, so that General Gressot, Reynier's chief-of-staff, actually hurried off to check what he took for over-eagerness; but he found that he had none but enemies before him. This desertion of an entire army corps not only produced an alarming gap in the French line, but rekindled the ardour of the Allied forces, and the Wurtemberg cavalry instantly followed the example of the Saxons. Bernadotte welcomed the traitors into his ranks, calling upon their artillery to assist his; and even begged the English commissioner to lend him the battery of Congreve rockets which he had brought. These the former marshal of France directed upon the French.

No sooner was the Saxon corps in the ranks of the enemy than it notified its treachery by a volley from all its guns – the commander exclaiming that he had burnt half his ammunition for the French, and would now fire the rest at them! Therewith he launched a hail of projectiles at us, of which my regiment received a large share. I lost some 30 men, including Captain Bertin, a most deserving officer, whose head was taken off by a round-shot. And it was Bernadotte a Frenchman, for whom the blood of Frenchmen had earned a crown, that gave us this finishing stroke!

Among this general disloyalty the King of Wurtemberg formed an honourable exception. As I have said, he warned Napoleon that circumstances would force him to leave his cause; but even after taking this supreme decision, he carried it out with perfect loyalty, ordering his troops to take no action against the French without giving them ten days' notice. Even when he had become our enemy, he expelled from his army the general and several of the officers who had taken their troops over into the Russian ranks during the battle of Leipzig, and deprived the deserting regiments of all their decorations.

Meanwhile Probstheida continued to be the scene of a murderous struggle. The Old Guard was deployed in rear of the village, ready to aid its defenders. Bulow's corps, trying to advance, was crushed, but we lost General Delmas, a distinguished soldier and honourable man, who had fallen out with Napoleon at the creation of the Empire and lived ten years in retirement, but demanded to serve when his country was in danger. The French were maintaining their position all along the line. On the left, where Macdonald and Sebastiani had held their ground between Probstheida and Stotteritz in the teeth of frequent attacks from Klenau's Austrians and Doctoroff's Russians, we were suddenly assailed by a charge of more than 20,000 Cossacks and Bashkirs. Their efforts were chiefly directed against Sébastiani's cavalry, and in a moment the barbarians surrounded our squadrons with loud shouts, letting off thousands of arrows. The loss these caused was slight, for the Bashkirs are totally undrilled and have no more notion of any formation than a flock of sheep. Thus they cannot shoot horizontally in front of them without hitting their own comrades, and are obliged to fire their arrows parabolically into the air, with more or less elevation according to the distance at which they judge the enemy to be. As this method does not allow of accurate aiming, nine-tenths of the arrows are lost, while the few that hit are pretty well spent, and only fall with the force of their own weight, which is inconsiderable; so that the wounds they cause are usually trifling. As they have no other weapons, they are certainly the least dangerous troops in the world. However, as they were coming up in myriads, and the more of these wasps one killed the more came on – the vast number of arrows with which they filled the air were bound sooner or later to inflict some severe wounds. Thus one of my non-commissioned officers, named Meslin; was pierced from breast to back by an arrow. Seizing it in both hands he broke it and drew the two portions from his body, but died a few minutes later. I fancy this was the only case of death caused by the Bashkirs' arrows: but I had several men and horses hit, and was myself wounded by the ridiculous weapon. I had my sword in my hand, and was giving orders to an officer. As I raised my arm to indicate the direction in which he was to go, I felt my sword unexpectedly checked, and perceived a slight pain in the right thigh. Looking down I saw that an arrow four feet long was sticking an inch deep in my right thigh, though in the excitement of the fight I had not perceived the wound. I got Dr Parot to take it out and place it in the regimental ambulance, for I wished to preserve it as a curious relic; but I am sorry to say it has been mislaid. As you may suppose, I did not leave my regiment for so slight a wound: and, indeed, the moment was very critical. The reinforcements brought up by Bernadotte and Blücher were attacking the suburb of Schönfeld, not far from the point where the Partha enters the town of Leipzig. Generals Lagrange and Friederichs repulsed seven assaults on this important point, driving the Allies from the houses which they carried. General Friederichs was killed in the combat; he was an excellent and brave officer, and had the further advantage of being the handsomest man in the French army. The enemy would, however, have probably captured Schönfeld, had not Marshal Ney flown to the support of that village. He himself received a contusion in the shoulder, which compelled him to leave the field.

When night fell, the two armies were over most part of their lines in the same position as when the battle began. That evening my troopers, and indeed all Sébastiani's corps, tethered their horses to the same pickets which they had used for the three previous days, and most of the battalions occupied the same bivouacs. Thus this battle, so vaunted as a victory by our enemies, was indecisive. We were inferior in numbers, with nearly all the nations of Europe against us and a crowd of traitors in our ranks, and yet did not lose an inch of ground. The English general, Sir Robert Wilson, who was present at Leipzig as British commissioner and whose evidence cannot be suspected of partiality, says: "In spite of the defection of the Saxon army in the middle of the battle, in spite of the ardent and persevering courage of the Allied troops, they could not carry a single one of the villages which the French proposed to hold as vital to their position. The action was closed by night, leaving to the French, and especially to the defenders of Probstheida, the glory of having inspired a generous envy in their enemies."

When darkness came on, I received orders to bid the useless sharpshooting, which usually follows engagements, cease along the front of my regiment. It is not easy in these cases to separate the men who have just been fighting each other, all the more so that in order to prevent the enemy knowing what is done one cannot use drums or trumpets to sound the "cease firing" and the "recall," but one has to give the word in a low voice to the section leaders, and they send sergeants to take the order quietly to the outposts. On his side, the enemy does the same, and the fire gradually slackens, and soon ceases entirely.

In order to be sure that no vedette was forgotten on the ground, and that the little retreat towards the bivouac was carried out in good order, my practice was to have it seen to by an adjutant. The one on duty that evening was named Captain Joly, a capable soldier and very courageous. He had given proof of this some months before, when, being entrusted with the distribution of the re-mounts which the Emperor presented to such of the officers as had served in the Russian campaign, M. Joly, in spite of all that I and his friends could say, had selected for himself a splendid white horse which the rest of us had declined on account of his too conspicuous vesture, and which I had at first assigned to the trumpeters. Now on the evening of the battle of Leipzig, as M. Joly was passing at a walk behind the skirmishing line, his white horse was so plainly seen by the enemy, in spite of the darkness, that horse and man were both severely wounded. The captain was shot through the body, and died in the course of the night in a house in the suburb of Halle, where I had had Major Pozac taken the day before. His wound was not dangerous, but he was melancholy at the thought that the French army would probably retire and leave him in the hands of the enemy, who then would get possession of the sword of honour which he had received when a sergeant from the hands of the First Consul after the battle of Marengo. But I calmed his natural regrets by making myself responsible for the glorious sword. One of the surgeons of the regiment took charge of it, and it was handed back to Pozac when he returned to France.

In the calm of the night which fell on the fields of Leipzig after the terrible battle which they had witnessed, the chiefs on both sides could consider their position. Napoleon's was most unfavourable, and indeed if that great man has been blamed for not having retired behind the Saale a week before the battle, when he might still have avoided endangering the safety of his army, around which infinitely superior forces were about to form a ring of steel, it is with much greater reason that many soldiers have disapproved his dispositions when he allowed himself to be completely surrounded on the battlefield of Leipzig. I say completely, because, when Lichenstein's Austrians captured the village of Zschochern on the left bank of the Elster at 11 a.m. on the 18th, there was a moment when the road from Leipzig to Weissenfels, the only way of retreat open to the French, was intercepted, and Napoleon's army completely hemmed in. It is true this state of things only lasted half an hour, but was it prudent to expose himself to all the evils which might have resulted from it, and would it not have been better worth while, before the French army was surrounded by the united forces of the enemy, for its chief to have sheltered it behind the mountains of Thuringia?

We are now approaching a critical moment. The French had maintained their positions during the three days which the battle had lasted, but this success had only been obtained at the cost of much bloodshed, for they had had nearly 40,000 men disabled. The enemy had, it is true, lost 60,000, a difference which must be attributed to their persistency in attacking villages which we had entrenched, but as the number of their troops was infinitely greater than ours, our army was proportionately far more weakened by its losses than theirs. It must be added that as the French artillery had in the three days fired 220,000 rounds our reserves were exhausted, and we had only 16,000 rounds left – enough, that is, for two hours' fighting. This lack of ammunition, which ought to have been foreseen before engaging superior forces at a distance from our frontier, rendered Napoleon incapable of giving battle again, and he was compelled to make up his mind to order a retreat.

It was no easy matter to carry this out. The ground which we occupied, being damp meadows with brooks between them and intersected by three streams, offered a number of small valleys, and these we had to pass close under the eyes of the enemy, who would find it easy to throw our march into disorder. There was only one way to secure our retreat: namely, the provision of a number of plank roads across the meadows, ditches, and watercourses, and of larger bridges across the three streams, especially the Elster, into which the others flow at the very gates of Leipzig. Nothing was easier to effect, since any amount of planks, beams, nails, &c., were close at hand in the town and suburbs.

The whole army was under the impression that all this had been done on its first arrival, and the work added to on the 17th when there was no fighting. But by a series of unfortunate circumstances, and by inconceivable neglect, no steps had been taken. Among the documents which are extant about the battle, there is absolutely no official statement to show that any measures had been taken, if a retreat was necessary, to facilitate the outflow of the columns from either the river valleys or the streets of Leipzig. No officer among the survivors, no author who has written on the battle, has been able to show that the chiefs of the army did anything to increase the number or the efficiency of the existing ways of communication. Only General Pelet, who pushed his admiration for Napoleon sometimes to the point of extravagance, wrote, 15 years after the battle, than he had heard more than once from M. Odier, sub-intendant of the Imperial Guard, that he was present in the morning (he does not say of what day) when the Emperor gave a general on the staff orders to attend to the construction of the bridges, specially charging him with that duty. General Pelet does not mention the name of the general officer to whom the Emperor gave that order – rather an important detail. Napoleon's secretary, M. Fain, says in his *Memoirs* that the Emperor ordered several new passages across the marshes to be constructed in order to facilitate the crossing. How far posterity will admit the truth of these assertions, made long after date, I know not; but even supposing them accurate, many writers think that the head of the French army should not have been satisfied with "giving orders" to a general, who, perhaps, had neither sappers nor materials at his disposal; but that several officers, at least one per regiment in every corps, should have been charged with the duty. One thing is certain – no one carried it out. The real reason, which at the time very few people knew, was as follows.

The Emperor's chief of the headquarters staff was Prince Berthier, who had been with him since the Italian campaign of 1796. He was a man of capacity, accuracy, and devotion to duty, but he had often felt the effects of the imperial wrath, and had acquired such a dread of Napoleon's outbreaks that he had vowed in no circumstance to take the initiative or ask any question, but to confine himself to executing orders which he received in writing. This system, while keeping the chief-of-the-staff on good terms with his master, was injurious to the interests of the army; for great as were the Emperor's activity and talents, it was physically impossible for him to see to everything, and thus, if he overlooked any important matter, it did not get attended to.

So it seems to have been at Leipzig. Nearly all the marshals and generals commanding army corps pointed out to Berthier, over and over again, the necessity of providing many passages to secure the retreat in the event of a reverse but he always answered: "The Emperor has given no orders." Nothing could be got out of him, so that when, on the night of the 18th the Emperor gave the order to retreat on Weissenfels and the Saale, there was not a beam or a plank across a single brook.

The losses of the Allies had been so great that they did not venture to attack afresh, and they were themselves on the point of withdrawing when they saw our heavy baggage being taken towards Weissenfels by way of Lindenau. Then they understood that Napoleon was preparing to retreat, and made their dispositions to profit by any chance in their favour which might result from his movement.

The most terrible moment of a retreat, especially for a commanding officer, is when he has to leave his wounded to the mercy of the enemy, who often have none, but plunder or put an end to the unhappy men who are unable to follow their comrades. However, as the worst thing of all is to be left lying on the ground, I had all my wounded taken up under cover of night and collected in two neighbouring houses, both to remove them from the first fury of the enemy, who would be flushed with wine, and to enable them to aid each other, and keep up each other's courage. M. Bordenave, assistant-surgeon, offered to remain with them. At the peace I got the Legion of Honour for that estimable doctor, by whose care many men's lives were saved.

Meanwhile, the troops were marching from that field which had witnessed their prowess and been watered by so much of their blood. The Emperor left his bivouac at 8 p.m., and took up his position in the town at the "Prussian Arms" in the horsemarket. After giving his orders, he visited the King of Saxony, whom he found making arrangements to follow him. The King, a model friend, expected that, to punish him for his fidelity to the Emperor of the French, the Allied sovereigns would deprive him of his crown, but he was most afflicted by the thought that his army had disgraced itself. Napoleon could not console the good old man, and only with difficulty persuaded him to stay at Leipzig and send one of his ministers to make terms with the Coalition. The Emperor then took leave of the King, the Queen, and their daughter. The parting was the more touching by the fact of news having come that the Allies declined to enter into any engagement as to the course they meant to take with regard to the Saxon monarch. He would, therefore, be at their mercy, and in his rich provinces they had strong motives for severity.

About eight o'clock in the evening the corps of Victor and Augereau, the ambulances, part of the artillery, the cavalry, and the Imperial Guard began to retreat. While they were passing through Lindenau, Ney, Marmont, and Reynier guarded the suburbs of Halle and Rosenthal. Lauriston, Macdonald, and Poniatowski entered the town and established themselves behind the gates, the walls of which had battlements. Thus all was ready for an obstinate resistance by the rear-guard, and the army was free to retreat in good order. Still, Napoleon, wishing to spare the town the horrors of street fighting, had allowed the magistrates to petition the Allied sovereigns for an armistice of a few hours that the evacuation might be conducted with order. This humane proposal was rejected, and the Allies, in hope of profiting by any disorder which might arise in the French rear-guard, scrupled not to expose one of the largest towns in Germany to total destruction. Then, in their indignation, several generals proposed to the Emperor to secure the retreat of his army by concentrating it within the town, and setting fire to all the suburbs except that of Lindenau. I think that the refusal to allow us to retreat unmolested justified us in employing all possible means of defence, and that as fire was the most effective we should have made use of it; but Napoleon could not make up his mind to it. This excessive magnanimity lost him his crown, for the fight, which I am going to relate cost us nearly as many men as the three days' battle. Indeed, it was more disastrous, for it demoralized the army, which would otherwise have reached France in considerable strength; and the fine way in which our weak remnant opposed the Allies for three months shows pretty well what we could have done if the survivors of the great battle had recrossed the Rhine without losing their arms and their organization. France would probably have repelled the invaders.

But it was not to be so; for while Napoleon, with a too chivalrous generosity – mistaken, as I think – was refusing to burn an enemy's town and thus secure without a blow the safe retreat of his army, Bernadotte, the unworthy Crown Prince of Sweden, blaming the lack of zeal which his allies showed in the destruction of his fellow-countrymen, launched all his troops against the suburb of Taucha, captured it, and entered the town. Following his example, Blücher with his Prussians, the Russians, and the Austrians attacked the rear of the French columns in their retreat towards the Lindenau bridge over the Elster; and finally, to fill our cup full, a smart musketry-fire opened near that bridge, the only way of retreat open to our troops. This fire came from the battalions of the Saxon guard, who had been left in the town with their King. Regretting that they had not been able to desert with the rest of their army, and wishing to testify their German patriotism, they attacked the French in rear, before the palace of their sovereign. In vain did the unfortunate prince, appearing on the balcony, where the bullets were flying, exclaim to his officers and men, "Cowards! kill me, your sovereign, and spare me the sight of your dishonour." The scoundrels continued to assassinate the French, and the King, returning to his apartments, seized the colours of his guard and flung them into the fire.

The last kick was given to our troops by a Baden battalion which, being notorious for cowardice, had been left in the town during the battle to chop wood for the bakehouses. These miscreants, from the shelter of the windows of the great bakery, also fired on our soldiers, killing a great number. The French, meanwhile, made a brave resistance, defending themselves in the houses, and, in spite of their losses, disputing the ground foot by foot with the allied Armies, while, they retired in good order towards the bridge of Lindenau.

The Emperor had with difficulty got out of the town, and reached the suburb. At the last bridge, called the Millbridge, he dismounted, and not till then gave orders to charge the mine under the main bridge. Further, he sent orders to Ney, Macdonald, and Poniatowski to hold the town 24 hours longer, so as to allow the artillery and baggage time to get through the suburb and across the bridges. Then he remounted; but he had hardly ridden a thousand paces along the road to Lutzen when a fearful explosion was heard. The great bridge over the Elster had blown up. And the troops under Macdonald, Lauriston, Reynier, and Poniatowski, with more than 200 guns, were still in Leipzig, and their retreat was wholly cut off. It was a climax to our disasters.

To explain this catastrophe, people said afterwards that

Prussian and Swedish skirmishers had slipped along to the neighbourhood of the bridge, and, joining the Saxon guards, had taken possession of some houses, and begun to fire on the French columns; and that the sapper who had to fire the mine was misled into thinking that the enemy was coming up, and that the moment had come to blow up the bridge, and had therefore set fire to the powder. Others attributed the deplorable mistake to Colonel Montfort of the engineers, alleging that he had given the order in consequence of seeing the enemy's skirmishers. This version was adopted by the Emperor, who made a scapegoat of M. de Montfort, and ordered him to be brought to trial; but it was proved later on that he had nothing to do with it. Whatever the truth may have been, the army accused the chief-of-the-staff of neglect; and it was said with reason that he ought to have entrusted the guardianship of the bridge to an entire brigade, making the general personally responsible for giving the order to fire the mine at the proper moment. But Berthier defended himself with his usual answer: "The Emperor had given no orders."

After the destruction of the bridge, some of the French threw themselves into the Elster, in the hope of swimming across. Some succeeded, including Marshal Macdonald; but the greater number, Prince Poniatowski among them, were drowned, because when they had crossed the river they could not get up the muddy banks, which were lined, moreover, with the enemy's skirmishers. Those of our men who remained in the town, thinking only how to sell their lives dearly, barricaded themselves behind the houses, and fought valiantly all the day and part of the night; but their ammunition failed, their hastily-raised entrenchments were forced, and nearly all were slain. The slaughter did not cease till two in the morning.

All this time the Allied sovereigns, Bernadotte among them, assembled in the chief square, were relishing their victory, and deliberating how best to make sure of its results.

The number of French massacred in the houses is reckoned at 13,000, and 25,000 were made prisoners. The enemy took also 250 guns.

After this general account of the events which followed the battle of Leipzig, I ought to tell you what specially befell my regiment, and Sébastiani's corps, to which it belonged. As we had for three days beaten off the enemy and held our part of the field, the troops were much astonished and grieved to hear on the evening of the 18th that for want of ammunition we were going to retreat. We hoped (and it seems to have been the Emperor's design) that he would at least go no further than beyond the Saale; where we might, in the neighbourhood of the fortress of Erfurt, replenish our powder wagons and recommence hostilities. We mounted then at 8 p.m. on October 18, and quitted the field where we had fought for three days, and where so many of our comrades had fallen with honour. Hardly were we out of our bivouac, when we felt the inconvenience arising from the neglect of the imperial staff to prepare for the retreat of so large an army. Every minute the columns were stopped by broad ditches, by marshes and brooks, which might so easily have been bridged. Horses and wheels stuck in the mud; and as the night was dark there were blocks everywhere. Our march was, therefore, very slow, and my regiment, being at the head of Exelmans', the leading division, did not reach the Lindenau bridge till 4 a.m. on the 10th. As we crossed it, we were far from foreseeing the frightful catastrophe which it was in a few hours to witness.

Day broke; the broad road was covered with troops of all arms in great number, which showed that the army would be still strong when it reached the Saale. The Emperor came by; but as he galloped along the flank of the column he heard none of the acclamations which were wont to proclaim his presence. The army was ill-content with the little care which had been taken to secure its retreat; but what would the troops have said if they had known with how little foresight the passage of the Elster had been arranged? They had crossed it; but many of their comrades were about to find their deaths there. We were halting at Markranstadt, a little town three leagues from Leipzig, when we heard the explosion of the mine; but instead of being grieved, all rejoiced, for we doubted not that it had been fired to prevent the passage of the enemy after all our columns were safe across.

During the few hours' rest which we took at Markranstadt I was able to look at our squadrons in detail, and learn the losses of the regiment in the three days' fighting. I was horrified to find that they amounted to 149, of which 60, including two captains, three lieutenants, and eleven non commissioned officers, were killed; a terrible proportion out of 700, which had been the strength of the regiment on the morning of the 16th. Nearly all the wounds were caused by grape or round shot, which unhappily allowed small hope of recovery. But my losses would, perhaps, have been two-fold if I had not taken the precaution of keeping my regiment as much as possible out of artillery-fire. To explain this, I may point out that there are positions in which the most humane general finds himself under the painful necessity of exposing his men to the fire of cannon; but it also often happens that they are exposed quite unnecessarily, especially in the case of cavalry, who are able to move quickly from place to place. It is just in the case of large bodies of cavalry and on great battlefields that precautions are most needed, but least taken. Now on October 16, at Leipzig, General Sébastiani having placed his three divisions between the villages of Wachau and Liebertvolkwitz, and indicated to each divisional commander approximately the ground which his division should take up, it fell to that of Exelmans to be posted on undulating ground, broken into small mounds and hollows. The enemy's cavalry was a long way off, and therefore could not surprise us; and I took advantage of the hollows in the ground to cover my regiment. Thus sheltered from artillery-fire, and at the same time all ready to act, we had the satisfaction of seeing a great part of the day go by without our having a single man hit, while the regiments in our neighbourhood were losing pretty heavily.

I was congratulating myself on having placed my men so well when General Exelmans, on the plea that everyone should take his share of danger, ordered me, in spite of the remonstrances of my brigadier, to advance my regiment a hundred paces. I obeyed, and in a short time lost Captain Bertin killed and a score of men disabled. Then I tried a new plan, namely, to send troopers, well apart, to fire at the enemy's gunners with their carbines. This made the enemy also send out skirmishers, and when skirmishing was thus going on between the lines the enemy's guns could not fire on us for fear of hitting their own people. Ours were of course similarly hampered; but to get the artillery silenced on even a small part of the line was all in our favour, as the enemy was far superior in that arm. Moreover, our infantry was just then at close quarters with that of the enemy in the villages, and the cavalry on both sides had nothing to do but await the issue; so it was of no use for either side to be smashing up the other with cannon-balls. A skirmishing engagement, in which for the most part more powder is burnt than damage done, was a much better way of spending the time. Accordingly, all the colonels followed my example, and much bloodshed was saved. Still more would have been, if General Exelmans had not given the order to recall the skirmishers: which was the signal to the enemy to pour a hail of shot on our squadrons. Luckily it was near the end of the day.

This was the evening of the 16th. All the cavalry colonels of the 2nd corps approved so highly this plan of economizing human life that we all agreed to employ it on the 18th. When the enemy's guns opened we sent out skirmishers; and as these would have captured the guns had they been left undefended, our opponents had also to send out skirmishers, thus paralyzing their artillery. The commander of the enemy's cavalry, probably divining our motive, did the same, with the result that on that day the artillery attached to the cavalry on both sides was much less employed. None the less we met in vigorous charges, but these had always a definite object, and in that case one must not spare oneself. But an artillery duel between two cavalry corps only leads to the useless slaughter of brave men. That was what Exelmans would not see, but as he was always rushing from one wing to another, as soon as he was a little way from a regiment the colonel would send out his skirmishers and the artillery would cease to speak. So persuaded were Sébastiani and all the cavalry generals of the merit of this plan, that Exelmans at last got orders to leave off teasing the enemy's gunners by firing at them when our squadrons were merely in observation. Two years later I employed the same system with the English artillery at Waterloo, and lost much less heavily than I otherwise should have done.

While the Emperor and the divisions from Leipzig were halted at Markranstadt came the disastrous news of the destruction of the Lindenau bridge. The army had lost by this nearly all its artillery; half the troops were left as prisoners, and thousands of our wounded comrades handed over to the outrage of the hostile soldiery, hounded on by its infamous officers to the slaughter. Grief was universal, for each man had a relation or a friend to mourn. The Emperor appeared overwhelmed; but he ordered Sébastiani's cavalry to return as far as the bridge for the protection of individuals who might succeed in crossing the river at one point or another. My regiment and the 24th, being the best mounted, were ordered to lead the column and to go at full trot. General Wathiez being unwell, it fell to me, as senior colonel, to command the brigade. Hardly had we traversed half the distance when we heard frequent shots, and as we drew near the suburb we could distinguish the despairing cries of the unhappy French, who, unable to retreat, and without cartridges, were being hunted from street to street, and butchered in a cowardly manner by Prussians, Badeners, and Saxons.

The fury of my two regiments was indescribable. Every man breathed vengeance, and regretted that vengeance was almost impossible, since the Elster, with its broken bridge, lay between us and the assassins. Our rage increased when we met about 2,000 French, mostly without clothing, and nearly all wounded, who had only escaped death by leaping into the river and swimming across under the fire from the other bank. Among them was Marshal Macdonald, who owed his life to his bodily strength and his practice in swimming. He was completely naked, and his horse had been drowned. I hastily got him some clothes and lent him my lead horse, which allowed him to rejoin the Emperor at once and report the disaster he had witnessed, one of the chief episodes in it being the death by drowning of Prince Poniatowski.

The remainder of the French who had crossed the river, having had to get rid of their arms in order to be able to swim, were without means of defence; they were running across the fields to escape from some 400 or 500 Prussians and others, who, not content with the bath of French blood which they had had in the town and suburbs, had laid planks across the pieces of the exploded bridge and had come over to kill such of our unhappy soldiers as they could overtake on the road to Markranstadt. When I caught sight of this band of murderers I ordered M. Schneit, colonel of the 24th, to make a combined movement with my regiment, by means of which we enclosed these brigands in a vast semicircle. Then I gave the order to sound the charge. The effect was terrible. The bandits, taken by surprise, offered only a feeble resistance, and there was a very great slaughter, for no quarter was given. So enraged was I, that before the charge I had vowed to run my sword through all who came within my reach. Yet when I was in the thick of them and saw that they were drunk, in disorder, and with no commanders but two Saxon officers, who trembled before the approaching vengeance, I saw that it was no case of fighting, but an execution, in which it did not become me to take a part. I dreaded lest I might actually find pleasure in killing some of the scoundrels with my own hand. So I sheathed my sword, and left the task of exterminating the assassins to my troopers. Two-thirds of them fell on the spot; the rest, among them two officers and several men of the Saxon guards, fled towards the bridge in hope of recrossing the river by the planks. But as they could only go in single file, and our men were pressing them hard, they made for a large inn close by, whence they set to work to fire on my people, some Badish and Prussian pickets on the further bank aiding.

As it was probable that the noise of the fight might attract large forces towards the bridge, who, without crossing the river, could destroy my two regiments by musketry and artillery fire, I resolved to lose no time. I ordered most of my men to dismount, and taking a good supply of cartridges, to attack the inn in rear, and set fire to the stables and hay-lofts. On this, the assassins, finding themselves about to be caught by the flames, made an effort to escape; but as fast as they appeared at the gates the chasseurs shot them down. In vain did they send one of the Saxon officers to me: I refused to treat the monsters who had butchered our comrades as soldiers who surrendered honourably. The Prussian, Saxon, and Badish assassins who had crossed the foot-bridge were therefore all exterminated. I announced the fact to General Sébastiani, and he halted the other brigades half-way.

The fire which we had kindled soon reached the neighbouring houses. A great part of the village of Lindenau was burnt, and the reconstruction of the bridge and passage of the enemy's troops in pursuit of the French army thereby delayed.

Our expedition ended, I brought back the brigade to Markranstadt, as well as the 2,000 French who had escaped the disaster at the bridge. Among them were officers of all ranks. The Emperor questioned them as to what they knew regarding the explosion of the mine and the massacre of the French prisoners by the Allies. It is probable that the sad tale made Napoleon regret that he had not followed the advice which had been given him that morning to secure the retreat of the army and prevent any attack from the enemy by setting fire to the suburbs, and, even, if necessary, to the town of Leipzig. I may say that nearly all the inhabitants had left the place during the three days' battle.

In our counter-attack at the bridge of Lindenau, only three men in my brigade had been wounded, and only one of my regiment, but he was one of my bravest and best non-commissioned officers, named Foucher. In the attack on the inn a bullet had made four holes in him, passing through both his thighs. In spite of this severe wound, the brave Foucher went through the retreat on horseback, refused to go into hospital at Erfurt, and accompanied the regiment into France. His comrades and all the troopers of his section took, indeed, particular care of him, and in all respects he deserved it.

When I left Leipzig I was in fear for the wounded men of my regiment whom I had left there, among them Major Pozac. But, fortunately, the distant suburb in which I had left them was not visited by the Prussians.

You will remember that during the last day of the battle an Austrian corps had wished to cut off our retreat by occupying Lindenau, and the Emperor had caused General Bertrand's troops to drive it back. After thus reopening communications Bertrand had reached Weissenfels, and we fell in with him there. After the losses caused by the destruction of the Lindenau bridge, there could be no more thought of halting on the Saale, so Napoleon passed that river. A fortnight before the battle, that stream had offered him an impregnable position, which he had then despised, in order to risk a general engagement in an open country with three rivers in his rear, besides a large town with its narrow streets. The great captain had reckoned too much on his star, and on the incapacity of the enemy's generals. These did, indeed, commit such gross blunders that, in spite of their immense superiority in numbers, not only were they unable in three days to take a single one of the villages which we held, but I have heard the King of the Belgians, who then was serving in the Russian army, admit to the Duke of Orleans that the allies were on two occasions in such confusion that the order for retreat was given. However, the state of affairs changed, and it was our army which had to yield to misfortune.

After crossing the Saale Napoleon thanked and bade farewell to the officers and some troops of the Confederation of the Rhine who, whether from honourable feeling or for want of an opportunity to desert, were still in our ranks. He carried his magnanimity so far as to allow these soldiers to retain their arms, although, as their sovereigns had joined his enemies, he had the right to detain them as prisoners. The French army continued its retreat to Erfurt, with no event except the combat of Kosen, where a single French division beat an Austrian army corps, and took its commander Count Gyulai prisoner.

Always beguiled by the hope of returning to the attack of Germany, in which case the fortresses which he was compelled to leave would be of great service to him, Napoleon established a strong garrison at Erfurt. He had left 25,000 men under Saint-Cyr at Dresden, 30,000 at Hamburg under Davout, while the various fortresses on the Oder and the Elbe were garrisoned in proportion to their importance. These were additional losses to those which Dantzig [Danzig] and the other places on the Vistula had already cost us. I need not repeat here what I have said about the inconvenience of distributing forces to hold places from which one is about to retire, but will merely say that Napoleon left in the fortresses of Germany 80,000 soldiers, not one of whom saw France again before the fall of the Empire; which they might, perhaps, have prevented if they had been united on our frontiers.

Our artillery repaired its losses in the arsenal of Erfurt. The Emperor, who up till then had borne his reverses with stoic fortitude, was affected by the desertion of his brother-in-law. Under the pretext of going to defend his kingdom of Naples, Murat left Napoleon, to whom he owed everything. Formerly so brilliant in war, he had done nothing remarkable during this campaign. It is certain that while he was still among us he had been keeping up a correspondence with Metternich, and the Austrian minister, placing before his eyes the example of Bernadotte, had, in the name of the Allied sovereigns, guaranteed him the preservation of his kingdom if he would take his place among Napoleon's enemies. Murat left the French army at Erfurt, and no sooner had he reached Naples than he prepared to make war upon us.

AN ARTILLERYMAN AT WATERLOO, 1815

Captain Alexander Cavalie Mercer, Royal Horse Artillery

Despite defeat at Leipzig and the Allied incursion into southern France, Napoleon refused to concede the war, and in a spate of brilliant defensive battles – often with scratch troops, sometimes mere boys ("Marie Louises") – slowed the Allied advance on all fronts. Yet, he could only stall the overwhelming tide, never stop it, and the Allies steadily neared Paris. Eventually, Napoleon's weary marshals mutinied and on 6 April 1814 Napoleon signed his first abdication.

Louis XVIII assumed the French throne, Napoleon set off for exile on the Island of Elba and Europe celebrated the end of hostilities.

The celebrations were premature. The Bourbons were unpopular with the Republican-minded French, especially the Army, which bridled against the imposition of emigre, Royalist commanders. Meanwhile, the Allied Coalition had fallen to squabbling over territorial settlements.

Napoleon saw his chance. On 1 March 1815 he landed on the coast of the south of France with a boatload of supporters and marched on Paris. The Army was sent against him, but every time units met their former commander they capitulated to his charisma. On 20 March Napoleon, having been joined by almost

the entire Army, entered Paris for the "One Hundred Days".
The Eagles flew again. An aghast Europe declared war and
mobilized its resources. Meanwhile, Napoleon, rather than
taking a defensive position around Paris, as he had done in
1814, decided to make one desperate strike against the only
Allied armies in the field – Wellington's mixed force and Field
Marshal Blücher's Prussians – in the hope that their removal
would deter others. Thus, on 15 June 1815 Napoleon sent
l'Armee du Nord rolling over the River Sambre at Charleroi
towards Brussels. Unfortunately for the Emperor, momentum
slowed badly on the left flank, where the fumble-fingered
Marshal Ney could only manage a draw with Wellington at
Quatre Bras on the 16th, although Napoleon himself trounced
Blücher at Ligny on the same day. Late on the 17th Napoleon
led the Reserve to a rendezvous with Ney's left wing, intending
to deal with Wellington himself. The most famous battle in
modern history opened the next day on the small battleground of
Waterloo (some four miles in extent) near Mont St Jean.
Napoleon's forces numbered 49,000 infantry, 15,750 cavalry,
7,250 gunners, with 246 guns; Wellington fielded a mixed Allied
force of 68,000. However, Blücher commanded 89,000 Prussians at nearby Wavre and over the course of the day would
extricate himself from the attention of Marshal Grouchy to join
the main battle at Waterloo. Here, meanwhile, Ney severely
mismanaged the main French attack and by 1 p.m. on the 18th,
the Prussian reinforcements began to appear. Even despite Ney
and the Prussians, the French came within an ace of cracking
Wellington's centre near La Haie Sainte at about 6.00 p.m.,
with Ney desperately urging Napoleon to send up the Imperial
Guard to clinch the matter. However, the Guard was absorbed
in protecting the French right at Plancenoit from a Prussian
attack, and not until 7.30 p.m. did the Guard move up to La
Haie Sainte. When the Middle Guard was repulsed there, the
entire will of the French Army broke in almost a single moment.
The call went up "sauve qui peut", and the men of the Eagle
departed the field in a desperate rabble.

The "Great War" was over.

Captain Mercer was commissioned in the Royal Artillery in 1799. He missed the Peninsular War entirely, being sent to serve in South America. At Waterloo he commanded G Troop, Royal Horse Artillery.

June 18th. – Memorable day! Some time before daybreak the bombardier who had been despatched to Langeveldt returned with a supply of ammunition. He reported that he had been much impeded by the confusion on the road, which was everywhere crowded with waggons, etc. Many he had seen overturned, and many plundered, or being plundered; but his account by no means justified those who stated the road to be blocked up in such a manner as to be impassable. Indeed, considering all things, he had performed his journey in sufficiently reasonable time.

With the providence of an old soldier, he had picked up and brought on a considerable quantity of beef, biscuit, and oatmeal, of which there was abundance scattered about everywhere. Casks of rum, etc., there were, and having broached one of these – he and his drivers – every one filled his canteen – a most considerate act, and one for which the whole troop was sincerely thankful. Nor must I omit to remark that, amidst such temptations, his men had behaved with the most perfect regularity, and returned to us *quite sober*!

The rum was divided on the spot; and surely if ardent spirits are ever beneficial, it must be to men situated as ours were; it therefore came most providentially. The oatmeal was converted speedily into stirabout, and afforded our people a hearty meal, after which all hands set to work to prepare the beef, make soup, etc. Unfortunately, we preferred waiting for this, and passed the stirabout, by which piece of folly we were doomed to a very protracted fast as will be seen. Whilst our soup was cooking, it being now broad daylight, I mounted my horse to reconnoitre our situation. During the night another troop (I think Major Ramsay's) had established itself in our orchard, and just outside the hedge I found Major Bean's, which had also arrived during the night, direct from England. Ascending from the farm towards the ground we had left yesterday evening, the face of the slope, as far as I could see, to the right and left, was covered with troops *en bivouac* – here, I think, principally cavalry. Of these, some were cleaning their arms, some cooking, some sitting round fires smoking, and a few, generally officers, walking about, or standing in groups conversing. Many of the latter eagerly inquired where I was going, and appeared very anxious for intelligence, all expecting nothing less than to recommence our retreat. I continued on to the position we had occupied last, and thence clearly saw the French army on the opposite hill, where everything appeared perfectly quiet – people moving about individually, and no formation whatever. Their advanced-posts and vedettes in the valley, just beyond La Haye Sainte, were also quiet. Having satisfied my curiosity, I returned the way I came, communicating my observations to the many eager inquirers I met with. Various were the speculations in consequence. Some thought the French were afraid to attack us, others that they would do so soon, others that the Duke would not wait for it, others that he would, as he certainly would not allow them to go to Brussels; and so they went on speculating, whilst I returned to my people. Here, finding the mess not yet ready, and nothing to be done, I strolled into the garden of the farm, where several Lifeguardsmen were very busy digging potatoes – a fortunate discovery, which I determined to profit by. Therefore calling up some of my men, to work we went without loss of time.

Whilst thus employed, I noticed a very heavy firing going on in front, but this did not make us quit our work. Shortly, after, to my great astonishment, I observed that all the bivouacs on the hillside were deserted, and that even Ramsay's troop had left the orchard without my being aware of it, and my own was left quite alone, not a soul being visible from where I stood in any direction, the ground they had quitted presenting one unbroken muddy solitude. The firing became heavier and heavier. Alarmed at being thus left alone, when it was evident something serious was going on, I hastened back and ordered the horses to be put to immediately.

Away went our mess untasted. One of the servants was desired to hang the kettle with its contents under an ammunition waggon. The stupid fellow hung the kettle as desired, but first emptied it. Without orders, and all alone, the battle (for now there was no mistaking it) going on at the other side of the hill, I remained for a few minutes undecided what to do. It appeared to me we had been forgotten. All except only ourselves, were evidently engaged; and labouring under this delusion, I thought we had better get into the affair at once. As soon, therefore, as the troop was ready I led them up the hill on the highroad, hoping to meet some one who could give me directions what to do. We had not proceeded a hundred yards, when an artillery officer came furiously galloping down towards us. It was Major M'Lloyd, in a dreadful state of agitation – such, indeed, that he could hardly answer my questions. I learned, however, that the battle was very serious and bloody. Their first attack had been on that part of our position where his battery stood; but now the principal efforts were making against our right. All this was told in so hurried and anxious a manner, that one could hardly understand him. "But where are you going?" he added. I told him my plan. "Have you no orders?" "None whatever; I have not seen a soul." "Then, for God's sake, come and assist me, or I shall be ruined. My brigade is cut to pieces, ammunition expended, and, unless reinforced, we shall be destroyed." He was dreadfully agitated, and when I took his hand and promised to be with him directly, seemed transported with joy; so, bidding me make haste, he darted up the hill again, and went to receive that death-stroke which, ere long, was to terminate his earthly career. I trust before that termination he heard the reason why I never fulfilled that promise; for weeks elapsed ere he died, no doubt – otherwise he must have set me down for a base poltroon. My destiny led me elsewhere. My tutelary spirit was at hand: the eternal Major M'Donald made his appearance, and, giving me a sharp reprimand for having quitted my bivouac, desired me instantly to return to the foot of the hill, and there wait for orders. Sulkily and slowly we descended, and forming in line on the ground opposite the farm of Mont St Jean, with our left to the road, I dismounted the men that they might be a little less liable to be hit by shot and shells which, coming over the hill, were continually plunging into the muddy soil all around us. This was a peculiarly dismal situation – without honour or glory, to be knocked on the head in such a solitude, for not a living being was in sight.

It was while thus standing idle that a fine tall upright old gentleman, in plain clothes, followed by two young ones, came across our front at a gallop from the Brussels road, and continued on towards where we supposed the right of our army to be. I certainly stared at seeing three unarmed civilians pressing forward into so hot a fight. These were the Duke of Richmond and his two sons. How long we had been in this position, I know not, when at length we were relieved from it by our adjutant (Lieutenant Bell), who brought orders for our removal to the right of the second line. Moving, therefore, to our right, along the hollow, we soon began a very gentle ascent, and at the same time became aware of several corps of infantry, which had not been very far from us, but remained invisible, as they were all lying down. Although in this move we may be said to have been always under a heavy fire, from the number of missiles flying over us, yet were we still so fortunate as to arrive in our new position without losing man or horse. In point of seeing, our situation was much improved; but for danger and inactivity, it was much worse, since we were now fired directly at, and positively ordered not to return the compliment – the object in bringing us here being to watch a most formidable-looking line of lancers drawn up opposite to us, and threatening the right flank of our army. A scientific relation of this great struggle, on which the fate of Europe hinged, I pretend not to write. I write neither history, nor "Memoires pour servir à l'Histoire," etc. etc., but only pure simple gossip for my own amusement – just what happened to me and mine, and what I *did* see happen to others about me. Depend upon it, he who pretends to give a general account of a great battle from his own observation deceives you – believe him not. He can see no farther (that is, if he be personally engaged in it) than the length of his nose; and how is he to tell what is passing two or three miles off, with hills and trees and buildings intervening, and all enveloped in smoke? Busaco might have been tolerably described, but there are no Busacos in the Pays Bas. The back of the principal ridge on which our army was posted descended by a pretty regular slope in the direction of Waterloo, and but just in rear of its right another shorter and lower ridge ran a little way almost parallel to it. The highroad to Nivelle passed along the hollow between the two. Both ridges terminated in a ravine that enclosed our right flank, running down from the Château de Hougoumont (although it be pretended now that the name is "Goumont," I persist in the orthography which is found in all the old maps of this department) in the direction of Merke Braine; in short, a contracted continuation of the greater valley lying between the two armies and nearly at right angles to it.

The sides of this ravine (much steeper than any other ground near), as far as I can recollect, were partially covered with bushes; and, from the summit of the one opposite to us, the ground ascended by a very gradual slope for about 800 or 1000 yards; and there, on what appeared as the height of the land, there were several small clumps of wood. This slope itself was still covered with fine crops of standing corn. The crest was occupied by the long line of lancers already spoken of, whose movements I was ordered to watch, but on no account to interfere with, unless they attempted to pass the ravine.[1] Such was our front view.

To the right we looked over a fine open country, covered with crops and interspersed with thickets or small woods. There all was peaceful and smiling, not a living soul being in sight. To our left, the main ridge terminated rather abruptly just over Hougoumont, the back of it towards us being broken ground, with a few old trees on it just where the Nivelle road descended between high banks into the ravine. Thus we were formed *en potence* with the 1st line, from which we (my battery) were separated by some hundred yards. In our rear the 14th Regiment of infantry (in square, I think) lay on the ground. In our front were some light dragoons of the German Legion, who from time to time detached small parties across the ravine. These pushed cautiously up the slope towards the line of lancers to reconnoitre. The corn, down to the edge of the ravine nearer the Nivelle road and beyond it, was full of French riflemen; and these were warmly attacked by others[2] from our side of the ravine, whom we saw crossing and gradually working their way up through the high corn, the French as gradually retiring. On the right of the lancers, two or three batteries kept up a continued fire at our position; but their shot, which could have been only 4-pounders, fell short – many not even reaching across the ravine. Some, however, did reach their destination; and we were particularly plagued by their howitzer shells with long fuses, which were continually falling

1 The light cavalry of the 2nd Corps formed in three lines across the causeway from Nivelle, etc., nearly at the height of the first woods at Hougoumont, scouring all the plain by the left, and having main guards near Braine le Leude, and its battery of light artillery on the causeway of Nivelle. – *Memoir of Napoleon*, lib. ix. cap. vi. p. 134; O'Meara's translation.
2 Jägers of the Hanoverian corps.

about us, and lay spitting and sputtering several seconds
before they exploded, to the no small annoyance of man and
horse. Still, however, nobody was hurt; but a round-shot,
striking the ammunition-boxes on the body of one of our
waggons, penetrated through both and lodged in the back of
the rear one, with nearly half its surface to be seen from
without – a singular circumstance! In addition to this front
fire, we were exposed to another on our left flank – the shot
that passed over the main ridge terminating their career with
us. Having little to occupy us here, we had ample leisure to
observe what was passing there. We could see some corps at
the end near us in squares – dark masses, having guns
between them, relieved from a background of grey smoke,
which seemed to fill the valley beyond, and rose high in the
air above the hill. Every now and then torrents of French
cavalry of all arms came sweeping over the ridge, as if
carrying all before them. But, after their passage, the squares
were still to be seen in the same places; and these gentry, who
we feared would next fall on us, would evaporate, nobody
could well say how. The firing still increased in intensity, so
that we were at a loss to conjecture what all this could mean.

About this time, being impatient of standing idle, and
annoyed by the batteries on the Nivelle road, I ventured to
commit a folly, for which I should have paid dearly had our
Duke chanced to be in our part of the field. I ventured to
disobey orders, and open a slow deliberate fire at the battery,
thinking with my 9-pounders soon to silence his 4-pounders.
My astonishment was great, however, when our very first
gun was responded to by at least half-a-dozen gentlemen of
very superior calibre, whose presence I had not even suspected, and whose superiority we immediately recognised by
their rushing noise and long reach, for they flew far beyond
us. I instantly saw my folly, and ceased firing, and they did
the same – the 4-pounders alone continuing the cannonade as
before. But this was not all. The first man of my troop
touched was by one of these confounded long shot. I shall

never forget the scream the poor lad gave when struck. It was one of the last they fired, and shattered his left arm to pieces as he stood between the waggons. That scream went to my very soul, for I accused myself as having caused his misfortune. I was, however, obliged to conceal my emotion from the men, who had turned to look at him; so, bidding them "stand to their front," I continued my walk up and down, whilst Hitchins ran to his assistance.

Amidst such stirring scenes, emotions of this kind are but of short duration; what occurred immediately afterwards completely banished Gunner Hunt from my recollection. As a counterbalance to this tragical event, our firing produced one so comic as to excite all our risibility. Two or three officers had lounged up to our guns to see the effect. One of them was a medico, and *he* (a shower having just come on) carried an umbrella overhead. No sooner did the heavy answers begin to arrive amongst us than these gentlemen, fancying they should be safer with their own corps, although only a few yards in the rear, scampered off in double-quick, doctor and all, he still carrying his umbrella aloft. Scarcely, however, had he made two paces when a shot, as he thought, passing rather too close, down he dropped on his hands and knees – or, I should rather say, hand and knees, for the one was employed in holding the silken cover most pertinaciously over him – and away he scrambled like a great baboon, his head turned fearfully over his shoulder, as if watching the coming shot, whilst our fellows made the field resound with their shouts and laughter.

I think I have already mentioned that it was not until some days afterwards that I was able to resume my regular journal, consequently that everything relative to these three days is written from memory. In trying to recollect scenes of this nature, some little confusion is inevitable; and here I confess myself somewhat puzzled to account for certain facts of which I am positive. For instance, I remember perfectly Captain Bolton's brigade of 9-pounders being stationed to the left of us, somewhat in advance, and facing as we did, consequently not far from the Nivelle road. Bolton came and conversed with me some time, and was called hastily away by his battery commencing a heavy fire. Query – Who, and what, was he firing at? That he was himself under a heavy fire there is equally no doubt, for whilst we were not losing a man, we saw many, both of his men and horses, fall, and but a few minutes after leaving me, he was killed himself – this is a puzzle. I have no recollection of any troops attempting to cross the ravine, and yet his fire was in that direction, and I think must have been toward the Nivelle road. A distressing circumstance connected with this (shall I confess it?) made even more impression on my spirits than the misfortune of Gunner Hunt. Bolton's people had not been long engaged when we saw the men of the gun next to us unharness one of the horses and chase it away, wounded, I supposed; yet the beast stood and moved with firmness, going from one carriage to the other, whence I noticed he was always eagerly driven away. At last two or three gunners drove him before them to a considerable distance, and then returned to their guns. I took little notice of this at the time, and was surprised by an exclamation of horror from some of my people in the rear. A sickening sensation came over me, mixed with a deep feeling of pity, when within a few paces of me stood the poor horse in question, side by side with the leaders of one of our ammunition waggons, against which he pressed his panting sides, as though eager to identify himself as of their society – the driver, with horror depicted on every feature, endeavouring by words and gestures (for the kind-hearted lad could not strike) to drive from him so hideous a spectacle. A cannon-shot had completely carried away the lower part of the animal's head, immediately below the eyes. Still he lived, and seemed fully conscious of all around, whilst his full, clear eye seemed to implore us not to chase him from his companions. I ordered the farrier (Price) to put him out of misery, which, in a few minutes, he reported having accomplished, by running his sabre into the animal's heart. Even *he* evinced feeling on this occasion. Meantime the roar of cannon and musketry in the main position never slackened; it was intense, as was the smoke arising from it. Amidst this, from time to time, was to be seen still more dense columns of smoke rising straight into the air like a great pillar, then spreading out a mushroom-head. These arose from the explosions of ammunition waggons, which were continually taking place, although the noise which filled the whole atmosphere was too overpowering to allow them to be heard.

Amongst the multitudes of French cavalry continually pouring over the front ridge, one corps came sweeping down the slope entire, and was directing its course straight for us, when suddenly a regiment of light dragoons (I believe of the German Legion) came up from the ravine at a brisk trot on their flank. The French had barely time to wheel up to the left and push their horses into a gallop, when the two bodies came in collision. They were at a very short distance from us, so that we saw the charge perfectly. There was no check, no hesitation, on either side; both parties seemed to dash on in a most reckless manner, and we fully expected to have seen a horrid crash – no such thing! Each, as if by mutual consent, opened their files on coming near, and passed rapidly through each other, cutting and pointing, much in the same manner one might pass the fingers of the right hand through those of the left. We saw but few fall. The two corps reformed afterwards, and in a twinkling both disappeared, I know not how or where. It might have been about two o'clock when Colonel Gould, R.A., came to me, perhaps a little later. Be that as it may, we were conversing on the subject of our situation, which appeared to him rather desperate. He remarked that in the event of a retreat, there was but one road, which no doubt would be instantly choked up, and asked my opinion. My answer was, "It does indeed look very bad; but I trust in the Duke, who, I am sure, will get us out of it somehow or other." Meantime gloomy reflections arose in my mind, for though I did not choose to betray myself (as we spoke before the men), yet I could not help thinking that our affairs *were* rather desperate, and that some unfortunate catastrophe was at hand. In this case I made up my mind to spike my guns and retreat over the fields, draught-horses and all, in the best manner I could, steering well from the highroad and general line of retreat.

We were still talking on this subject, when suddenly a dark mass of cavalry appeared for an instant on the main ridge, and then came sweeping down the slope in swarms, reminding me of an enormous surf bursting over the prostrate hull of a stranded vessel, and then running, hissing and foaming, up the beach. The hollow space became in a twinkling covered with horsemen, crossing, turning, and riding about in all directions, apparently without any object. Sometimes they came pretty near us, then would retire a little. There were lancers amongst them, hussars, and dragoons – it was a complete *mêlée*. On the main ridge no squares were to be seen; the only objects were a few guns standing in a confused manner, with muzzles in the air, and not one artilleryman. After caracoling about for a few minutes, the crowd began to separate and draw together in small bodies, which continually increased; and now we really apprehended being overwhelmed, as the first line had apparently been. For a moment an awful silence pervaded that part of the position to which we anxiously turned our eyes. "I fear all is over," said Colonel Gould, who still remained by me. The thing seemed but too likely, and this time I could not withhold my assent to his remark, for it did indeed appear so. Meantime the 14th, springing from the earth, had formed their square, whilst we, throwing back the guns of our right and left divisions, stood waiting in momentary expectation of being enveloped and attacked. Still they lingered in the hollow, when suddenly loud and repeated shouts (not English hurrahs) drew our attention to the other side. There we saw two dense columns of infantry pushing forward at a quick pace towards us, crossing the fields, as if they had come from Merke Braine. Every one, both of the 14th and ourselves, pronounced them French, yet still we delayed opening fire on them. Shouting, yelling, and singing, on they came, right for us; and being now not above 800 or 1000 yards distant, it seemed folly allowing them to come nearer unmolested. The commanding officer of the 14th, to end our doubts, rode forward and endeavoured to ascertain who they were, but soon returned, assuring us they were French. The order was already given to fire, when, luckily, Colonel Gould recognised them as Belgians. Meantime, whilst my attention was occupied by these people, the cavalry had all vanished, nobody could say how or where.

We breathed again. Such was the agitated state in which we were kept in our second position. A third act was about to commence of a much more stirring and active nature.

It might have been, as nearly as I can recollect about 3 p.m., when Sir Augustus Frazer galloped up, crying out, "Left limber up, and as fast as you can." The words were scarcely uttered when my gallant troop stood as desired in column of subdivisions, left in front, pointing towards the main ridge. "At a gallop, march!" and away we flew, as steadily and compactly as if at a review. I rode with Frazer, whose face was as black as a chimney-sweep's from the smoke, and the jacket-sleeve of his right arm torn open by a musket-ball or case-shot, which had merely grazed his flesh. As we went along, he told me that the enemy had assembled an enormous mass of heavy cavalry in front of the point to which he was leading us (about one-third of the distance between Hougoumont and the Charleroi road), and that in all probability we should immediately be charged on gaining our position. "The Duke's orders, however, are positive," he added, "that in the event of their preserving and charging home, you do not expose your men, but retire with them into the adjacent squares of infantry." As he spoke, we were ascending the reverse slope of the main position. We breathed a new atmosphere – the air was suffocatingly hot, resembling that issuing from an oven. We were enveloped in thick smoke, and, *malgré* the incessant roar of cannon and musketry, could distinctly hear around us a mysterious humming noise, like that which one hears of a summer's evening proceeding from myriads of black beetles; cannon-shot, too, ploughed the ground in all directions, and so thick was the hail of balls and bullets that it seemed dangerous to extend the arm lest it should be torn off. In spite of the serious situation in which we were, I could not help being somewhat amused at the astonishment expressed by our kind-hearted surgeon (Hitchins), who heard for the first time this sort of music. He was close to me as we ascended the slope, and, hearing this infernal *carillon* about his ears, began staring round in the wildest and most comic manner imaginable, twisting himself from side to side, exclaiming, "My God, Mercer, what *is* that? What *is* all this noise? How curious! – how very curious!" And then when a cannon-shot rushed hissing past, "*There!* – *there*! What *is* it all?" It was with great difficulty that I persuaded him to retire: for a time he insisted on remaining near me, and it was only by pointing out how important it was to us, in case of being wounded, that he should keep himself safe to be able to assist us, that I prevailed on him to withdraw. Amidst this storm we gained the summit of the ridge, strange to say, without a casualty; and Sir Augustus, pointing out our position between two squares of Brunswick infantry, left us, with injunctions to remember the Duke's order, and to economise our ammunition. The Brunswickers were falling fast – the shot every moment making great gaps in their squares, which the officers and sergeants were actively employed in filling up by pushing their men together, and sometimes thumping them ere they could make them move. These were the very boys whom I had but yesterday seen throwing away their arms, and fleeing, panic-stricken, from the very sound of our horses' feet. Today they fled not bodily, to be sure, but spiritually, for their senses seemed to have left them. There they stood, with recovered arms, like so many logs, or rather like the very wooden figures which I had seen them practising at in their cantonments. Every moment I feared they would again throw down their arms and flee; but their officers and sergeants behaved nobly, not only keeping them together, but managing to keep their squares closed in spite of the carnage made amongst them. To have sought refuge amongst men in such a state were madness – the very moment our men ran from their guns I was convinced, would be the signal for their disbanding. We had better, then, fall at our posts than in such a situation. Our coming up seemed to reanimate them, and all their eyes were directed to us – indeed, it was providential, for, had we not arrived as we did, I scarcely think there is a doubt of what would have been their fate. Our first gun had scarcely gained the interval between their squares, when I saw through the smoke the leading squadrons of the advancing column coming on at a brisk trot, and already not more than one hundred yards distant, if so much, for I don't think we could have seen so far. I immediately ordered the line to be formed for action – *case-shot*! and the leading gun was unlimbered and commenced firing almost as soon as the word was given: for activity and intelligence our men were unrivalled. The very first round, I saw, brought down several men and horses. They continued, however, to advance. I glanced at the Brunswickers, and that glance told me it would not do; they had opened a fire from their front faces, but both squares appeared too unsteady, and I resolved to say nothing about the Duke's order, and take our chance – a resolve that was strengthened by the effect of the remaining guns as they rapidly succeeded in coming to action, making terrible slaughter, and in an instant covering the ground with men and horses. Still they persevered in approaching us (the first round had brought them to a walk), though slowly, and it did seem they would ride over us. We were a little below the level of the ground on which they moved – having in front of us a bank of about a foot and a half or two feet high, along the top of which ran a narrow road – and this gave more effect to our case-shot, all of which almost must have taken effect, for the carnage was frightful. I suppose this state of things occupied but a few seconds, when I observed symptoms of hesitation, and in a twinkling, at the instant I thought it was all over with us, they turned to either flank and filed away rapidly to the rear. Retreat of the mass, however, was not so easy. Many facing about and trying to force their way through the body of the column, that part next to us became a complete mob, into which we kept a steady fire of case-shot from our six pieces. The effect is hardly conceivable, and to paint this scene of slaughter and confusion impossible. Every discharge was followed by the fall of numbers, whilst the survivors struggled with each other, and I actually saw them using the pommels of their swords to fight their way out of the *mêlée*. Some, rendered desperate at finding themselves thus pent up at the muzzles of our guns, as it were, and others carried away by their horses, maddened with wounds, dashed through our intervals – few thinking of using their swords, but pushing furiously onward, intent only on saving themselves. At last the rear of the column, wheeling about, opened a passage, and the whole swept away at a much more rapid pace than they had advanced, nor stopped until the swell of the ground covered them from our fire. We then ceased firing; but as they were still not far off, for we saw the tops of their caps, having reloaded, we stood ready to receive them should they renew the attack.

One of, if not the first man who fell on our side was wounded by his own gun. Gunner Butterworth was one of the greatest pickles in the troop, but, at the same time, a most daring, active soldier; he was No. 7 (the man who sponged, etc.) at his gun. He had just finished ramming down the shot, and was stepping back outside the wheel, when his foot stuck in the miry soil, pulling him forward at the moment the gun was fired. As a man naturally does when falling, he threw out both his arms before him, and they were blown off at the elbows. He raised himself a little on his two stumps, and looked up most piteously in my face. To assist him was impossible – the safety of all, everything, depended upon not slackening our fire, and I was obliged to turn from him. The state of anxious activity in which we were kept all day, and the numbers who fell almost immediately afterwards, caused me to lose sight of poor Butterworth; and I afterwards learned that he had succeeded in rising and was gone to the rear; but on inquiring for him next day, some of my people who had been sent to Waterloo told me that they saw his body lying by the roadside near the farm of Mo[u]nt St Jean – bled to death! The retreat of the cavalry was succeeded by a shower of shot and shells, which must have annihilated us had not the little bank covered and threw most of them over us. Still some reached us and knocked down men and horses.

At the first charge, the French column was composed of *grenadiers à cheval* and cuirassiers, the former in front. I forget whether they had or had not changed this disposition, but think, from the number of cuirasses we afterwards found, that the cuirassiers led the second attack. Be this as it may, their column reassembled. They prepared for a second attempt, sending up a cloud of skirmishers, who galled us terribly by a fire of carbines and pistols at scarcely forty yards from our front. We were obliged to stand with port-fires lighted, so that it was not without a little difficulty that I succeeded in restraining the people from firing, for they grew impatient under such fatal results. Seeing some exertion beyond words necessary for this purpose, I leaped my horse up the little bank, and began a promenade (by no means agreeable) up and down our front, without even drawing my sword, though these fellows were within speaking distance of me. This quieted my men; but the tall blue gentlemen, seeing me thus dare them, immediately made a target of me, and commenced a very deliberate practice, to show us what very bad shots they were and verify the old artillery proverb, "The nearer the target, the safer you are." One fellow certainly made me flinch, but it was a miss; so I shook my finger at him, and called him *coquin*, etc. The rogue grinned as he reloaded, and again took aim. I certainly felt rather foolish at that moment, but was ashamed, after such bravado, to let him see it, and therefore continued my promenade. As if to prolong my torment, he was a terrible time about it. To me it seemed an age. Whenever I turned, the muzzle of his infernal carbine still followed me. At length bang it went, and whiz came the ball close to the back of my neck, and at the same instant down dropped the leading driver of one of my guns (Miller), into whose forehead the cursed missile had penetrated.

The column now once more mounted the plateau, and these popping gentry wheeled off right and left to clear the ground for their charge. The spectacle was imposing, and if ever the word sublime was appropriately applied, it might surely be to it. On they came in compact squadrons, one behind the other, so numerous that those of the rear were still below the brow when the head of the column was but at some sixty or seventy yards from our guns. Their pace was a slow but steady trot. None of your furious galloping charges was this, but a deliberate advance, at a deliberate pace, as of men resolved to carry their point. They moved in profound silence, and the only sound that could be heard from them amidst the incessant roar of battle was the low thunder-like reverberation of the ground beneath the simultaneous tread of so many horses. On our part was equal deliberation. Every man stood steadily at his post, the guns ready, loaded with a round-shot first and a case over it; the tubes were in the vents; the port-fires glared and sputtered behind the wheels; and my word alone was wanting to hurl destruction on that goodly show of gallant men and noble horses. I delayed this, for experience had given me confidence. The Brunswickers partook of this feeling, and with their squares – much reduced in point of size – well closed, stood firmly, with arms at the recover, and eyes fixed on us, ready to commence their fire with our first discharge. It was indeed a grand and imposing spectacle! The column was led on this time by an officer in a rich uniform, his breast covered with decorations, whose earnest gesticulations were strangely contrasted with the solemn demeanour of those to whom they were addressed. I thus allowed them to advance unmolested until the head of the column might have been about fifty or sixty yards from us, and then gave the word, "Fire!" The effect was terrible. Nearly the whole leading rank fell at once; and the round-shot, penetrating the column carried confusion throughout its extent. The ground, already encumbered with victims of the first struggle, became now almost impassable. Still, however, these devoted warriors struggled on, intent only on reaching us. The thing was impossible. Our guns were served with astonishing activity, whilst the running fire of the two squares was maintained with spirit. Those who pushed forward over the heaps of carcasses of men and horses gained but a few paces in advance, there to fall in their turn and add to the difficulties of those succeeding them. The discharge of every gun was followed by a fall of men and horses like that of grass before the mower's scythe. When the horse alone was killed, we could see the cuirassiers divesting themselves of the encumbrance and making their escape on foot. Still, for a moment, the confused mass (for all order was at an end) stood before us, vainly trying to urge their horses over the obstacles presented by their fallen comrades, in obedience to the now loud and rapid vociferations of him who had led them on and remained unhurt. As before, many cleared everything and rode through us; many came plunging forward only to fall, man and horse, close to the muzzles of our guns; but the majority again turned at the very moment when, from having less ground to go over, it were safer to advance than retire, and sought a passage to the rear. Of course the same confusion, struggle amongst themselves, and slaughter prevailed as before, until gradually they disappeared over the brow of the hill. We ceased firing, glad to take breath. Their retreat exposed us, as before, to a shower of shot and shells: these last, falling amongst us with very long fuses, kept burning and hissing a long time before they burst, and were a considerable annoyance to man and horse. The bank in front, however, again stood our friend, and sent many over us innocuous.

Lieutenant Breton, who had already lost two horses and had mounted a troop-horse, was conversing with me during this our leisure moment. As his horse stood at right angles to mine, the poor jaded animal dozingly rested his muzzle on my thigh; whilst I, the better to hear amidst the infernal din, leant forward, resting my arm between his ears. In this attitude a cannon-shot smashed the horse's head to atoms. The headless trunk sank to the ground – Breton looking pale as death, expecting, as he afterwards told me, that I was cut in two. What was passing to the right and left of us I know no more about than the man in the moon – not even what corps were beyond the Brunswickers. The smoke confined our vision to a very small compass, so that my battle was restricted to the two squares and my own battery; and, as long as we maintained our ground, I thought it a matter of course that others did so too. It was just after this accident that our worthy commanding officer of artillery, Sir George Adam Wood, made his appearance through the smoke a little way from our left flank. As I said, we were doing nothing, for the cavalry were under the brow re-forming for a third attack, and we were being pelted by their artillery. "D – n it, Mercer," said the old man, blinking as a man does when facing a gale of wind, "you have hot work of it here." "Yes, sir, pretty hot"; and I was proceeding with an account of the two charges we had already discomfited, and the prospect of a third, when, glancing that way, I perceived their leading squadron already on the plateau. "There they are again!" I exclaimed; and, darting from Sir George *sans cérémonie*, was just in time to meet them with the same destruction as before. This time, indeed, it was child's play. They could not even approach us in any decent order, and we fired most deliberately; it was folly having attempted the thing. I was sitting on my horse near the right of my battery as they turned and began to retire once more. Intoxicated with success, I was singing out, "Beautiful!–beautiful!" and my right arm was flourishing about, when some one from behind, seizing it, said quietly, "Take care, or you'll strike the Duke"; and in effect our noble chief, with a serious air, and apparently much fatigued, passed close by me to the front, without seeming to take the slightest notice of the remnant of the French cavalry still lingering on the ground. This obliged us to cease firing; and at the same moment I, perceiving a line of infantry ascending from the rear, slowly, with ported arms, and uttering a sort of feeble, suppressed hurrah – ankle-deep in a thick tenacious mud, and threading their way amongst or stepping over the numerous corpses covering the ground, out of breath from their exertions, and hardly preserving a line, broken everywhere into large gaps the breadth of several files – could not but meditate on the probable results of the last charge had I, in obedience to the Duke's order, retired my men into the squares and allowed the daring and formidable squadrons a passage to our rear, where they must have gone thundering down on this disjointed line. The summit gained, the line was amended, files closed in, and the whole, including our Brunswickers, advanced down the slope towards the plain.

Although the infantry lost several men as they passed us, yet on the whole the cannonade began to slacken on both sides (why, I know not), and, the smoke clearing away a little, I had now, for the first time, a good view of the field. On the ridge opposite to us dark masses of troops were stationary, or moving down into the intervening plain. Our own advancing infantry were hid from view by the ground. We therefore

recommenced firing at the enemies' masses, and the cannonade, spreading, soon became general again along the line.
Whilst thus occupied with our front, we suddenly became
sensible of a most destructive flanking fire from a battery
which had come, the Lord knows how, and established itself
on a knoll somewhat higher than the ground we stood on, and
only about 400 or 500 yards a little in advance of our left
flank. The rapidity and precision of this fire were quite
appalling. Every shot almost took effect, and I certainly
expected we should all be annihilated. Our horses and
limbers, being a little retired down the slope, had hitherto
been somewhat under cover from the direct fire in front; but
this plunged right amongst them, knocking them down by
pairs, and creating horrible confusion. The drivers could
hardly extricate themselves from one dead horse ere another
fell, or perhaps themselves. The saddle-bags, in many instances, were torn from the horses' backs, and their contents
scattered over the field. One shell I saw explode under the
two finest wheel-horses in the troop – down they dropped. In
some instances the horses of a gun or ammunition waggon
remained, and all their drivers were killed. The whole live-
long day had cost us nothing like this. Our gunners too – the
few left fit for duty of them – were so exhausted that they
were unable to run the guns up after firing, consequently at
every round they retreated nearer to the limbers; and as we
had pointed our two left guns towards the people who were
annoying us so terribly, they soon came altogether in a
confused heap, the trails crossing each other, and the whole
dangerously near the limbers and ammunition waggons,
some of which were totally unhorsed, and others in sad
confusion from the loss of their drivers and horses, many
of them lying dead in their harness attached to their carriages. I sighed for my poor troop – it was already but a
wreck.

I had dismounted, and was assisting at one of the guns to
encourage my poor exhausted men, when through the smoke

a black speck caught my eye, and I instantly knew what it was. The conviction that one never sees a shot coming towards you unless directly in its line flashed across my mind, together with the certainty that my doom was sealed. I had barely time to exclaim "Here it is then!" – much in that gasping sort of way one does when going into very cold water takes away the breath – "whush" it went past my face, striking the point of my pelisse collar, which was lying open, and smash into a horse close behind me. I breathed freely again.

Under such a fire, one may be said to have had a thousand narrow escapes; and, in good truth, I frequently experienced that displacement of air against my face caused by the passing of shot close to me; but the two above recorded, and a third which I shall mention, were remarkable ones, and made me feel in full force the goodness of Him who protected me among so many dangers. Whilst in position on the right of the second line, I had reproved some of my men for lying down when shells fell near them until they burst. Now my turn came. A shell, with a long fuse, came slop into the mud at my feet, and there lay fizzing and flaring, to my infinite discomfiture. After what I had said on the subject, I felt that I must act up to my own words, and, accordingly, there I stood, endeavouring to look quite composed until the cursed thing burst – and, strange to say, without injuring me, though so near. The effect on my men was good. We had scarcely fired many rounds at the enfilading battery when a tall man in the black Brunswick uniform came galloping up to me from the rear, exclaiming, "Ah! mine Gott! – mine Gott! vat is it you doos, sare? Dat is your friends de Proosiens; an you kills dem! Ah, mine Gott! – mine Gott! vill you no stop, sare? – vill you no stop? Ah! mine Gott! – mine Gott! vat for is dis? De Inglish kills dere friends de Proosiens! Vere is de Dook von Vellington? – vere is de Dook von Vellington? Oh, mine Gott! – mine Gott!" etc. etc., and so he went on raving like one demented. I observed that if these were our friends the Prussians they were treating us very uncivilly; and that it was not without sufficient provocation we had turned our guns on them, pointing out to him at the same time the bloody proofs of my assertion. Apparently not noticing what I said, he continued his lamentations, and, "Vill you no stop, sare, I say?" Wherefore, thinking he might be right, to pacify him I ordered the whole to cease firing, desiring him to remark the consequences. *Psieu, psieu, psieu,* came our *friends'* shot, one after another; and our friend himself had a narrow escape from one of them. "Now, sir," I said, "you will be convinced; and we will continue our firing, whilst you can ride round the way you came, and tell them they kill their friends the English; the moment their fire ceases, so shall mine." Still he lingered, exclaiming, "Oh, dis is terreebly to see de Proosien and de Inglish kill vonanoder!" At last darting off I saw no more of him. The fire continued on both sides, mine becoming slacker and slacker, for we were reduced to the last extremity, and must have been annihilated but for the opportune arrival of a battery of Belgic artillery a little on our left, which, taking the others in flank nearly at point blank, soon silenced and drove them off. We were so reduced that all our strength was barely sufficient to load and fire three guns out of our six.

These Belgians were all beastly drunk, and, when they first came up, not at all particular as to which way they fired; and it was only by keeping an eye on them that they were prevented treating us, and even one another. The wretches had probably already done mischief elsewhere – who knows? My recollections of the latter part of this day are rather confused; I was fatigued, and almost deaf. I recollect clearly, however, that we had ceased firing – the plain below being covered with masses of troops, which we could not distinguish from each other. Captain Walcot of the horse-artillery had come to us, and we were all looking out anxiously at the movements below and on the opposite ridge, when he suddenly shouted out, "Victory! – victory! they fly! – they fly!"

and sure enough we saw some of the masses dissolving, as it were, and those composing them streaming away in confused crowds over the field, whilst the already desultory fire of their artillery ceased altogether. I shall never forget this joyful moment! – this moment of exultation! On looking round I found we were left almost alone. Cavalry and infantry had all moved forward, and only a few guns here and there were to be seen on the position. A little to our right were the remains of Major M'Donald's troop under Lieutenant Sandilands, which had suffered much, but nothing like us. We were congratulating ourselves on the happy results of the day, when an aide-de-camp rode up, crying "Forward, sir! – forward! It is of the utmost importance that this movement should be supported by artillery!" at the same time waving his hat much in the manner of a huntsman laying on his dogs. I smiled at his energy, and, pointing to the remains of my poor troop, quietly asked, "How, sir?" A glance was sufficient to show him the impossibility, and away he went.

Our situation was indeed terrible: of 200 fine horses with which we had entered the battle, upwards of 140 lay dead, dying, or severely wounded. Of the men, scarcely two-thirds of those necessary for four guns remained, and these so completely exhausted as to be totally incapable of further exertion. Lieutenant Breton had three horses killed under him; Lieutenant Hincks was wounded in the breast by a spent ball; Lieutenant Leathes on the hip by a splinter; and although untouched myself, my horse had no less than eight wounds, one of which – a graze on the fetlock joint – lamed him for ever. Our guns and carriages were, as before mentioned, altogether in a confused heap, intermingled with dead and wounded horses, which it had not been possible to disengage from them. My poor men, such at least as were untouched, fairly worn out, their clothes, faces, etc., blackened by the smoke and spattered over with mud and blood, had seated themselves on the trails of the carriages, or had thrown themselves on the wet and polluted soil, too fatigued to think of anything but gaining a little rest. Such was our situation when called upon to advance! It was impossible, and we remained where we were. For myself, I was also excessively tired – hoarse, to making speech painful, and deaf from the infernal uproar of the last eleven hours. Moreover, I was devoured by a burning thirst, not a drop of liquid having passed my lips since the evening of the 16th; but although, with the exception of the chicken's leg last night, I may be said to have eaten nothing for two whole days, yet did I not feel the least desire for food.

The evening had become fine, and but for an occasional groan or lament from some poor sufferer, and the repeated piteous neighing of wounded horses, tranquillity might be said to reign over the field. As it got dusk, a large body of Prussian artillery arrived, and formed their bivouac near us. There was not light to see more of them than that their brass guns were kept bright, and that their carriages were encumbered with baggage, and, besides, appeared but clumsy machines when compared with ours. All wore their great-coats, which apparently they had marched in. As they looked at us rather scowlingly, and did not seem inclined to hold any communication with us, I soon returned to my own people, whom I found preparing to go supperless to bed – the two remaining officers, the non-commissioned officers and men having all got together in a heap, with some painted covers spread under and others drawn over them – at a distance from our guns, etc., the neighbourhood of which, they said, was too horrible to think of sleeping there. For my part, after standing all day amongst all these horrors, I felt no squeamishness about sleeping amongst them; so pulling down the painted cover of a limber over the footboard in the manner of a tent-roof, I crept under it, and endeavoured to sleep. The cramped situation in which I lay, and the feverish excitement of my mind, forbade, however, my obtaining that sound and refreshing sleep so much needed – I only dozed. From one of these dozes I awoke about midnight, chilled and cramped to death from the awkward doubled-up position imposed upon me by my short and narrow bed. So up I got to look around and contemplate a battle-field by the pale moonlight. The night was serene and pretty clear; a few light clouds occasionally passing across the moon's disc, and throwing objects into transient obscurity, added considerably to the solemnity of the scene. Oh, it was a thrilling sensation thus to stand in the silent hour of the night and contemplate that field – all day long the theatre of noise and strife, now so calm and still – the actors prostrate on the bloody soil, their pale wan faces upturned to the moon's cold beams, which caps and breast-plates, and a thousand other things, reflected back in brilliant pencils of light from as many different points! Here and there some poor wretch, sitting up amidst the countless dead, busied himself in endeavours to stanch the flowing stream with which his life was fast ebbing away. Many whom I saw so employed that night were, when morning dawned, lying stiff and tranquil as those who had departed earlier. From time to time a figure would half raise itself from the ground, and then, with a despairing groan, fall back again. Others, slowly and painfully rising, stronger, or having less deadly hurt, would stagger away with uncertain steps across the field in search of succour. Many of these I followed with my gaze until lost in the obscurity of distance; but many, alas! after staggering a few paces, would sink again on the ground, probably to rise no more. It was heart-rending – and yet I gazed! Horses, too, there were to claim our pity – mild, patient, enduring. Some lay on the ground with their entrails hanging out, and yet they lived. These would occasionally attempt to rise, but, like their human bed-fellows, quickly falling back again, would lift their poor heads, and, turning a wistful gaze at their side, lie quietly down again, to repeat the same until strength no longer remained, and then, their eyes gently closing, one short convulsive struggle closed their sufferings. One poor animal excited painful interest – he had lost, I believe, both his hind legs; and there he sat the long night through on his tail, looking about, as if in expectation of coming aid, sending forth, from time to time, long and protracted melancholy neighing. Although I knew that killing him at once would be mercy, I could not muster courage even to give the order. Blood enough I had seen shed during the last six-and-thirty hours, and sickened at the thought of shedding more. There, then, he still sat when we left the ground, neighing after us, as if reproaching our desertion of him in the hour of need.

The Prussian bivouac near at hand offered a far different and more cheering scene. There all was life and movement. Their handsome horses, standing harnessed and tied to the carriages, sent forth neighings of another character. Dark forms moved amongst them; and by the bivouac-fires sat figures that would have furnished studies for a Salvator. Dark, brown, stern visages, rendered still sterner by the long drooping mustache that overshadowed the mouth, from which appended their constant companion, the pipe. Many there were, too, busily occupied with the first great care of all animals – cooking, or eating the mess already cooked. Save these I have mentioned, no living being moved on the moon-lit field; and as I cast up my eyes at the lustrous lamp of heaven, I thought on the thousand dear connections far, far away, on whose peaceful dwelling it now looked down, their inmates sleeping in tranquil security, ignorant as yet of the fatal blow which had now for ever severed them from those they loved, whose bodies encumbered the ground around me. And here, even here, what a contrast between this charnel-house and the distant landscape within my ken! Over it the same fair planet shed her mild beams, illuminating its groves and yellow corn-fields, its still and quiet villages, whose modest spires here and there arose from the horizon – emblems of peace, tranquillity, and repose. Long I continued to gaze on this sad and solemn scene; and all this slaughter, I said, to gratify the ambition of one man, and that man –

whom? – one who has risen from a station humble as my own, has already devastated Europe, and filled it with blood and mourning – who only recently left behind him 400,000 gallant men, a prey to the sword and the intemperance of a northern clime – fearful holocaust on the altar of that ambition!

At length I again crept into my cell, and again slept by fits and starts, until the first blush of day reddened the eastern sky, and aroused us all to new exertion. As I emerged from under my cover a shudder crept over me, when the stronger light of day enabled me to see the corpse of one of my drivers lying mangled and bloody beneath my lair.

19th. – The cool air of the morning lasted not long; the rising sun soon burst in all his glory over our bloody bivouac, and all nature arose into renewed life, except the victims of ambition which lay unconscious of his presence. I had not been up many minutes when one of my sergeants came to ask if they might bury Driver Crammond. "And why particularly Driver Crammond?" "Because he looks frightful, sir; many of us have not had a wink of sleep for him." Curious! I walked to the spot where he lay, and certainly a more hideous sight cannot be imagined. A cannon-shot had carried away the whole head except barely the visage, which still remained attached to the torn and bloody neck. The men said they had been prevented sleeping by seeing his eyes fixed on them all night; and thus this one dreadful object had superseded all the other horrors by which they were surrounded. He was of course immediately buried, and as immediately forgotten. Our first care after this was to muster the remaining force, to disentangle our carriages from each other, and from the dead and dying animals with which they were encumbered. Many sound or only slightly-wounded horses, belonging to different corps of both armies, were wandering about the field. Of these we caught several in the course of the morning, and thus collected, with what remained of our own fit for work, sufficient to horse four guns, three ammunition waggons, and the forge. Of men we had nearly enough for these at reduced numbers, so we set to work equipping ourselves without delay. Although supplies of ammunition had been sent to us during the action, yet little remained. The expenditure had been enormous. A return had been called for yesterday evening just as we were lying down to rest, but, fatigued as we all were, it was impossible to give this correctly. As near as I could ascertain, we must have fired nearly 700 rounds per gun. Our harness, etc., was so cut to pieces, that but for the vast magazines around us from which we could pick and choose, we should never have got off the field. Soon after daybreak an officer came from headquarters to desire me to send all my superfluous carriages to Lillois, where a park was forming, and to inform me that a supply of ammunition would be found in the village of Waterloo. Accordingly the carriages were sent without delay; but this requiring all the horses, they were obliged to make a second trip for the ammunition. Whilst this was doing I had leisure to examine the ground in our immediate vicinity. Books and papers, etc., covered it in all directions. The books at first surprised me, but upon examination the thing was explained. Each French soldier, it appeared, carried a little accompt-book of his pay, clothing, etc. etc. The scene was now far from solitary; for numerous groups of peasants were moving about busily employed stripping the dead, and perhaps finishing those not quite so. Some of these men I met fairly staggering under the enormous load of clothes, etc., they had collected. Some had firearms, swords, etc., and many had large bunches of crosses and decorations; all seemed in high glee, and professed unbounded hatred of the French.

I had fancied we were almost alone on the field, seeing only the remains of Major Bull's troop of horse-artillery not far from us (the Prussians had gone forward about, or a little before, daybreak); but in wandering towards the Charleroi road I stumbled on a whole regiment of British infantry fast asleep, in columns of divisions, wrapped in their blankets, with their knapsacks for pillows. Not a man was awake. There they lay in regular ranks, with the officers and sergeants in their places, just as they would stand when awake. Not far from these, in a little hollow beneath a white thorn, lay two Irish light-infantry men sending forth such howlings and wailings, and oaths and execrations, as were shocking to hear. One of them had his leg shot off, the other a thigh smashed by a cannon-shot. They were certainly pitiable objects, but their vehement exclamations, etc., were so strongly contrasted with the quiet resolute bearing of hundreds, both French and English, around them, that it blunted one's feelings considerably.

I tried in vain to pacify them; so walked away amidst a volley of abuse as a hard-hearted wretch who could thus leave two poor fellows to die like dogs. What could I do? All, however, though in more modest terms, craved assistance; and every poor wretch begged most earnestly for water. Some of my men had discovered a good well of uncontaminated water at Hougoumont, and filled their canteens; so I made several of them accompany me and administer to the most craving in our immediate vicinity. Nothing could exceed their gratitude, or the fervent blessings they implored on us for this momentary relief. The French were in general particularly grateful; and those who were strong enough, entered into conversation with us on the events of yesterday, and the probable fate awaiting themselves. All the non-commissioned officers and privates agreed in asserting that they had been deceived by their officers and betrayed; and, to my surprise, almost all of them reviled Buonaparte as the cause of their misery. Many begged me to kill them at once, since they would a thousand times rather die by the hand of a soldier than be left at the mercy of those villanous Belgic peasants. Whilst we stood by them, several would appear consoled and become tranquil; but the moment we attempted to leave, they invariably renewed the cry, "*Ah, Monsieur, tuez moi donc! Tuez moi, pour l'amour de Dieu!*" etc. etc. It was in vain I assured them carts would be sent to pick them all up. Nothing could reconcile them to the idea of being left. They looked on us as brother soldiers, and knew we were too honourable to harm them: "But the moment you go, those vile peasants will first insult, and then cruelly murder us." This, alas! I knew, was but too true. One Frenchman I found in a far different humour – an officer of lancers, and desperately wounded; a strong square-built man, with reddish hair and speckled complexion. When I approached him he appeared suffering horribly – rolling on his back, uttering loud groans. My first impulse was to raise and place him in a sitting posture; but, the moment he was touched, opening his eyes and seeing me, he became perfectly furious. Supposing he mistook my intention, I addressed him in a soothing tone, begging he would allow me to render him what little assistance was in my power. This only seemed to irritate him the more; and on my presenting him the canteen with water, he dashed it from him with such a passionate gesture and emphatic "*Non!*" that I saw there was no use in teasing, and therefore reluctantly left him. Returning towards our position, I was forcibly struck by the immense heap of bodies of men and horses which distinguished it even at a distance; indeed, Sir Augustus Frazer told me the other day, at Nivelles, that, in riding over the field, he "could plainly distinguish the position of G troop from the opposite height by the dark mass which, even from that distance, formed a remarkable feature in the field." These were his very words. One interesting sufferer I had nearly forgotten. He was a fine young man of the *grenadiers à cheval*, who had lain groaning near us all night – indeed scarcely five paces from my bed; therefore was the first person I visited as soon as daylight came. He was a most interesting person – tall, handsome, and a perfect gentleman in manners and speech; yet his costume was that of a private soldier. We conversed with him some time, and were exceedingly pleased with his mild and amiable address. Amongst other things he told us that Marshal Ney had led the charges against us. In this, however (if we understood him rightly), he must have been mistaken, since that Marshal is an infantry general. Be that as it may, we all felt deeply interested for our unfortunate prisoner, and did all in our power for him, which consisted in kind words and sending two careful men to lead him to the village – a most painful undertaking, for we now found that, besides one ball in the forehead, he had received another in his right thigh, which, together with his being barefooted, could not but render his journey both tedious and painful.

I now began to feel somewhat the effects of my long fast in a most unpleasant sense of weakness and an inordinate craving for food, which there were no means of satisfying. My joy, then, may be imagined when, returning to our bivouac, I found our people returned from Lillois, and, better still, that they had brought with them a quarter of veal, which they had found in a muddy ditch, of course in appearance then filthy enough. What was this to a parcel of men who had scarcely eaten a morsel for three days? In a trice it was cut up, the mud having been scraped off with a sabre, a fire kindled and fed with lance-shafts and musket-stocks; and old Quartermaster Hall, undertaking the cooking, proceeded to fry the dirty lumps in the lid of a camp-kettle. How we enjoyed the savoury smell! and, having made ourselves seats of cuirasses, piled upon each other, we soon had that most agreeable of animal gratifications – the filling our empty stomachs. Never was a meal more perfectly military, nor more perfectly enjoyed.

We had not yet finished our meal, when a carriage drove on the ground from Brussels, the inmates of which, alighting, proceeded to examine the field. As they passed near us, it was amusing to see the horror with which they eyed our frightful figures; they all, however, pulled off their hats and made us low bows. One, a smartly dressed middle-aged man, in a high cocked-hat, came to our circle, and entered into conversation with me on the events of yesterday. He approached holding a delicately white perfumed handkerchief to his nose; stepping carefully to avoid the bodies (at which he cast fearful glances *en passant*), to avoid polluting the glossy silken hose that clothed his nether limbs. May I be pardoned for the comparison: Hotspur's description of a fop came forcibly to my mind as we conversed; clean and spruce, as if from a bandbox, redolent of perfume, he stood ever and anon applying the 'kerchief to his nose. I was not leaning on my sword, but I arose to receive him from my seat of armour, my hands and face begrimed and blackened with blood and smoke – clothes too. "I do remember when the fight was done," etc. etc. It came, as I said, forcibly to my mind as I eyed my friend's costume and sniffed the sweet-scented atmosphere that hovered round him. The perfumed handkerchief, in this instance, held the place of Shakespeare's "pouncet-box" – the scene was pleasant to remember! With a world of bows my man took leave, and proceeded, picking his steps with the same care as he followed the route of his companions in the direction of Hougoumont.

Having despatched our meal, and then the ammunition waggons to Waterloo, and leaving the people employed equipping as best they could, I set off to visit the chateau likewise; for the struggle that had taken place there yesterday rendered it an object of interest. The same scene of carnage as elsewhere characterised that part of the field over which I now bent my steps. The immediate neighbourhood of Hougoumont was more thickly strewn with corpses than most other parts of the field – the very ditches were full of them. The trees all about were most woefully cut and splintered, both by cannon-shot and musketry. The courts of the chateau presented a spectacle more terrible even than any I had yet seen. A large barn had been set on fire, and the conflagration had spread to the offices, and even to the main building. Here numbers, both of French and English, had perished in the flames, and their blackened swollen remains lay scattered about in all directions. Amongst this heap of ruins and misery many poor devils yet remained alive, and were sitting up endeavouring to bandage their wounds. Such a scene of horror, and one so sickening, was surely never witnessed.

Two or three German dragoons were wandering among the ruins, and many peasants. One of the former was speaking to me when two of the latter, after rifling the pockets, etc., of a dead Frenchman, seized the body by the shoulders, and, raising it from the ground, dashed it down again with all their force, uttering the grossest abuse, and kicking it about the head and face – revolting spectacle! – doing this, no doubt, to court favour with us. It had a contrary effect, which they soon learned. I had scarcely uttered an exclamation of disgust, when the dragoon's sabre was flashing over the miscreants' heads, and in a moment descended on their backs and shoulders with such vigour that they roared again, and were but too happy to make their escape. I turned from such scenes and entered the garden. How shall I describe the delicious sensation I experienced!

The garden was an ordinary one, but pretty – long straight walks of turf overshadowed by fruit-trees, and between these beds of vegetables, the whole enclosed by a tolerably high brick wall. Is it necessary to define my sensations? Is it possible that I am not understood at once? Listen then. For the last three days I have been in a constant state of excitement – in a perfect fever. My eyes have beheld nought but war in all its horrors – my ears have been assailed by a continued roar of cannon and cracking of musketry, the shouts of multitudes and the lamentations of war's victims. Suddenly and unexpectedly I find myself in solitude, pacing a green avenue, my eyes refreshed by the cool verdure of trees and shrubs; my ear soothed by the melody of feathered songsters – yea, of sweet Philomel herself – and the pleasing hum of insects sporting in the genial sunshine. Is there nothing in this to excite emotion? Nature in repose is always lovely: here, and under such circumstances, she was delicious. Long I rambled in this garden, up one walk, down another, and thought I could dwell here contented for ever. Nothing recalled the presence of war except the loopholed wall and two or three dead Guardsmen;[3] but the first caused no interruption, and these last lay so concealed amongst the exuberant vegetation of turnips and cabbages, etc., that, after coming from the field of death without, their pale and silent forms but little deteriorated my enjoyment. The leaves were green, roses and other flowers bloomed forth in all their sweetness, and the very turf when crushed by my feet smelt fresh and pleasant. There was but little of disorder visible to tell of what had been enacted here. I imagine it must have been assailed by infantry alone; and the havoc amongst the trees without made by our artillery posted on the hill above to cover the approach to it – principally, perhaps, by Bull's howitzer battery.

I had satisfied my curiosity at Hougoumont, and was retracing my steps up the hill, when my attention was called to a group of wounded Frenchmen by the calm, dignified, and soldier-like oration addressed by one of them to the rest. I cannot, like Livy, compose a fine harangue for my hero, and, of course, I could not retain the precise words, but the import of them was to exhort them to bear their sufferings with fortitude; not to repine, like women or children, at what every soldier should have made up his mind to suffer as the fortune of war, but, above all, to remember that they were surrounded by Englishmen, before whom they ought to be doubly careful not to disgrace themselves by displaying such an unsoldier-like want of fortitude. The speaker was sitting on the ground, with his lance stuck upright beside him – an

3 In some accounts of the battle, and visits to the field, etc., it has been stated that this garden was a scene of slaughter. Totally untrue! As I have stated in the text, I did not see above two or three altogether. There certainly might have been more concealed amongst the vegetation, but they could not have been many [Mercer].

old veteran, with a thick bushy grizly beard, countenance like a lion – a lancer of the Old Guard, and no doubt had fought in many a field. One hand was flourished in the air as he spoke, the other, severed at the wrist, lay on the earth beside him; one ball (case-shot, probably) had entered his body, another had broken his leg. His suffering, after a night of exposure so mangled, must have been great; yet he betrayed it not. His bearing was that of a Roman, or perhaps of an Indian warrior, and I could fancy him concluding appropriately his speech in the words of the Mexican king, "And I too; am I on a bed of roses?" I could not but feel the highest veneration for this brave man, and told him so, at the same time offering him the only consolation in my power – a drink of cold water, and assurances that the waggons would soon be sent round to collect the wounded. He thanked me with a grace peculiar to Frenchmen, and eagerly inquired the fate of their army. On this head I could tell him nothing consolatory, so merely answered that it had retired last night, and turned the conversation to the events of yesterday. This truly brave man spoke in most flattering terms of our troops, but said they had no idea in the French army we should have fought so obstinately, since it was generally understood that the English Government had, for some inexplicable reason, connived at Napoleon's escape from Elba, and therefore had ordered their army only to make a show of resistance. After a very interesting conversation, I begged his lance as a keepsake, observing that it never could be of further use to him. The old man's eyes kindled as I spoke, and he emphatically assured me that it would delight him to see it in the hands of a brave soldier, instead of being torn from him, as he had feared, by those vile peasants. So I took my leave, and walked away with the lance in my hand.[4] Every since, my groom (Milward) has been transformed into my lancer-orderly; and I propose, if ever I return to England, consecrating it to the memory of the interesting old hero. In passing Bull's bivouac it was my fate to witness another very interesting scene. A wounded hussar had some-how or another found his way there from another part of the field, and, exhausted by the exertion, had just fainted. Some of those collected round him cried out for water, and a young driver, who, being outside the throng, had not yet seen the sufferer, seized a canteen, and ran away to fill it. Whilst he was absent the hussar so far recovered as to be able to sit up. The driver returned at this moment, and, pushing aside his comrades, knelt down to enable the hussar to drink, holding the canteen to his lips, and in so doing recognised a brother whom he had not seen for years! His emotion was extreme, as may be supposed.

On regaining my own bivouac I found the ammunition arrived, and, what was still more satisfactory, Mr Coates with his whole train of Flemish waggons – our baggage and provisions. He had got intelligence in time of the battle of Quatre Bras and its results, and therefore altered his route to meet us on our retreat. On approaching the Charleroi road he had been swept away by the torrent of fugitives, and actually carried, *malgré lui*, beyond Brussels, some way on the road to Antwerp, before he could succeed in disentangling his train from the rabble rout, which he described as exceeding all

4 During the remainder of the campaign Milward carried it; and on returning to England I even rode into Canterbury followed by my lancer – a novelty in those days. Whilst in retirement on half-pay, it was suspended in my library; but on going to America in 1823 I deposited it in the Rotunda at Woolwich. On my return in 1829 the lance was gone. In 1823 or 1824 it seems Lieutenant-Colonel Vandaleur, of the 9th Lancers, came to Woolwich to look for a model. Mine pleased him, and he took it to St John's Wood Riding-House, where it was tried against others in presence of the Duke of York, and approved of as a model for arming the British lancers. After a long hunt I at last found it at the Enfield manufactory, spoilt completely, the iron work and thong taken off, and flag gone. It cost me a long correspondence with the Board before I succeeded in getting it restored and put together. When I received it from him who had so long wielded it, the flag was dyed in blood, the blade notched, and also stained with blood; inside the thong was cut Clement, VII., probably the number of his troop [Mercer]

imagination. As he brought the where-withal, etc., of course his joining was hailed with joy by every one.

Since the order to send away my carriages I had received none; but as my diminished troop was completed as far as could be done here, I resolved to move off this horrid place; and accordingly, at 3 p.m., we joyfully took to the Nivelles road – by instinct, perhaps, for I knew nothing of the movements of the army, nor by what road they had gone forward. About a mile or so from the field I formed our bivouac for the night in a sweet and wholesome orchard near the road, with a turf like velvet, and perfectly dry. This in itself was a luxury; it was a luxury to breathe pure unconta-minated air; it was a luxury to be out of hearing of groans, cries, and lamentations. This was not all. Mr Coates brought us a ham and a cheese; the neighbouring farmhouse supplied us with eggs, milk, and cider: so that in due time we sat down to an excellent dinner, seasoned with that sauce which no cook, however *scientific*, has yet learned to equal – hunger. Hilarity reigned at our board – if we may so term the fresh turf at the foot of an apple-tree; and over our grog and cigars we managed to pass a most pleasant evening. Previously, I had caused my servant to bring me a bucket of water, and prepared myself for our repast by the enjoyment of that first of luxuries, a thorough wash and clean clothes. This was the first time I had undressed since leaving Strytem – four whole days and three whole nights. It may be imagined with what joy I got rid of my bloody garments. Like the birds, we all retired to rest with the close of day, and the delicious sleep I enjoyed it is impossible to describe.

SOURCES

Captain William Bragge, *Peninsular Portrait, 1811–1814: The Letters of Captain William Bragge*, ed. S.A.C. Cassels (London, Oxford University Press, 1963)

Captain Jean-Roch Coignet, *The Narrative of Captain Coignet: Soldier of the Empire*, translated Mrs M. Carey (London, Chatto & Windus, 1897)

Captain T.C. Fenton, "The Peninsula and Waterloo Letters of Captain Thomas Charles Fenton," *Journal of the Society for Army Historical Research*, vol 53, Winter 1975, pp. 210–31

William Grattan, *Adventures with the Connaught Rangers, 1809–1814*, ed. Charles Oman (London, Edward Arnold, 1902)

Rifleman Harris, *The Recollections of Rifleman Harris*, ed. H. Curling (London, 1848)

George Hennell, *A Gentleman Volunteer: The Letters of George Hennell from the Peninsular War, 1812–1813*, ed. Michael Glover. Copyright C. Elizabeth Hennell, 1979 (London, William Heinemann Ltd, 1979)

Baron Lejeune, *Memoirs of Baron Lejeune*, trans. and ed. Mrs Arthur Bell (London, Longmans, Green & Co., 1897)

Marshal Macdonald, *Recollections of Marshal Macdonald, Duke of Tarentum* (New York, Scribner's, 1893)

Baron de Marbot, *Memoirs of Baron de Marbot*, 2 vols (London, Longmans, Green, 1892)

General Cavalie Mercer, *Journal of the Waterloo Campaign*, edited by his son, C.A. Mercer (London, 1870)

Thomas Morris, *Napoleonic Wars* (London, Longmans, 1967, ed. John Selby; first published as *Recollections of Military Service in 1813, 1814, and 1815, through Germany, Holland and France* (London, James Madden & Co., 1845)

Sergeant D. Robertson, *The Journal of Sergeant D. Robertson* (Perth, J. Fisher, 1842)

Corporal Samuel Stubbs, *The Magazine of History*, (USA, 1929)

Lieutenant-Colonel Tomkinson, *The Diary of a Cavalry Officer in the Peninsular War and Waterloo Campaign*, edited by his son James Tomkinson (London, Swan Sonnenschein & Co., 1895; first published 1894)